Religion and Equality

This volume presents an analysis of controversial events and issues shaping a rapidly changing international legal, political, and social landscape. Leading scholars and experts in law, religious studies, and international relations thoughtfully consider issues and tensions arising in contemporary debates over religion and equality in many parts of the world.

The book is in two parts. The first section focuses on the anti-discrimination dimension of religious freedom norms, examining the developing law on equality and human rights and how it operates at national and international levels. The second section provides a series of case studies exploring the contemporary issue of same-sex marriage and how it affects religious groups and believers.

This collection will be of interest to academics and scholars of law, religious studies, political science, and sociology, as well as policymakers and legal practitioners.

W. Cole Durham, Jr. is Susa Young Gates Professor of Law and Director of the International Center for Law and Religion Studies at Brigham Young University, Utah, United States, and Director of the International Consortium for Law and Religion Studies, based in Milan, Italy.

Donlu Thayer is Senior Editor at the International Center for Law and Religion Studies at Brigham Young University Law School and an Associate Editor and Case Note Editor of the *Oxford Journal of Law and Religion.*

ICLARS Series on Law and Religion

Series Editors:

The *ICLARS Series on Law and Religion* is a new series designed to provide a forum for the rapidly expanding field of research in law and religion. The series is published in association with the International Consortium for Law and Religion Studies, an international network of scholars and experts of law and religion founded in 2007 with the aim of providing a place where information, data and opinions can easily be exchanged among members and made available to the broader scientific community. The series aims to become a primary source for students and scholars while presenting authors with a valuable means to reach a wide and growing readership.

Titles in this series:

Religion and Equality
Edited by W. Cole Durham, Jr. and Donlu Thayer, Brigham Young University, USA

Church and State in Scotland
Francis Lyall, University of Aberdeen, UK

Religion as Empowerment
Edited by Kyriaki Topidi and Lauren Fielder, both at University of Lucerne, Switzerland

Religion and Equality

Law in conflict

Edited by
W. Cole Durham, Jr., and
Donlu Thayer

Routledge
Taylor & Francis Group
LONDON AND NEW YORK

First published 2016
by Routledge
2 Park Square, Milton Park, Abingdon, Oxon OX14 4RN

and by Routledge
711 Third Avenue, New York, NY 10017

First issued in paperback 2018

Routledge is an imprint of the Taylor & Francis Group, an informa business

British Library Cataloguing in Publication Data
A catalogue record for this book is available from the British Library

Library of Congress Cataloging-in-Publication Data
Religion and equality : law in conflict / [edited] by W. Cole Durham, Jr. and Donlu Thayer.
pages cm. — (ICLARS series on law and religion)
Includes bibliographical references and index.
ISBN 978-1-4724-5915-2 (hardback : alk. paper) — ISBN 978-1-4724-5916-9 (ebook) — ISBN 978-1-4724-5917-6 (epub)
1. Freedom of religion. 2. Religion and state. 3. Same-sex marriage—Law and legislation. 4. Religious discrimination—Law and legislation. 5. Equality before the law. I. Durham, W. Cole, Jr., 1948– editor. II. Thayer, Donlu D., editor.
K3258.R435 2016
342.08′52—dc23
2015034758

ISBN 13: 978-1-138-60568-8 (pbk)
ISBN 13: 978-1-4724-5915-2 (hbk)

Typeset in Times New Roman
by Apex CoVantage, LLC

Contents

Notes on Contributors

Rex Ahdar is Professor, Faculty of Law, University of Otago, Dunedin, New Zealand and Adjunct Professor, University of Notre Dame Australia School of Law, Sydney. He is a Barrister and Solicitor of the High Court of New Zealand. He lectures on Competition Law, Contract Law, Law and Sport, and Law and Religion. He was a Fulbright Senior Scholar at Boalt Hall School of Law, University of California Berkeley. He is author or editor of *Competition Law and Policy in New Zealand* (1991); [with John Stenhouse] *God and Government: The New Zealand Experience* (2000); *Law and Religion* (2000); *Worlds Colliding: Conservative Christians and the Law* (2001); [with Nicholas Aroney] *Sharia in the West* (2010); and [with Ian Leigh] *Religious Freedom in the Liberal State* (2nd edn, 2013). He has published articles in journals such as *Oxford Journal of Legal Studies, Cambridge Law Journal, Modern Law Review, McGill Law Journal, Ratio Juris, Stanford Journal of Civil Rights & Civil Liberties, Journal of Church & State, Journal of Law & Religion, Religion & Human Rights, Ecclesiastical Law Journal,* and *Rutgers Journal of Law & Religion.*

Helen M. Alvaré is Professor of Law, George Mason University School of Law, Arlington, Virginia (USA). She is faculty advisor to the law school's Civil Rights Law Journal, president of the Chiaroscuro Institute (New York, New York), a consultor for the Pontifical Council of the Laity (Vatican City), and an advisor to the US Conference of Catholic Bishops (Washington, DC). She publishes regularly on matters concerning marriage, parenting, non-marital households, and the First Amendment religion clauses. Professor Alvaré received her law degree from Cornell University School of Law and her master's degree in Systematic Theology from the Catholic University of America. Prior to joining the faculty of George Mason University, she taught at the Columbus School of Law at the Catholic University of America, represented the United States Conference of Catholic Bishops, and practiced commercial litigation for the Philadelphia law firm of Stradley, Ronon, Stevens & Young.

Rodrigo Vitorino Souza Alves is a member of the Academic Staff of the Faculty of Law of the Federal University of Uberlândia, Brazil. He was an Academic Visitor at the Faculty of Law of the University of Oxford (2014–2015). His teaching and research interests include Constitutional Law, Human Rights, and Law and Religion. He is the Coordinator of the Law and Religion Research Group (Brazil), which focuses on religious freedom, religious minorities, anti-discrimination norms, and religion-state relations. He served as guest speaker at the Sixth Session of the Forum on Minority Issues of the United Nations, on the rights of religious minorities. He is a member of the International Consortium for Law and Religion Studies (ICLARS) and of the Law and Religion Scholars Network

(LARSN), and is a guest academic at The Sacred and Secular Blog (The Open University). He is licensed to practice law in Brazil.

Ursula C. Basset has a PhD in Law. She is Director of the Center of Research in Family Law and Chair holder in Family Law and Law of Successions at Pontificia Universidad Católica Argentina. She has been actively involved in the same-sex marriage debate in her country, producing an alternative bill to the marriage reform. She was also a member to the Committee to reform the Argentine Civil and Commercial Code (2011–2014). She was the first woman in her country to win the Accésit Prize of the National Academy of Jurisprudence (2012). She is VicePresident of the International Academy for the Study of the Jurisprudence of the Family and member of the Executive Board of the International Society of Family Law. She has published more than one hundred articles and has written and co-authored several books.

Thomas C. Berg is the James L. Oberstar Professor of Law and Public Policy at the University of St. Thomas School of Law, Minnesota (USA). He is the author of four books, dozens of scholarly and popular articles, and many appellate briefs on religious liberty and free speech issues. He supervises a religious liberty appellate clinic, and he has often testified to Congress concerning religious freedom legislation. He received the Religious Liberty Defender of the Year Award from the Christian Legal Society in 1996 and is past chair of the Law and Religion Section of the Association of American Law Schools; a member of the European-American Consortium on Church-State Relations; and a current or past member of boards or advisory committees for the National Council of Churches, the Pew Forum on Religion & Public Life, the DePaul University Center for Church-State Studies, and the Democrats for Life of America. He has degrees from the University of Chicago, in both Law and Religious Studies; from Oxford University, in Philosophy and Politics (as a Rhodes Scholar); and from Northwestern University, in Journalism. He was executive editor of the law review at Chicago, clerked for Judge Alvin Rubin of the US Court of Appeals for the Fifth Circuit, and practiced law in Chicago with Mayer, Brown and Platt.

Heiner Bielefeldt was appointed as United Nations Special Rapporteur for Freedom of Religion or Belief on 18 June 2010. Holding both a PhD in Philosophy from the University of Tübingen and a post-doctoral Habilitation Degree in Philosophy from the University of Bremen, following on undergraduate studies in Philosophy and Catholic Theology at both institutions, Professor Bielefeldt teaches in the areas of political science, philosophy, law, and history. He has taught in faculties of law and philosophy at the universities of Tübingen, Mannheim, Heidelberg, Toronto, and Bielefeld. From 2003–2009 he served as Director of the German Institute for Human Rights, and during 2008–2009 he was Chair of the Subcommittee on Accreditation of National Human Rights Institutions, International Coordinating Committee, Office of the United Nations High Commissioner for Human Rights. In 2009, he was appointed professor in the newly created Chair of Human Rights and Human Rights Policy at the University of Erlangen, which position he held at the time of his appointment as Special Rapporteur.

Pieter Coertzen is a retired professor of Theology at the University of Stellenbosch, South Africa. He teaches a yearly course in Comparative Canon Law at the KU Leuven, Belgium. He is chairperson of the Unit for the Study of Law and Religion in the Beyers Naudé Centre for Public Theology, Faculty of Theology, University of Stellenbosch, and President of the African Consortium for Law and Religion Studies (ACLARS). He holds seven degrees: BA, BA Hons, and MA in Philosophy (Pothefstroom University for Christian Higher Education); Bachelor of Theology, Licentiate in Theology, and Master of Theology in Ecclesiology, and a doctoral degree in Theology (Ecclesiology) (University of Stellenbosch). For the Dutch Reformed Church he has served in many capacities, including Parish Minister, Actuarius, and on Church Law Committees. He was Senior Lecturer in Ecclesiology, Professor, and Dean of the Faculty of Theology at the University of Stellenbosch. He has published 36 articles in NGTT (the *Dutch Reformed Theological Journal*, now *Stellenbosch Theological Journal*), (of which he was editor for many years). He has written 14 books and is co-author or editor of more than 30 other publications. Among many honors and activities he is Chairman of the Huguenot Memorial Museum in Franschhoek.

W. Cole Durham, Jr. is Susa Young Gates University Professor of Law and Director of the International Center for Law and Religion Studies at Brigham Young University, Utah, United States and Director of the International Consortium for Law and Religion Studies, based in Milan, Italy. He is a Founding Editor of the *Oxford Journal of Law and Religion* and an Associate Member of the International Academy of Comparative Law in Paris. He has served as Chair both of the Comparative Law Section and the Law and Religion Section of the American Association of Law Schools. He is a Vice President of the International Academy for Freedom of Religion and Belief and has served as a board member of church-state centers at DePaul and Baylor Universities, of the International Religious Liberty Association, and of the International Advisory Board of the Oslo Coalition on Freedom of Religion or Belief. He has also been active in work on laws governing the civil society sector, having served as Chairman of the Board of the International Center for Not-for-Profit Law in Washington DC, and as a member of its board for many years. He was the 2009 recipient of the International First Freedom Award from the First Freedom Center of Richmond, Virginia.

Nicolae V. Dură holds a PhD in Theology, Canon Law, and Law. Professor Emeritus since 2013, he was Professor and Vice Dean of the Faculty of Law and Vice Rector of 'Ovidius' University of Constanţa for International Relations. He has received honorary doctorates from universities in Ukraine, Bulgaria, and Georgia. He is a Member of the Academy of Romanian Scientists, of the Society of the Law of the Oriental Churches (Vienna), of the International Consortium of Law and Religion Studies (Milan), and of the Union of Jurists in Romania. He has been a member of scientific boards and boards of editors in many countries, including Georgia, Poland, Moldova, and Canada. Among his many honors, he received the National Order of Merit (France); the AD Xenopol Award (Romanian Academy); the Pontifical Medal 'Ut Unum Sint' (Rome); the Order of St. Vladimir (Moscow); the Patriarchal Grammata 'Sofronie Vracianski' (Sofia); the Prize 'Mircea Manolescu' and the Gold Medal (both from the Union of Jurists in Romania). He is author of books and studies on Theology, Canon Law, Law, Philosophy, History, Ecclesiology, and the History of Ancient Literature, published in Romanian, French, English, Bulgarian, Ethiopian, and Georgian. In 2001 and 2004 he was awarded the prestigious 'Man of the Year' designation by the American Biographical Institute (New York).

Silvio Ferrari is Professor of Canon Law at the University of Milan and recently retired as Professor of Church-State Relations at the University of Leuven in Belgium. He has been visiting professor in Paris (École Pratique des Hautes Études) and Berkeley (University of California) and works for many international organizations, including the European Union and the Organization for Security and Cooperation in Europe. He has founded, together with other professors, the European Consortium for Church and State Research. Professor Ferrari is a member of the Scientific Committee of the Institut européen en sciences des religions (EPHE, Paris) and of the Board of Experts of the International Religious Liberty Association (Silver Spring, Maryland). His main fields of interest are Law and Religion issues in Western Europe; Comparative Law of Religions (in particular Jewish Law, Canon Law and Islamic Law); and relations between Israel and the Vatican. Professor Ferrari is Life Honorary President of the International Consortium for Law and Religion Studies (ICLARS) and is a Founding Editor of the *Oxford Journal of Law and Religion*. He received the 2012 Distinguished Service Award from the International Center for Law and Religion Studies (ICLRS).

Mark Hill QC is a leading barrister with chambers in London and specializes in litigation concerning religious matters in the domestic courts in the United Kingdom and at the European Court of Human Rights in Strasbourg. He is a recorder on the Midland Circuit (sitting in criminal, civil, and family cases) and Deputy Judge of the Upper Tribunal, Immigration and Asylum Chamber. He sits as judge in ecclesiastical courts of the Church of England and is Honorary Professor at Cardiff University and Extraordinary Professor at the University of Pretoria. His publications include *Magna Carta, Religion and the Rule of Law* (2015, Cambridge University Press); *Religion and Discrimination Law in the European Union* (2012, Institute for European Constitutional Law); *Ecclesiastical Law* (3rd edn, 2007, Oxford University Press); *Religious Liberty and Human Rights* (2002, University of Wales Press); and *English Canon Law* (1998, University of Wales Press). He is Ecumenical Fellow in Canon Law at the Venerable English College in Rome, and a former President of the European Consortium for Church and State Research. An accredited mediator, he is current co-chair and a founder of BIMA, a charity which promotes faith-based mediation.

Douglas Laycock is the Robert E. Scott Distinguished Professor of Law and Professor of Religious Studies at the University of Virginia, and Alice McKean Young Regents Chair in Law Emeritus at the University of Texas at Austin, in the United States. He is Vice President of the American Law Institute and a fellow of the American Academy of Arts and Sciences. Laycock has testified frequently before Congress and has argued many cases in the courts, including some of the most important religious liberty decisions in the US Supreme Court. He is the author of the leading casebook *Modern American Remedies*; the award-winning monograph *The Death of the Irreparable Injury Rule*; and many articles in the leading law reviews. He has co-edited a collection of essays, *Same-Sex Marriage and Religious Liberty*, and he recently published *Religious Liberty, Volume I: Overviews and History*, and *Volume II: The Free Exercise Clause*. These two volumes are the first half of a four-volume collection of his many writings on religious liberty. In 2009, he received the National First Freedom Award from the Council on America's First Freedom, and in 2012 he was given the International Religious Liberty Award of the J. Reuben Clark Law Society.

Russell Sandberg is the Managing Editor of Ashgate's ICLARS Series on Law and Religion. He is a senior lecturer in law at Cardiff University, where he researches at the Centre for Law and Religion. His publications include *Law and Religion* (2011, Cambridge University Press) and *Religion, Law and Society* (2014, Cambridge University Press). He is co-author of *Religion and Law in the United Kingdom* (2011/2014, Kluwer Law International) which forms part of the International Encyclopaedia of Laws Series. He is also co-editor of *Law and Religion: New Horizons* (2010, Peeters) and editor of *Religion and Legal Pluralism* (2015, Ashgate). He is a contributor to Westlaw UK Insight and was a specialist Contributing Editor for *Jowitt's Dictionary of English Law* (2010, Sweet & Maxwell). He is the author or co-author of more than 50 articles and book chapters addressed to legal, sociological, and general readerships. His recent research has included an empirical study into the operation of religious tribunals in Britain, funded by the AHRC / ESRC Religion and Society programme.

Donlu Thayer is Senior Editor at the International Center for Law and Religion Studies at Brigham Young University Law School and an Associate Editor and Case Note Editor of the *Oxford Journal of Law and Religion.* She received BA and MA degrees in Languages and Literature and a JD degree with emphasis in family, international, and constitutional law from Brigham Young University. She has been a family, juvenile court, small claims, and high-risk victim/offender mediator and was for a time Executive Director of Community Dispute Resolution Services of Utah County. She is a member of the Utah State Bar. A professional editor for more than 45 years, she also for many years taught writing in the Brigham Young University English Department and Honors Program. Publications include *Law, Religion, Constitution*, ed. with W. Cole Durham, Jr., Silvio Ferrari, and Cristiana Cianitto (2013, Ashgate) and *Religion and the Secular State: National Reports*, ed., with Javier Martínez-Torrón and W. Cole Durham, Jr., General Reporters (2015, Universidad Complutense Madrid), and more than 35 case notes for the *Oxford Journal of Law and Religion.*

María J. Valero Estarellas was awarded a Bachelor of Law degree (Universidad Pontificia de Comillas ICAI-ICADE) in 1998. She is at present a PhD candidate and a lecturer for Law and Religion at the Villanueva University Centre, Universidad Complutense Madrid. She was a practicing lawyer in the Litigation Department of the firm Cuatrecasas (Madrid) between 2002 and 2007. Specializing in educational rights and in the collective religious freedom of religious communities, she is the author of several published papers on homeschooling and faith-schools in Europe and has participated as a speaker and discussant in various national and international conferences. She currently focuses her research on the relationship between the autonomy of religious groups and the right to non-discrimination in the workplace.

Greg Walsh is Senior Lecturer, School of Law, the University of Notre Dame Australia. He was educated at the Australian National University, where he completed a combined Bachelor of Laws/Science degree and a Graduate Diploma in Legal Practice. He completed a Master of Laws at the University of Sydney and a PhD at Curtin University. He has lectured at the University of Western Sydney and the University of New South Wales. Greg has worked in various legal roles in Australia and overseas, including as a prosecutor and a medical negligence solicitor. Greg's research interests include torts, medical law, human rights law, and the intersection between law and religion. Publications include *Religious Schools and Discrimination* (2015, Central Press) and *Torts*, ed. with Sarah Withnall and Patrick Rooney (2015, LexisNexis Butterworths).

Series Introduction

Issues concerning law and religion are increasingly the subject of scholarship around the globe. The study of law and religion is well developed in continental Europe and the Americas, and is beginning to blossom in Australia, South Africa, the United Kingdom, and elsewhere. As scholarly communities develop, research groupings have been set up, including centers and research units at the local level as well as national and pan-national associations.

In 2007, a global association, the International Consortium for Law and Religion Studies (ICLARS), was established as an international network of scholars and experts in law and religion, with the aim of providing a forum where information, data, and opinions could easily be exchanged among members and be made available to the broader scientific community. ICLARS hosts a resource-rich website and has organized and sponsored impressive international conferences. ICLARS members are prolific in their teaching, consulting, speaking, and publishing; a number of them serve as editors and advisors to first-class specialist journals. Four books have resulted to date from ICLARS members focusing on the themes of the first three ICLARS Conferences, held in Milan, Italy (2009), in Santiago, Chile (2011), and in Virginia, United States (2013).[1] As this book goes to press, plans are underway for the fourth ICLARS Conference, in Oxford, United Kingdom, in September 2016.[2]

We have established the ICLARS Series on Law and Religion to provide further opportunities and support for those interested in this rapidly expanding field of research, to become a primary source for students and scholars, while presenting authors with a valuable means to reach a wide and growing readership. It is intended that the Series will publish both monographs and edited collections. The Series Editors are Professor Pieter Coertzen (University of Stellenbosch, South Africa), Professor Tahir Mahmood (Amity International University, New Delhi, India), and the three of us. We are supported by an Editorial Advisory Board which comprises Professors Anver Emon, Asher Maoz, Benjamin Berger, Carolyn Evans, Domenico Francavilla, Gerhard Robbers, Juan Navarro Floria, Linda Woodhead, Liu Peng, Marie-Claire Foblets, Rajeev Bhargava, Renáta Uitz, Richard Helmholz, and Willy Zeze. The composition of the Board underscores our ambition to produce an international, interdisciplinary, and innovative series at the forefront of law and religion scholarship. Law and religion is a blossoming field of studies covering both international and national

1 *Law and Religion in the 21st Century: Relations between States and Religious Communities*, Silvio Ferrari and Rinaldo Cristofori, eds (Ashgate 2010); *Law, Religion, Constitution: Freedom of Religion, Equal Treatment, and the Law*,W. Cole Durham, Jr., Silvio Ferrari, Cristiana Cianitto, and Donlu Thayer, eds (Ashgate 2013), as well as the present volume and the forthcoming *Religion, Pluralism, and Reconciling Difference*, both edited by W. Cole Durham, Jr. and Donlu Thayer.

2 Further information can be found on the ICLARS website: http://www.iclars.org/.

laws affecting religions and also the religious legal systems of different faith groups. The increasing religious diversity and visibility that characterize many parts of the world have shown the inadequacy of the traditional systems of regulation of the relations between states, international organizations, and religious communities and has highlighted the need for new legal strategies and tools. This explains the increasing interest in law and religion studies and provides us with an initial rationale for defining the identity of this new Series.

The first defining characteristic of the Series is its international focus. It is not possible to speak of law and religion as universal and well-defined categories with a univocal content. The notions of law and religion need to be contextualized. They do not have the same meaning and do not perform the same social roles in all parts of the world. The need to contextualize these categories and to understand how they are conceived in different social settings is a precondition to any attempt to regulate their relationship. It also needs to be remembered that the relationship between law and religion differs across time and space. For some commentators, the 'law and religion' category is itself the product of a specific Western history, and therefore other categories may be needed to provide a sound legal regulation of religion globally. Only a more intense and continuous dialogue between law and religion scholars from different cultural areas of the world can truly advance mutual understanding. The Series is dedicated to furthering comparative work by providing a home for analysis of the regulation of religion and religious law across the globe. Some of the books will be comparative in nature, while others will focus on particular jurisdictions. Taken as a whole, however, the focus of the Series will be international.

The second defining characteristic of the Series is its interdisciplinary focus. Too often, work on law and religion focuses exclusively on national and international law, in particular human rights law. However, these are only two normative orders among many. Limiting the analysis to the way in which states and international law deal with religion amounts to focusing on just one layer (and sometimes the most superficial) of the complex regulation of religion, neglecting the existence of a normative web made of overlapping and interacting rules. Comparative lawyers have been discussing this topic for a long time, and the outcomes of their research can provide useful hints to law and religion scholars. However, there is a need for more than comparative legal studies. There is a risk that law and religion studies, as practiced by legal scholars, are too legalistic, focusing solely upon formal regulation and paying little attention to how things are enforced, experienced, and lived. There is, therefore, a need for historical, sociological, anthropological, philosophical, and theological knowledge that lawyers may not possess. Without this, no sound and effective regulation of the relations between law and religion is possible. Although the Series will publish doctrinal legal analyses, we will also include works that draw upon theology, sociology, anthropology, history, philosophy, and so on.

The third defining feature of the Series will be its focus on innovation. The studies and researches of law and religion need not only to keep up with the progress of other disciplines and fields of study but also to engage with them, sharing ideas and insight. We will publish monographs and edited collections that innovate in terms of the questions they ask, the approaches they take, and the answers they provide. The Series will explore areas that have been neglected to date in law and religion scholarship and will provide a platform for both established and new voices. For this reason, the Series is especially committed to publishing monographs based on doctoral theses. The Series will also publish collections of papers from leading conferences, including those organized by ICLARS itself.

This edited book is the first of two volumes of selected revised papers from the third ICLARS conference, which was held in the United States, in Richmond, Williamsburg, and

Virginia, from 21–23 August 2013. Co-sponsored by ICLARS, the International Center for Law and Religion Studies at Brigham Young University (ICLRS), the University of Virginia School of Law, the Institute of Bill of Rights Law of William & Mary Law School, and the First Freedom Center, the Virginia conference was a remarkable event, bringing together approximately125 speakers and guests in 'Jefferson country', to consider the topic 'Religion, Democracy, and Equality'. The theme for the conference was developed by the ICLARS Steering Committee – eminent law and religion scholars from Italy, Spain, India, Argentina, Germany, Israel, and South Africa – in response to timely issues that continue to intensify. Fittingly, the central venue for the conference was in Richmond, near where the language was crafted that ultimately became the protections – in the First Amendment to the United States Constitution – of the free exercise of religion and against a government establishment of religion.

ICLARS III opened with a day of 'young scholars' 'sessions, capped with a keynote address – 'Freedom of Religion or Belief: A Classical Human Right under Fire?' – delivered byUnited Nations Special Rapporteur on Freedom of Religion or Belief, Heiner Bielefeldt. Ensuing presentations from international experts in the fields of law, religion, and human rights explored new instantiations of classic tensions between liberty and equality, and differing ideas about how modern secular states can best institutionalize respect for plurality and difference.

The issues discussed at the Virginia conference, presented in this volume and in the forthcoming companion volume, *Religion, Pluralism, and Reconciling Difference*, are representative of the broader array of complex social issues that ICLARS and its members are uniquely qualified to address, and with respect to which they can help promote deeper understanding. We look forward to sharing such explorations with our readers in this new Series.

Professor Silvio Ferrari
(University of Milan, Italy), Series Coordinator

Professor Cole Durham
(Brigham Young University, United States), Series Editor

Dr. Russell Sandberg
(Cardiff University, United Kingdom), Series Manager
October 2015

Comments, queries, and proposals will be gratefully received by the Series Manager at SandbergR@cf.ac.uk, or by Alison Kirk, the Publisher, at Alison.kirk@informa.com.

Foreword

Equality and Diversity in Conceptualizing Freedom of Religion or Belief

Equality is one of the architectural principles upon which the entire system of human rights protection is based. The first sentence of the preamble of the first-ever international human rights document, the 1948 Universal Declaration of Human Rights (UDHR), recognizes 'the inherent dignity' and 'the equal and inalienable rights of all members of the human family' as 'the foundation of freedom, justice and peace in the world'. There is a compelling logic underlying this connection. If respect for human dignity is to serve as the axiomatic condition for any meaningful normative interaction among human beings, then the institutionalization of this foundational respect, in the form of human rights, must necessarily include all human beings equally. Human rights are conceivable only as equal rights of everyone. Article 1 of the UDHR corroborates this overarching normative structure by proclaiming: 'All human beings are born free and equal in dignity and rights.'

The principle of equality defines the normative profile of the human rights approach in general – and thus of each and every human right, including the right to freedom of thought, conscience, religion, or belief. This is not only a right to freedom, but also a right to equality. Hence, it is no coincidence that all comprehensive human rights documents contain the prohibition of discrimination on various grounds, including the grounds of religion or belief. The 1981 Declaration on the Elimination of All Forms of Intolerance and of Discrimination on the Basis of Religion or Belief spells out this prohibition more specifically by addressing the various societal spheres in which religious discrimination may occur. Its Article 3 sends a strong message by reminding states that 'discrimination between human beings on the grounds of religion or belief constitutes an affront to human dignity and a disavowal of the principles of the Charter of the United Nations.'

However, when it comes to conceptualizing equality more precisely in order to make it applicable in practice, vexing complications may arise. What makes equality and non-discrimination in the area of freedom of religion or belief particularly difficult is, above all, the experience that religious or belief communities – Jews, Christians, Muslims, Baha'is, Hindus, Buddhists, Taoists, indigenous communities, and numerous others – have *very different* needs and demands. They follow different liturgical calendars, celebrate different holidays, practice a huge variety of different rituals, prescribe all sorts of dietary rules, and may employ totally different forms of religious self-organization. One should not forget that freedom of religion or belief also protects atheists or agnostics, which adds yet another layer of complexity. Where is the common denominator that nonetheless allows us to strive for equality within this vastly complex and diverse landscape?

The first step to an answer is easy: it is human beings who provide that common denominator. Due to its nature as a human right, freedom of religion or belief protects human beings rather than religions or belief systems in themselves. Hence, the basic respect institutionalized in freedom of religion or belief always relates to human beings who, strictly speaking, act as the only rights holders in the framework of human rights. In order to avoid a widespread misunderstanding, it may be useful to add that when exercising their rights, human beings usually do so in community with others, and they may furthermore need an appropriate infrastructure to be able to practice their religion. That is why the focus on human beings as right holders should not be confused with a narrowly 'individualistic' conceptualization of freedom of religion or belief. Taking seriously the community dimension of freedom of religion or belief, however, does not alter the fact that it is up to human beings to tell legislators, judiciaries, and other state agencies what precisely they need in order to be able fully to enjoy their freedom of religion or belief in practice. Like other human rights, freedom of religion or belief presupposes, and at the same time facilitates, the free articulation of human beings. It is they who have to define what really matters and how they wish to be respected and protected in their various religious or belief-related identities.

Free articulation thus brings us to the concept of freedom, which is another architectonic principle underpinning the human rights approach in general. Freedom and equality are inextricably intertwined. One could even say that they represent two sides of one and the same foundational principle, i.e. the principle of equal freedom for all. Without equality, rights of freedom would sink to mere privileges, and without regard to freedom, the principle of equality could easily be mistaken for uniformity or 'sameness'.[3] In other words, human rights empower all human beings equally to pursue their freely chosen life plans, to enjoy equal respect for their irreplaceable personal biographies, to freely express their diverse political opinions, and to freely manifest their different faith-related convictions and practices, as individuals and in community with others. Instead of leading to a homogeneous or uniform society, the equal implementation of human rights for everyone will contribute to the flourishing of the existing and emerging diversity in society. In the framework of human rights equality has always been, and can only be, a diversity-friendly equality. Freedom of religion or belief may be the most obvious example in this regard.

Pointing to human beings and their freedom to articulate what matters to them provides only the first element of an answer to the above question about how to conceptualize equality in the area of religious diversity. What about public holidays, for example? Do they not usually privilege certain predominant religious traditions at the expense of equal treatment of all? If so, would it not be logical to either abolish all public holidays linked to a particular liturgical calendar or, alternatively, enlarge the list of public holidays in such a way as to take on board the festivities of all religions and beliefs which happen to exist in the country (which in practice would be impossible)? Although few people would draw such radical conclusions, the problem remains that even in a society committed to everyone's equal freedom of religion or belief the existing normative standards will most likely reflect – and thus also reinforce – the country's predominant religious or cultural traditions, with discriminatory implications for people of alternative orientations.

The example of public holidays is evident and in that sense easy. In reality this may just be the tip of a huge iceberg. Whereas the tip is visible, we may in many cases not even be aware

3 This misunderstanding already occurred in Edmund Burke, *Reflection on the Revolution in France* (J.M. Dent & Sons 1910; original James Dodsley 1790).

of the existence of the iceberg, i.e. the manifold issues of discriminatory treatment which may be hidden under the veneer of everyday practices, general rules, and regulations. Although seemingly applying to everyone equally, the existing normative structure in a society may reflect the implicit standpoints of majority religions, predominant cultures, and hegemonic ways of life. Dress codes in public institutions which, for the majority, may seem totally 'natural' may impose a heavy burden on some members of religious minorities. Working schedules in companies may create problems for people who, due to religious prescripts, feel obliged not to work on specific days. And in some situations certain professional duties, as defined for those employed by hospitals or other institutions, may collide with deeply held conscientious convictions.[4]

Apart from direct, straightforward, and unconcealed manifestations of discrimination which continue to cause violations of human rights, less salient forms of discrimination – indirect or structural discrimination – also exist. Frequently, people involved in such discrimination may not even be aware of what they are doing. This experience has given rise to demands for a more nuanced understanding of equality, which would also allow us to better address concealed forms of discrimination.

In the literature, broader understanding of equality sometimes figures under the heading of 'substantive equality'. The assumption is that we should move away (and partially have already moved away) from mere 'formal' towards a more 'substantive' equality. Whereas formal equality treats everyone equally without sufficiently taking into account relevant specificities of certain people – such as their specific needs or specific vulnerabilities – substantive equality is thought to be more accommodating towards relevant differences. For instance, based on empirical evidence on persisting religious discrimination in many European States, the EU-sponsored RELIGARE project has recommended substantive equality in order to do justice to persons belonging to religious minorities.[5] One measure designed to promote this purpose is 'reasonable accommodation' of specific needs of minorities in the workplace or other spheres of societal life. This may include exemptions from generally binding rules in order to avoid conflicts with deeply held convictions or certain conviction based practices. In the words of Gabrielle Caceres, 'Reasonable accommodation aims at relaxing generally applicable rules in order to guarantee a more substantive equality in which the specificities of everyone are taken into account.'[6]

Calls for substantive equality generally have a great deal of persuasive force because it seems evident that, without accommodating relevant differences, the principle of equality might simply prolong existing hegemonic standards. Empirical research indicates that in many situations this is actually the case. At the same time, it often remains somewhat unclear which differences or specificities should be accommodated in practice. Of course, in a spirit of respect for everyone's free self-identification and self-articulation, the starting point must always be human beings who have to take the first step by requesting accommodation of their specific religious or belief-related needs. But which arguments should count in this regard?

4 One example is the conscience-based refusal of doctors or nurses to get involved with carrying out abortions.

5 Marie-Claire Foblets, Katayoun Alidadi, Jorgen Nielsen, and Zeynep Yanasmayan, eds, *Belief, Law and Politics. What Future for a Secular Europe?* (Ashgate 2014).

6 Gabrielle Caceres, 'Reasonable Accommodation as a Tool to Manage Religious Diversity in the Workplace: What about the "Transposability" of an American Concept in the French Secular Context?', in Katayoun Alidadi, Marie-Claire Foblets and Jogchum Vrielinek, eds, *A Test of Faith? Religious Diversity and Accommodation in the European Workplace* (Ashgate 2012), 284.

The challenge is to accommodate relevant differences without simply blurring the contours of the principle of equality. How can we avoid the danger that the element of 'difference', when built into a new and possibly more accommodating conceptualization of equality, could lead to arbitrariness or even cause retrogressive effects? The above quote from Caceres gives a hint by insisting that what should be taken into account is 'the specificities of *everyone*' (emphasis added). Of course, this does not mean that specific accommodations or exemptions granted to one person in recognition of his or her specific religious needs should actually be made available to everyone else, which would be absurd. Instead, what it means is that measures of specific accommodation should be applicable to all those who can plausibly claim that they live, roughly speaking, in an analogous situation and would be faced with an analogously existential conflict if measures of accommodation were denied. Admittedly, what an 'analogous situation' is may often be debatable and the actual application of this rule will most likely be controversial in many situations. And yet, this way of reasoning seems to be the only plausible course to steer out of the dilemma of either denying any accommodation of specific religious needs *in toto* or opening the floodgate of arbitrary and privileged treatment.

Measures of accommodation or the granting of specific exemptions are, by definition, always contextual. They refer to the contextualized specificities of individual cases or situations. At the same time, however, their justification depends on the possibility of discussing and assessing them within the broader normative horizon of equality for everyone. Even though the actual measure of accommodation may be limited to just very few people, *the criteria of justification* of such a specific measure must do justice to the egalitarian spirit underlying human rights in general.

Within the framework of human rights, substantive equality cannot be mere compromise between formal equality and some vague accommodation of differences, nor can it be the middle ground between strictly equal treatment of everyone and a more lenient attitude. Such a diffuse compromise would be less, not more, than formal equality; it would be a step backwards instead of moving ahead. At the end of the day, a diffuse compromise between equality and difference might amount to the very dissolution of equality as a systematically applicable principle. The Aristotelian formula of treating 'equal things equally and unequal things unequally'[7] – which strangely enough continues to be frequently cited as a guiding idea in legal literature even today – is no help in this regard. If taken literally, it would actually pave the way to fragmentation in normative issues and the loss of any critical stance against arbitrary privileges and discrimination.[8]

For the concept of equality to retain its foundational function in human rights, it must provide the horizon *within which* any 'specificities' must be claimed, negotiated, and finally assessed. In practice, this requirement is less difficult to apply than it may seem at first glance. Indeed, the egalitarian spirit underpinning the human rights approach in general has never precluded the possibility, and indeed advisability, of according additional attention to people who live in situations of increased vulnerability – such as refugees, migrant workers, persons with disabilities, and individuals belonging to religious minorities. Such extra

7 'But that the unequal should be given to equals, and the unlike to those who are like, is contrary to nature, and nothing which is contrary to nature is good.' Aristotle, *Politics*, Book 7, Part III, trans. Benjamin Jowett (1984), University of Adelaide, https://ebooks.adelaide.edu.au/a/aristotle/a8po/book7.html (updated 15 July 2015, accessed 30 October 2015).

8 It should not be forgotten that Aristotle justified slavery as a 'natural' and just institution.

attention given to people in vulnerable situations usually finds broad endorsement, as long as it is based on universalistic criteria which do not single out certain individuals or groups while turning a blind eye to the special needs and problems of others.

What follows from this reflection? The notion of 'substantive equality' should be not be mistaken as a move away from 'formal equality', but instead should be conceptualized as a more nuanced and sophisticated continuation of 'formal equality'. Rather than promoting a gradual de-formalization of equality, which in the end would leave us with congeries of unrelated diversity claims, substantive equality may remind us of the never-ending task of spelling out the practical implications of equality in the light of different and often changing demands put forward by the subjects of human rights: i.e. human beings and indeed all of them.

While philosophers have tried to clarify the meaning of substantive equality by designing thought experiments, such as the Rawlsian 'veil of ignorance',[9] lawyers usually operate more pragmatically in a case-by-case manner. This is fine. It should be borne in mind, however, that a case-by-case approach is more than just ad-hoc decision-making. In dealing with specific claims for accommodations or exemptions, those in charge of deciding should know (and usually do know) that, whatever decision they take, their judgment will have repercussions on other cases that will inevitably arise in the future. Any decided case can serve as a precedent to which others may legitimately refer, provided they can claim plausibly to live in an analogous situation of increased vulnerability or to have comparable religious or belief-related needs which would warrant similar accommodation. In this way, the precise contours of a more substantive equality remain historically open, while the principle of equality itself provides the general normative horizon within which any claims, debates, negotiations, and assessments must strictly remain.

The chapters that follow probe the boundaries and the internal domains of this general normative horizon, bringing the vantage points of different regions and different normative perspectives to bear on the enduring yet recurring challenges of religion and equality.

Heiner Bielefeldt

9 The 'veil of ignorance' within the original position as constructed in Rawls's Theory of Justice does not filter out contextual factors in general, as many critics have asserted, but merely illustrates the need of abstracting from personal egoistic interests and biases.

Abbreviations and Terms

1981 Declaration	Declaration on the Elimination of All Forms of Intolerance and Discrimination based on Religion or Belief
ACHR	American Convention on Human Rights (Pact of San José)
Amsterdam Treaty	Treaty of Amsterdam amending the Treaty of the European Union, the Treaties establishing the European Communities and certain related acts
BLAG	Bipartisan Legal Advisory Group
CEDAW	Convention on the Elimination of all Forms of Discrimination Against Women
CDF	(Catholic) Congregation for the Doctrine of the Faith
CFR	Charter of Fundamental Rights of the European Union (Treaty of Nice)
CJEU	Court of Justice of the European Union (EU institution encompassing the entire judiciary)
COE	Council of Europe (having 47 member states)
CorteIDH	Corte Interamericana de Derechos Humanos (Inter-American Court of Human Rights)
DOMA	Defense of Marriage Act (USA)
ECHR	European Convention on Human Rights (a Council of Europe institution, formally the Convention for the Protection of Human Rights and Fundamental Freedoms)
ECJ	European Court of Justice (European Union)
ECmHR	European Commission of Human Rights (Council of Europe)
ECtHR	European Court of Human Rights (Council of Europe)
EU	European Union (having 28 member states)
FRA	European Union Agency for Fundamental Rights
IACourtHR/ICH	Inter-American Court of Human Rights (Corte Interamericana de Derechos Humanos)
ICCPR	International Covenant on Civil and Political Rights
ICESCR	International Covenant on Economic, Social and Cultural Rights
ICLARS	International Consortium for Law and Religion Studies (Italy)
ICLRS	International Center for Law and Religion Studies (USA)
LGBTI	Lesbian, Gay, Bi-sexual, Transgender, Intersex
OAS	Organization of American States
NGO	Non-governmental Organization
PACE	Parliamentary Assembly of the Council of Europe

PCANZ	Presbyterian Church of Aotearoa New Zealand
RELIGARE	Religious Diversity and Secular Models in Europe
RFRA	Religious Freedom Restoration Act (USA)
RLUIPA	Religious Land Use and Institutionalized Person Act (USA)
SABJE	South African Board of Jewish Education
SAHRC	South African Human Rights Commission
SSM	Same-sex marriage
TEEC	Treaty establishing the European Economic Community (original Treaty of Rome)
TEC	Treaty establishing the European Community (Treaty of Rome renamed following the Maastricht Treaty)
TEU	Treaty on European Union (Maastricht Treaty)
TFEU	Treaty on the Functioning of the European Union (Treaty of Rome after Treaty of Lisbon)
Treaty of Lisbon	'Reform Treaty' modifying the Treaties of Rome and Maastricht
TWU	Trinity Western University (Canada)
UDHR	Universal Declaration of Human Rights
VA	Voluntary Association (South Africa)

Introduction

1 Conscience and Equality

Negotiating Emerging Tensions

Russell Sandberg

A New Atmosphere

The present volume represents a new stage in the work of the International Consortium for Law and Religion Studies (ICLARS): the launch of a series of publications dedicated to the academic study of law and religion. Although collections based on papers from previous ICLARS conferences have been published,[1] this is the first collection of such papers to be published as part of ICLARS' own Series on Law and Religion.

The establishment of this series is entirely appropriate. In the opening decades of the twenty-first century, issues concerning law and religion are never far from the global news headlines. Acts of terrorism committed in the name of religion; moral panics concerning the operation of religious courts; controversies about the relationship between freedom of expression and freedom of religion; disputes about the wearing of religious dress and symbols; the role of religion in marriage law and in the education system; and questions about the autonomy of religious groups are just some of the issues that continue to excite controversy in society at large. Thoroughly different and often entrenched views exist as to the role of religion in the public sphere.

These controversies often have a legal dimension. Lawyers – both practitioners and academics – are increasingly focusing upon law and religion matters. In some jurisdictions, law and religion is becoming regarded as an academic subject for the first time, studied and researched like family law or employment law. Elsewhere, where aspects of law and religion have long been studied and taught, there has also been a significant change: the focus has mutated to increasingly include the study of religious freedom as a human right and the religious laws of religious minorities.

The academic study of law and religion has become more visible and more important in recent years as a result of the same changes that have made the role of religion in the public sphere controversial. The ICLARS initiative has played an important role in this development.[2] The new ICLARS Series on Law and Religion takes this activity a stage further, providing a forum for the rapidly expanding field of research in law and religion. The Series will be a home not only for edited collections resulting from ICLARS conferences

1 Silvio Ferrari and Rinaldo Cristofori, eds, *Law and Religion in the 21st Century: Relations between States and Religious Communities* (Ashgate 2010); and W. Cole Durham, Jr., Silvio Ferrari, Cristiana Cianitto and Donlu Thayer, eds, *Law, Religion, Constitution: Freedom of Religion, Equal Treatment and the Law* (Ashgate 2013).

2 Further information can be found on the ICLARS website: http://www.iclars.org/.

and other ICLARS events but also for the very best law and religion scholarship from across the globe. The term 'law and religion' will be widely defined,[3] and the Series will include both edited collections arising from important events and cutting-edge monographs by both established names and new voices. The Series will include interdisciplinary works, comparative examinations, and detailed studies of particular jurisdictions.[4] In short, it will be home to the wide-ranging and dynamic scholarship produced by academics with an interest in and passion for law and religion around the globe, reflecting the increasing societal, political and legal interest in religion.

Taking the Temperature

The emergence of the ICLARS Series on Law and Religion Series might seem unsurprising, even inevitable. However, the fact that religion is receiving more scholarly attention in the twenty-first century than the twentieth and that this is especially the case in relation to legal scholarship is actually rather surprising.

Speaking in 1888 as part of a course of lectures on 'The Constitutional History of England', Frederic Maitland suggested that 'religious liberty and religious equality is complete.'[5] The extent to which lawyers in the twenty-first century are concerned with matters of 'religious liberty and religious equality', both in Maitland's home country and around the world, clearly would have surprised England's greatest legal historian.

In many respects, it is important not to be too critical of Maitland's assertion. His understanding of 'religious liberty and religious equality' was narrowly related to the toleration of the right of religious groups to worship and of adherents of all faiths to hold public offices. In these respects, his statement remains broadly accurate. And Maitland's account of the historical development of religion under English law continues to be the starting point for the subject.[6] However, what Maitland failed to see is that the question of religious freedom – at both a collective and an individual level – would not only continue to be important and irresolvable but would grow in significance, giving rise to a large body of law.

It is perfectly understandable that Maitland would not have predicted this situation. A number of complex political, religious, and sociological changes have affected the place of religion within society since 1888. These include not only the increased religious pluralism and diversity that has come about as a result in part of increased mobility and immigration; it is also the consequence of new ways of thinking. Modern technology has made the world a much smaller place and has put information at our finger tips. These changes have all

3 For discussion of the definition of the term see Russell Sandberg, *Law and Religion* (Cambridge University Press 2011), 6, which proposes that 'the study of law and religion is *at least* the study of religion law and religious law': that is, 'religion law', the 'external' temporal laws made by the state, international bodies and sub-state institutions that affect religious individuals and groups and 'religious law; the 'internal' spiritual laws or regulations made by religious groups themselves which affect the members of those groups and how that group interacts with the secular legal regime.

4 See, further, the Series Introduction in this volume.

5 Frederic W. Maitland, *Constitutional History of England* (Cambridge University Press 1908), 520.

6 In particular, Frederic W. Maitland, *Roman Canon Law in the Church of England* (Methuen, 1898). For appraisal see, for example, James R. Cameron, *Frederick William Maitland and the History of English Law* (University of Oklahoma Press 1961), Chapter IV; ,and H. Edith Bell, *Maitland: A Critical Examination and Assessment* (Adam & Charles Black 1965), Chapter VIII and Russell Sandberg, 'F W Maitland: Faithful Dissenter' in Richard H Helmholz and Mark Hill, eds, *Great Christian Jurists in English History* (Cambridge University Press forthcoming)

impacted what we believe and what we consider the role of the law ought to be in terms of accommodating freedom of thought, conscience, and religion.

There have also been significant changes in terms of religious beliefs and practices. The picture is complex, and there is significant variation from place to place as a result of a myriad of factors that are historical, geographical, sociological, cultural, political, economic and theological. Any single attempt to explain the picture is bound to be over-simplistic, whether it is in the form of Enlightenment era inspired prophecies about the social decline of religion or of twenty-first century statements that religion has returned.[7] Predictions about the death of God and the demise of the secularization thesis are both premature.[8] However, both also have elements of truth about them. Most societies are no longer mono-creedal, and several societies, especially those in Europe, are clearly more secular than they once were, though, of course, the meaning and consequence of the term 'secular' is open to much debate. Moreover, sophisticated versions of the secularization thesis, which provide a more nuanced assessment than simply stating that God is dead in modern society, have not been debunked by the so-called 'return of religion'.[9] Secularization theories are limited: they can only provide a limited account of the role of religion in society because they are what Charles Taylor has called 'subtraction stories' in that they only explain the fortunes of those forms of religiosity which were previously dominant.[10] However, such theories can provide part of the picture, provided it is remembered that patterns of religious change are historically and geographically specific and operate at different levels, affecting social institutions, religious institutions, and individuals in different ways.[11]

One explanation is to suggest that two waves of secularization have occurred in the Western world.[12] The first wave consisted of the (on-going) battles of modernity which began with the Enlightenment. The key process was that of differentiation.[13] Rather than one institution (the Church) performing a myriad of social functions, a range of specialist institutions developed (the state, the education system, the media, the family, the churches, etc.) each performing specific functions. The result of this was that the Church moved away from the center of social life: it was no longer the main or unique educator, discipliner, instiller of societal values). The second wave of secularization can be said to have affected the individual rather than the societal level and to have occurred following the Second World War and in the sixties in particular, provided 'the hinge moment, at least symbolically', ushering in 'an individuating revolution'.[14] This led to what

7 See, further, Russell Sandberg, *Religion, Law and Society* (Cambridge University Press 2014).

8 See, by way of comparison, Steve Bruce, *God is Dead* (Blackwell 2002), and Rodney Stark, 'Secularisation RIP', (1999) 60 *Sociology of Religion* (3) 249.

9 This is true of the work of Steve Bruce despite the sensationalist title of his 2002 book. See, in particular, Steve Bruce, *Secularization: In Defence of an Unfashionable Theory* (Oxford Universty Press 2011).

10 Charles Taylor, *A Secular Age* (Harvard University Press 2007), 22.

11 Karel Dobbelaere, *Secularization: An Analysis at Three Levels* (Peter Lang 2002).

12 Sandberg, *Religion, Law and Society*, supra note 7 at 171.

13 See further, Sandberg, *Religion, Law and Society*, supra note 7 at 64. The concept of differentiation is also central to the social systems theory of Niklas Luhmann. For a discussion of its potential application in relation to law and religion see Russell Sandberg, 'Religious Law as a Social System', in Russell Sandberg, ed., *Religion and Legal Pluralism* (Ashgate 2015), and Russell Sandberg, 'A Sociological Theory of Law and Religion' in Frank Cranmer, Mark Hill QC, Celia Kenny and& Russell Sandberg, eds, *The Confluence of Law and Religion: Interdisciplinary Reflections on the Work of Norman Doe* (Cambridge University Press 2016).

14 Charles Taylor, *Varieties of Religion Today* (Harvard University Press 2002), 80.

has been referred to as the 'subjective turn';[15] the way in which the 'subjectivities of each individual became a, if not the, unique source of significance, meaning and authority'.[16] This describes the increased focus people placed upon the construction and re-construction of personal identities.[17] This has resulted from a lack of trust in public institutions and a death of deference. We are now less deferential to authority than we once were and we tend to define ourselves much more by our achieved status rather than by our ascribed positions. Following the end of the Cold War and the collapse of Communism old certainties continued to collapse. And such trends have escalated in recent years. The closing years of the twentieth century and the start of the twenty-first century have been the era of globalization, the fragmentation of politics, the rise of the Internet, and a number of scandals concerning the financial industries, the political classes, the media and the historical churches.

The result of these complex and often contradictory social changes is that the place of religion in the public sphere has become controversial. We are now much more questioning of all forms of authority, including religious authority. Most societies are now much more diverse in terms of life experiences, including religious experiences. In an ever-changing world, older traditional ways of life are misunderstood but newer seemingly different beliefs and practices are also treated with caution, if not hostility, since an age of declining certainties provides a climate for increased fears. The traditionalist and the outsider both become the Other. This is affecting the very way in which we talk about religion. Issues concerning law and religion are now inherently divisive and contentious in our post-9/11 age, where the very suggestion that some people may owe a loyalty to a source of authority other than the nation state causes suspicion.

These social changes have resulted in a lack of consensus about the place of religion. This has been partially reflected in a significant increase in legislation and litigation about religious matters in many jurisdictions, while other jurisdictions have seen existing laws affecting religion become increasingly controversial, with disputes being reported, simplified, and played out in the media. This trend has been referred to as the 'juridification of religion' and can be said to have three dimensions:[18] first, 'legal explosion', that is the process 'through which law comes to regulate an increasing number of different activities'; second, the increase in litigation whereby 'conflicts increasingly are being solved by or with reference to law'; and third, 'legal framing', that is the process 'by which people increasingly tend to think of themselves and others as legal subjects'.[19] 'Legal framing' denotes the way in which reference to law is used outside the courtroom as both a way of solving conflict and also to shape policy. This is shown by the way in which the language of religious rights has begun to enter into the public discourse as a result of the new legal obligations and the media reporting of litigation and is evident in the number of courses, guidelines, and policies which employers and public authorities now have concerning religion.

15 See, for example, Charles Taylor, *The Ethics of Authenticity* (Harvard University Press 1991), 26; Sandberg, *Religion, Law and Society*, supra note 7 at 161.

16 Paul Heelas and Linda Woodhead, *The Spiritual Revolution* (Blackwell 2005).

17 See, further, Russell Sandberg, 'The Impossible Compromise', in Sandberg, ed., *Religion and Legal Pluralism*, supra note 13 at 1.

18 Sandberg, *Law and Religion*, supra note 3, Chapter 10.

19 Lars C. Blicher and& Anders Molander, 'Mapping Juridification', (2008) 14 *European Law Journal* (1) 36.

This 'juridification of religion' has led to an increase in the profile of law and religion, but at a cost. The fact that contentious issues and cases have enjoyed a high media profile has been unfortunate, given that the media reception of the issues has often been informed by a base fear of religious difference.[20] Complex issues have been over-simplified by a media perplexed by the complex social changes that have occurred. And the political haste in passing new laws or revising existing laws has often required judges to reach sociological decisions which they are ill-equipped to do.[21] A number of unfortunate shortcuts have been taken: decision – makers have favoured 'binary' solutions where adherents are forced to choose between following their religious beliefs and enjoying the citizenship rights they would otherwise enjoy under state law; and it is often assumed that religious groups are homogenous entities where all believers share identical beliefs and a direct link between creedal assent and behaviour can be assumed.[22]

The Same Rain

It is possible, however, to overestimate the novelty of the situation in which we find ourselves. The number of moral panics concerning religion in recent years suggests that the lack of consensus about how to accommodate religious difference is a new problem. It is not. It is true, of course, that recent years have seen a number of often unexpected storm clouds concerning religion and that even experts in the field have been taken aback by the torrential nature of the downpour. But while the causes of such storms are new, the storms themselves have been experienced before. It is the same rain. Concerns about apparently religiously motivated acts of violence are not new. Moral panics about the otherness of those who practice Islam rehearse fears that were previously reserved for those who practiced non-sanctioned forms of Christianity. We have been here before. The current position is the product of both change and continuity.

However, it is not simply a case of history repeating itself. The storm clouds do differ from place to place. This underlines the need to understand particular downpours in context. Our analysis of any particular storm – say the clash between religious and non-religious views on the nature of marriage – will be enriched if we understand it in the context of other storms across the ages and if we are able to compare the situation across jurisdictions. Explorations of issues concerning law and religion can benefit from the work that has already been done, whether that is historical or comparative in nature.

This is one of the reasons why networks of law and religion scholars such as ICLARS are important. They provide a home for such historical and comparative work, whether that be the product of one academic or the opportunity for scholars to collaborate or to learn from each other's research. Academic networks provide a number of means by which we

20 This has been epitomized by the ill-informed public debate concerning Sharia law and Sharia courts, on which see, for example, Ralph Grillo, *Muslim, Families, Politics and the Law* (Ashgate 2015). For an example of research which has sought to replace this heat with light see the 'Social Cohesion and Civil Law: Marriage, Divorce and Religious Courts' Research Project carried out by Gillian Douglas and her colleagues at Cardiff University, funded by the AHRC/ESRC Religion and Society Programme (http://www.law.cf.ac.uk/clr/research/cohesion.html, accessed 11 October 2015).

21 An example of this is the growing emphasis on proportionality, on which see Megan Pearson, 'Proportionality: A Way Forward for Resolving Religious Claims?' in Nick Spencer, ed., *Religion and Law* (Theos 2012), 35.

22 See, further, Russell Sandberg, 'The Impossible Compromise', in Sandberg, *Religion and Legal Pluralism* supra note 13 at 1.

can ensure that today's scholarship builds upon yesterday's achievements and that we do not simply constantly re-invent the wheel. Conferences and other symposiums, specialist journals, and email updates allow us to be aware of what others are doing. They allow us to draw upon each other's work and to make comparisons across time and place.

The present volume, in line with the work of ICLARS generally, seeks to facilitate this by bringing to a larger audience revised papers from the third ICLARS conference on 'Religion, Democracy and Equality' which was held in the United States, in Virginia, from 21–23 August 2013.

A Changing Climate

This book is the first of two collections of revised papers from the third ICLARS conference. It focuses on religion and equality in two respects: the first is the focus on the development of religion as an anti-discrimination norm generally; the second is the focus on religion within the context of the recognition same-sex marriage. These focuses are connected.

The development of religion as an anti-discrimination norm has occurred as a result of the impact of international and national laws dealing with equality upon religious groups and believers. On the one hand, the tension between the law of the state and the autonomy of belief communities is not new.[23] Yet, on the other hand, the issue has become markedly more important in recent years not only as a result of the social changes discussed above but also because of changes in the legal regulation. The major change has been the development of international legal human rights standards following the Second World War. Although provisions protecting religious freedom were commonplace in many national constitutions before this time, the development of religious freedom as a human right in an international framework provided a watershed moment. The post-War period has seen the development of human rights instruments at global and regional levels, with provisions being interpreted and refined by the creation of soft law and judicial decisions. These judicial decisions have furthered the 'juridification of religion'. Recourse to arguments based on constitutional or international human rights law and equality provisions have become commonplace in disputes concerning religion. International standards have influenced in several respects the interpretation of religious freedom and equality provisions at a state and sub-state level.

Moreover, religious equality is not the only protected ground under the plethora of international, national, and sub-national legal instruments. Laws protecting equality based on race, sex, and sexual orientation in particular have had an impact upon religious freedom. There has been much talk of the 'clash of rights'. The question of to what extent, if any, religious groups and individuals should be able to apply different standards as to religious, race, sex, and sexual orientation discrimination has been asked in several different contexts. Should religious groups be able to insist that their leaders and representatives follow doctrinal teachings in terms of both what they preach and what they practice? Should religious institutions be able to reserve certain offices to members of one sex only? Should religious courts be able to make rulings that breach state law standards as to gender equality? Should a religious registrar be able to refuse to conduct same-sex marriages? Should religious organizations be obliged to provide services for such couples?

23 The underlying tension can be seen in the New Testament instruction to 'render unto Caesar the things that are Caesar's and unto God, the things that are God's' (Matthew 22:21).

These last two questions refer to a particular tension that has emerged in many states in recent years: the clash between the right to religious freedom and the right not to be discriminated against on grounds of sexual orientation. In most jurisdictions, the legal regulations of religious and sexual identities have taken a similar trajectory.[24] Historically, the law discriminated against people of certain religions and sexual orientations, often by the criminalization of activities on grounds of the sex of participants.[25] Over time, however, many but not all of these disadvantages and criminal offences were removed. The previously illegal forms of religiosity and sexual identity became tolerated but they were still seen as being unusual. This toleration was achieved on an *ad hoc* and piecemeal basis. This stance of non-discrimination was then gradually superseded by the active promotion of anti-discrimination. This involved the promulgation of laws forbidding discrimination on grounds of religion and sexual orientation and the development of the notion that these forms of identity were protected as subjective constitutional and/or human rights. This stance of anti-discrimination has led to the revisiting of laws and practices which explicitly or implicitly discriminate against minorities by normalizing majority practices and assumptions. This has meant changes, for instance, to how the law defines terms such as religion, the family, and marriage.

Although the journeys of the legal regulation of religion and sexual orientation have been similar, the journey began much later in relation to sexual orientation than religion and has been far quicker. The move from the law discriminating against homosexuality to the law prohibiting such discrimination has occurred over decades rather than centuries. Much has changed in the early years of the twenty-first century. Many jurisdictions created legal relationships and institutions that are functionally equivalent to marriage and many states have now gone further in their quest for equality to recognize same-sex marriages. These rapid social changes have posed particular problems for some religious groups and believers. Opinions and stances which were the norm just a few decades ago are now regarded as being discriminatory, prejudiced, and even bigoted. Changing societal understandings of marriage in particular have proved challenging given the role that religious groups have traditionally played, with marriages often taking place in religious settings using religious rites.[26]

24 Russell Sandberg, 'The Right to Discriminate' (2011) 13 *Ecclesiastical Law Journal* (2) 157–181.

25 For an examination of the historical development of laws protecting sexual orientation, see Stephen Cretney, *Same Sex Relationships: From Odious Crime to 'Gay Marriage'* (Oxford University Press 2006).

26 There is considerable variation, however, in the extent to which state law recognizes religious marriages. For example, in his study of the laws of European states, Norman Doe noted that it is a principle of religion law common to the states of Europe that 'The State must permit the celebration of marriage in a religious context following a civil marriage' and 'may recognize a marriage conducted in accordance with a religious rite as having a civil effect either from the moment of its ritual celebration or from the moment of its civil registration provided the conditions set down by law are met.' Doe pointed out that, although all states permitted the celebration of a religious marriage following a civil marriage, there are three models in terms of the formation and recognition of religious marriages. The first model consists of 'States which recognize the validity and public effects of certain religious marriages formed at the time of their ritual celebration, provided the conditions of civil law are met'. The second comprises 'States which recognize Catholic marriages as religious marriage with civil effect from the time of their ritual celebration'. The third consists of 'States which do not recognize religious marriages at all, but may permit a religious ceremony subsequent to a civil marriage, or indeed penalize their solemnization under criminal law if conducted prior to a civil marriage'. Norman Doe, *Law and Religion in Europe* (Oxford University Press 2011), 264, 216.

This book falls into two sections. The first, 'Religion and Anti-Discrimination Norms', explores how religion has developed as an anti-discrimination norm, examining the developing law on equality and human rights and how it operates at international and national levels. The second section, 'Religion and Same Sex Marriage', then provides a case study, exploring the contemporary issue of same-sex marriage and how it affects religious groups and believers.

The first section begins with a chapter by Romanian scholar Nicolae Dură that sets the scene by providing a *tour de force* on how religion is protected by international laws at both a global and regional level. The chapter introduces and analyzes the legal framework concerning freedom of religion at the international level before exploring the instruments and institutions at a pan-European level. The chapter distinguishes the separate but increasingly connected protections afforded by the Council of Europe and the European Union, a theme which is developed in the chapter that follows by Mark Hill QC. While the European Court of Human Rights at Strasbourg – a product of the Council of Europe – has spent the last two decades generating an increasingly complex case law concerning religious freedom, the Court of Justice of the European Union in Luxembourg – an institution of the European Union – has only started to deal with religious matters in enforcing EU directives forbidding discrimination on grounds of religion. Hill's chapter compares the two courts and their interrelationship, an issue that is likely to become increasingly important. The next chapter, by María J. Valero Estarellas, furthers this analysis by focusing on the jurisprudence of the European Court of Human Rights, looking in particular at the recent controversial case law concerning religion in the workplace. The chapter explores not only the decisions themselves but also the changes in the interpretation of Article 9, identifying new principles being developed by the Strasbourg Court. The chapter underscores how, although the text of instruments protecting religious freedom remain unchanged, the interpretation of such provisions evolves in light of changing social tensions and also as a result of a growing confidence by court actors. The jurisprudence of the European Court of Human Rights on religion is no longer in its infancy; it has now entered a period of adolescence and the growing pains are often all too evident.

Similar experiences can be found at the national level in both Europe and elsewhere. This is underscored in the last two chapters in this first section. The chapter by Rodrigo Alves provides an examination of how anti-discrimination law concerning religion has developed and is developing in Brazil. The Brazilian experience should be of much wider interest since the chapter reveals how the country is peacefully undergoing one of the most dramatic religious shifts in the world today. It is important, however, not simply to focus upon developments at a constitutional level, be that internationally or nationally. And so the final chapter in this section, by Greg Walsh, zooms in to a particular issue: the employment decisions of religious schools under anti-discrimination legislation in the Australian State of New South Wales. This provides a concrete case study of many of the themes explored in the section as a whole. The chapter also raises the issue of exceptions or exemptions afforded in the name of religion: should religious schools be exempt from generally applicable laws forbidding discrimination? This issue concerning what may be referred to as 'the right to discriminate' has led to a significant literature by scholars interested in law and religion in recent years, including a number of important works in political and philosophical theory, which has explored the interplay between laws protecting freedom of religion and forbidding discriminating on grounds of sexual orientation.

The second section, 'Religion and Same Sex Marriage', focuses on these concerns. It begins with another *tour de force*, this time by Rex Ahdar, who explores how laws on same-sex marriage in New Zealand, Canada, and the United Kingdom interact with religious freedom. In particular, the chapter explores the extent to which exemptions have been provided for celebrants (that is, religious ministers, clergy, marriage celebrants, commissioners, and registrars) to enable them to refuse to conduct same-sex marriages. In all three jurisdictions studied by Ahdar, the reformulation of marriage law has been fairly recent, though Canada provides a significantly earlier experience, and has been shaped by the aim to provide equality on grounds of sexual orientation. In contrast, in other jurisdictions there has been a much longer experience of reformulating marriage laws for other purposes. Pieter Coertzen's chapter provides a detailed exploration of the development of the law relating to marriage in South Africa, exploring the earlier and much more wide-ranging re-definition of marriage that has occurred there.

The issues present in both Adhar and Coertzen's chapters are then revisited in a chapter by Argentine family law scholar Ursula C. Basset, who not only takes a step back to explore the redefinition of marriage in Europe but provides not-often-seen information about these issues as developed in the Americas, through General Assembly resolutions of the Organization of American States, provisions of the American Convention on Human Rights, and relevant opinions of the Inter-American Court of Human Rights. This section concludes with two chapters by U.S. scholars, the first by Helen Alvaré, who provides a detailed view of the Catholic understanding of marriage, in the light of imputations of animus in all opposition to same-sex marriage made in the majority opinion of the Supreme Court case *United States v. Windsor*.[27] Such concerns as Alvaré raises about potential threats to religious autonomy, arising from such a high-level imputation of malign motives for holding a traditional religious belief, have been amplified for many by the Court's subsequent decision in *Obergefell v. Hodges*,[28] which found a federal constitutional right to same-sex marriage. These issues are developed in the final chapter in this section, by Thomas Berg and Douglas Laycock, which adopts a synoptic approach to explore the current state of U.S. law in relation to same-sex marriage and the protection of religious autonomy. The book then closes with a chapter by W. Cole Durham that explores the themes of the book as a whole, examining amongst other things the role of exemptions and the concept of reasonable accommodation, to engage with the work of Heiner Bielefeldt, who kindly provided the preface to this volume and a keynote address at the third ICLARS conference.

The issue of same-sex marriage and the wider tensions between religious and sexual identities is just one of the ways in which religion is interacting with equality laws in the twenty-first century. Other interactions will be explored not only in the second collection of chapters originally presented at the third ICLARS conference but also in other books which will be published under the auspices of ICLARS Series on Law and Religion. The chapters that appear here, together with those published in the earlier volumes resulting from ICLARS conferences,[29] underscore how dynamic, controversial, and important interactions between law and religion can be. However, the work published to date is just the tip of the iceberg. The ambition of the Series is to reflect the wide-ranging ambit and ambition of scholarship in this and related fields and to stimulate and encourage its further growth. The early years of the twenty-first century have seen storm clouds gather as social and political tensions have

27 *United States v. Windsor*, 133 S. Ct. 2675 (2013).

28 *Obergefell v. Hodges*, 135 S. Ct. 2584 (2015).

29 Ferrari and Cristofori, *Law and Religion in the 21st Century*, supra note 1; and Durham et al., eds, *Law, Religion, Constitution*, supra note 1.

erupted in a downpour of issues, laws, and decisions that have affected religious freedoms. It would be foolish to speculate as to what weather is likely to lie ahead. But even if calmer or sunnier times are to come, there will remain the need for scholars to address the short- and long-term effects of the storm in a calm and erudite manner, away from the glare and sensationalism of the media. There will need to be a place whereby increasingly ambitious analyses can be disseminated to scholars around the world who, although they experience local variations, invariably share experiences of common issues. ICLARS in general and the ICLARS Series on Law and Religion in particular are designed to provide that place for formulating, sharing, and discussing insights, ideas and speculations. It is hoped that this volume provides the start of a new stage of the ICLARS initiative, bringing even closer those around the world who have an interest in and passion for the study of law and religion.

Religion and Anti-Discrimination Norms

2 The Right to Religion

Some Considerations of the Principal International and European Juridical Instruments

Nicolae V. Dură

Religious Freedom as a Human Right

The notion of the right to religious freedom, as a fundamental human right, is not new. According to Roman jurisprudence, the manifestations of a specific religious belief and, it follows, a religion, must be conducted and regulated first of all according to the rules enforced by *jus divinum* (divine law) and *jus naturale* (natural law), which 'nature itself has made along with humankind', and only afterwards by *civilia iura* (civil rights), which 'have been created when the cities were built, the magistrates were elected, and the laws were written down'.[1]

Examination of the texts of the main international and European juridical instruments indicates that religious freedom is itself above all a *jus*, that is a right, which is founded on *jus divinum*, *jus naturale*, and *jus positivum*, i.e. *jus scriptum* (written law),[2] hence its characteristic of *jus cogens* (peremptory norm, fundamental principle of international law). People can only be subjected to the penalties established by the law. They can be deprived of the right to religious freedom when their actions detrimentally affect the rights and freedoms

1 *Institutiones Justiniani*. Lib. II, Tit. I, para. 6, in Paul Frédéric Girard, *Textes de droit romain, entièrement revue et augmentée par Félix Senn* (Librairie Arthur Rousseau, 6th edn, 1937). Translations from the Latin text are provided by the author.

2 Regarding *vetus jus positivum* (ancient positive law), it is perhaps enough to mention the legendary Edict of Cyrus the Great of Persia, typically dated to 539 BCE, which has been held to be emblematic of tolerant imperial rule (see, for example, Amélie Kuhrt, 'The Cyrus Cylinder and Achaemenid Imperial Policy', (1983) 25 *Journal for the Study of the Old Testament* (8) 83), and the Edict of Milan, an agreement between the Roman emperors Constantine I (West) and Lincinus (East) in 313 CE, which has 'an epochal significance because it marks the initium libertatis [beginning of (religious) freedom] for modern man', Gabrio Lombardi, 'Persecuzioni, laicità, libertà religiosa. Dall'Editto di Milano alla "Dignitatis humanae"' (*Studium Roma* 1991), 128, quoted in Angelo Scola, 'The Edict of Milan: Initium Libertatis', 6 December 2012, *Oasis: Christians and Muslims in a Global World*, http://www.oasiscenter.eu/articles/religious-freedom/2013/01/09/the-edict-of-milan-initium-libertatis (accessed 12 October 2015); see generally Nicolae V. Dură, 'Edictul de la Milan (313) şi impactul lui asupra relaţiilor dintre Stat şi Biserică. Câteva consideraţii istorice, juridice şi ecleziologice (The Edict of Milan (313) and its impact on the relationships between the State and the Church. Some legal and ecclesiological historical considerations'), (2012) 64 *Mitropolia Olteniei (Metropolia of Oltenia)* (5–8) 28–43; and Nicolae V. Dură and Catalina Mititelu, 'The State and the Church in IV-VI Centuries. The Roman Emperor and the Christian Religion', *SGEM 2014 Conference on Political Sciences, Law, Finance, Economics & Tourism*, 1–10 (Albena, Bulgaria, September 2014), 923–930.

or others, in other words when a right does not comply with *juris praecepta* (rules of the rights): 'to live honestly, not to harm another person, and give everyone what is deserved'.[3]

Today, international law similarly protects the right to religious freedom and recognizes that the right to manifest religion can be subject to limitations, including the need to protect the rights of others.[4] Provisions protecting religious freedom as a human right are to be found within the constitutional law of states.[5] This chapter provides an overview of how religious freedom is protected by the instruments found in international law, focusing upon both the United Nations model and the regional human rights protection afforded under the Council of Europe (COE)[6] and the European Union (EU).[7]

The principal international instruments with implications for religious freedom are the Universal Declaration of Human Rights (UDHR), adopted by the United Nations General Assembly on 10 December 1948, and two international treaties – the International Covenant on Economic, Social and Cultural Rights (ICESCR) and the International Covenant on Civil and Political Rights (ICCPR) – both enacted by the General Assembly on 16 December 1996 and together termed the International Bill of Rights.[8] There also exists the Declaration on the

3 *Institutiones Justiniani* Lib. I, tit. I, para. 3

4 Concerning religious freedom, see Nicolae V. Dură, 'Drepturile şi libertăţile fundamentale ale omului şi protecţia lor juridică. Dreptul la religie şi libertatea religioasă (Human Fundamental Rights and Liberties and their Juridical Protection. The Right to Religion and Religious Liberty)', (2005) 56 *Ortodoxia* (3–4) 7–55; Nicolae V. Dură, 'The Fundamental Rights and Liberties of Man in the E.U. Law', (2010) 4 *Dionysiana* (1) 431–464; Nicolae Dură and Catalina Mititelu, 'The Freedom of Religion and the Right to Religious Freedom', *SGEM 2014 Conference on Political Sciences, Law, Finance, Economics & Tourism* (Albena, Bulgaria, 1–10 September 2014), 831–838.

5 See, for example, the jurisprudence of the Supreme Court of the United States, including the recent important decision in *Hosanna-Tabor Evangelical Lutheran Church and School v. Equal Employment Opportunity Commission*, 132 S. Ct. 694 (2012). See generally W. Cole Durham, Jr., 'Perspectives on Religious Liberty: A Comparative Framework', in Johan D. van der Vyver and John Witte Jr., eds, *Religious Human Rights in Global Perspective: Religious Perspectives* (Martinus Nijhoff Publishers 1996), 10; W. Cole Durham, Jr. and Brett G. Scharffs, 'State and Religious Communities in the United States: The Tension between Freedom and Equality', *Church and State: Towards Protection for Freedom of Religion*, Japanese Association of Comparative Constitutional Law, Proceedings of the International Conference on Comparative Constitutional Law (2–4 September 2005), 362. For discussion of the protection of religion in constitutional laws generally see the essays in W. Cole Durham. Jr., Silvio Ferrari, Cristiana Cianitto, and Donlu Thayer, eds, *Law, Religion, Constitution* (Ashgate 2013).

6 The Council of Europe (COE) is an advisory human rights organization established in 1950 by the Convention for the Protection of Human Rights and Fundamental Freedoms (commonly, European Convention on Human Rights, ECHR) and comprising 47 member states, including Russia and Turkey and all members of the European Union. The court of the ECHR is the European Court of Human Rights (ECtHR). Previously there also existed a European Commission of Human Rights which served as a filter for the Court. The Council of Europe's statutory institutions are the Committee of Ministers (the foreign ministers of each member state) and the Parliamentary Assembly (PACE, composed of members of the parliaments of each member state).

7 The European Union, comprising 28 member states, had its origins in economic collaboration. Its governing institutions include the European Commission, the European Council, the Council of the European Union (formerly Council of Ministers), and the European Parliament. Its court is the Court of Justice of the European Union (CJEU or ECJ). The European Commission is the EU executive body responsible for proposing legislation, implementing decisions, upholding the EU treaties, and managing the day-to-day business of the EU. The European Council is an institution comprising the heads of government of the EU member states, its own president, and the president of the Commission. The Council of the European Union (representing governments of the member states) and the European Parliament (composed of 751 directly elected members) constitute a sort of bicameral EU legislature.

8 See further, for example, Paul Taylor, *Freedom of Religion: UN and European Human Rights Law and Practice* (Cambridge University Press 2005) and Malcolm D. Evans, 'The UN and Freedom of Religion', in Rex J. Ahdar, ed., *Law and Religion* (Ashgate 2000), 35.

Elimination of All Forms of Intolerance and Discrimination based on Religion or Belief, a resolution passed by the General Assembly on 25 November 1981. The '1981 Declaration' is not endowed with the force of international law, but this was the first legal instrument devoted exclusively to the freedom of religion and it was in consequence of this resolution that the position of UN Special Rapporteur on Religious Intolerance, changed in 2000 to Special Rapporteur on Freedom of Religion or Belief, was created.

The relevant European instruments begin with the Convention for the Protection of Human Rights and Fundamental Freedoms, commonly called the European Convention of Human Rights (ECHR), an international treaty drafted in 1950 to which all member states (currently numbering 47) of the Council of Europe are party.[9] The two fundamental treaties of the European Union are the Treaty on the Functioning of the European Union (TFEU/ Treaty of Rome), effective since 1958, and the Treaty on European Union (TEU/Maastricht Treaty), effective since 1993 and substantially modified by the Treaty of Amsterdam, which entered into force in 1999. The Charter of Fundamental Rights of the European Union (CFR/ Treaty of Nice) was proclaimed on 7 December 2000. Finally, the TFEU and the TEU were together modified by the Treaty of Lisbon, which entered into force in 2009.[10]

International Juridical Instruments with Implications for Religious Freedom

We begin our analysis with the international instruments. 'The Peoples of the United Nations', through their representatives gathered in San Francisco in June 1945 for the United Nations Conference on International Organization, reaffirmed above all 'faith in fundamental human rights, in the dignity and worth of the human person' and, recognizing that 'the inherent dignity and . . . the equal and inalienable rights of all members of the human family is the foundation of freedom, justice and peace in the world', declared their determination to establish the 'conditions under which justice and respect for the obligations arising from treaties and other sources of international law can be maintained'.[11] The Charter of the United Nations, signed at this conference, provides that, among the basic objectives of the trusteeship system for the administration and supervision of the territories, the United Nations should 'encourage respect for human rights and for fundamental freedoms for all without distinction as to race, sex, language, or religion'.[12] Thus, the right to religion and religious freedom has expressly been provided in the text of the first international juridical instrument.

The Universal Declaration of Human Rights (UDHR), adopted on 10 December 1948 by the United Nations General Assembly, is the most fundamental international human rights document: it is the authoritative interpretation of the term 'human rights'. Formally, the UDHR is merely a resolution of the General Assembly and is not binding under international

9 See further, for example, Malcolm D. Evans, *Religious Liberty and International Law in Europe* (Cambridge University Press 1997) and Caroline M. Evans, *Freedom of Religion under the European Convention on Human Rights* (Oxford University Press 2001).

10 See further, for example, Ronan McCrea, *Religion and the Public Order of the European Union* (Oxford University Press 2010) and Norman Doe, *Law and Religion in Europe* (Oxford University Press 2011), Chapter 10.

11 The Charter of the United Nations, Preamble, http://www.un.org/en/documents/charter/ (accessed 12 October 2015).

12 Art. 76 para. C.

law. However, it is referred to by other international instruments and some national constitutions.[13] Among the rights and the freedoms proclaimed by the UDHR is the right to freedom of religion. This right, protected under Article 18, has become 'one of the most influential statements of the religious rights of mankind yet devised'.[14] It provides that:

> Everyone has the right to freedom of thought, conscience and religion; this right includes freedom to change his religion or belief, and freedom, either alone or in community with others and in public or private, to manifest his religion or belief in teaching, practice, worship and observance.

It is commonly said that there are two different rights under Article 18: first, the right to freedom of thought, conscience and religion; and second, the right to manifest religion or belief. The first right may be understood as a passive right, the second as an active right. The United Nations Human Rights Committee[15] has recognized that protection extends to 'theistic, non-theistic and atheistic beliefs, as well as the right not to profess any religion' and that it 'is not limited to traditional religions' or those with 'practices analogous to those of traditional religions'.[16] The Human Rights Committee has further stated that while the right to freedom of thought, conscience, and religion is absolute, the right to manifest religion or belief is qualified.[17] Article 18 of the UDHR differs from subsequent freedom of religion clauses in that it does not contain its own limitation clause. Rather, it is subject to the general limitation provision found in Article 29(2).[18] Article 26 further states that respect for human rights and fundamental freedoms – among them religious freedom – must be promoted by all forms of education (elementary, gymnasium, technical, professional, and higher education) and education must also promote 'understanding, tolerance and friendship among all nations, racial or religious groups'.

Another international juridical instrument, this one enforced with binding power, is the International Covenant on Economic, Social and Cultural Rights (ICESCR), adopted by the UN General Assembly on 16 December 1966 and entered into force on 3 January 1976. The ICESCR provides that 'in accordance with the principles proclaimed in the Charter of the United Nations, recognition of the inherent dignity and of the equal and inalienable rights of all members of the human family is the foundation of freedom, justice and peace in the world'.[19] Although the ICESCR does not expressly mention religious freedom, nevertheless the text provides that States Parties 'undertake to guarantee that the rights enunciated in the present Covenant will be exercised without discrimination of any kind as to race, colour, sex, language, religion, political or other opinion, national or social origin, property, birth or

13 It is disputed whether the Declaration has the status of customary international law, though it is often conceded that at least some of its provisions (such as the prohibition of slavery and torture) enjoy this status. See Manfred Nowak, *Introduction to the International Human Rights Regime* (Martinus Nijhoff 2003), 75–76.

14 M.D. Evans, *Religious Liberty . . .*, supra note 9 at 192.

15 The Human Rights Committee of the Office of the UN High Commissioner for Human Rights is the body charged with monitoring the implementation of the ICCPR by its State Parties.

16 CCPR General Comment No. 22: Article 18 (Freedom of Thought, Conscience or Religion), UN Human Rights Committee, CCPR/C/21/Rev.1/Add.4, 30 July 1993, paras 1–2.

17 CCPR General Comment No. 22: Article 18 para. 3.

18 This provides that 'In the exercise of his rights and freedoms, everyone shall be subject only to such limitations as are determined by law solely for the purpose of securing due recognition and respect for the rights and freedoms of others and of meeting the just requirements of morality, public order and the general welfare in a democratic society.'

19 ICESCR, Preamble.

other status' (Art. 2 para. 2). Thus, discriminations of any kind were forbidden on reasons related to religion. The text of the ICESCR also mentions that the States Parties recognize that education 'shall promote understanding, tolerance and friendship among all nations and all racial, ethnic or religious groups' (Art. 13 para. 1), and stipulates that States Parties 'undertake to have respect for the liberty of parents . . . to ensure the religious and moral education of their children in conformity with their own convictions' (Art. 13 para. 3).

The UN General Assembly also adopted on 16 December 1966 the International Covenant on Civil and Political Rights (ICCPR). The freedom of religion clause can be found in Article 18:

1 Everyone shall have the right to freedom of thought, conscience and religion. This right shall include freedom to have or adopt a religion or belief of his choice, and freedom, either individually or in community with others and in public or private, to manifest his religion or belief in worship, observance, practice and teaching.
2 No one shall be subject to coercion which would impair his freedom to have or to adopt a religion or belief of his choice.
3 Freedom to manifest one's religion or belief may be subject to such limitations as are prescribed by law and necessary to protect public safety, order, health or morals or the fundamental rights and freedoms of others.
4 The States Parties to the present Covenant undertake to have respect for the liberty of parents and, where applicable, legal guardians to ensure the religious and moral education of their children in conformity with their own convictions.

Although there are a number of differences between Article 18 of the UDHR and Article 18 of the ICCPR,[20] the most important difference is the inclusion of the limitation clause in 18.3. This provides that states can limit the right to manifest religion or belief (as opposed to the right to freedom of thought, conscience and religion) provided that certain tests are met. However, it has been noted that the Human Rights Committee so far has not applied Article 18(3) 'either rigorously or, indeed, even methodically in practice'.[21] The Committee has noted that: 'The fact that a religion is recognized as a state religion or that it is established as official or traditional or that its followers comprise the majority of the population, shall not result in any impairment of the enjoyment of any of the rights under the Covenant . . . nor in any discrimination against adherents to other religions or non-believers.'[22]

The former State Council of the Socialist Republic of Romania declared that some of the provisions in these two covenants were not 'in accordance' with the principles mentioned in certain 'International Treaties'.[23] The Council did specify how human rights and freedoms were respected and applied at that time in Romania, though it was well known outside the borders of the country in that time that religious freedom was not in practice respected.[24]

20 See, for example, Paul Taylor, *Freedom of Religion* . . . supra note 8, Chapter 2.

21 M.D. Evans, 'The UN and Freedom of Religion', supra note 8 at 35, 51.

22 General Comment 22 (1993), para. 9.

23 Decree n. 212 issued on 31October 1974 for the ratification of the International Covenant on Economic, Social, and Cultural Rights and the International Covenant on Civil and Political Rights, *Official Gazette* 146, issued on 20 November 1974, http://www.cdep.ro/pls/legis/legis_pck.htp_act_text?idt=63815 (accessed 12 October 2015).

24 For further discussion of freedom of religion and the application in Romania of the principles discussed in this chapter, see Nicolae V. Dură, 'Proselytism and the Right to Change Religion: The Romanian Debate', in Silvio Ferrari and Rinaldo Crisofori, eds, *Law and Religion in the 21st Century: Relations between State and Religious Communities* (Ashgate 2010), 279–287.

The Declaration on the Elimination of All Forms of Intolerance and Discrimination based on Religion or Belief ('1981 Declaration') does not have the legal status of an international agreement but rather of an international legal decision.[25] Article 1 protects freedom of religion in terms very similar to those of the UDHR and ICCPR, since 'it proved impossible to forge a consensus around a more detailed formulation.'[26] However, Article 6 of the 1981 Declaration provides a list of freedoms that are included in this general right.[27] The freedom of religion clause in Article 1 is accompanied by Article 2, which prohibits discrimination on grounds of religion or belief. This is the focus of the remainder of the Declaration, which is the most comprehensive international law document on religious discrimination, using language borrowed from similar UN instruments on racial discrimination.

European Juridical Instruments with Implications for Religious Freedom

The first European instrument with constitutional value was the Convention for the Protection of Human Rights and Fundamental Freedoms (European Convention on Human Rights, ECHR), adopted in Rome on 4 November 1950 and entered into force on 3 September 1953. Article 9 ECHR not only reiterated the text of Article 18 UDHR, but also followed Article 18 ICCPR by emphasizing that 'Freedom to manifest one's religion or beliefs shall be subject only to such limitations as are prescribed by law and are necessary in a democratic society in the interests of public safety, for the protection of public order, health or morals, or for the protection of the rights and freedoms of others.' Article 14 provided that 'The enjoyment of the rights and freedoms set forth in this Convention shall be secured without discrimination on any ground such as sex, race, colour, language, religion, political or other opinion, national or social origin, association with a national minority, property, birth or other status.' However, this provision has been understood as not providing a general prohibition on religious discrimination. Rather it only forbids discrimination in regard to 'the rights and

25 See, for example, Donna J. Sullivan, 'Advancing the Freedom of Religion or Belief through the UN Declaration on the Elimination of Religious Intolerance and Discrimination', (1988) 82 *American Journal of International Law* 487–502.

26 M.D. Evans, 'The UN and Freedom of Religion', supra note 8 at 35, 36.

27 These include the following freedoms:

- (a) To worship or assemble in connection with a religion or belief, and to establish and maintain places for these purposes;
- (b) To establish and maintain appropriate charitable or humanitarian institutions;
- (c) To make, acquire and use to an adequate extent the necessary articles and materials related to the rites or customs of a religion or belief;
- (d) To write, issue and disseminate relevant publications in these areas;
- (e) To teach a religion or belief in places suitable for these purposes;
- (f) To solicit and receive voluntary financial and other contributions from individuals and institutions;
- (g) To train, appoint, elect or designate by succession appropriate leaders called for by the requirements and standards of any religion or belief;
- (h) To observe days of rest and to celebrate holidays and ceremonies in accordance with the precepts of one's religion or belief;
- (i) To establish and maintain communications with individuals and communities in matters of religion and belief at the national and international levels.

freedoms set forth in this Convention'. Article 1 of Protocol 12 extended this to 'any right set forth by law' but this has not been ratified by all Member States. Article 17 provided that no state, group, or person is allowed to be engaged in any activity or perform any act aimed at the destruction of the rights and freedoms set forth in its text.

The first additional Protocol to the ECHR – adopted in Paris on 20 March 1952 and entered into force on 18 May 1954 – mentions that 'in the exercise of any functions which it assumes in relation to education and to teaching, the State shall respect the right of parents to ensure such education and teaching in conformity with their own religious and philosophical convictions.'[28] This provision, however, does not include the right to education at a particular school.[29]

Unlike the rights guaranteed by UN instruments, those freedoms found in the ECHR are policed by the European Court of Human Rights (ECtHR) at Strasbourg. In religious matters the Court presumes that there is a 'margin of appreciation' allowing states to differ from each other in relation to their laws and policies to some extent to allow for their different cultures. However, there has been a vast increase in the number of such cases in recent years, including a number of controversial decisions.[30] The ECtHR has stated that 'a State Church system cannot in itself be considered to violate Article 9 of the Convention . . . However, a State Church system must, in order to satisfy Article 9, include specific safeguards for the individual's freedom of religion.'[31] Moreover, the ECtHR has suggested that states are required to facilitate religious freedom.[32]

In addition to the Council of Europe (COE), attention also needs to be paid to the growing regulation of religion by the European Union (EU). The European Union is based on two treaties having 'the same legal value':[33] the Treaty on the Functioning of the European Union (TFEU, establishing the European Economic Community and setting out the 'functioning' of the proposed Union) and the Treaty on European Union (TEU, formally establishing the European Union). In addition, one of the main European juridical instruments is the Charter of Fundamental Rights of the European Union (CFR), adopted in Nice in 2000 and proclaimed on 12 December 2007 by the European Parliament, the EU Council (that is, heads of governments of the Member States), and the European Commission. The CFR 'works politically, because all EU institutions and Member States have this yardstick to go by when promulgating and applying civil law'.[34] It has been said of the CFR – which according to Article 6 paragraph 1 of the Treaty on European Union (TEU) has the same juridical value as

28 Article 2.

29 As a matter of interest, a number of Romanian jurists have remarked that under Article 4 paragraph 2 of Romania's Law n. 30/1994, 'Romania considers Article 2 of the Additional Protocol to the Convention as non-binding in terms of supplementary financial obligations referring to the private education institutions, other than those established by the national legislation' (Additional Protocol to the Convention . . . 406, n.1).

30 The first significant case was *Kokkinakis v. Greece*, App. No. 14307/88 (ECtHR, 25 May 1993). Recent decisions include *Lautsi v. Italy*, App. No. 30814/09 (ECtHR Grand Chamber, 18 March 2011) and *Eweida and Others v. United Kingdom*, App. Nos. 48420/10, 59842/10, 51671/10, 36516/10 (ECtHR, 15 January 2013), as discussed in Chapters 3 and 4 of this volume.

31 *Darby v. Sweden*, App. No. 11581/85 (ECtHR, 23 October 1990).

32 See, for example, *Refah Partisi v. Turkey*, App. Nos. 41340/98, 41342/98, 41343/98 (ECtHR Grand Chamber, 13 February 2003), § 91.

33 *The Treaty on European Union*, Art. 1, The European Union. Consolidated Treaties . . ., 16.

34 EPP-ED, *Charter of Fundamental Rights of the European Union* (CFR) 5 para. 2, http://arc.eppgroup.eu/Activities/docs/cd-rom/charter-en.pdf (accessed 12 October 2015).

the EU Treaties – that it 'also works in legal terms' and that it 'is an important reference point and an interpretive aid for the European Court of Justice in its jurisprudence'.[35]

It has been suggested that 'one third of the text of the European Charter of Fundamental Rights' has been copied from the text of 'the European Convention on Human Rights', and the Charter 'sets out safeguards for the individual against the power of the state'.[36] The Declaration by the Czech Republic on the CFR stressed that 'its provisions are addressed to the Member States only when they are implementing Union law, and not when they are adopting and implementing national law independently from Union law.[37]

Consequently, the CFR confirms fundamental human rights – among them the right to religious freedom – as guaranteed by the ECHR, but it also recognizes and confirms the rights resulting from 'the common constitutional traditions of Member States'. It has been said that 'the Charter reaffirms the rights, freedoms and principles recognised in the [European] Union and makes those rights more visible, but does not create new rights or principles.[38] Among such rights, freedoms, and principles are those linked to religion and, *ipso facto,* the right of those persons who have a religious belief to freely confess and practice. These concern, however, only 'the common constitutional traditions' of the states regarding fundamental human rights, not those where the term 'human' has been replaced – following the example inherited from the French Revolution of 1789 – by the word 'individual' or 'citizen'.[39]

In *Kingdom of the Netherlands v. European Parliament and Council of the European Union,*[40] the European Union's Justice Court, the European Court of Justice (ECJ), affirmed its obligation 'to ensure that the fundamental right to human dignity and integrity is observed'. Indeed, the fundamental right to human dignity 'is part of the substance of the rights laid down in this Charter, [which] must therefore be respected, even where a right is restricted'.[41] For the jurisprudence of the ECJ, 'a fundamental right to human dignity is part of (European) Union law'.[42]

35 CFR para. 2.

36 CFR para. 2.

37 Declaration by the Czech Republic on the Charter of Fundamental Rights of the European Union, Art.1, http://europa.eu/pol/pdf/qc3209190enc_002.pdf, 355 (accessed 12 October 2015). 'The Law of European Union' is addressed 'to the Member States only when they are implementing Union Law' (CFR Art. 51 para. 1). Along with the obligation to comply with both the rights and the principles, the states must promote 'the application thereof in accordance with their respective powers, under the condition and within the limits defined by those Treaties' (CFR Art. 51 para. 1). The same EU juridical instruments have stipulated that the principles may only be implemented 'by legislative and executive acts taken by institutions, bodies, offices and agencies of the Union, and by acts of Member States when they are implementing Union law, in the exercise of their respective powers' (CFR Art. 52 para. 5). As regards the invocation of the principles in the court, they 'shall be judicially cognisable only in the interpretation of such acts and in the ruling on their legality' (CFR Art. 52 para. 5).

38 On the Application of the Charter of Fundamental Rights of the European Union to Poland and to the United Kingdom, *Consolidated Treaties*, March 2010, Preamble to Protocol No. 30, 313, http://europa.eu/pol/pdf/qc3209190enc_002.pdf (accessed 12 October 2015).

39 Hence, the complete elusion of the expression *dignitas humana*, which 'is not only a fundamental right in itself but constitutes the real basis of fundamental rights': Explanations Relating to the Charter of Fundamental Rights of the European Union (2007/C303/02), in the *Official Journal of the European Union*, issued on 14 December 2007 (C 303/17) (Explanations . . . CFR), Title I – Dignity, *Explanation on Article 1 – Human dignity,* C 303/21.

40 [2001] ECR I-7079, at grounds 70–77.

41 Explanations . . . CFR, Title I – Dignity, C 303/21.

42 Explanations . . . CFR, Title I – Dignity, C 303/21.

Beginning with its Preamble, the CFR emphasized that the EU is 'conscious of its spiritual and moral heritage'; however, the text does not mention the European (i.e. the Judeo-Christian) religious-spiritual heritage.[43] As regards religious freedom, the CFR reiterates word-by-word the text of Article 9 ECHR, with the sole addendum that 'The right to conscientious objection is recognised, in accordance with the national laws governing the exercise of this right.'[44] It has been suggested that 'the right guaranteed in paragraph 2 corresponds to national constitutional traditions and to the development of national legislation on this issue.'[45] The CFR also provides 'the right of parents to ensure the education and teaching of their children in conformity with their religious, philosophical and pedagogical convictions' in private educational institutions.[46]

According to Article 21 of the CFR, any discrimination is forbidden on grounds of 'citizenship, sex, race, colour, ethnic or social origin, genetic features, language, religion, political or any other opinion, membership of a national minority, property, birth, disability, age, or sexual orientation'.[47] Article 52 of the CFR provides that 'any limitation on the exercise of the rights and freedoms recognised by this Charter must be provided for by law and respect the essence of those rights and freedoms.' Article 54 mentions the prohibition of abuse of rights performed against 'any of the rights and freedoms recognised in this Charter'.

On 1 December 2009 the Treaty of Lisbon ('Consolidated Treaties') entered into force, modifying both the TFEU and the TEU as it had been amended by the Treaty of Amsterdam. Article 17 of the Consolidated Version of the TFEU asserts that 'the Union respects and does not prejudice the status under national law of churches and religious associations or communities in the Member States' and that, 'recognising their identity and their specific contribution, the Union shall maintain an open, transparent and regular dialogue with these churches'. Article 22 of the CFR also expressly provides that 'the Union shall respect cultural, religious and linguistic diversity.' This Article was inspired by Declaration 11 of the Final Act of the Treaty of Amsterdam, which had been signed on 2 October 1997 by the representatives of fifteen EU Member States.[48] One of the Declarations annexed in 2010 to the Final Act of the Intergovernmental Conference, which adopted the Treaty of Lisbon, mentions that the treaty 'has legally binding force' and it only 'confirms the fundamental rights guaranteed by the European Convention for the Protection of Human Rights and

43 By contrast, the Preamble of the Treaty of Lisbon mentions that the authors were drawing inspiration 'from the cultural, religious and humanist inheritance of Europe, from which have developed the universal values of the inviolable and inalienable rights of the human person, freedom, democracy, equality and the rule of law': *Consolidated Treaties* at 15.

44 CFR Art. 10 para. 2.

45 Explanations . . . CFR, *Explanation on Article 10 – Freedom of thought, conscience and religion*, C 303/21.

46 Art. 14 para. 3.

47 Paragraph 1 of Article 21 is inspired by Article 13 of the EU Treaty, which has been replaced by Article 19 of the Treaty on the Functioning of the European Union and Article 14 of the European Charter of Human Rights (see Explanations . . . CFR, *Article 21*). For fuller discussion of religious discrimination law in Europe see the essays in Mark Hill, ed., *Religion and Discrimination Law in the European Union* (Institute for European Constitutional Law, 2012).

48 The Treaty of Amsterdam amending the Treaty on European Union, the Treaties establishing the European Communities and certain related acts, as signed in Amsterdam on 2 October 1997, http://www.europarl.europa.eu/topics/treaty/pdf/amst-en.pdf (accessed 12 October 2015).

Fundamental Freedoms and as they result from the constitutional traditions common to the Member States'.[49]

Numerous provisions and references (directly or indirectly expressed) about human rights and freedoms can be found in the Consolidated Treaties, which confers on the Union exclusive competence in a specific area. Article 10 of the TFEU (Consolidated Version) Treaty also provides that 'in defining and implementing its policies and activities, the Union shall aim to combat discrimination', including discrimination 'based on religion'. At the same time, in order to realize its policy, the EU can make decisions and take the 'needed actions' – through the European Council[50] – 'in accordance with a special legislative procedure and after obtaining the consent of the European Parliament . . . to combat discrimination . . . based on a number of reasons, including "religion"'.[51] Moreover: 'The European Parliament and the Council, acting in accordance with the ordinary legislative procedure, may adopt rules designed to prohibit such discrimination' (Art. 18).[52]

In spite of the general provisions of the principal international and European juridical instruments however, the right to religious freedom so far has not been entirely guaranteed, either on a universal level or on all national levels. Struggles for affirmation of human dignity and the defense of rights continue, and lawmakers on international, European, and national levels must continue to work to enact both general and specific norms regarding the right to religious freedom and its juridical protection in states where only principles[53] regarding the protection of religious liberty, but not yet adequate laws, prevail.

The national constitutions and religion laws in every EU Member State not only recognize the autonomous status of religions but also expressly provide the right to religion, implicitly the right to religious freedom.[54] In many cases, these national constitutional provisions predate and extend further than the rights found in both global and regional international laws. These laws need to be taken into account in order to understand the application of religious rights.

As prominent European jurists have noted, the European Union has become aware of the importance of religion.[55] Globalization is now a fact of life both politically and socially. Analysis of any area of law can no longer stop with the nation state. Indeed, in some respects this represents a return to the past. The right to religious freedom is a *jus cogens* of the present day, initially founded on both *jus divinum* and *jus naturale*.

49 European Union, Consolidated Treaties / Charter of Fundamental Rights (March 2010), Treaty on the Functioning of the European Union (Consolidated Version), Declaration 1 (337), http://europa.eu/pol/pdf/consolidated-treaties_en.pdf (accessed 31 October 2015).

50 The European Council, an institution of the European Union, must be distinguished from the Council of Europe. See discussion of the relevant institutions, supra notes 6 and 7.

51 Article 19.

52 Article 18, *Consolidated Treaties*, Preamble at 49.

53 Nicolae V. Dură, 'General Principles of European Union Legislation Regarding the Juridical Protection of the Human Rights', (2013) 3 *Journal of Danubius Studies and Research* (2), 7–14.

54 See, for example, Doe, *Law and Religion in Europe*, supra note 10.

55 See the work of the European Consortium for Church and State Research, http://www.churchstate.eu/ (accessed 12 October 2015).

3 Freedom of Religion

Strasbourg and Luxembourg Compared

Mark Hill QC

Two Pan-European Courts

Europe has the benefit of (or is burdened by, depending on one's viewpoint) two pan-national courts, which are distinctly different in a number of ways. The European Court of Human Rights (ECtHR) in Strasbourg was established in 1959 pursuant to the European Convention on Human Rights (ECHR) under the auspices of the Council of Europe. The Convention charges the Court with the enforcement and implementation of the ECHR in all 47 member states of the Council of Europe.

The Court of Justice of the European Union (ECJ) in Luxembourg is not related to the ECtHR. However, all European Union (EU) states are members of the Council of Europe and signatories to the ECHR. The ECJ refers to the case-law of the ECtHR and treats the ECHR as though it were part of the EU's legal system, since the legal principles of the ECHR apply to EU member states. All EU institutions are bound under Article 6 of the EU Treaty of Nice to respect human rights under the ECHR. Furthermore, since the Treaty of Lisbon took effect on 1 December 2009, the EU is expected to become a party to the ECHR. This would mean that the ECJ will be bound by the case law of the ECtHR.[1]

This chapter considers religious liberty claims brought in the ECtHR under Article 9 (freedom of religion) and Article 14 (prevention of discrimination) of the ECHR. In parallel, it considers the role and function of the ECJ, in the exercise of its pan-national jurisdiction overseeing EU treaties and directives. It examines the emergent trajectories of the jurisprudence of these key European institutions in promoting and safeguarding religious liberty and equality, and considers their relative effectiveness in securing such rights. It also considers the likely impact for litigants of developments within both courts, as the dynamic of collaboration or conflict amongst the two jurisdictions evolves.

1 For some hints on collaborative practice as between the Strasbourg and Luxembourg courts, see the views expressed by a former President of the European Court of Human Rights when delivering the 2013 *Sir David Williams Annual Lecture*: Jean-Paul Costa, 'The Relationship between the European Court of Human Rights and National Constitutional Courts', University of Cambridge, 15 February 2013.

Freedom of Religion in the ECtHR

For a systematic overview of the protection of religious freedom in Strasbourg, readers must look elsewhere.[2] For present purposes, this chapter considers the relevant features refracted through the prism of the ECtHR's seminal judgment in the recent case of *Eweida and Others v. UK.*[3] In these conjoined applications the principles were already well known and had earlier been adverted to in a lecture by Sir Nicolas Bratza.[4] They are helpfully gathered up in paragraphs 79 and 80 of the Court's judgment, which include the following succinct propositions. As enshrined in Article 9, freedom of thought, conscience, and religion is one of the foundations of a democratic society. In its religious dimension it is one of the most vital elements that go to make up the identity of believers and their conception of life. But it is also a precious asset for atheists, agnostics, sceptics, and the unconcerned. Religious freedom is primarily a matter of individual thought and conscience, which is absolute and unqualified. Manifestation of belief, alone and in private, but also in community with others and in public (in worship, teaching, practice, and observance)[5] may have an impact on others. Article 9(2) qualifies the right by such that any limitation placed on a person's freedom to manifest religion or belief must be prescribed by law and necessary in a democratic society in pursuit of one or more legitimate aims.

After setting out these broad, well-established, and non-controversial statements of principle, the majority opinion then identifies three subtle but significant elucidations through which the Article 9 right to freedom of religion is reinforced. In re-articulating the ambit of Article 9, through this carefully voiced judgment, the effective reach of the provision as an instrument for securing religious liberty is significantly increased.[6] First, the ECtHR has made plain that, provided a religious view demonstrates a certain level of cogency, seriousness, cohesion, and importance, the duty of neutrality of individual governments 'is incompatible with any power on the state's part to assess the legitimacy of religious beliefs or the way those beliefs are expressed'.[7] Second, the judgment outlaws the narrow interpretation

2 For an authoritative analysis of the history of the Court's treatment of Article 9 applications, see Javier Martínez-Torrón, 'Religious Liberty in European Jurisprudence', in Mark Hill, ed., *Religious Liberty and Human Rights* (University of Wales Press 2002), 99–127. See also, for example, Maria J. Valero Estarellas, 'State Neutrality, Religion and the Workplace in the Recent Case Law of the European Court of Human Rights', Chapter 4 of this volume, as well as Paul Taylor, *Freedom of Religion: UN and European Human Rights Law and Practice* (Cambridge University Press, 2006); Ian Leigh, 'New Trends in Religious Liberty and the European Court of Human Rights', (2010) 12 *Ecclesiastical Law Journal* (3) 266–279; Marie A. Failinger, ed., AALS Symposium: The Freedom of Religion and Belief Jurisprudence of the European Court of Human Rights I, (2010–2011) 26 *Journal of Law and Religion* (1) xiii–xv.

3 *Eweida and Others v. United Kingdom*, App. Nos. 48420/10, 59842/10, 51671/10, 36516/10 (ECtHR Fourth Section, 15 January 2013). For a detailed analysis of the decision, see Mark Hill, 'Religious Symbolism and Conscientious Objection in the Workplace: An Evaluation of Strasbourg's Judgment in *Eweida and others v United Kingdom*', (2013) 15 *Ecclesiastical Law Journal* (2) 191–203. See also analysis by Maria J. Valero Estarellas in Chapter 4 of this volume.

4 Nicolas Bratza, 'The "Precious Asset": Freedom of Religion under the European Convention on Human Rights', (2012) 14 *Ecclesiastical Law Journal* (2) 256–271.

5 See *Kokkinakis v. Greece*, App. No. 14307/88 (ECtHR, 25 May 1993), § 31; also *Leyla Şahin v. Turkey*, App. No. 44774/98 (ECtHR Grand Chamber, 10 November 2005), § 105.

6 Significantly, this is the first adverse determination for the United Kingdom on Article 9 since it became a signatory to the Convention. It also runs counter to the trend identified by Professor Silvio Ferrari in his systematic analysis of Strasbourg judgments on pan-European violations of religious freedom: Silvio Ferrari, 'Law and Religion in a Secular World: A European Perspective', (2012) 14 *Ecclesiastical Law Journal* (3) 363.

7 *Eweida* § 81.

of manifestation which required a doctrinal mandate. While rightly acknowledging that liturgical acts are self-evidently outward expressions of belief, the ECtHR made clear that the manifestation of religion is much wider than this. The third, and most significant, aspect of the Court's judgment is the laying to rest of a principle that had been gaining currency in both Strasbourg and domestic jurisprudence, to the effect that if a person can take steps to circumvent a limitation placed upon him or her, such as resigning from a particular job, then there is no interference with the Article 9 right.[8]

The development of a European jurisdiction is valuable as a counter balance to denominational majorities and religious nationalism.[9] From the *Kokkinakis* case (1993) to the French case *Association Les Témoins de Jéhovah* (2011),[10] the ECtHR has developed a robust protection of the rights and interests of religious minorities. Sometimes national courts have paved the way, but the contribution of the ECtHR cannot be ignored. The role of the ECJ in Luxembourg, enforcing emerging principles of European Union law, has been as important as that of the ECtHR in Strasbourg.

Freedom of Religion in the ECJ

Article 10 of the EU Charter of Fundamental Rights is in very similar terms to Article 9 of the ECHR. The ECJ characterizes the ECHR as an instrument having 'special relevance' for the determination and interpretation of EU law.[11] Article 52(3) of the EU Charter (whose status is equivalent to a treaty)[12] states that Charter rights are to be interpreted consistently with corresponding rights guaranteed by the ECHR. The EU Charter, unlike the ECHR, is not a universal document of human rights protection. Instead the provisions of the Charter only apply to EU institutions and member states when they are 'implementing EU law'.[13]

Directive 2004/113,[14] implementing the principle of equal treatment between men and women in the access to and supply of goods and services, was adopted under Article 19 of the Treaty on the Functioning of the European Union (TFEU).[15] Recital 3 of the Preamble to the Directive states: 'While prohibiting discrimination, it is important to respect other fundamental rights and freedoms, including [. . .] the freedom of religion.' The *EU Guidelines on the Promotion and Protection of Freedom of Religion or Belief (2013)*[16] were adopted on

8 As the Court states in the opinion of the majority: 'Given the importance in a democratic society of freedom of religion, the Court considers that, where an individual complains of a restriction on freedom of religion in the workplace, rather than holding that the possibility of changing job would negate any interference with the right, the better approach would be to weigh that possibility in the overall balance when considering whether or not the restriction was proportionate.'

9 See Marco Ventura, 'The Changing Civil Religion of Secular Europe', (2010) 41 *George Washington International Law Review* (4) 947–961.

10 *Association Les Témoins de Jehovah v. France*, App. No. 8916/05 (ECtHR, 30 June 2011).

11 Joined cases 46/87 and 227/88 *Hoechst* [1989] ECR 2859.

12 The Lisbon Treaty, which entered into force on 1 December 2009, accords the EU Charter the 'same legal value as the Treaties': Article 6(1) of the Treaty on European Union (TEU).

13 Article 51 of the EU Charter.

14 OJ L373 13 December 2004, http://eur-lex.europa.eu/LexUriServ/LexUriServ.do?uri=OJ:L:2004:373:0037:0043:en:PDF (accessed 12 October 2015).

15 Formerly Article 13 of the Treaty establishing the European Community.

16 See http://www.consilium.europa.eu/uedocs/cms_data/docs/pressdata/EN/foraff/137585.pdf (accessed 12 October 2015).

24 June 2013 by the EU Council of Foreign Affairs. The guidelines seek to promote this fundamental right in countries beyond EU borders. The *Guidelines* detail the EU's approach to the freedom of religion or belief which the EU will promote in its negotiations with other countries.

Article 19 of the TFEU (introduced by the Treaty of Amsterdam) allows the Council to pass legislation combating discrimination on grounds of sex, racial or ethnic origin, religion or belief, disability, age or sexual orientation. It requires unanimity in the Council. It does not prohibit discrimination in itself, but acts as a legal mechanism for the adoption of legislation designed to combat discrimination, for example Directive 2000/78[17] and Directive 2000/43.[18]

Article 21 of the EU Charter states that: 'Any discrimination based on any ground such as sex, race, colour, ethnic or social origin, genetic features, language, religion or belief, political or other opinion, membership of a national minority, property, birth, disability, age, or sexual orientation, shall be prohibited.'

Directive 2000/78 establishing a general framework for equal treatment in employment and occupation aimed at combating discrimination on the grounds of religion or belief, disability, age or sexual orientation as regards employment and occupation[19] was adopted on the basis of Article 19 TFEU. It requires all member states to protect against discrimination on grounds of religion and belief in employment, occupation and vocational training, and applies to everybody in the private or public sector and public bodies. The Directive prohibits direct and indirect discrimination,[20] harassment,[21] instructions to discriminate[22] and victimization[23] based on religion or belief. These terms are not defined in the Directive itself, leaving it to the member states to do so.

Member states are required to transpose Directive 2000/78 into their domestic legal systems. They are free to extend the prohibition of discrimination on grounds of religion or belief beyond employment, occupation and vocational training.[24] When interpreting Directive 2000/78, the ECJ is required to have due regard to Strasbourg jurisprudence, the 1961 European Social Charter and the 1996 Revised European Social Charter.

The proposal for Council Directive 2008/426 on implementing the principle of equal treatment between persons irrespective of religion or belief, disability, age or sexual orientation[25] was announced by the European Commission on 2 July 2008. As with Directive 2000/78, the proposal for Council Directive 2008/426 applies to everybody in the private or public sector and to public bodies. However, the scope of the proposal is much broader, covering social protection (including social security and health care), social

17 Directive 2000/78/EC establishing a general framework for equal treatment in employment and occupation aimed at combating discrimination on the grounds of religion or belief, disability, age or sexual orientation as regards employment and occupation (OJ L303 2 December 2000).

18 Directive 2000/43/EC implementing the principle of equal treatment between persons of racial or ethnic origin (OJ L180 29 June 2000).

19 OJ L303 2 December 2000, http://eur-lex.europa.eu/LexUriServ/LexUriServ.do?uri=CELEX:32000L0078:en:HTML (accessed 1 November 2015).

20 Article 2(2) Directive 2000/78.

21 Article 2(3) Directive 2000/78.

22 Article 2(4) Directive 2000/78.

23 Article 11 Directive 2000/78.

24 For example, the UK Equality Act 2010 prohibits discrimination on grounds of religion or belief in relation to housing and education.

25 See http://eur-lex.europa.eu/LexUriServ/LexUriServ.do?uri=COM:2008:0426:FIN:EN:HTML (accessed 12 October 2015).

advantages and education, as well as access to and supply of goods and services, such as housing and transport. The principle of equal treatment, as provided for in the proposal for Council Directive 2008/426, does not apply to differences in treatment based on religion or beliefs vis-à-vis access to educational institutions founded on a particular religion or belief. As with Directive 2000/78, member states may introduce or maintain more protective provisions than the minimum requirements provided for in the proposed Directive.

A *Corrigendum* to Directive 2004/58 on the right of citizens of the EU and their family members to move and reside freely within the territory of the member states[26] was adopted by virtue of Articles 18, 21, 46, 50 and 59 TFEU.[27] The Corrigendum sought to remedy the piecemeal approach to the right of free movement and residence by providing a single, all-encompassing legislative provision. Recital 31 of the Preamble to Corrigendum states that: 'Member States should implement this Directive without discrimination between the beneficiaries of this Directive on grounds such as [. . .] religion or beliefs [. . .].'

The document, *Communication from the Commission to the Council, the Parliament, the European Economic and Social Committee and the Committee of the Regions on Non-Discrimination and Equal Opportunities for All: A Framework Strategy*[28] sets out the Commission's strategy for the positive and active promotion of non-discrimination and equal opportunities for all. The Commission's strategy includes ensuring effective legal protection against discrimination on grounds of religion or belief across the EU through the full transposition by all member states of the Community legislation in this field, notably Directives 2000/78 and Directive 2000/43, discussed above. Decision No 771/2006 of the European Parliament and of the Council, establishing the European Year of Equal Opportunities for All: Towards a Just Society,[29] sought to raise public awareness of the substantial Community *acquis* in the field of equality and non-discrimination.

So far, the ECJ has not engaged with religious disputes, particularly equality cases relating to religious dress. The Directives relating to non-discrimination are relevant, particularly in the employment context.[30] An early example is the ECJ decision on the *Steymann* case.[31] The Court had been asked to decide on whether a member of a religious community was entitled to a pension for his work. Facing the problem of assessing whether the question pertained to a purely religious matter or had an economic dimension, thus falling within the competence of the Court, the judges stated that Article 2 of the EEC Treaty must be interpreted as meaning that activities performed by members of a community based on religion or another form of philosophy as part of the commercial activities of that community constitute economic activities in so far as the services which the community provides to its members may be regarded as the indirect quid pro quo for genuine and effective work.

26 OJ 2004 L158 30 April 2004, http://eur-lex.europa.eu/LexUriServ/LexUriServ.do?uri=CELEX:32004L0038R(01):en:HTML (accessed 1 November 2015).

27 Formerly Articles 12, 18, 40, 44, and 52 TEC.

28 OJ C236 of 24 September 2005, http://eur-lex.europa.eu/LexUriServ/LexUriServ.do?uri=CELEX:52005DC0224:EN:HTML (accessed 12 October 2015).

29 OJ L146 of 31 May 2006, http://eur-lex.europa.eu/LexUriServ/LexUriServ.do?uri=CELEX:32006D0771:EN:HTML (accessed 1 November 2015).

30 See, for discrimination on grounds of race or ethnic origin: Directive 2000/43/EC of 29 June 2000, *OJ 180 L*, 19/7/2000, 22 (Race directive), for sex discrimination: Directive 2006/54/EC of 5 July 2006, *PJ 204 L*, 26.7.2006, 23 (Recast directive) and for discrimination on grounds of (amongst others) religion: Directive 2000/78/EC of 27 November 2000, *OJ 303 L*, 2/12/2000, 16 (Employment Equality Directive).

31 ECJ, *Udo Steymann v. Staatssecretaris van Justitie*, 1988.

The Key Differences between the Courts

There are a number of significant differences which, from a litigant's point of view, might tend to favor the ECJ over the ECtHR.

1. Exhaustion of Domestic Remedies

It is a requirement of the ECHR and the procedural rules of the ECtHR that any potential applicants exhaust their domestic remedies before they claim relief in the supra-national court. This means that many years can be taken up in domestic first instance and appellate courts before an application is filed in the ECtHR.[32] Referrals to the ECJ can be made at any time and declarations are generally given more speedily in respect of interpretative decisions on EU Directives.

2. Delay

The backlog of cases in the ECHR means that many years will elapse between the incident complained about and the determination of the ECtHR.[33] The caseload at the ECJ is growing but it does not have such a long backload of cases.

3. Margin of Appreciation

The ECtHR consistently defers to national legislators in relation to political, social, cultural and other considerations. Whist the ECJ openly acknowledges and applies the principle of subsidiarity, No such elasticity is afforded the ECJ in the enforcement of EU Directives.

4. Political Considerations

Some critics have commented on a lack of clarity and inconsistency of decision making within the ECtHR. Others have pointed to the ideological and political underpinning of its case law. It straddles jurisprudence and politics and, as one commentator has indicated, it occasionally overreaches itself.[34] The ECJ, though not immune to political pressures, is not required to make sensitive value judgments of this type.

5. Parties

In the ECtHR, proceedings can only be brought against member states and the Government of that member state is the Respondent.

32 In the case of Nadia Eweida, she was refused permission openly to wear the cross in 2006, but did not obtain declaratory relief from the ECtHR until 2013.

33 At the end of 2011, the backlog of cases exceeded 152,000: http://www.bbc.co.uk/news/uk-politics-17762341 (accessed 12 October 2015). By December 2014, however, after the streamlining effects of ECHR Protocol 14 had taken effect, the case backlog had been reduced to 69,900: http://www.echr.coe.int/Documents/Facts_Figures_ 2014_ENG.pdf.

34 See the comments of Lord Hoffmann and of David Cameron.

Melting Pots of Ideologies

National courts are indebted to Strasbourg and Luxembourg for their distinct methodology and analysis, for the exposure of conceptual, cultural, terminological and linguistic misunderstandings amongst European lawyers, and for the development of substantive jurisprudence.[35]

In his concurring opinion for the Grand Chamber of the Court of Strasbourg in the 2011 appeal judgment on *Lautsi*, Justice Bonello warned:

> A court of human rights cannot allow itself to suffer from historical Alzheimer's. It has no right to disregard the cultural continuum of a nation's flow through time, nor to ignore what, over the centuries, has served to mould and define the profile of a people. No supranational court has any business substituting its own ethical mock-ups for those qualities that history has imprinted on the national identity.[36]

He clearly referred to the stance taken by the Chamber in its 2009 'anti-crucifix' ruling, and maybe in many other cases in which European Courts stood for transformative justice instead of acquiescing to what was deemed the untouchable identity of a given country.

Similarly, in the *Refah Partisi* decisions, the idea of the state's role 'as the neutral and impartial organiser of the exercise of various religions, faiths and beliefs' encapsulates what is sometimes referred to as 'the European project':

> The Court has frequently emphasised the State's role as the neutral and impartial organiser of the exercise of various religions, faiths and beliefs, and stated that this role is conducive to public order, religious harmony and tolerance in a democratic society. It also considers that the State's duty of neutrality and impartiality is incompatible with any power on the State's part to assess the legitimacy of religious beliefs . . . and that it requires the State to ensure mutual tolerance between opposing groups.[37]

The endeavour of the European courts was very much about reconciling principles with reality. Justice Tulkens' momentous dissenting opinion in *Leyla Şahin* affirmed this point:

> [T]the Court's review must be conducted *in concreto*, in principle by reference to three criteria: first, whether the interference, which must be capable of protecting the legitimate interest that has been put at risk, was appropriate; second, whether the measure that has been chosen is the measure that is the least restrictive of the right or freedom concerned; and, lastly, whether the measure was proportionate, a question which entails a balancing of the competing interests.[38]

35 The benefits also extend beyond the territorial borders of Europe. In the 2007 *Pillay* case, Justice Pius Langa for the South African Constitutional Court referred to the application of the margin of appreciation to faith-based cases in Strasbourg, in his discussion of the autonomy of school boards in determining uniform codes impinging on religious rights. Constitutional Court of South Africa, *MEC for Education: Kwazulu-Natal and Others v. Pillay (*CCT 51/06) [2007] ZACC 21; 2008 (1) SA 474 (CC); 2008 (2) BCLR 99 (CC) (5 October 2007), at para 80.

36 *Lautsi v. Italy*, App. No. 30814/09 (ECtHR Grand Chamber, 18 March 2011), concurring opinion of Judge Gonello § 1.1.

37 *Refah Partisi v. Turkey*, App. Nos. 41340/98, 41342/98, 41343/98 (ECtHR Grand Chamber, 13 February 2003), § 91.

38 *Leyla Şahin*, dissenting opinion of Judge Tulkens § 2.

National Autonomy

How much discretion will the ECJ leave to the national authorities to implement and apply the non-discrimination provisions of the equality directives in this sensitive area? A strict interpretation could entail far-reaching obligations to accommodate religion in the workplace that may not be acceptable to all member states. The Dutch interpretation of non-discrimination law, for instance, which does not allow for a refusal to employ a Muslim woman as a public school teacher because she wishes to wear a headscarf in class, would appear unacceptable for France.[39] Although EU directives may leave the forms and methods chosen to the discretion of the member states, the stated objective is binding. This suggests that a generally uniform outcome of discrimination claims across Europe should be achieved, at least as far as minimum standards are concerned. In the area of sex discrimination this seems to be the case. The ECJ's case law has provided detailed rules and principles that govern the interpretation and transposition of the directives in all member states. They ensure that the levels of protection against discrimination to be derived from EU law are similar between countries.[40]

The ECtHR leaves national governments a wide margin of appreciation to regulate relationships between state and religion. The ECtHR has shown itself particularly deferential in its case law concerning headscarf bans in public education. In the landmark case *Şahin v. Turkey* it has elaborated its approach. This case concerned a university student who objected to the dress regulations of a Turkish state university. The regulations contained a ban on all religious attire being worn in the university. The ECtHR held the ban to be compatible with the rights enshrined in the ECHR. In its decision the ECtHR kept its distance and emphasized the margin of appreciation to be left to the states party to the Convention: 'Where questions concerning the relationship between State and religions are concerned, on which opinion in a democratic society may reasonably differ widely, the role of the national decision-making body must be given special importance.'[41]

The ECtHR accorded particular importance to the lack of a common view among contracting states which are party to the Convention concerning the regulation of wearing religious symbols in public education. Consequently the Turkish government was given a significant margin of appreciation to decide whether it is indeed necessary in the Turkish context to prohibit wearing religious symbols in teaching institutions. The ECtHR accepted the arguments put forward by the government, especially those that referred to the specific Turkish history of secularism, and the strong political significance of wearing a headscarf in Turkey connected with the growing influence of extremist political movements in that country. As a result Turkey was allowed to prohibit not just teachers, but also adult students from wearing religious symbols in educational institutions. Even in France, well-known for its strict *laïcité*, the legal ban introduced in 2004 extends only to primary and secondary education, not to universities.[42]

39 See generally Titia Loenen, 'Accommodation of Religion and Sex Equality in the Workplace under the EU Equality Directives: A Double Bind for the European Court of Justice' in Katayoun Alidadi, Marie-Claire Foblets, and Jogchum Vrielink, eds, *A Test of Faith* (Ashgate 2012), Chapter 5; and Blandine Chelini-Pont and Nassima Ferchiche, 'Religion and the Secular State in France', in Javier Martínez-Torrón and W. Cole Durham, Jr., General Reporters, *Religion and the Secular State: National Reports* (Universidad Complutense Madrid 2015), 315–317.

40 For an overview of sex discrimination case law see for example Evelyn Ellis, *EU Anti-Discrimination Law* (Oxford University Press 2005).

41 *Leila Şahin* § 109.

42 Mention might be made here of France's 2010 'anti-burqa law' which prohibited face coverings in public (not specifically restricted to those worn by Muslim women, though this was the group obviously most affected by the law). The ban was challenged at the ECtHR by a Muslim woman. In *S.A.S. v. France*, App. No. 43835/11

A similarly deferential approach would be politically attractive for the ECJ as well. As has been pointed out by Bell, the EU often tries to avoid getting involved in moral controversies. He refers to the transnational (non)recognition of same sex partnerships as an example. In this context the ECJ has taken pains to stay away from imposing a specific position. As Bell remarks: 'This is perhaps best described as a form of "moral subsidiarity," which regards issues of cultural or moral sensitivity as best left to national discretion.'[43]

Though politically understandable, such an approach might leave vulnerable minority groups with less human rights protection than majority groups. The German experience may provide an example of how this may turn out. As mentioned before, in Germany the *Bundesverfassungsgericht* was confronted with the question of whether it was constitutional for a public school to prohibit a Muslim teacher from wearing a headscarf in the class room. The Court held that this issue should be decided through the democratic process and that any restriction would have to be based on a formal act of the legislatures of the German states. Subsequently several states adopted such legislation restricting the right to manifest religion through certain forms of dress. These restrictions will predominantly affect members of minority religions such as Muslims. Several German states even introduced legislation which more or less explicitly bars Muslim religious symbols, leaving the wearing of Christian attire untouched. In fact, in some states this was for the explicit purpose of allowing nuns or monks to teach in public schools while wearing their habit. The difference in treatment was sometimes justified by the argument that Christian symbols are to be perceived as religiously neutral as they have become part of the Western cultural tradition. As such the legislation was presented as not privileging one religion over another, but as just protecting a neutral educational setting. So far, such regulations have not been struck down by German courts as incompatible with equality and non-discrimination.[44]

A deferential approach by the ECJ could lead to widely diverging outcomes when transposing the equality directives in this area: they may come to mean entirely different things in different countries. This is perhaps all the more problematic as some of the issues clearly engage potential sex discrimination, an area where the ECJ traditionally has been strict in not allowing widely diverging practices between states. One wonders whether a relaxation of the standards regarding non-discrimination on grounds of gender in one area could lead to a relaxation in other areas as well.

(ECtHR Grand Chamber, 1 July 2014), the Court found no violation of the ECHR in this law, largely due to what the Court termed 'respect for the minimum set of values of an open democratic society', specifically the minimum requirements for 'living together'. By 'raising a veil concealing the face' an individual could violate the 'right of others to live in a space of socialisation which made living together easier'.

43 Mark Bell, *Anti-Discrimination Law and the European Union* (Oxford University Press 2002), 120.

44 For an overview of the German developments see Ute Sachsofsky, 'Religion and Equality in Germany: The Headscarf Debate from a Constitutional Perspective', in Dagmar Schiek and Victoria Chege, eds, *European Union Non-Discrimination Law: Comparative Perspectives on Multidimensional Equality Law* (Routledge/Cavendish 2009), 353–370. In early 2015 the German Federal Constitutional Court issued a 'new teacher headscarf case' in which it held that a general prohibition against teachers wearing headscarves in public schools is unconstitutional under Article 4 (1) and (2) of the German Basic Law. 'The Court emphasized the "margin of appreciation" the [ECtHR] has awarded the national states in this area. Nonetheless, a fascinating open question now is this: How will Headscarf II interact with recent decisions of the ECtHR?' Claudia Haupt, 'The "New" German Teacher Headscarf Decision', *The International Journal of Constitutional Law Blog,* 17 March 2015, http://www.iconnectblog.com/2015/03/the-new-german-teacher-headscarf-decision (accessed 12 October 2015).

Only time will tell how the ECJ will deal with this situation. Will it impose a uniform standard on all member states in such controversial cases or leave them wide discretion? On the one hand the directives would seem to call for the former. Although member states may choose the means to implement the non-discrimination standards laid down in the equality directives, they are required to achieve an equal outcome that guarantees the same level of protection against discrimination on grounds of religion, sex and race. Yet, it is hard to conceive of a substantively uniform level of protection that would be politically acceptable in all EU countries. Approaches in the UK and France, to name but two, are worlds apart. In this context a 'light touch' approach focusing only on broad principle may be inevitable; although this would strip the anti-discrimination directive of much of its meaning.

Some Concluding Observations

To date, the ECtHR has concentrated largely on religious liberty and far less on anti-discrimination norms as such. Where a breach of a substantive right is established the ECtHR rarely proceeds to an examination of the alternative plea that there has been a violation of Article 14 and, in consequence, the jurisprudence addressing the stand-alone anti-discrimination provision of the ECHR is not well developed. Conversely, the ECJ, in addition to enforcing the EU Charter, is responsible for securing compliance with EU Equality Directives in fact-specific decisions where anti-discrimination will be to the fore. The real question for the future is whether the ECJ in Luxembourg will be robust in its interpretation of the Directives, and their enforcement throughout EU member states, or whether it will allow some degree of 'moral subsidiarity' to gain currency and become the unpredictable equivalent of the 'margin of appreciation' as invoked in Strasbourg.

4 State Neutrality, Religion, and the Workplace in the Recent Case Law of the European Court of Human Rights

*María J. Valero Estarellas**

Religion in Employment: Two Questions

Given the current focus in international and comparative law on preventing any sort of discrimination in employment and occupation, it is perhaps unsurprising that many recent decisions by the European Court of Human Rights (ECtHR) dealing with the freedom of religion or belief protections of Article 9 of the European Convention on Human Rights (ECHR) are set against a very specific backdrop, that of the workplace. From the 2010 decisions against Germany of *Obst* and *Schüth*,[1] to the 2014 judgments of *Eweida and others v. United Kingdom*,[2] *Sindicatul 'Păstorul cel Bun' v. Romania*,[3] and *Fernández Martínez v. Spain*,[4] this recent body of employment-related decisions offers a vantage point from which to analyze the ECtHR's most recent elaborations on the notions of state neutrality, church autonomy, and the individual right to freedom of religion in pluralistic democratic societies. To begin, we may ask two seminal questions: Can religion or religious beliefs lawfully affect employment? How is the principle of state neutrality engaged in labor relations where there is a religious element in the employment equation?[5]

Individual Religious Freedom in the Workplace: *Eweida and Others v. United Kingdom*

The ECtHR judgment in *Eweida and others v. United Kingdom* has been welcomed by some academics as a positive turning point in the protection of the right to individual freedom of religion in the case law of the Court.[6]

* The author would like to express her gratitude to Professor Dr. Javier Martínez-Torrón for his insightful suggestions and comments during the process of drafting of this article.

1 *Obst v. Germany*, App. No. 425/03 (ECtHR, 23 September 2010) and *Schüth v. Germany*, App. No. 1620/03 (ECtHR, 23 September 2010).

2 *Eweida and others v. United Kingdom,* App. Nos. 48420/10, 59842/10, 51671/10, 36516/10 (ECtHR, 15 January 2013). See further discussion in Mark Hill QC, 'Freedom of Religion: Strasbourg and Luxembourg Compared', Chapter 3 of this volume.

3 *Sindicatul 'Păstorul cel Bun' v. Romania*, App. No. 2330/09 (ECtHR, 9 July 2013).

4 *Fernández Martínez v. Spain*, App. No. 56030/07 (ECtHR Third Section, 15 May 2012, and Grand Chamber, 12 June 2014).

5 As indicated by Christoper Dwyer, 'How Far Can Religion Affect Employment?', (2009) 163 *Law & Justice – The Christian Law Review* 142, and Mark R. Freedland and Lucy Vickers, 'Religious Expression in the Workplace in the United Kingdom', (2008–2009) 30 *Comparative Labour Law & Policy Journal* 599. On the notion of neutrality in a religious context, see Rafael Palomino, 'Religion and Neutrality: Myth, Principle, and Meaning,' (2011) 2011 *Brigham Young University Law Review* (3) 657–668.

6 See Mark Hill, 'Religious Symbolism and Conscientious Objection in the Workplace: An Evaluation of Strasbourg's Judgment in *Eweida and others v United Kingdom*', (2013) 15 *Ecclesiastical Law Journal* (2) 193, as

The ruling jointly decided four applications, lodged by Christian UK citizens who claimed that employment action taken against them by their employers had breached their rights to manifest belief and to not be discriminated against for religious reasons. Nadia Eweida and Shirley Chaplin were both devout Christians who desired to be granted exceptions to uniform codes in their respective jobs in order to visibly wear small crosses around their necks as a symbol of commitment to their faith.[7] Lillian Ladele and Gary McFarlane made conscientious objections to providing professional services for gay and lesbian couples within organizations – one public, one private – that had a strong commitment to non-discrimination.[8]

As with most decisions by the ECtHR, the largest section of this judgment is dedicated to the articulation of the general principles that the Court's case law has distilled over time when interpreting the rights enshrined in Article 9. The novelty is that in *Eweida* these general principles were subtly re-articulated by the majority judges in a twofold way that, at least theoretically, has served to clarify, reinforce, and advance the protection of individual religious freedom by significantly enlarging the number of situations in which Article 9 may be *a priori* deemed to be engaged.[9] However, a critical analysis of the particular outcome of some of the individual cases in *Eweida*, and more specifically of the Court's rationale when reaching these decisions, may be slightly discouraging for those who anticipated a new trend in Strasbourg for the protection of conscience- and religion-related issues. It would appear that the Court's initial articulation of more nuanced general principles has not been subsequently followed by a carefully balanced and solid application of those principles.

A Promising Start: Two Newly Articulated General Principles

Overcoming a Burdensome Dichotomy: Religious Manifestation v. Religious Motivation

The first general principle re-worked in *Eweida* is the Court's former restrictive stance that not every expression of belief that has attained a certain level of cogency, seriousness, cohesion, and importance constitutes a *manifestation of belief* protected under Article 9 of the Convention. It is common ground that Article 9.1 protects the unqualified and absolute right to hold and change any religious beliefs (*forum internum*), as well as the freedom to manifest one's beliefs through worship, teaching, practice, and observance, in private or publicly, alone or in a community with others (*forum externum*). Therefore, only *manifestations* of belief, and not beliefs themselves, may be qualified in the manner set out in Article 9.2; namely they have to be prescribed by law, pursue a legitimate aim, and be necessary in a democratic society.[10]

---

well as Chapter 3 of this volume; Helen Hall and Javier García Oliva, 'Simbología religiosa en el ámbito laboral. A propósito del caso Chaplin y sus implicaciones en el derecho británico', (2013) 23 *Revista General de Derecho Canónico y Derecho Eclesiástico del Estado* 2.

7 *Eweida* § I A and B.

8 *Eweida* § I C and D.

9 See Javier Martínez-Torrón, 'The (Un)protection of Individual Religious Identity in the Strasbourg Case Law', (2012) 1 *Oxford Journal of Law and Religion* (2) 364365; and Hill, 'Religious Symbolism . . . ' supra note 6 at 192, 193, 199.

10 *Eweida* § 80.

As far back as 1978, in *Arrowsmith v. United Kingdom*,[11] the ECtHR differentiated between conduct which was *motivated by religion* and conduct which was *a manifestation of religion*. The latter warranted the protection accorded in Article 9 ECHR, while religiously motivated activities that were only remotely connected to a precept of faith did not. If interference with what were merely religiously motivated acts did not amount to a violation of the right to religious freedom under Article 9.1, no review of the proportionality or necessity of the limitation was required under Article 9.2 and, consequently, the scope of protection offered *a priori* by the Convention as interpreted by the Court was rather narrow.[12]

This restrictive approach faced two significant practical problems. First, it left civil courts to decide whether a particular act motivated by conscience was central or reasonable enough to qualify as a manifestation of religion or belief. The ECtHR struggled with this problem in the 1996 judgments of *Valsamis v. Greece* and *Efstratiou v. Greece*,[13] where it assessed that disciplinary measures taken against two young Greek Jehovah's Witnesses, for having conscientiously decided not to attend the school parade organized to commemorate the beginning of the war between Greece and Italy in 1940, could not be considered an interference with the right to freedom to manifest belief, as neither the purpose nor the arrangement of the parade could offend the students' religious or pacifist convictions.[14] Second, the approach proved particularly restrictive and discriminatory for individuals who felt compelled to adapt their everyday life to the dictates of their own conscience, perhaps in a stricter way than is customary and even beyond the mandatory duties of the denomination to which they admittedly belonged.

In *Eweida*, the Court has taken what seems a decisive step towards a broader interpretation of Article 9 by extending its protective umbrella, at least in principle, to every individual expression of belief, regardless of whether it is religiously mandated or merely motivated by religion. On the one hand, it has tackled the obstacle of civil courts having to establish the degree of religious motivation of individual conduct by resorting to its well-established doctrine on church autonomy, thus linking the state's duty of neutrality and impartiality to a prohibition of assessing the legitimacy or validity of religious beliefs or the ways in which those beliefs are expressed beyond proof of their cogency, seriousness, cohesion, and importance.[15] But also, it has eliminated the requirement for the individuals to act in fulfilment of a duty doctrinally mandated by a religion, and has expanded the concept of *manifestation of belief* to encompass not only

11 *Arrowsmith v. United Kingdom*, App. No. 7050/75 (ECtHR, 16 May 1977). The applicant was a pacifist who was trying to convince soldiers not to go to Northern Ireland by handing out flyers. Although she was able to prove her pacifist beliefs, in the view of the ECtHR the actual practice of distributing anti-war flyers was an act motivated by those beliefs which did not qualify as legitimate manifestation under Article 9 ECHR.

12 See Javier Martínez-Torrón, 'Limitations on Religious Freedom in the Case Law of the European Court of Human Rights', (2005) 19 *Emory International Law Review* (2) 595–596.

13 *Valsamis v. Greece*, App. No. 21787/93 and *Efstratiou v. Greece*, App No. 24095/94 (ECtHR, 18 December 1996). To the applicants' argument that refusal to attend a school event commemorating war was based on religious beliefs, the ECtHR retorted that these pacifist convictions could not have been offended by the event, its purpose, or the arrangements for it, and observed that the commemoration of national events served not only the public interest, but also pacifist purposes.

14 *Efstratiou* § 37; *Valsamis* § 36.

15 See Hill, 'Religious Symbolism . . . ' supra note 6 at 194–195. In *Eweida* § 81, 'The right to freedom of thought, conscience and religion denotes views that attain a certain level of cogency, seriousness, cohesion and importance. Provided this is satisfied, the State's duty of neutrality and impartiality is incompatible with any power on the State's part to assess the legitimacy of religious beliefs or the ways in which those beliefs are expressed.'

expressions of worship and devotion which form part of the practice of a religion or belief in a generally recognized form, but also any act for which a sufficiently close and direct nexus to the underlying belief can be found.[16]

Not quite two years after the Grand Chamber's landmark ruling of *Bayatyan v. Armenia*,[17] in which for the first time the ECtHR extended the scope of Article 9 to conflicts between deeply and genuinely held religious beliefs and national laws of general applicability, the Court seems to have further strengthened freedom of religion by embracing a broad construction of the right to manifest one's religion as one that generally protects all individual acts mandated by conscience except when they can be subjected to limitation under the parameters set forth in Article 9.2.[18]

Venturing into Uncharted Territory: Farewell to the Specific Situation Rule?

The second general principle re-articulated in *Eweida* is the significance accorded to the possibility of resigning from a job and finding new employment elsewhere as a guarantee of freedom of conscience and religion in the workplace.

Traditionally, the Court and the now extinct European Commission of Human Rights had called on the *specific situation rule* in cases involving restrictions placed by employers on an employee's ability to observe religious practice in the workplace, on the grounds that the possibility of changing employment meant that there was no interference with the employee's religious freedom.[19] The right to opt out of the employment contract was seen as the ultimate protection of the freedom of conscience and religion of the employee, given the voluntary nature of a labor relationship.[20] Again, if there was no interference with the right to religious freedom under Article 9.1, no review was required under Article 9.2.

In *Eweida*, the Court has re-worked this former rather formulistic – and drastic – approach in a manner that is more protective of the right to freedom of religion in the workplace and more consistent with the actual trends in comparative law of privileging the reasonable accommodation of the religious beliefs of employees.[21] The Court has taken into account two circumstances: first, that this interpretation of the right to resign would be inconsistent with the Court not having applied a similar approach in respect to employment sanctions imposed on individuals where other Convention protected rights were at stake – such as the right to private life or the right to freedom of expression; and second, that due to the acknowledged importance of freedom

16 *Eweida* § 82: 'However, the manifestation of religion or belief is not limited to such acts: the existence of a sufficiently close and direct nexus between the act and the underlying belief must be determined on the facts of each case. In particular, there is no requirement on the applicant to establish that he or she acted in fulfilment of a duty mandated by the religion in question.'

17 *Bayatyan v. Armenia*, App. No. 23459/03 (ECtHR Grand Chamber, 7 July 2011). The applicant was a male Jehovah's Witness who objected to compulsory military service because of his religious beliefs. Although he was willing to perform alternative civilian service, the applicant was arrested and sentenced to imprisonment for draft evasion. See Petr Muzny, '*Bayatyan v Armenia*: The Grand Chamber Renders a Grand Judgment', 12 *Human Rights Law Review* (2012): 135–47. On the 2009 Chamber judgment, see Zachary R. Calo, 'Pluralism, Secularism and the European Court of Human Rights', (2010–2011) 26 *Journal of Law & Religion* (1) 266, 267.

18 As anticipated by Martínez-Torrón, 'The (Un)protection . . . ' supra note 9 at 373. See also Hill, 'Religious Symbolism . . . ' supra note 6 at 199.

19 *Eweida* § 83.

20 Lucy Vickers, *Religious Freedom, Religious Discrimination and the Workplace* (Hart 2008), 45, 46.

21 See Heiner Bielefeldt, 'Misperceptions of Freedom of Religion or Belief', (2013) 35 *Human Rights Quarterly* 56 ff.

of religion in a democratic society, the possibility of changing jobs should not operate as an element that eliminates interference with the right, but rather as an additional element to take into account when weighing whether a particular restriction was proportionate or not.[22]

Although construing this new approach to the right to resign as a *carte blanche* for employees to see all their religious demands accommodated by employers would be too far-fetched, making the stepping-out argument part of the proportionality equation instead of using it to foreclose interference with freedom of religion – and therefore barring review under Article 9.2 – shows once more a theoretical disposition of the Court to extend its protection of freedom of religion in work environments.[23]

A Half-Hearted Conclusion: Déjà-vu Justifications to Limitations of Freedom of Conscience and Religion

In Eweida, the transposition of the general principles discussed above to the facts of each of the four particular applicants resulted in the Court's finding that the employment decisions taken against them by their employers had amounted to interferences with their right to manifest religion.[24] However, after measuring the necessity and proportionality of the limitations in question, the Court could only find a violation of Article 9 of the Convention in the case of Ms. Eweida, but not in the cases of Ms. Chaplin, Ms. Ladele, and Mr. McFarlane.

In the disposition of the four cases there seems to be a *déjà-vu* tendency of the Court to be overly deferential to the margin of appreciation of the respondent state and to make little use of the doctrine of the reasonable accommodation of religious beliefs in the workplace, particularly in the face of politically unpopular cases of conscientious objection. As a matter of fact, the Court still appears to be struggling with an understanding of state neutrality and the place of manifestations of belief in the public sphere that informed some of its former – and perhaps most controversial – decisions.

Hanging on to the Doctrine of the Margin of Appreciation

The doctrine of the *margin of appreciation* was developed by the ECtHR as a correcting parameter for assessing the proportionality of limitations to Convention rights imposed by national laws or courts against the *necessary in a democratic society* clause, in order to allow the Contracting States some flexibility to organize the domestic system for the enforcement of human rights.[25] The trouble with the margin of appreciation is that, when used too extensively, it

22 *Eweida* § 83: 'However, the Court has not applied a similar approach in respect of employment sanctions imposed on individuals as a result of the exercise by them of other rights protected by the Convention, for example the right to respect for private life under Article 8; the right to freedom of expression under Article 10; or the negative right, not to join a trade union, under Article 11 . . . Given the importance in a democratic society of freedom of religion, the Court considers that, where an individual complains of a restriction on freedom of religion in the workplace, rather than holding that the possibility of changing job would negate any interference with the right, the better approach would be to weigh that possibility in the overall balance when considering whether or not the restriction was proportionate.'

23 For a critical analysis, see Hall and García Oliva, 'Simbología religiosa . . . ' supra note 6 at 13–14.

24 *Eweida* §§ 91, 97, 103 and 108.

25 *Handyside v. the United Kingdom*, App. No. 5493/72 (ECtHR, 7 December 1976), §§ 49 and 50. See Carolyn M. Evans, *Freedom of Religion under the European Convention on Human Rights* (Oxford University Press 2001), 142–144

has the potential to undermine the protection afforded by the Convention and, where individual religious freedom is concerned, the Court has a record of being highly deferential to respondent states when they play the card of limiting manifestations of belief in the interest of advancing a religiously neutral public space or of protecting public order and health.[26] The ECtHR has also been reluctant to narrow the states' margin of appreciation when adjudicating claims based on a joint reading of Articles 9 and 14 of the Convention.

The tendency to almost automatically defer to the state's margin of appreciation without requesting solid justification for restrictions to freedom of religion when public order is at stake seems to weigh heavily in the *Chaplin* case, consolidated under *Eweida*. Ms. Chaplin is a practising Christian who worked as a qualified nurse in the geriatric ward of a public hospital. When, in 2007, the hospital's uniform codes were modified, she was asked to remove a chain and a small cross that she always wore around her neck and which now became visible and accessible, in order to prevent health or security hazards. Ms. Chaplin and the hospital were not able to reach an agreement on how to accommodate the nurse's expression of belief; she was eventually transferred to a non-nursing position that disappeared less than a year later, and she subsequently became jobless. The ECtHR found against Ms. Chaplin, stating that, even if the refusal by the health authority to allow her to remain in her former nursing post while wearing a cross was an interference with the freedom to manifest her religion, this interference was justified in the interest of protecting health and safety in a hospital ward, adding that hospital managers were better placed to make decisions about clinical safety than courts, particularly international courts, which hear no direct evidence.[27] So the ECtHR first deferred to the judgment of the hospital managers and then to the oversight carried out by British courts,[28] apparently renouncing all control over the state's national margin of appreciation and forgetting its role as the ultimate guarantor of individual fundamental rights founded on human dignity.[29]

Although it might be argued that it is not the work of the ECtHR to get involved in the evaluation of factual evidence,[30] it is certainly its role to ensure that restrictions to manifestations of freedom of religion or belief are enacted with minimum interference and that limitations are not the result of mere conjectures but rather of real and substantial risks of actual harm for which convincing evidence has been provided.[31] For a restriction on freedom of religion to be considered necessary there has to be a pressing social need assessed on

26 Evans, *Freedom of Religion* . . . supra note 25 at 143. As pointed out by T. Jeremy Gunn in 'Permissible Limitations on Religion', (2010) *Fides et Libertas* 158,, '[S]tates and public authorities are more likely to emphasize an expansive reading of limitations clauses and their responsibility to limit manifestations of religion that they believe are not in the interest of the state or the public.'

27 *Eweida* §§ 97, 99, 100.

28 See David H. McIlroy, 'A Marginal Victory for Freedom of Religion', (2013) 2 *Oxford Journal of Law and Religion* (1) 215.

29 See Zoila Combalía Solís, 'Relación entre laicidad del Estado y libertad religiosa en la jurisprudencia reciente del Tribunal Europeo de Derechos Humanos', (2010) 24 *Revista General de Derecho Canónico y Derecho Eclesiástico del Estado* 18, 19.

30 Hall and García Oliva, 'Simbología religiosa . . . ' supra note 6 at16.

31 See Bielefeldt, 'Misperceptions . . .' supra note 21 at 38. In the recent case law of the ECtHR see *Sindicatul* §§ 159, 162; and *Vojnity v. Hungary*, App. No. 29617/07 (ECtHR, 12 February 2013), § 38: '[N]o convincing evidence was presented to substantiate a risk of actual harm, as opposed to the mere unease, discomfort or embarrassment which the child may have experienced on account of his father's attempts to transmit his religious beliefs.' On *Vojnity*, see note 37 below.

a case-to-case basis through a thorough appraisal of evidence and states have to bear the burden of justifying proportional limitations of external manifestations of belief.[32]

In *Chaplin*, the Court simply accepted as clear empirical evidence the mere argument advanced by the hospital's managers that they *considered* there was a risk in wearing a small cross around the neck with a magnetic clasp that would open with minimum effort. The Court seems overly deferential towards the hospital manager's statement without questioning the lack of evidence provided, excusing this omission by stating that hospital managers are better placed to make decisions about clinical safety than courts. Had the hospital managers, or ultimately the government, been able to provide substantive proof that Ms. Chaplin's visible chain and cross were a real and measurable threat to the health and security of patients and staff, the Court's allowance for the national margin of appreciation would indeed have been the result of the correct appraisal of the proportionality of the interference with the applicant's right to manifest her religious beliefs at work. Instead, the Court accepted at face value claims about an abstract threat to public health and about the proportionality of the action taken against Ms. Chaplin, without considering whether the hospital had succeeded in providing sufficient evidence that the measures adopted were indeed the least restrictive mean available to them to accommodate their employee's religious demands without compromising the patients' wellbeing and safety.[33] Although it is true that the hospital managers did propose what they believed to be a middle ground solution to accommodate the applicant's request, securing the cross and chain to the lanyard with her identity badge,[34] the alleged health and safety reasons for refusing Ms. Chaplin's proposed alternatives still remained mere conjectures which should have deserved a more thorough consideration.

The doctrine of the margin of appreciation has also played an important role in the Court's jurisprudence with regard to claims based on a joint reading of Articles 9 and 14 of the Convention, as is the case with *Eweida's* third and fourth applicants, Ms. Ladele and Mr. McFarlane.[35] While Article 14 expressly prohibits discrimination in the enjoyment of the

32 Martínez-Torrón, 'Limitations . . .' supra note 12 at 599. On the burden of proof, see Gunn, 'Permissible Limitations . . .' supra note 26 at 165–166.

33 See Rafael Navarro-Valls and Javier Martínez-Torrón, *Conflictos entre conciencia y ley: las objeciones de conciencia* (Iustel, 2nd edn, 2011), 367, and Gunn, 'Permissible Limitations . . .' supra note 26 at 163. In fact, not long before *Eweida*, in *Bayatyan*, the Grand Chamber of the ECtHR indicated how the margin of appreciation accorded to the States must not allow for the disproportionate interference with Convention-protected rights, particularly when a least restrictive alternative is readily available: 'According to its settled case-law, the Court leaves to States party to the Convention a certain margin of appreciation in deciding whether and to what extent an interference is necessary. This margin of appreciation goes hand in hand with European supervision embracing both the law and the decisions applying it. The Court's task is to determine whether the measures taken at national level were justified in principle and proportionate' (*Bayatyan* GC § 121). The Court ruled that because no alternative civilian service was available in Armenia at the material time for conscience-based objections to compulsory military service, the State had failed 'to strike a fair balance between the interests of society as a whole and those of the applicant.' The imposition of a penalty on the applicant could not be considered as the least restrictive means with which to interfere with Mr. Bayatyan's right to freedom of religion or belief (*Bayatyan* GC § 124).

34 *Eweida* § 20.

35 The Court has a well-seasoned doctrine on Article 14 ECHR, and has repeatedly stated that although it exists in relation to the rights and freedoms safeguarded by other substantive Convention provisions, it is autonomous to the extent that it does not necessarily presuppose a breach thereof, but becomes applicable also when the facts of a case fall within the ambit of another substantive provision of the Convention or its Protocols (*Eweida* § 85).

rights and freedoms set forth in the ECHR on a number of specific grounds, including religion, it has also been used to protect other forms of unequal treatment such as those based on birth out of wedlock or sexual orientation.[36] Over time, the decisions of the ECtHR have created a hierarchy of discrimination grounds by grouping them in two not fully individualized categories, *suspect grounds of differentiation* and *non-suspect grounds of differentiation*. Suspect grounds of differentiation are those considered to be directly involved in a person's identity and should not be expected to change in order to be allowed fair and equal treatment in society. They therefore require justification by *very weighty reasons* that considerably narrow the state's margin of appreciation. Surprisingly enough, although expressly listed under Article 14 ECHR, religion has not always been treated as a suspect class by the Court's case law,[37] as opposed to sexual orientation, which is not specifically mentioned in Article 14 of the Convention but has long been considered by the Strasbourg Court as a highly protected category.[38]

In both *Ladele* and *McFarlane*, the Court had to examine claims for indirect discrimination in employment based on religion, which had been dismissed by the respondent state on the argument that the differences in treatment endured by the applicants were proportionate to the legitimate aim of preventing unequal treatment on grounds of sexual orientation.[39] Two forms of discrimination were therefore pitted against one another and required appropriate balancing: discrimination on religious grounds and discrimination on grounds of sexual orientation. In *Ladele*, the Court recalled that in its case-law under Article 14 ECHR it has held that differences in treatment based on sexual orientation are a suspect category that limits the state's margin of appreciation since they require particularly serious reasons by way of justification, but did not extend the same treatment to discrimination based on religious grounds.[40] In *McFarlane*, the Court prioritized the protection against discrimination based on sexual orientation over the right to manifest religious beliefs by stating that, in the balancing exercise, the most important factor to be taken into account was that the employer's action was intended to secure the implementation of a policy of providing a service without discrimination, even above the convincing and weighty argument that the applicant had voluntarily chosen to enter into an employment relationship in a private company that operated on an equality policy that – as he was aware – was likely to conflict

36 *Eweida* § 86.

37 In *Hoffman v. Austria*, App. No. 12875/87 (ECtHR, 23 June 1993) the Court held that a distinction based essentially on a difference in religion alone is not acceptable (§ 36). Post *Eweida*, in *Vojnity* the Court has included 'religion' in the same category as other suspect grounds of discrimination such as sex, birth status, sexual orientation and nationality: '[I]n the light of the importance of the rights enshrined in Article 9 of the Convention in guaranteeing the individual's self-fulfillment, such a treatment will only be compatible with the Convention if very *weighty reasons exist*' (*Vojnity* § 36, emphasis added). See Kristin Henrard, 'A Critical Appraisal of the Margin of Appreciation Left to States Pertaining to "Church-State Relations" under the Jurisprudence of the European Court of Human Rights', in Kristin Henrard, ed., *The Interrelation between the Right to Identity of Minorities and Their Socio-Economic Participation* (Martinus Nijhoff, 2013), 245–247, and Olivier de Schutter, *The Prohibition of Discrimination under European Human Rights Law. Relevance for the EU non-discrimination directives – an update* (European Communities, 2011), 14 ff.

38 The first time the ECtHR acknowledged sexual orientation as a concept undoubtedly covered by Article 14 ECHR was in *Salgeiro da Silva Mouta v. Portugal*, App. No. 33298/96 (ECtHR, 21 December 1999), § 28. The need for a heightened scrutiny in cases of potential discrimination based on sexual orientation and the narrow margin of appreciation enjoyed by States has been recently stressed by the Court in *X. and others v. Austria*, App. No. 19010/07 (19 February 2013), § 99.

39 *Eweida* § 63.

40 *Eweida* § 105.

with his right to manifest his religious beliefs.[41] Since Ms. Ladele's and Mr. McFarlane's claims for indirect discrimination based on religion were not treated as a suspect category which required justification by very weighty reasons, the state was not required to narrow its margin of appreciation and, particularly in *Ladele*,[42] the Court largely overlooked any balancing of the competing rights at stake by prioritizing the protection of sexual-orientation equality over the accommodation of religious beliefs in the workplace.[43]

Ignoring the Doctrine of the Reasonable Accommodation of Religious Beliefs in the Workplace

The first general principle cited in *Eweida* is that freedom of thought, conscience, and religion is one of the foundations of a democratic society, and that the pluralism of this democratic society is largely dependent on it.[44] Despite this promising overture, the outcome of the *Ladele* case may reveal that the theoretical importance accorded to promoting pluralism in society receives a lukewarm enforcement when religious diversity in the workplace is perceived as an uncomfortable threat to equality policies regarding sexual orientation.

Ms. Ladele had been a registrar of births, deaths, and marriages in service with the London Borough of Islington since before the 2004 Civil Partnership Act came into force in the United Kingdom.[45]Adhering to a *Dignity for All* equality and diversity policy, Islington decided to designate all existing registrars as civil partnership registrars, although it was not under a legal obligation to do so. The applicant, who holds the strong religious belief that same-sex marriage is opposed to God's will, was initially allowed to accommodate her refusal to perform civil partnership ceremonies. Eventually, complaints about rota difficulties, the excessive burdening of colleagues and claims of victimization from gay and lesbian co-workers, resulted in the opening of disciplinary proceedings that culminated in the registrar's dismissal.[46] The ECtHR was ready to admit that Ms. Ladele's objection to participating in the

41 *Eweida* § 109.

42 In McFarlane the ECtHR did pay more attention to the balancing of competing interests by focusing on the applicant's knowingly finding employment in a private organization that operated on an equality policy that prohibited any filtering of clients on the ground of sexual orientation. The Court stated that although an individual's voluntary decision to enter into a contract of employment which will have an impact on his freedom to manifest religious belief is not determinative, 'it is a matter to be weighed in the balancing process.' (*Eweida* § 109).

43 *Eweida* §§ 106 and 109.

44 *Eweida* § 79 quoting *Kokkinakis v. Greece*, App. No. 14307/88 (ECtHR, 25 May 1993), § 31.

45 Initially she held office under the aegis of the Registrar General. With judicial proceedings underway before the Employment Tribunal, a change in the law caused Ms. Ladele to become an employee of the local authority. It was advanced before the Employment Tribunal that if the applicant lost the proceedings, she likely would be dismissed by the Islington authorities.

46 Following disciplinary hearings, she was required to sign a new job description that exempted her from conducting same-sex civil partnership ceremonies, but which required her to carry out signings of the register and administrative work in connection with them. She complained before the national courts for direct and indirect discrimination on grounds of religion or belief and harassment, and her claims were upheld by the Employment Tribunal, which stated that the local authority had 'placed a greater value on the rights of the lesbian, gay, bisexual, and transsexual community than it placed on the rights of Ms. Ladele as one holding an orthodox Christian belief'. The Employment Appeal Tribunal later reversed this first decision, stating that the local authority had used proportionate means to achieve the legitimate aim of providing registrar service on a non-discriminatory basis. The Court of Appeal upheld the Employment Appeal Tribunal's decision and concluded that Islington was not merely entitled but obliged to require Ms. Ladele to perform civil partnerships.

registration of same-sex partnerships was directly motivated by her religious beliefs,[47] but found no violation of Article 14 taken in conjunction with Article 9 because her employer's limitation of her freedom of religion, and its subsequent endorsement by domestic courts, did not exceed the margin of appreciation available and was based on a proportional protection of the rights of others, namely, the right of same-sex couples to be provided public services free of discrimination.[48]

There are two surprising elements in this judgment that may suggest that the Court ultimately carries out the proportionality test on limitations to acts motivated by conscience as a results-oriented exercise rather than by a consistent application of its own general principles. First, although the Court uses the term *objection* to refer to the applicant's refusal to conduct same-sex civil partnership ceremonies, it omits any application of the doctrine on conscientious objection developed by Grand Chamber in *Bayatyan* as recently as 2011.[49] Second, despite express reference to the development in comparative law of the doctrine of the *reasonable accommodation* of religious practices in the workplace, in the judgment there is a regrettable lack of implementation thereof.[50]

Indeed, *Ladele* may have toned down the expectation raised by *Bayatyan* that the Court was moving towards a stronger accommodation of freedom of conscience when confronted by neutral laws that pursue legitimate secular goals.[51] As in the Armenian case, for Ms. Ladele there was a serious and insurmountable moral conflict between her newly imposed professional duties and the strength of her religious conviction, and therefore the question that the ECtHR should have addressed is whether a public employer such as the Borough of Islington did not have a particularly strong duty to accommodate Ms. Ladele's conscientious objection in a way that was respectful of her freedom of religion or belief, other than dismissing her, without impinging on the rights of the couples who wished to register same-sex civil partnerships.[52] Although the Court has a well-established doctrine that states must be neutral and impartial organizers of religion[53] who cannot remove tension at

47 *Eweida* § 103.

48 *Eweida* § 106.

49 See also Resolution 1928 (2013) of the Parliamentary Assembly of the Council of Europe, that states in Article 9.10: 'The Assembly therefore calls on member States to ensure the right to well-defined conscientious objection in relation to morally sensitive matters, such as military service or other services related to health care and education, in line also with various recommendations already adopted by the Assembly, provided the rights of others to be free from discrimination are respected and that the access to lawful services is guaranteed.'

On the meaning and implications of conscientious objection, see Navarro-Valls and Martínez-Torrón, *Conflictos entre conciencia y ley* . . . supra note 33 at 33ff. According to Professors Navarro-Valls and Martínez-Torrón, a democratic society shows not weakness, but strength, when the majority renounces the imposition of its will on the dissident minority, and conscientious objection only reinforces one of the political elements that underpin a democratic system (33). Furthermore, conflicts between conscience and law should not be addressed as a rivalry between private interests and the public good, but rather as situations where equally placed lawful interests call for a special analysis (38).

50 *Eweida* §§ 48 and 49. See McIlroy, 'A Marginal Victory . . . ' supra note 28 at 213. For an overview on Spain, see Silvia Meseguer Velasco, 'La integración de la diversidad religiosa en el ámbito de las relaciones laborales: la cuestión de las prácticas religiosas', (2012) 28 *Revista General de Derecho Canónico y Derecho Eclesiástico del Estado* 1–28.

51 As anticipated in Martínez-Torrón, 'The (Un)protection . . . ' supra note 9 at 384.

52 See McIlroy, 'A Marginal Victory . . .' supra note 28 at 215 and Francisca Pérez-Madrid, 'Objeción de conciencia a uniones civiles entre personas del mismo sexo: comentarios acerca del caso Ladele c. Reino Unido', (2013) 32 *Revista General de Derecho Canónico y Derecho Eclesiástico del Estado* 18.

53 *Sindicatul* § 165; *Bayatyan* GC § 120; and *Hasan and Chaush v. Bulgaria*, App. No. 30985/96 (ECtHR, 26 October 2000), § 78.

the cost of erasing true religious pluralism,[54] the decision in *Ladele* does not give a moment's consideration to the possible effects of the following principles in state employment: Should state employment reflect the religious and ideological make-up of society thorough reasonable accommodation?[55] Can a public employer act on an equality and diversity policy that *de facto* discriminates against religious employees?[56] What does state neutrality entail in the specific context of public employment?

As the minority judges pointed out, the *Dignity for All* preached by the Borough of Islington at the end of the day proved to be non-pluralistic, unequal, and certainly not neutral,[57] showing more zeal to avoid discrimination to same-sex couples than to accommodate religious beliefs,[58] and exposing the apparent paradox that laws and policies protecting equality on grounds of sexual orientation may excel at limiting religious freedom.[59] The Court has apparently failed to grasp the consequences for social pluralism and inclusiveness of endorsing equality for same-sex couples at the expense of denying a reasonable accommodation of religious conduct or absence of conduct in the workplace.

Conscientious objection to specific work-tasks connected with same-sex couples is an emerging and highly sensitive issue[60] that should not be played out as an easy game of win-all or lose-all. The fight against discrimination in the workplace ought not to be conquered at the expense of consistently trumping religious interest. This dialectic would oversimplify a complex debate, often at the cost of sacrificing the freedom of conscience of citizens who feel compelled under their religious beliefs to object to policies largely accepted by the majority of society.[61] Ladele should not be welcome as a victory of same-sex couples' rights over dated religious worldviews that have no place in modern societies, but regretted as a lost opportunity for the Strasbourg Court to encourage states to advance the visibility of a mosaic society in the particularly sensitive context of public employment while at the same time ensuring the protection against *any* form of discrimination in the rendering of public services.[62] Non-discrimination is important within state institutions themselves and access to public positions should be open to anyone regardless of religious or philosophical orientation, as long as the rights of others to access lawful services free from discrimination are guaranteed.[63]

54 *Serif v. Greece*, App. No. 38178/97 (14 December 1999), § 53.

55 See Martínez-Torrón, 'The (Un)protection . . . ' supra note 9 at 380.

56 See Alejandro González-Varas Ibáñez, 'Objeción de conciencia al tratamiento psicológico de homosexuales', (2013) 32 *Revista General de Derecho Canónico y Derecho Eclesiástico del Estado*1–23 and María José Roca Fernández, 'Incidencia de las políticas de igualdad en el desarrollo armónico de los derechos fundamentales. (Especial referencia al derecho de libertad religiosa)', (2009) 20 *Revista General de Derecho Canónico y Derecho Eclesiástico del Estado* 1–30.

57 *Eweida*, dissenting opinion, 7; Vickers, *Religious Freedom* . . . supra note 20 at 67 ff.

58 See Dwyer, 'How Far Can Religion . . . ' supra note 5 at 148.

59 Russell Sandberg, 'El derecho a discriminar', (2011) 21 *Revista General de Derecho Canónico y Derecho Eclesiástico del Estado* 29. We have to look no further than the UK. After *Ladele*, the Marriage (Same Sex Couples) Act of 2013 has omitted any provision that addresses the possibility of conscientious objection to same-sex civil marriage by registrars, http://services.parliament.uk/bills/2012–13/marriagesamesexcouplesbill.html (accessed 29 July 2015).

60 Patrick Parkinson, 'Accommodating Religious Belief in a Secular Age. The Issue of Conscientious Objection in the Workplace', (2011) 34 *UNSW Law Journal* (1) 282.

61 See Dwyer, 'How Far Can Religion . . ., supra note 5 at 294 on moral multiculturalism. Also Parkinson, 'Accommodating Religious . . . ' supra note 60 at 294.

62 See Bielefeldt, 'Misperceptions . . .,' supra note 21 at 51.

63 See González-Varas, *Objeción de conciencia* . . ., supra note 56 at 18. Pérez-Madrid, *Objeción de conciencia y uniones*, supra note 52 at 23. Also Resolution 1928 (2013) of the Parliamentary Assembly of the Council of Europe, Article 9.10, supra note 49.

Quoting the UN Special Rapporteur on Freedom of Religion or Belief, human rights protection is not about making the world uniform, equality cannot be mistaken for uniformity or sameness, and '[t]here is not the slightest tension, let alone an inherent antagonism, between equality and diversity'.[64] Indeed, as the Court pointed out in *Bayatyan*, respecting individuals who hold non-mainstream moral positions by providing them with the opportunity to serve society as dictated by their consciences might, far from creating unjust inequalities or discrimination, rather ensure cohesive and stable pluralism and promote religious harmony and tolerance in society.[65] Perhaps Strasbourg is not prepared to place on equal footing the now widely accepted conscientious objection to compulsory military service of an Armenian Jehovah's Witness and the politically incorrect serious moral conflict of a Christian registrar who is forced to provide services to same-sex couples at the risk of losing her job, when the same services could be easily performed by any other civil servant without detrimental effects on receivers.

The Court seems to have missed a good opportunity to consolidate the overarching principle that employers should try to accommodate individual acts motivated by conscience in the workplace, not because the underlying religious beliefs are reasonable and not only when they coincide with mainstream social trends, but because failure to do so undermines human dignity and constitutes yet another case of what professor Martinez-Torrón has very vividly described as the *mutilation of pluralism*.[66]

Church Autonomy and Labor Relations: *Obst*, *Schüth*, *Siebenhaar*, and *Fernández Martínez*

If the recent case law of the ECtHR shows some positive advances in the protection of individual religious freedom in the workplace, the trend may be veering towards a more restricted protection of the collective dimension of freedom of religion in the specific labor context, particularly where the right of religious groups to manage their employment decisions without undue interference from the state collides with their employees' fundamental rights.[67]

The basic doctrinal lines developed by the Court regarding the right to self-determination of religious groups[68] suggest that the collective dimension of religion carries such weight for believers and for pluralism in society alike, that Articles 9 and 11 of the Convention

64 Bielefeldt, 'Misperceptions . . .' supra note 21 at 51 and *Bayatyan* GC § 126: 'The Court further reiterates that pluralism, tolerance and broadmindedness are hallmarks of a "democratic society". Although individual interests must on occasion be subordinated to those of a group, democracy does not simply mean that the views of the majority must always prevail: a balance must be achieved which ensures the fair and proper treatment of people from minorities and avoids any abuse of a dominant position. Thus respect on the part of the State towards the beliefs of a minority religious group like the applicant's by providing them with the opportunity to serve society as dictated by their conscience might, far from creating unjust inequalities or discrimination, as claimed by the Government, rather ensure cohesive and stable pluralism as promote religious harmony and tolerance in society.'

65 *Bayatyan* GC § 126.

66 See Martínez-Torrón, 'The (Un)protection ...' supra note 9 at 369, 375, 381.

67 See Christopher McCrudden, 'Religion, Human Rights, Equality and the Public Sphere', (2011) 13 *Ecclesiastical Law Journal* (1) 35.

68 The turn-of-the-century judgments of *Serif v. Greece, Hasan and Chaush v. Bulgaria,* and *Metropolitan Church of Bessarabia v. Moldova*, App. No. 45701/99 (ECtHR, 13 December 2001), gave the Court a chance to establish a set of principles that addressed the right to self-determination of religious groups as a manifestation of the right to freedom of religion enshrined in Article 9 of the Convention.

grant churches a right to manage their internal affairs free, to a certain extent, from any state interference, therefore barring any statist assessment of the legitimacy of religious beliefs or of the ways in which those beliefs are expressed.[69] It is also clear under the Convention, and under EU law, that religious group autonomy requires limits to the freedom of clergy or employees that originate in voluntarily accepted duties of loyalty towards the ethos of the denomination.[70] In the case of ministers, their fundamental rights are safeguarded by their right to exit the church. In the case of lay employees, they are in principle protected by their right to resign from the employment in question.[71]

Despite this strong protection of the institutional immunity of religious groups from state interference, the Court has traditionally been reluctant to exclude secular oversight of ecclesiastical decisions which may potentially limit the fundamental rights of lay employees. Over the years, the Strasbourg Court has moved from a limited review of the compliance of church employment decisions with fair-procedure or fair-trial standards that foreclosed any validation or assessment of underlying religious motivations,[72] to a growing endorsement of an in-depth balancing of the autonomy of the religious organisation and the individual rights of employees.[73] As already discussed above for religious workers in secular employment, in the case of religious employers, the Court seems also to be moving away from its traditional *specific situation rule*,[74] turning the right to find employment elsewhere into an element of

69 See *Hasan and Chaush* § 78; and *Metropolitan Church of Bessarabia* § 117.

70 Ian Leigh, 'Balancing Religious Autonomy and Other Human Rights under the European Convention', (2012) 1 *Oxford Journal of Law and Religion* (1) 115. Council Directive 2000/78/ EC of 27 November establishing a general framework for equal treatment in employment and occupation. Article 4.2.2: 'Provided that its provisions are otherwise complied with, this Directive shall thus not prejudice the right of churches and other public or private organisations, the ethos of which is based on religion or belief, acting in conformity with national constitutions and laws, to require individuals working for them to act in good faith and with loyalty to the organisation's ethos.'

71 Leigh, 'Balancing Religious . . .' supra note 70 at 115. See also María J. Valero Estarellas, 'El derecho de los profesores de religión católica al respeto de su vida privada y familiar', (2013) 33 *Revista General de Derecho Canónico y Derecho Eclesiástico del Estado* 15 ff.

72 *Lombardi Vallauri v. Italy*, App. No. 39128/05 (ECtHR, 20 October 2009). The Court had to decide on an application lodged by a professor who had been denied a renewal of his contract to teach philosophy at the Law Faculty of the Florentine University of the Sacred Heart, which belonged to the Roman Catholic Church. The reasons alleged by the University were that since certain opinions of the applicant manifestly opposed Catholic doctrine, the students' interests justified the non-renewal of the professor's contract. The case – in which the Court found in favour of the applicant – was decided in the light of the rights to freedom of expression and of teaching enshrined in Article 10 of the Convention, as well as on due process arguments under Article 6. The ECtHR argued that although the reasons behind the decision not to renew the contract were founded on the University's legitimate aim to ensure that teaching was inspired by Catholic doctrine, it could not go as far as to injure the substance of the procedural guarantees accorded to the applicant. Carolyn M. Evans and Anna Hood, 'Religious Autonomy and Labor Law: A Comparison of the Jurisprudence of the United States and the European Court of Human Rights', (2012) 1 *Oxford Journal of Law and Religion* (1) 94 ff. See also McCrudden, 'Religion . . .' supra note 67 at 30.

73 *Schüth* § 67 and *Siebenhaar* § 45. On these judgments, see Frank Cranmer, 'Employment Rights and Church Discipline: *Obst* and *Schüth*', (2011) 13 *Ecclesiastical Law Journal* (2) 208–15; Santiago Cañamares Arribas, 'Autonomía de las confesiones religiosas y discriminación laboral', (2012) 155 *Revista Española de Derecho del Trabajo* 41 ff. On these cases prior to the ECtHR's decisions, see Gerhard Robbers, 'Church Autonomy in the European Court of Human Rights – Recent Developments in Germany', (2010–2011) 26 *Journal of Law & Religion* (1) 281–320.

74 Although it has been noted that the recent *Fernandez Martinez GC* may have taken a step back again on the doctrine of the 'freedom to resign'. See Stijn Smet, 'Fernández Martínez v. Spain: The Grand Chamber Putting the Brakes on the "Ministerial Exception" for Europe?' *Strasbourg Observers*, 23 June 2014, http://strasbourgobservers.com/2014/06/23/fernandez-martinez-v-spain-the-grand-chamber-putting-the-breaks-on-the-ministerial-exception-for-europe/ (accessed 27 July 2015).

the balancing process. The trouble with this shifting approach is that, so far, the Court has carried out this balancing exercise by inquiring into substantive aspects of ecclesiastical labour decisions, putting at risk both the institutional autonomy of religious groups and the neutrality of the Court and of the domestic tribunals.[75]

Sowing the Seeds: Obst, Schüth, and Siebenhaar

Endorsement of substantive civil oversight of ecclesiastical employment decisions is particularly noticeable in the 2010–2011 cases of *Obst v. Germany*, *Schüth v. Germany*, and *Siebenhaar v. Germany*. These cases follow a common pattern: a lay employee of a religious institution is summarily dismissed from a position on grounds of breach of contractual duties of loyalty owed to the employer's ethos. After unsuccessfully seeking the protection of the German courts, the employees lodged applications before the ECtHR for violation of their rights to family and private life (*Obst*, *Schüth*) or to individual religious freedom (*Siebenhaar*). In the three cases the Court argued that, when reviewing labor relations, national courts have to give full and proper consideration to the rights of the employees and evaluate the impact of church dismissals in their personal lives, regardless of any voluntary contractual duties of loyalty. This means that courts and tribunals have to settle whether a particular limitation of an employee's fundamental right is proportional to the legitimate aim of protecting church autonomy. An immediate consequence of this balancing process is that, depending on the evaluation criteria used, civil tribunals risk violating the Court's own doctrine on church autonomy and state neutrality, by substituting their own judgment for the church's appraisal of the religious significance of a position or even of the doctrinal value accorded to individual moral misbehavior. In other words, courts have to evaluate and adjudicate issues concerning the internal organization and doctrine of a religious group which only the affected denomination can rightly assert.

This interference with the internal affairs of churches is far from hypothetical. Both Mr. Schüth and Mr. Obst were employees of religious groups who had voluntarily accepted contractual clauses that subjected them to duties of loyalty to their religious employers which, as both were aware, extended to moral aspects of their private lives beyond the strict professional realm. Both committed adultery (in the case of *Schüth*, there was also a *de facto* cohabitation with a second woman), an immoral behavior which is of special significance for The Church of Jesus Christ of Latter-day Saints (Obst) and for the Catholic Church (Schüth). In both cases, the denominations in question justified the contractual duties of loyalty in the special significance of the position held by the plaintiffs to the mission of the Church. And yet, the Court reached a different decision in each case, upholding Mr. Schüth's claim that his right to private life under the Convention had been interfered with, and rejecting the claim of Mr. Obst.

75 This doctrine can however be traced back to an older case decided in 1989 by the European Commission of Human Rights, relating to an alleged violation of Article 10 of the Convention (freedom of expression). In *Rommelfanger v. Germany*, App. No. 12242/86 (ECmHR, 6 September 1989), the Commission rejected the admissibility of a request lodged by a doctor who was a former employee of a hospital owned by a Catholic foundation. The applicant had publicly and repeatedly manifested his personal opinion on abortion, which was in stark opposition to the doctrine held by the Catholic Church. The dismissal was based on the violation of duties of loyalty owed by the employee to its employer, and which were set out in the contract. Although the Commission found the doctor's dismissal lawful because, under the Convention, employees may voluntarily and freely accept contractual loyalty duties towards their employers which limit to some extent their fundamental rights, it also indicated that courts must take into account the actual position held by the employee and its meaning within the religious community, in order to prevent churches from burdening their employees beyond what may be considered reasonable.

The reason for these different outcomes seems to lie in the circumstantial evaluation by the Court of the profile of the employee, of the fact that Mr. Obst was a director of public relations for his religious employer, while Mr. Schüth was only the organist and choir director of a German Catholic parish. The Court struggles with not finding the logic in treating both employees in the same way, even though the churches in question attributed the same moral relevance to adultery and insisted on the high pastoral significance attached to both positions. In the opinion of the Court, voluntarily accepted loyalty duties that affect private life and marital fidelity may be required to a greater degree of a director of public relations than of an organist who has a minor participation in church liturgy, regardless of what the position of the relevant church on the subject may be. Unfortunately, in reaching this conclusion, the Court failed to provide solid legal rationale – strictly based on the core content of the right to private and family life – to justify this overriding of the autonomy of the religious employer, resorting instead to ambiguous criteria and giving the impression that it was trying to accommodate the balancing test to a pre-conceived notion of what the logic outcome of each particular case should be, even at the cost of aiming dead center at the core of the churches' right to institutional self-determination.[76]

The applicant in *Siebenhaar* was a Catholic childcare assistant working in a day nursery run by a Protestant parish. She was dismissed because of her active involvement in a religious community (the Universal Church/Brotherhood of Humanity) whose teachings were deemed to be incompatible with those of the Protestant Church. The ECtHR found reasonable the ruling of the German labor court that though her Catholic confession had not raised issues of loyalty, Ms Siebenhaar could no longer be counted on to respect the ideals of her employer, since she 'had been, or should have been, aware from the moment of signing her employment contract that her activities for the Universal Church [would be] incompatible with her work for the Protestant Church' (*Siebenhaar* § 46). There was, therefore, no violation of the applicant's Article 9 freedom of religion rights in the dismissal.[77]

Reaping the Harvest: Fernández Martínez v. Spain and Sindicatul 'Pastorul cel Bun' v. Romania

The uncomfortable footing of the Court with the new doctrine established in the German cases, as well as its yet unsettled position regarding the autonomy of religious organizations in

76 But see Johan D. van der Vyver, 'State Interference in the Internal Affairs of Religious Institutions', (2012) 26 *Emory International Law Review* (1) 1–9. Professor van der Vyver has observed that the Court upheld Mr. Obst's dismissal 'on the basis that the labor courts of Germany, in reviewing the legality of his dismissal, adequately considered the impact of the applicant's discharge on his personal and family life', while in the case of Mr. Schüth 'the legal protection afforded to the rights of the applicant by the European Convention was never mentioned in proceedings before the labor courts [which] consequently failed to strike a balance between the interests of the Catholic Church and the rights of the applicant'. The Court noted a difference in that Mr. Obst 'was, or should have been, aware of the special premium placed by the Mormon Church on marital fidelity', while Mr. Schüth's 'signature . . . on his contract of employment could not be interpreted as an indisputable undertaking to lead a life of abstinence following the breakup of his marriage or in the event of a divorce'.

77 According to Saïla Ouald Chaib, this might be seen as continuing evidence of a 'step forward' from the perspective of the Court's previous case law concerning the church as an employer, while at the same time, from the perspective of the Court's Article 10 (freedom of speech) jurisprudence it might be, in its 'ignoring the personal conduct of the applicant and by stating that no weight can be given to the fact that her activities took place outside the professional sphere,' a 'step backward'. See Chaib, 'Freedom of Religion in Conflict: Siebenhaar v. Germany', *Strasbourg Observers*, 4 March 2011, http://strasbourgobservers.com/2011/03/04/freedom-of-religion-in-conflict-siebenhaar-v-germany/ (accessed 29 July 2015).

employment-related issues, could be inferred from the 2012 Chamber decision of *Fernández Martínez v. Spain* and perhaps also indirectly from the Grand Chamber's ruling in *Sindicatul 'Pastorul cel Bun' v. Romania*,[78] which shares with the Spanish case the singular coincidence of being a sort of hybrid-situation where applicants are both secular employees and clergy.

The ECtHR's Grand Chamber ruling in *Fernández Martínez v. Spain*, the final judgment in an 18-year legal process, upheld the resolution of the Court's Third Section – and before that, of the Spanish Constitutional Court – in finding no violation of the appellant's right to respect for his private and family life protected by Article 8 of the Convention, while at the same time addressing some of the shortcomings of the 2012 Third Section decision.[79] But while the decision against the plaintiff and in favour of Spain was to some extent predictable, the Grand Chamber's rationale reaching it has created some uneasiness concerning the future protection of the collective dimension of religious freedom.[80]

First, the final tight 9/8 vote seems to reflect a Court that was sharply divided over a subject that has proven more controversial than perhaps could have been anticipated. This sense of division only becomes more prominent in view of the four separate opinions that give voice to the eight dissenting magistrates, one of which goes so far as to surrender any legal language or reasoning in favor of a clearly visceral line of personal thought far removed from what should be expected in a national judge appointed before the ECtHR.[81]

But more importantly, this resolution appears to be yet another step in the consolidation of a doctrine that addresses the protection of the fundamental rights of lay church employees – or of employees whose position depends on the standing of ecclesiastical declarations of suitability – by increasingly weakening the self-determination right of religious groups on doctrinal or internal disciplinary issues.

78 See, for example, *Sindicatul* § 159: '[R]eligious communities are entitled to their own opinion on any collective activities of their members that might undermine their autonomy and this opinion must be in principle respected by the national authorities.' Also § 161: '[T]he aims set out in the union's constitution were incompatible with the duties accepted by priests by virtue of their ministry and their undertaking towards the archbishop. It asserted that the emergence within the structure of the Church of a new body of this kind would seriously imperil the freedom of religious denominations to organise themselves in accordance with their own traditions, and that the establishment of the trade union would therefore be likely to undermine the Church's traditional hierarchical structure.' § 165: 'Respect for the autonomy of religious communities recognised by the State implies, in particular, that the State should accept the right of such communities to react, in accordance with their own rules and interests, to any dissident movements emerging within them that might pose a threat to their cohesion, image or unity.' See Eric Rassbach and Diana Verm, 'Analysis of Sindicatul "Păstorul cel Bun" v. Romania', http://www.strasbourgconsortium.org/common/document.view.php?docId=5847, and Roger Kiska, 'The Question of Church Autonomy in Affaire Sindicatul "Păstorul cel Bun" c. Roumanie', http://www.strasbourgconsortium.org/common/document.view.php?docId=5848 (both accessed 27 July 2015).

79 On the Third Section decision, see José María Coello de Portugal, 'La jurisprudencia europea sobre profesores de religión' and María J. Valero Estarellas, 'La jurisprudencia europea sobre profesores de religión. La autonomía institucional de las confesiones religiosas', both in Isabel Cano Ruiz, ed., *La enseñanza de la religión en la escuela pública. Actas del VI simposio internacional de Derecho concordatario. Alcalá de Henares, 16–18 de octubre de 2013* (Comares 2014), 86–206 and 207–220 respectively.

80 See, for example, Smet, 'Fernández Martínez v. Spain . . .' supra note 74; Neil Addison, 'Fernandez Martinez v Spain – Priestly Celibacy and the European Convention', *Religion Law Blog*, 18 June 2014, http://religionlaw.blogspot.com.es/2014/06/fernandez-martinez-v-spain-priestly.html, and Frank Cranmer, 'Marriage, Roman Catholic clergy and Article 8 ECHR: *Fernández Martínez v Spain*', *Law & Religion UK*, 16 June 2014, http://www.lawandreligionuk.com/2014/06/16/marriage-roman-catholic-clergy-and-article-8-echr-fernandez-martinez-v-spain/ (all accessed 29 July 2015).

81 See *Fernández Martínez* GC separate opinions, dissenting opinion of Judge Dedov.

Mr. Jose Antonio Fernández Martínez was a secularized Spanish priest who for some years had found employment as a teacher of Catholic religion at a public school in a small town in south-east Spain. Although he was appointed by the Diocese on a year-to-year basis, he was an employee of the Spanish Ministry of Education. After he spoke publicly in a local newspaper about his status as a married priest and against the church's doctrine on certain sensitive subjects such as divorce and contraception, the Bishop decided not to renew the mandatory ecclesiastical authorization necessary for Mr. Fernández to be eligible for employment as a teacher of Catholic religion at a public school in Spain, and therefore the Ministry was unable to hire him for subsequent years. Mr. Fernández started proceedings before the ECtHR, claiming that the Bishop's decision to exclude him from the list of eligible appointees amounted to interference with his right to family and private life.

The Third Section of the Court found that the Spanish authorities had not breached their positive obligations towards the applicant and particularly focused on the status of Mr. Fernández as a Catholic priest, disregarding the fact that under Spanish and Canon Law the degree of loyalty legally required to be eligible for appointment as a teacher of Catholic religious education does not differ for laymen and clergy. By building the outcome of the case on the fact that the applicant was a priest, the Court omitted the secular element of the equation that would have led to the rationale of *Obst*, *Schüth*, and *Siebenhaar*.[82] The Third Section instead opted for the Court's former stance of preserving the institutional autonomy of religious groups and of favoring an understanding of the principle of state neutrality that precludes any examination of religious decisions. The strictly religious motivation of the ecclesiastical decision was as a result left unquestioned on the basis of the principles of religious freedom and neutrality, and the ambiguous argumentation of the German cases was replaced by a straightforward affirmation of the importance of the heightened duties of loyalty of religious education teachers towards the Church and of the conscious and voluntary decision of these teachers to accept the effect of those duties in their private lives.[83] However, this argumentation prompted the unsettling question of what would have been the outcome if the Court had elucidated the case of a lay teacher of Catholic religion who had lost the confidence of the Church thorough personal moral misbehavior, and how the application of the balancing criteria in *Obst* and *Schüth* would have played out.

The answer to that question lay with the Grand Chamber. In its final decision on *Fernández Martínez* in June 2014, the Court decided to step away from the argument of preserving church autonomy and state neutrality and work a balancing appraisal of the case based on the voluntary and conscious breach by Mr. Fernández of the special duty of loyalty that bound him to the Church. Reassessing the Third Section's opinion, the Grand Chamber downplayed the significance of the precise status of the actor by placing the emphasis on the fact that, regardless of where this obligation originated, the applicant was bound to the Church by a qualified duty of loyalty which he had voluntary accepted throughout his career as a teacher of Catholic religion and ethics. This is the duty that he had consciously breached.

By shifting the focus from what constituted the core of the Third Section's reasoning, the Grand Chamber transformed a straightforward case about the scope and rightful limits

82 *Fernández Martínez* §§ 85 and 86. For an in-depth analysis of this decision, see María J. Valero Estarellas, 'Autonomía institucional de las confesiones religiosas y derecho al respeto de la vida privada y familiar en Estrasburgo: la sentencia de la Gran Sala del TEDH Fernández Martínez c España', (2014) *Revista General de Derecho Canónico y Derecho Eclesiástico del Estado* 1–21.

83 *Fernández Martínez* § 84.

of church autonomy into an elaborate balancing exercise of duties of loyalty in religiously significant positions. At first look it might seem that it is precisely through the balancing that church autonomy is best protected. However, a closer look at both the Grand Chamber's stance on the source of the state's interference with Mr. Fernández's right to respect for privacy and family life and its rationale for reaching its decision makes the seemingly linear defense of the right of autonomy of religious denominations seem less sure.

Contrary to the Third Section decision, which grounded the source of the state's potential interference with Mr. Fernández's right to private and family life, protected by Article 8 ECHR, in a breach of the state's *positive obligations* to protect Convention rights even in the sphere of relations between private parties, the Grand Chamber places the collision with Article 8 within the scope of the Spanish authorities' *negative obligations*.[84] This different approach is not without consequences for the protection afforded by the Court to the internal autonomy of religious groups, even if in both instances the respondent state was acquitted of any responsibility and, albeit indirectly, the Catholic Church was confirmed in its decision.

Although the ECtHR has repeatedly stated that the boundaries between the state's positive and negative obligations under Article 8 do not lend themselves to precise definition, since in both instances regard must be had to the fair balance that has to be struck between the general interest and the interests of the individual,[85] adopting one or the other of these positions as an initial stance may lead to consequences that differ significantly. One of the main differences between negative and positive obligations is that, while finding failure with the former leads in principle to only one consequence – the elimination of the interference with the unduly compromised fundamental right – breach of the latter may be remedied by several possible actions not defined in advance, which leaves the state a wide margin of discretion when seeking balance between competing interests. In *Fernández Martínez* this disparity between negative and positive obligations is evidenced by the different solutions proposed by the majority and minority judges, and by the varying degrees of protection each of these solutions potentially affords to the autonomy of religious denominations.

If the Grand Chamber had concluded that the Spanish authorities had breached their negative obligation to protect the right to private and family life of the applicant as a result of having executed the ecclesiastical decision not to renew his teaching contract, the state's only possible remedy would have been to not enforce this decision and to renew the applicant's contract, reinstating Mr. Fernández[86] in his position as a teacher for Catholic religion and morals in spite of his no longer being in possession of the mandatory *missio canonica*. The disruptive effect of such a renewal on the autonomy of religious groups and their core fundamental rights to appoint representatives and to lay down the requisites to become or remain such a representative should not be underestimated. Mr. Fernández was indeed an employee of the Spanish Ministry of education, but only because, first and foremost, he was a *representative* of the Catholic Church, entrusted with performing an ecclesiastical function – teaching Catholic doctrine. He was the means whereby the Church was able to realize its collective right to manifest religion through teaching, as protected under Article 9.1 ECHR. The interest at stake for the Church did not concern a minor or circumstantial issue that affected its internal organization, but was hefty and substantive, and one that

84 *Fernández Martínez* GC § 115.

85 *Fernández Martínez* GC § 114.

86 Hypothetically, as Mr. Fernández had already reached the age of retirement when the Grand Chamber's decision was issued.

immediately fell within the core content of the right of a religious group to carry out its proclamatory mission free from undue state interference.

This shortcoming in the Grand Chamber's decision may have ultimately triggered the minority judges' quest for a less disruptive approach. Without making express reference to positive state obligations, the dissenting magistrates do seem to find through this second category a more feasible way to protect the plaintiff's private and family life without weakening the institutional autonomy of the Church. In their opinion, the Spanish education authorities erred in failing to consider whether the state could have taken any active measure that, while less detrimental to the private sphere of Mr. Fernández, would have at the same time ensured the immunity of the ecclesiastical decision. By appointing Mr. Fernández to a position in the public education system unrelated to his former religious teaching activities, the state would have protected the teacher's private and family life without impinging upon the Church's internal autonomy.[87]

The Grand Chamber's rationale in this case also deserves some close attention. When carrying out an analysis of the proportionality of such interests as those at stake in *Fernández Martínez*, the Court cannot overstep a certain inherent boundary: it cannot make a secular assessment of the legitimacy of religious beliefs.[88] The Grand Chamber appears to circumvent this boundary by articulating its legal reasoning around the consequences of two voluntary and conscious acts by the applicant: his acceptance of the qualified duty of loyalty towards the Catholic Church on which his appointment as teacher depended, and the breach of that bond as a result of the publicity given to certain aspects of his private and family life. But in its assessment, the Grand Chamber also pauses to weight favorably the Church's interests in the matter. It recalls that under certain conditions voluntarily accepted duties of loyalty are compatible with the Convention;[89] it notes the need for qualified adherence by those who, like Mr. Fernández, have been appointed to be representatives of the Church charged with the specific task of conveying its doctrine;[90] it accepts the close proximity between the role of a teacher of religious doctrine and the proclamatory mission of the Church;[91] it justifies the notion that Mr. Fernández's decision to publicize certain aspects of his personal life might have raised doubts about his suitability as a Catholic religion teacher;[92] and, finally, it supports the notion that the Bishop's decision was the most effective means to ensure the credibility of the Church.[93]

But when the Grand Chamber *accepts*, *justifies,* or *supports*, it implicitly trespasses that inherent boundary, because what it is actually doing is delving into the internal logic of an ecclesiastical decision and second-guessing the religious grounds of a church's internal decision. By accepting that one specific religiously significant position is sufficiently close to the core mission of a church to call for a qualified duty of loyalty, by justifying the impact on a denomination's credibility of particular acts carried out by their employees or representatives, or by supporting a certain ecclesiastical reaction to such acts, the Court is

87 *Fernández Martínez* GC separate opinions, joint dissenting opinions of judges Spielmann, Sajò, Karakaş, Lemmens, Jäderblom, Vehabović, Dedov, and Saiz-Arnaiz § 35.

88 *Fernández Martínez* GC § 129.

89 *Fernández Martínez* GC § 135.

90 *Fernández Martínez* GC §§ 135, 137, 138 and 142.

91 *Fernández Martínez* GC § 140.

92 *Fernández Martínez* GC § 138.

93 *Fernández Martínez* GC § 141.

substituting the church's criteria on issues foreclosed to external determination by the right of religious autonomy and by the principle of state neutrality.[94] The ECtHR places itself once more in the awkward and inappropriate position of arbiter of purely religious issues.

***

Although it may be difficult to draw general conclusions or to extrapolate principles of general application from the actual outcomes of these work-related Strasbourg decisions, when analyzed as a whole they allow some insight into the Court's current stance on the protection of the individual and collective dimensions of freedom of religion or belief. And the result is bitter-sweet.

On one sweet side, it would seem that Strasbourg is finally moving towards an understanding of the individual right to freedom of religion as one deserving a broad protection not only of the *forum internum* but also of the *forum externum*. Blurring the formerly strict divide between the concepts of manifestation of belief and motivation by belief, and turning filters that were previously used in the case law of the Court to rule out interference with religious freedom into elements of the test on the proportionality of the restriction, conveys the message that the Court is prepared to admit that Article 9 ECHR deserves at least the same degree of protection as other Convention rights. Similarly, a new approach towards religious employment that is more attentive to preventing arbitrariness and discrimination against lay employees should also be celebrated, provided it does not impinge upon the autonomy of religious groups or interfere with the state's religious neutrality.

On the not-so-sweet side is the reflection that the particular outcome of some of the actual cases may show that this new elucidation of general principles may not result in a significant future strengthening of the amount of actual protection given to religious interests at work, unless the Court refines some of its balancing criteria. While the general principles concerning the significance of religion in the work context seem to be evolving in the right direction – more so where individual freedom of religion is concerned than where it is the autonomy of a religious employer that is at stake – the actual decisions are in fact leaving the interest of religious employers and of morally conscious employees largely unprotected.

This disparity between principle and practice could arise from any of several reasons: the Court's excessive workload and the impossibility for judges of taking time to play out the general principles according to the actual facts of the cases; the challenges posed by the internal workings of decision panels composed of national judges who come from quite different legal backgrounds; the influence of politics and ideology; or the added difficulty of operating on purely legal grounds due to social pressure or active lobbying.

But there may also be other more subtle reasons that, if true, will continue to have far-reaching consequences in the protection of freedom of religion and belief at domestic levels, affecting the understanding of the religious neutrality of the state. The Court's ready acceptance of the state's margin of appreciation without sufficient factual evidence, or its

94 Again, the dissenting opinions of the minority judges address these arguments, omitted by the majority judgment, and propose two alternative legal analyses of the case. The joint opinion drafted by all eight minority judges tries to safeguard the autonomy of the Catholic Church by keeping the religious element out of the civil overview in the name of the principle of State neutrality; while the separate opinion signed by judge Sajó takes into account the effects of the ecclesiastical decision – not its internal motives – since it concludes that the right of religious groups to autonomy may not entail breach of other rights protected under the Convention.

reluctance to use the doctrine of reasonable accommodation to promote religious diversity and the visibility of socially unpopular moral options, as well as its deviation from the longstanding principle of the incompetence of public authorities to take positions in doctrinal matters or to interfere with the internal affairs of religious communities, may suggest that the judges at Strasbourg are still grappling with an understanding of state neutrality that is almost synonymous with secularism and with a growing privatization of religion.

In our ever-changing Western societies, where religious resurgence has not become synonymous with a disposition to make concessions on the basis of religion or belief, cases concerning the place of religion in the workplace are likely to keep courts busy for years to come. It is to be hoped that the ECtHR will live up to its own words expressed in *Bayatyan*: 'It is of crucial importance that the Convention is interpreted in a manner which renders its rights practical and effective, not theoretical and illusory.'[95]

95 *Bayatyan* GC § 98.

5 Religious Freedom, Anti-Discrimination, and Minority Rights in Brazil

Rodrigo Vitorino Souza Alves

Religious Freedom and the Protection of Minorities

'Religious freedom, both as a term and as an ideal, is a staple of modern liberal discourse.'[1] Certain dimensions of this right, however, have been identified as problematic. Tensions arise between religious freedom and other human rights, such as the right to be protected from intolerance and discrimination. By guaranteeing all dimensions of freedom of religion or belief, as well as protection against discrimination, we specially protect minority religious cultures and communities, and guarantee their right to existence.[2] In this way, the freedom to believe and to manifest religion or belief is guaranteed not only to members of majority and traditional religions, but also to members of minority groups and new religious movements.

The Federal Republic of Brazil is a notably successful part of the worldwide spread of national and international commitments to freedom of religion or belief and to the protection of members of religious minorities. Contemporary Brazilian society is complex, characterized by increasing religious diversity and a robust secularism. Brazilian law, however, 'recognizes and protects religious freedom, recognizing each faith equally. This legal framework has reinforced a pattern of peaceful accommodation of minority faiths.'[3] With very few legal restrictions on religion and a climate of relatively low social hostilities related to religion, Brazil makes an impressive showing in studies by the Pew Research Center's Religion & Public Life Project. Data collected between 2007 and 2013 show Brazil with the lowest or near-lowest government restrictions on religion among the world's 25 most-populous countries during the entire period of the study, moving into first place in 2011 and thereafter.[4]

Concerning the protection of minorities, the Declaration on the Rights of Persons Belonging to National or Ethnic, Religious and Linguistic Minorities of 1992, which was inspired by Article 27 of the International Covenant on Civil and Political Rights (ICCPR),[5]

1 Arvind Sharma, *Problematizing Religious Freedom* (Springer 2011), 3.

2 See Anat Scolnicov, *The Right to Religious Freedom in International Law: Between Group Rights and Individual Rights* (Routledge 2011), 46.

3 'Religious Freedom in Brazil', Berkley Center for Religion, Peace & World Affairs, Georgetown University, at http://berkleycenter.georgetown.edu/essays/religious-freedom-in-brazil (accessed 3 August 2015).

4 See *Pew Research Center: Religion & Public Life*, 'Restrictions and Hostilities in the Most Populous Countries' (from 'Latest Trends in Religious Restrictions and Hostilities'), 26 February 2015, http://www.pewforum.org/2015/02/26/restrictions-and-hostilities-in-the-most-populous-countries-2013/ (accessed 30 July 2015).

5 ICCPR, Art. 27: 'In those states in which ethnic, religious or linguistic minorities exist, persons belonging to such minorities shall not be denied the right, in community with the other members of their group, to enjoy their own culture, to profess and practise their own religion, or to use their own language.'

acknowledges the rights of persons belonging to religious minorities and entrusts states with duties. Under the Declaration, on the one hand states shall protect the existence and identity of religious minorities, ensure that members of religious minorities may exercise their rights, protect them against discrimination, create favorable conditions for the expression and development of the group characteristics, and create measures so that they may participate in the progress of the country. In short, states shall observe and enforce the cornerstone principles of equality, non-discrimination, non-exclusion, and non-assimilation of religious minorities. On the other hand, persons have the right under the declaration to enjoy their own culture, to profess and practice their own religion and to use their own language, to participate effectively in every area of social life and in political decisions, and to associate and establish or keep contact with others, including members of other minority groups and of the mainstream society. In other words, those belonging to minorities must be able to exercise all of their human rights individually or with others.[6]

Protection of Minority Groups: Evolution of a Process

Religious minorities have not always enjoyed the unhindered exercise of all rights granted to the majority in Brazil. After gaining independence from Portugal in 1822 and until the late nineteenth century (during the entire period of the Monarchy),[7] the country's official religion was Roman Catholicism,[8] and all other faiths suffered restrictions. Minority faiths could be practiced privately or in specific places, but these places could not have the form of a traditional church building. During this period, almost the entire population was Catholic.

Although the Roman Catholic Church remains the majority religion in Brazil, the number of its adherents has declined considerably in past decades, while the number of Protestants, members of other religious groups, and non-religious people has been rising. According to the last census, in 2010[9] (when the population was almost 191 million) 64.6 percent of the population remained Catholics, while 22 percent were Protestants, 8 percent had no religion, 3.2 percent declared themselves followers of other religions, and 2 percent were Spiritualists. This religious switching in Brazil was facilitated by the expansion of legal protection of religious freedom and the institutional separation between religion and state since the late nineteenth century.

Religion has always held a special position in Brazilian society, and legislation has protected its exercise. The right to believe and to express a faith has been granted to Brazilians since the first Constitution in 1824, though this initial provision was more a declaration of

6 In order to propose some practical and concrete measures for the implementation of the Declaration, the UN Independent Expert on Minority Issues, Mrs. Rita Itzak presented before the Human Rights Council, during its 25th Regular Session (March 2014), a set of Recommendations on Guaranteeing the Rights of Religious Minorities (A/HRC/25/66). The document is an outcome of the VI Session of the Forum on Minority Issues (November 2013). It is based on the Declaration, as well as on other international and regional human rights standards and principles, jurisprudence, general comments, and relevant reports. The set of recommendations also reflects all inputs received from participants in the Forum, numbering more than 500.

7 The Republic was instituted on 15 November 1889.

8 Article 5, the Imperial Constitution of 1824.

9 The agency responsible for official statistics is the Brazilian Institute of Geography and Statistics (IBGE). It performs a national census every ten years. Information on age, household income, religion, education, occupation and other subjects can be found in the IBGE's reports published at http://www.ibge.gov.br (accessed 16 October 2015).

toleration than a religious freedom clause in its full sense, as there were some restrictions for non-Catholics. This situation was changed when the new Constitution was promulgated in 1891. Since the 1891 Constitution, freedom of religion has been largely ensured to every individual.[10] It must be said, nevertheless, that during authoritarian periods, particularly the military dictatorship that ruled Brazil from 1964 to 1985, civil rights such as freedom of conscience and expression were restricted. Even recently there have been reports of societal abuses or discrimination based on religious affiliation, belief, or practice, including incidents involving anti-Semitism and intolerance towards followers of Afro-Brazilian religions.[11]

The current Federal Constitution,[12] which was promulgated in October 1988, prohibits discrimination based on grounds of belief.[13] Individuals are entitled to the rights of conscience and to practice religion. Religious assistance in collective establishments is granted. Religious societies have autonomy to make decisions internally, and their members receive protection against discrimination. Places of worship and rites have to be protected by the government. The Constitution, in order to keep religious autonomy, also guarantees that places of worship are given tax immunity.[14] A right to conscientious objection is also provided for.[15] In federal legislation, several rules ensure and advance religious freedom. For example, Brazil recognizes that religious marriage equates to civil marriage (if practiced in accordance with the law),[16] and religious practices are protected by the Criminal Code[17] (see below). These clauses compel respect for religious diversity, accommodate religious beliefs, and forbid discrimination against religious minorities.

10 Article 72, para. 3 of the 1891 Constitution guaranteed Brazilians and foreigners residing in the country the inviolability of the rights to liberty, security of person and property: 'All individuals and religious groups can publicly and freely exercise their religion, associating for that purpose and acquiring assets, subject to the provisions of law.'

11 See the International Religious Freedom Report for 2013 of the U.S. Department of State, *Brazil,* http://www.state.gov/j/drl/rls/irf/religiousfreedom/index.htm?year=2013&dlid=222361 (accessed 16 October 2015).

12 The text of the Constitution of 1988 is available (Portuguese and English) at http://www.planalto.gov.br (accessed 16 October 2015).

13 Article 5. All persons are equal before the law, without any distinction whatsoever, Brazilians and foreigners residing in the Country being ensured of inviolability of the right to life, to liberty, to equality, to security and to property, on the following terms: (. . .)

VI – freedom of conscience and of belief is inviolable, the free exercise of religious cults being ensured and, under the terms of the law, the protection of places of worship and their rites being guaranteed;

VII – under the terms of the law, the rendering of religious assistance in civil and military establishments of collective confinement is ensured;

VIII – no one shall be deprived of any rights by reason of religious belief or philosophical or political conviction, unless he invokes it to exempt himself from a legal obligation required of all and refuses to perform an alternative obligation established by law (. . .).

14 Article 150. Without prejudice to any other guarantees ensured to the taxpayers, the Union, the states, the Federal District and the municipalities are forbidden to: (. . .)

VI – institute taxes on: (. . .)

b) temples of any denomination (. . .).

15 Article 5, item VIII, the Brazilian Constitution.

16 Article 1.515, Law n. 10.406 of 2002. In July 2013, for the first time, the Superior Court of Justice recognized the civil effects of a marriage annulment made by the Catholic Church.

17 Executive Order n. 2.848, of 1940.

In adopting the principle of non-discrimination, the Brazilian Constitution follows the American Convention on Human Rights and also United Nations declarations and treaties. According to Article 5, item XLII of the Constitution, the practice of racism is a non-bailable and imprescriptible crime, subject to the penalty of confinement, under the terms of the law.

Under the Constitution and legislation, the non-discrimination principle includes the protection of the members of religious communities against discrimination (to ensure freedom of religion or belief) and the prohibition of discrimination practiced by members of a religious community (equal treatment).

According to the Constitution, no one shall be deprived of any rights due to religious belief or philosophical or political conviction, unless one invokes the right to exempt oneself from a legal obligation required of all and refuses to perform an alternative obligation established by law (Art. 5, item VIII). In relation to military service, the Constitution establishes that clerics are exempt from military service during times of peace and that the Armed Forces may require from the objectors an alternative service (such as community service).[18]

Granting conscientious exemptions is a way to protect freedom of religion and to accommodate diversity. A conscientious exemption is called for when a deeply held belief based on the deeply held moral values of a group or an individual conflicts with the demands of the law. In other words, the conscientious objector seeks an exemption from the law not because of his status, but because he holds an alternative set of basic values or an alternative way of balancing basic values that derive from his conscience and conflict with the ends, the means, or the values of a specific law. His conscience, therefore, ultimately contradicts the demands of that law.[19]

Legislation protects religious practices, making it a crime to disturb a ceremony or worship service or to mock someone for their religion;[20] it further prohibits biased or discriminatory language and practices by and against members of religious communities. The Criminal Code defines bias-motivated verbal injury as a distinct crime, which consists in intentionally offending someone's dignity based on race, color, ethnicity, religion, origin, or condition as an elderly or disabled person (Art. 140 para. 3). In addition, the Anti-Discrimination Law[21] states that acts of prejudice or discrimination are crimes and they consist in practicing,

18 Article 143. Military service is compulsory as set forth by law.

Paragraph 1. It is within the competence of the Armed Forces, according to the law, to assign an alternative service to those who, in times of peace, after being enlisted, claim imperative of conscience, which shall be understood as originating in religious creed and philosophical or political belief, for exemption from essentially military activities.

Paragraph 2. Women and clergymen are exempt from compulsory military service in times of peace, but are subject to other duties assigned to them by law.

19 Yossi Nehushtan, 'Religious Conscientious Exemptions', (2011) 30 *Law and Philosophy* (2) 143–144.

20 Article 208. Publicly mock someone for reasons of belief or religious function, prevent or disrupt ceremony or practice of religious worship; publicly vilify act or object of worship:

Penalty – imprisonment of one month to one year or a fine.

Sole Paragraph – If there is use of violence, the penalty is increased by one third, not to mention the penalty for the corresponding violence.

21 Law n. 7716 of 1989.

inducing or inciting discrimination or prejudice based on race, color, ethnicity, religion, or national origin. Examples of discrimination are to deny or impede employment in private enterprise (Art. 3), and to decline or prevent access to business premises, refusing to serve or receive customer or buyer (Art. 5).

Brazil also ratified the Convention on the Prevention and Punishment of the Crime of Genocide of 1948 and approved its own Anti-Genocide Law,[22] which severely punishes the crime of genocide, defined as an act committed with intent to destroy, in whole or in part, a national, ethnic, racial or religious group.

Protection of Minority Groups: Religious Freedom and Freedom of Speech

Although religious speech is protected by freedom of religion or belief and free speech, which encompasses also a right of the individual to be inquisitive and critical about religion, there are limits.[23] Religious extremist speech (especially the discourse that incites someone to practice discrimination or violence on religious grounds or against a religious group) should enjoy a lower standard of protection (or, preferably, no protection) than other speech, for it presents a threat to individuals, internal communities, and society as a whole. Precisely because of the danger presented by such extremist religious speech, there is a compelling need to expand restrictions on religious speech. Imposing limits, while difficult, is necessary.[24]

In accordance with Brazilian Supreme Court case law, extremist speech is an act of discrimination and must be punished. The leading case in this matter is *Ellwanger*.[25] The Supreme Court ruled that 'hate speech,' which consists of expressions that promote hatred against religious, ethnic or racial minorities, is unconstitutional. The defendant, a writer and associate publisher, was convicted of the crime of discrimination against Jews for exclusively publishing, distributing, and selling anti-Semitic works. Acquitted in a lower level court, the defendant's condemnation at the appellate level was only possible because the statute of limitations (period of prescription) was not applicable in his case pursuant to Article 5, XLII of the Federal Constitution, which states: 'the practice of racism is a non-bailable and imprescriptible crime, subject to the penalty of confinement, under the terms of the law.' The defendant filed a petition for writ of *habeas corpus* claiming that the crime of discrimination

22 Law n. 2889, of 1956.

23 Scolnicov, supra note 4 at 195–196. Commenting on the American context, S. Cagle Juhan ('Free Speech, Hate Speech, and the Hostile Speech Environment', (2012) 98 *Virginia Law Review* 1578) notes that 'the first amendment protests a wide array of distasteful, disturbing, defamatory or factually false, profane, "anti-American," and hateful speech. Such protection has been justified, at least in part, by the sentiment that the First Amendment prevents the government from prescribing orthodoxy "in politics, nationalism, religion, or other matters of opinion." Officials must not regulate speech based on their disagreement with it or because society finds it offensive or unsavory. Unfortunately, the liberty interest inherent in the freedom of speech can collide with the equality interest that law and society hold dear.'

24 Amos N. Guiora, *Freedom from Religion: Rights and National Security* (Oxford University Press 2013), 66. Caleb Yong ('Does Freedom of Speech Include Hate Speech?' (2011) 17 *Res Publica* (4)396) suggests that 'targeted vilification is uncovered because it does not promote any free speech interests and its regulation would not violate any free speech rights; indeed, the concerns of the free speech justifications are barely implicated in this category of hate speech at all. This category of hate speech simply is not what the free speech principle is concerned with, and as such is uncovered and regulable.'

25 Habeas Corpus n. 82424-RS, 2003.

against Jews does not have racial connotation and seeking to avoid the application of the racism clause. The question was: Are Jews considered a race for the effects of race crimes? The Full Court by majority concluded that racism is, first and foremost, a social and political reality. This reflected, in truth, a reproachable behavior that stems from the conviction that there is a sufficient hierarchy among human groups to justify acts of segregation and even the killing of people. There were three dissenting opinions, which did not consider Jews as a race (biological criteria). Two of these dissents were also based on freedom of speech and on the absence of a conduct constituting incitement to discrimination. The Full Court by majority denied the petition of *habeas corpus*.[26]

Protection of Minority Groups: Religion, Discrimination and Gender

One of the most heated debates between religious groups and gender movements in Brazil relates to Bill n. 122, of 2006,[27] which sought to criminalize homophobia. The main problem identified by critics of the project was the potential threat to religious manifestation, that is, the excessive restriction on freedom of religious expression.[28] Bill n. 122 aimed to change some existing laws, especially the Anti-Discrimination Law,[29] aiming to add to this statute gender characteristics, namely, gender, sex, sexual orientation, and gender identity. Although the Bill died in 2015, because of the delay in the legislative process (limited to two periods of four years each), the legislative bylaws authorize the return of the Bill for another period of four years, if required by a third of the senators.

The Anti-Discrimination Law criminalizes many forms of behavior in Articles 3 to 19, such as banning a person with one of a number of enumerated characteristics from entering a public place, refusing service in a restaurant or similar places to such a customer, and preventing someone from becoming a civil servant based on those grounds. However, Article 20 of this law has a very vague wording that would allow a more restrictive interpretation of freedom of expression.[30]

The religious sectors fear that the LGBT movement, which is gaining strength in Brazil, might use this Article to restrict religious rights, in particular the freedom to preach against or criticize homosexual practices. On the one hand, though homosexuals need protection from violence, discrimination, and intolerance, homosexual practices should not be granted legal protection against religious or ideological criticism or

26 Concerning the limits of free speech and religious expression, some members of Afro-Brazilian religions feel disadvantaged by the way pastors of Neo-Pentecostal churches preach in the media, as they demonize their deities and rituals (sometimes, exorcism practices are broadcast on TV, radio and Internet). There is a case in Brazilian courts related to the display of videos with messages against those religions on YouTube, which was filed by the Attorney's Office in Rio de Janeiro. This case raises the question of the limits of the offensive speech against a religion – not properly extremist speech or defamation of an individual person. The Federal Court granted temporary injunctive relief to compel Google to refrain from displaying the videos, but (as of August 2015) the case is still pending (TRF-2, Processo n. 0004747–33.2014.4.02.5101 / 2014.51.01.004747–2).

27 http://www.senado.gov.br/atividade/materia/detalhes.asp?p_cod_mate=79604 (accessed 16 October 2015).

28 http://veja.abril.com.br/noticia/brasil/religiosos-entregam-1-milhao-de-assinaturas-contra-pl-122 (accessed 16 October 2015).

29 Law n. 7716 of 1989.

30 Article 20. Practice, induce or incite discrimination or prejudice based on race, color, ethnicity, religion or national origin. Penalty: Imprisonment for one to three years and fine.

moral disapproval. On the other hand, even though religious speech is protected by the freedoms of conscience, religion, belief and expression which encompass the right of the individual to be inquisitive and critical about religion, ideologies, and human behavior, it has limitations.[31] Religious extremist speech that incites someone to commit acts of discrimination or violence should not enjoy legal protection.

Church-State Relations in Brazil

The Federal Constitution outlines the relation between state and religions. While it declares in its Preamble that it was promulgated 'under the protection of God', the Constitution kept in its text an establishment clause. Article 19 forbids the state to establish churches, subsidize them, impede their activities, or maintain relationships of dependence or alliance with them.[32]

Civil legislation ratifies the separation when it states that religious organizations are free to define their organizational structures. Until 2003, all religious organizations had to adapt their structures to the requirements of the Civil Code[33] – they were treated like associations or foundations in general. However, in 2003 the Civil Code was reformed and it was established that religious organizations may be created and organized freely and that the government is forbidden to deny the recognition or registration of their incorporation and other necessary acts.

Although state and church are separated, the Constitution allows the government to support religious schools, because of their social relevance.[34] Concerning religious education in public schools, the Constitution states that religious education has to be taught in elementary public schools. However, such education must not have a proselytizing or dogmatic character, and students' participation shall not be mandatory.[35] Curiously, however, the government made an

31 See quotations from Scolnicov and Juhan, supra note 23.

32 Article 19. The Union, the states, the Federal District and the municipalities are forbidden to:

I – establish religious sects or churches, subsidize them, hinder their activities, or maintain relationships of dependence or alliance with them or their representatives, without prejudice to collaboration in the public interest in the manner set forth by law.

33 Law n. 10.825.

34 Article 213. Public funds shall be allocated to public schools, and may be channeled to community, religious or philanthropic schools, as defined by law, which:

I – prove that they do not seek profit and that they apply their surplus funds in education;
II – ensure that their assets shall be assigned to another community, religious or philanthropic schools, or to the Government in case they cease their activities.

Paragraph 1. The funds provided by this Article may be allocated to elementary and secondary school scholarships, as provided by law, for those who prove insufficiency of means, when there are no vacancies or no regular courses are offered in the public school system of the place where the student lives, the Government being placed under the obligation to invest, on a priority basis, in the expansion of the public system of the locality.

Paragraph 2. Research and extension activities at university level may receive financial support from the Government.

35 Article 210. Minimum curricula shall be established for elementary schools in order to ensure a common basic education and respect for national and regional cultural and artistic values.

Paragraph 1. The teaching of religion is optional and shall be offered during the regular school hours of public elementary schools.

Agreement ('Concordat') with the Holy See in 2008 to guarantee some rights to the Catholic Church, which include the teaching of Catholic doctrine in public schools during religious education classes (as one of the religious doctrines that should be taught).

Although the Brazilian legal framework related to the protection of freedom of religion or belief certainly meets the international standards on the protection of human rights, some tensions in the socio-political landscape since the last National Constituent Assembly are relevant in the discussion about religion and non-discrimination.

During the National Constituent Assembly of 1987–1988,[36] a competition arose concerning religious symbols. On the one hand, the crucifix on the wall of the National Congress represented the majority presence of Catholicism in Brazil. On the other hand, Evangelical deputies (Evangelical churches were already growing rapidly) demanded the amendment of the Bylaws of the Constituent Assembly (Amendment n. 681). Based on their proposal, the Constituent Assembly included Article 46 in the Bylaws, to determine that 'The Holy Bible should be on the desk of the National Constituent Assembly, available to those who want to make use of it.'

This was not of minor importance. First, it was an affirmation of the Evangelical presence in the Brazilian political scene, indicating the ascension of a religious minority group. Second, it reinforced the symbolic recognition of Christian values in the new constitutional order – the Crucifix on the wall and the Bible on the table. Third, it inspired the use of Bible verses and authority in the debates to justify political claims.

The symbolic presence of religion is also recognized in the Preamble of the Constitution. The Constituent Assembly, when it promulgated the Federal Constitution of 1988, recognized that it was acting 'under the protection of God' and this expression was included in the Preamble of the Constitution,[37] like the traditional *invocationes dei* present in many of the world's constitutions.[38]

Although it has never been interpreted as the establishment of a religion or the prohibition of atheism in Brazil, the invocation of God in the Preamble of the Constitution has been a point of contention. In the course of the Constituent Assembly, Deputy José Genuíno issued Amendment n. 523 to exclude from the Preamble the expression 'under the protection of God', based on comparative law and on the demands of a pluralistic society. However, only one Deputy voted in favor of the Amendment. The Assembly considered that the expression reflected the beliefs and the religious sentiments of the Brazilian people.

A few years later, a complaint was filed in the Supreme Court in order to identify the legal effects of the Preamble. In 1999, the Social Liberal Party required that the Supreme Court should compel the Constituent Assembly of Acre (a Member-State) to include in the Preamble of the Constitution of Acre the expression 'under the protection of God', replicating

36 These issues are discussed in Douglas Antônio Rocha Pinheiro, *Direito, Estado E Religião* (Fino Traço Editora, 2008).

37 'We, the representatives of the Brazilian People, convened in the national constituent assembly to institute a democratic state for the purpose of ensuring the exercise of social and individual rights, liberty, security, well-being, development, equality and justice as supreme values of a fraternal, pluralist and unprejudiced society, founded on social harmony and committed, in the internal and international orders, to the peaceful settlement of disputes, promulgate, under the protection of God, this Constitution of the Federative Republic of Brazil.'

38 For an extensive account on the reference to God in the world constitutions, see Jeroen Temperman, *State-Religion Relationships and Human Rights Law: Towards a Right to Religiously Neutral Governance* (Martinus Nijhoff Publishers 2010).

the Preamble of the Federal Constitution. In this case (named ADI 2076[39]), the Supreme Court ruled that the Preamble of the Federal Constitution does not have a normative force. Therefore, it must not be used to impose duties or to grant rights.

More recently, the Catholic Church, through the National Conference of Bishops of Brazil, appeared as *amicus curiae* in lawsuits against same-sex unions, namely the cases ADPF 132[40] and ADI 4277.[41] The Conference also sought to act as *amicus curiae* in ADPF 54,[42] which was a landmark case about the abortion of anencephalic fetuses, but its participation was rejected by Justice Marco Aurélio. Justice Aurélio's controversial opinion, which guided the court's decision, was based on the argument of separation between church and state. The Conference of Catholic Bishops also appeared as *amicus curiae* in the case ADI 3510,[43] which questioned the legalization of research with embryonic stem cells. It is noteworthy that in all these cases, the majority of the Brazilian Supreme Court ruled in opposition to the Conference's claims.

Among the Evangelicals, especially Pentecostals and neo-Pentecostals, there is intense political involvement of some sectors, which causes tensions between secular and religious sectors of the society. Marcos Feliciano, who is a Federal Deputy and a member of the Christian Social Party, is also an Evangelical pastor of the Cathedral Church of Revival. Reverend Feliciano was elected as President of the Commission of Human and Minority Rights of the Brazilian Chamber of Deputies, an event which had major repercussions in Brazil, since the Congressman had made quite provocative statements on social networks, considered by some as racist and homophobic, such as 'Africa is a cursed continent because of the Old Testament Canaan curse' and 'homosexual feelings cause social problems.'[44] Silas Malafaia, the leader of a branch of the Assemblies of God Pentecostal denomination, who is in charge of the oldest religious television program in Brazil, is known for his forceful protest addressed to political actions that can violate Christian values. Reverend Malafaia participates in many public debates and organized a protest march in Brasilia in front of the Capitol against same-sex marriage and Bill n. 122, which criminalizes discrimination and prejudice against homosexuals.[45]

In the National Congress (which includes the Chamber of Deputies and the Senate), there is an Evangelical Parliamentary Group, established in 2003, whose members are connected to some branches of the Evangelical movement (although the group itself has no institutional connection with churches). The group opposes the legalization of abortion, euthanasia, and recreational drugs and the criminalization of 'homophobia', as well as the dissolution of the traditional family structure, *inter alia*. In most of these controversial debates, the National Congress has remained more conservative.

While the news reported by the media is almost always related to the opposition to the so-called 'homosexual agenda' (mostly the Bill n. 122) and other contentious moral issues, the religious sectors seek or have sought also to influence other important social and political matters. For example, a theme that is often mentioned by the Evangelical Parliamentary Group, mostly by Senator Magno Malta, is the problem of sexual abuse of children. Senator Malta, Chairman of the Parliamentary Inquiry Committee on Pedophilia, has been the leader

39 Direct Action of Unconstitutionality n. 2076, 8 August 2003.

40 Allegation of Disobedience of Fundamental Precept n. 132, 5 May 2011.

41 Direct Action of Unconstitutionality n. 4277, 5 May 2011.

42 Allegation of Disobedience of Fundamental Precept n. 54, 5 May 2011.

43 Direct Action of Unconstitutionality n. 3510, 29 April 2008.

44 See http://veja.abril.com.br/noticia/brasil/marco-feliciano-outro-deputado-contra-gays-e-negros (accessed 16 October 2015).

45 See http://noticias.gospelmais.com.br/pastor-silas-malafaia-organiza-grande-protesto-contra-pl-122–19608.html (accessed 16 October 2015).

of the applauded national campaign 'All Against Pedophilia', which aims to raise awareness about the issue of child sexual abuse.[46]

In addition, religious sectors have aimed to support political decisions beneficial to the protection of the rights of indigenous peoples. In this respect, the opposition of religious organizations to the Proposed Constitutional Amendment n. 215 of 2000 and to the Bill n. PLC/227 of 2012, was remarkable. Such proposals, which aim to reduce the rights of indigenous peoples over their lands, have been criticized by the Secretary-General of the Conference of Catholic Bishops and by important Evangelical associations, such as the Brazilian Evangelical Alliance, the Brazilian Association of Transcultural Missions, and the Council of Indigenous Pastors, in a joint declaration.[47]

Religious performance of both Catholics and Evangelicals in the political and judicial arenas causes outrage in certain social groups, which are mostly represented by humanist, gender, and Afro-Brazilian religious organizations. For example, LGBT groups have often vigorously protested in front of churches where the Deputy Reverend Marco Feliciano visited as a preacher, and the congressman's life has been much reported upon in the news. Furthermore, during World Youth Day in Brazil (July 2013), which was attended by Pope Francis, the so-called 'SlutWalk' was organized by a feminist movement with various claims. On that occasion, women broke statues of Catholic saints and used crucifixes in acts of a sexual nature. Certainly, the political debate between the LGBT movement, feminists, Afro-Brazilian religious groups, humanists, and Christian sectors has become more intense over the last decade.

Proposed Constitutional Amendment about Abstract Constitutional Control

Proposed Amendment to the Constitution n. 99 of 2011[48] intends to grant religious organizations the power to file legal actions related to the abstract constitutional control by the Supreme Federal Court (original jurisdiction), inserting Item X into Article 103 of the Constitution. Currently, only the persons or institutions included in the Article 103[49] may file 'Direct Action of Unconstitutionality' (ADI)[50] and 'Declaratory Actions of Constitutionality' (ADC).[51]

46 See http://www.fpebrasil.com.br/portal/index.php/component/k2/item/289-contraapedofilia (accessed 1 November 2015).

47 See http://www.aliancaEvangelica.org.br/index.php/declaracoes/item/171-demarcacao-terras-indigenas (accessed 16 October 2015).

48 See http://www.camara.gov.br/proposicoesWeb/fichadetramitacao?idProposicao=524259 (accessed 16 October 2015).

49 Article 103. The direct action of unconstitutionality and declaratory actions of constitutionality may be filed by:

I – the President of the Republic;
II – the Bureau of the Senate;
III – the Bureau of the Chamber of Deputies;
IV – the Bureau of Legislative Assembly or the Legislative Chamber of the Federal District;
V – the Governor of the State or the Federal District;
VI – the Attorney General's Office;
VII – the Federal Council of the Bar Association of Brazil;
VIII – a political party represented in the National Congress;
IX – union confederation or nationwide class entity.

50 The Direct Action of Unconstitutionality is the instrument that aims to drawn into question the constitutionality of federal or state laws and normative acts (abstract control).

51 The Declaratory Action of Constitutionality is the instrument destined to affirm the constitutionality of a federal law or normative act, in order to solve relevant controversies on the interpretation of the Constitution (abstract control).

The Committee on Constitution, Justice, and Citizenship gave assent to the proposal on 27 March 2013, following the opinion of Deputy Bonifacio de Andrada, who did not find any unconstitutionality in the proposal. A special commission of the Chamber of Deputies will scrutinize it before it is debated and voted on by the Chamber and the Senate (both houses will vote twice).

Expanding the list to include religious organizations might raise problems beyond religion-state relations. The proposed amendment suggests that nationwide religious organizations should have the legal power to require abstract control from the Supreme Court. However, what would be a nationwide religious entity? In the proposal, the General Convention of the Assemblies of God, the National Conference of Bishops of Brazil, the Supreme Council of the Presbyterian Church, the National Baptist Convention, and the College of Bishops of the Methodist Church are noted. Nonetheless, as the creation and organization of religious entities are not subjected to many legal rules, how is one to define which entity is nationwide? There are thousands of independent religious organizations, and most of them could claim to be nationwide religions or to have nationwide aims – and many are already found in all Brazilian states.

On the one hand, the intention to protect religious freedom is legitimate, that is, to allow religious organizations to directly challenge before the Supreme Court the constitutionality of a law that may violate freedom of religion or belief, or other human rights. On the other hand, besides the problem of selecting which religious organizations are entitled to that right, there are two further issues. First, why not include any other nationwide cultural or philosophical association? Second, the multiplication of the entities that may file a constitutional challenge will greatly increase the number of cases before the Court.

Equality and Religion-State Separation

In 2009, Bill n. 160[52] was proposed, also known as the General Law of Religions, which provides for the guarantees and rights to freedom of religion or belief. The proposal of the pastor of the Universal Church of the Kingdom of God and Congressman George Hilton aimed to establish mechanisms that ensure the free exercise of religion, organizational autonomy, protection of places of worship and of rites, the inviolability of belief, and religious education in public schools (as an elective course).

The purpose of the Bill is to ensure that every religion enjoys the same conditions as those granted to the Catholic Church in the general Agreement signed between Brazil and the Holy See in 2008 by President Luiz Inácio Lula da Silva and Pope Benedict XVI (Decree n. 7101/2010).[53] The arrangement gives the Roman Catholic Church express legal protection concerning religious education in public schools (although it mentions that other religious doctrines should be allowed to be taught as well) and ensures that their priests will not be subject to labor law and that parochial schools and other social projects may receive public aid. The Agreement also reaffirms the recognition of the civil effects of religious marriage[54] and tax immunity, among others.

52 http://www.senado.gov.br/atividade/materia/detalhes.asp?p_cod_mate=92959 (accessed 16 October 2015).

53 Brazil had already adopted a specific Agreement in 1989, concerning the pastoral care in the army.

54 Because of the adoption of the Agreement, for the first time the Superior Court of Justice recognized an ecclesiastical judgment of annulment of marriage, which had been confirmed by the Supreme Tribunal of the Apostolic Signatura, in the Vatican. The ruling was based on the Agreement, which grants the religious judgments made

Although the Catholic Church has a different nature when compared to other religious organizations, because of its international nature and its connection to the Holy See, the arrangement suffers from problems related to its necessity and constitutionality, or possibly, the lack of both.

Two issues can be highlighted. First, what is the reason for the existence of such an Agreement? Was the Church suffering or threatened by unwarranted restrictions by the state? It seems not. Second, while all faiths have constitutional and civil protection (by general laws), the special legal status of this enhanced protection given to the Catholic Church possibly violates the Constitution. The Attorney's Office filed a lawsuit challenging the constitutionality of the Agreement before the Supreme Court, giving special emphasis to the unconstitutionality of the teaching of Catholic doctrine in public schools demanded by the Agreement[55] (pending case ADI 4439). However, although the Constitution certainly adopts a separation and non-preferential regime regarding religions (which contradicts the establishment of a special relationship with the Catholic Church), it is worth noting that the Constitution does not forbid religious education in schools. On the contrary, according to the Constitution, religious education is a regular discipline in primary education (although participation is non-mandatory).

Regarding the General Law of Religions, the proposal aims to ensure rights to religious entities that require isonomic treatment by the Brazilian state. However, the bill faces some resistance by politicians and religious people because they are afraid of state interference in religious matters (to date, there is no statute that regulates religious freedom). Members of unorganized religions, mainly the Afro-Brazilian religious groups, are especially reluctant, since they fear being unprotected, as was declared in the Social Affairs Committee meetings.[56] Nonetheless, the bill does not distinguish between religions; instead, it aims to promote equal treatment for all religious organizations.

During an extraordinary meeting held on 12 June 2013, the Social Affairs Committee approved the bill, which had already been examined and approved by the Committee on Education, Culture, and Sports on 6 July 2010. The justification of its approval was to ensure equality between religious organizations operating in Brazil. In 2014, the Government (Executive Branch) declared support for the bill.[57] As of August 2015, it is still pending in Congress.

A Way Forward

In the Pew Research studies cited at the opening of this chapter, Brazil's rank on the Government Restrictions on Religion index in the most recent data year (2013) is both the lowest of the world's 25 most populous countries and the lowest Brazil had achieved

by the Holy See the status of foreign judgments. The details of the case were not disclosed by the Court because of the judicial secrecy statute rules (Family Law).

55 Article 11. Paragraph 1. Religious education, both Catholic and of other religious denominations, while optional, is a regular discipline in normal hours of state schools in primary education, so long as respect for the religious diversity of Brazil is ensured, in accordance with the Constitution and other laws, without any form of discrimination.

56 http://www12.senado.gov.br/noticias/materias/2013/05/23/debatedores-pedem-rejeicao-de-projeto-de-lei-que-regula-religiao (accessed 16 October 2015).

57 http://www12.senado.leg.br/noticias/materias/2014/09/04/lei-geral-das-religioes-segue-sem-definicao (accessed 16 October 2015).

over the course of the study, with an index approaching zero. Former Pew researcher, Brian Grim, now president of the Religious Freedom & Business Foundation, has noted that one of the most important factors in Brazil's 'peaceful navigation of the past decades of religious change is the position taken by the majority faith – Catholicism – toward religious freedom'. As a result, 'Brazil is peacefully undergoing one of the most dramatic religious shifts in the world today.'[58] Most of the shift, says Grim, has been from Roman Catholicism to energetic and conservative forms of Pentecostalism and other minority denominations. In 'other parts of the world, active and conservative religion is sometimes equated with extremism and political destabilization.'[59] In Brazil, however, though it has the world's largest Catholic population, 'religious freedom is more keenly appreciated by religious minorities'.[60]

To be sure, on the Social Hostilities index, Brazil has risen gradually, from a very 'low' ranking in 2007 to nudge into a 'high' ranking in 2013. Though this is still a rank below all but a few of the world's 25 most populous countries, and is characteristic of a general worldwide rise in social hostilities involving religion,[61] this is nothing to be sanguine about. However, while it perhaps would not be prudent to over-interpret these statistics, we can assert with confidence that developments in this complex country would be worth watching and perhaps emulating.

At an 'historic meeting' in Brasilia on 11 August 2015, the first Parliamentary Committee for Religious Freedom 'announced the signed participation of 207 Deputies and 12 Senators in the common goal of guaranteeing the free exercise of religion'. With the slogan 'Don't just believe. We must respect!' the group of '[g]overnment officials, religious leaders, non-governmental organizations and the business sector united to support this right, highlighting the need for greater tolerance as a way to peace.'[62]

Congressman Moroni Torgan, who created the multi-party Parliamentary Committee in February 2015, summed up its work as 'an instrument for the institutions of the most varied religions and denominations, for believers and even for atheists, to ensure everyone has the right to believe or not . . . [R]especting the diversity of beliefs is as important as the very right to believe or not to believe; then we can also learn from each other.'[63]

58 Quoted in Claudia Augelli, 'Brazil Celebrates First Place, but not in Soccer', *Religion Press Release Services*, 4 May 2015, http://pressreleases.religionnews.com/2015/05/04/brazil-celebrates-first-place-but-not-in-soccer/ (accessed 16 October 2015).

59 Augelli, supra note 58.

60 Augelli, supra note 58. See also 'Oldest Mosque Hosts Religious Freedom & Business Celebration: Event Kicks Off Focus on Religious Freedom and Business', *Religious Freedom and Business Foundation*, 9 May 2015, http://religiousfreedomandbusiness.org/2/post/category/brazil, and 'Global Forum – Business, Interfaith Understanding & Peace, http://religiousfreedomandbusiness.org/global-forums (both accessed 16 October 2015).

61 In 2007, 12 of the 25 most populous countries were in the low or moderate range on the Social Hostilities index. In 2013, only South Africa ranked 'Low' on this index, with only four other countries – Japan, DR Congo, Philippines, and theUnited States – securely in the 'Moderate' range. Italy, Mexico, and Vietnam, like Brazil, were nudging into the 'High' range. See Pew Research Center, supra note 4; also Pew's report of 14 January 2014, 'Religious Hostilities Reach Six-Year High', http://www.pewforum.org/2014/01/14/religious-hostilities-reach-six-year-high/ (accessed 16 October 2015).

62 All quotations in this paragraph are from the Press Release, 'Brazil: Historic Meeting, with 207 Deputies, 12 Senators Supporting Religious Freedom', 13 August 2015, *Religious Freedom & Business Foundation*, http://religiousfreedomandbusiness.org/2/post/2015/08/brazil-historic-meeting-with-207-deputies-12-senators-supporting-religious-freedom.html (accessed 16 October 2015).

63 'Brazil: Historic Meeting', supra note 62.

6 Anti-Discrimination Legislation and Regulation of Employment Decisions of Religious Schools in Australia

Greg Walsh

Regulating Religious Employment Decisions

This chapter evaluates the current approach to regulating the employment decisions of religious schools under anti-discrimination legislation in the Australian State of New South Wales (NSW), focusing specifically on the central role of the right to religious liberty in debates concerning how religious schools should be regulated, and analyzing the extent to which the current protections provided to the employment decisions of religious schools (referred to as the 'general exception approach') is consistent with the right to religious liberty.

Under anti-discrimination legislation, religious schools in Australia are often provided with the ability to make employment decisions based on an individual's compatibility with the school's religion. These provisions have the capacity to adversely affect a considerable number of individuals employed or seeking employment at these schools. In 2011, for example, there were 9,435 schools in Australia, comprising 6,705 government schools, 1,710 Catholic schools, and 1,020 Independent schools (the majority being religious schools)[1] – with the Catholic and Independent schools together employing 104,779 teachers.[2] The actual number of employees who could be adversely affected would be much higher than this, as this figure does not include management, support, or maintenance staff or the employees of educational institutions other than schools. Further, all members of the community have the potential to be adversely affected by the employment decisions of religious schools if they decide to apply for a teaching or non-teaching employment position.

Further concerns about the protections provided to religious schools under anti-discrimination legislation include the view that the protections can contribute to a school environment that is harmful to the wellbeing of students, can interfere with the effective promotion of human rights standards, and can undermine the social cohesion that is essential to a successful multicultural society.[3] The extent of the possible adverse impact from the operation of religious schools in Australia is increasing, considering that the percentage of students attending non-government schools is rising, from 31 percent in 2001 to 34.6 percent in 2011.[4]

1 Australian Bureau of Statistics, *Schools* (3 May 2012), http://www.abs.gov.au/ausstats/abs@.nsf/Lookup/4221.0main+features202011 (accessed 1 November 2015).

2 Australian Bureau of Statistics, *Teaching Staff (Number)* (3 May 2012), http://www.abs.gov.au/ausstats/abs@.nsf/Lookup/4221.0main+features502011 (accessed 1 November 2015).

3 See generally Jennifer Buckingham, *The Rise of Religious Schools* (The Centre for Independent Studies 2010); Deb Wilkinson, Richard Denniss and Andrew Macintosh, 'The Accountability of Private Schools to Public Values' (The Australia Institute 2004), http://www.tai.org.au/documents/dp_fulltext/DP71.pdf (accessed 16 October 2015).

4 Australian Bureau of Statistics, *Students* (3 May 2012), http://www.abs.gov.au/ausstats/abs@.nsf/Lookup/4221.0main+features302011 (accessed 29 October 2015).

In New South Wales, employment decisions are regulated by the *Anti-Discrimination Act 1977* (NSW) (*ADA 1977*), which makes it unlawful for a person in an employment decision to discriminate on the grounds of race, sex, transgender status, marital or domestic status, disability, a person's responsibilities as a caregiver, homosexuality, or age.[5] An example of the protection that *ADA 1977* gives to employees in relation to the specified grounds can be provided in relation to discrimination on the ground of marital status. Section 40 states:

> (1) It is unlawful for an employer to discriminate against a person on the ground of marital status:
>
> (a) in the arrangements the employer makes for the purpose of determining who shall be offered employment,
> (b) in determining who should be offered employment, or
> (c) in the terms on which the employer offers employment.
>
> (2) It is unlawful for an employer to discriminate against an employee on the ground of marital status:
>
> (a) in the terms or conditions of employment which the employer affords the employee,
> (b) by denying the employee access, or limiting the employee's access, to opportunities for promotion, transfer or training, or to any other benefits associated with employment, or
> (c) by dismissing the employee or subjecting the employee to any other detriment.[6]

However, an exception from the operation of these provisions is provided not just to religious educational institutions but to any organization that qualifies as a 'private educational authority', which is defined as:

> . . . a person or body administering a school, college, university or other institution at which education or training is provided, not being:
>
> (a) a school, college, university or other institution established under the *Education Reform Act 1990* (by the Minister administering that Act), the *Technical and Further Education Commission Act 1990* or an Act of incorporation of a university, or
> (b) an agricultural college administered by the Minister for Agriculture.[7]

Under *ADA 1977* private educational authorities can make employment decisions on the grounds of sex, transgender status, marital or domestic status, disability, and homosexuality that would otherwise be unlawful.[8] However, no exceptions are provided on the grounds of race, age or a person's responsibilities as a carer.[9] As religion is not a characteristic protected

5 *Anti-Discrimination Act 1977* (NSW) [*ADA 1977*] ss 8–16, 25–31, 38C–38J, 40–46, 49D–49K, 49V–49ZC, 49ZH–49ZN, 49ZYB–49ZYK.
6 *ADA 1977* (NSW) ss 40(1)–(2).
7 See *ADA 1977* (NSW) s 4 (definition of 'private educational authority').
8 *ADA 1977* (NSW) ss 25(3)(c), 38C(3)(c), 40(3)(c), 49D(3)(c), 49ZH(3)(c).
9 *ADA 1977* (NSW) ss 8, 49ZYB, 49V.

in *ADA 1977*, an adverse employment decision made by a private educational authority on the grounds of religion does not breach *ADA 1977*. Although *ADA 1977* defines race to include 'ethno-religious' origin, which covers groups such as Jews, this has been held to not allow discrimination complaints on the grounds of religion.[10]

Advocates of strong protections being provided for religious schools under anti-discrimination legislation typically rely heavily on the right to religious liberty to justify the appropriateness of protection being provided.[11] Considering the central position that the right to religious liberty has in debates concerning the merits of these protections it is appropriate to examine the religious liberty claim in detail to determine the extent to which it can legitimately be held to support approaches such as the general exception approach.

Religious liberty is only one of many important criteria that need to be considered in determining the appropriateness of any approach to regulating religious schools under anti-discrimination legislation. Any comprehensive assessment would also include the right to equality, the welfare of children, the rights of parents and minorities, the right to privacy, and freedom of association. Nevertheless, considering the centrality of the right to religious liberty in discussions concerning the merits of any approach adopted in the area, it is useful to undertake a detailed analysis of this right and assess the extent to which it can support the general exception approach.

Religious Schools and the Right to Religious Liberty

To accurately determine the extent to which the general exception approach is consistent with the right to religious liberty it is necessary to understand the importance and scope of the right, the religious dimensions of religious schools, and the important role employment decisions play in maintaining religious schools as religious institutions.

The Importance of the Right to Religious Liberty

The importance of the right to religious liberty is recognized in an extensive range of international human rights treaties.[12] Although these instruments also emphasize the

10 *A on behalf of V and A v. NSW Department of School Education* [2000] NSWADTAP 14, [16]. Although the focus of this chapter is on the merits of the current approach adopted in *ADA 1977* to regulating religious schools, it should also be noted that section 351(1) of the *Fair Work Act 2009* (Cth) prohibits an employer from taking adverse action against an employee or prospective employee on a variety of grounds, including religion. However, this prohibition is limited in its application to private educational authorities as the prohibitions do not apply in any jurisdiction where the conduct is not unlawful under that jurisdiction's anti-discrimination legislation: id. 351(2)–(3). A complaint concerning an employment decision of a religious school in NSW can also be made to the Australian Human Rights Commission; however, the Commission has no coercive powers and can only attempt to conciliate the matter between the parties and provide a report on the matter to the Commonwealth Attorney-General: *Australian Human Rights Commission Act 1986* (Cth) ss 31(b), 32(1)(b).

11 Although terms such as 'exceptions' and 'exemptions' are commonly used to refer to limitations provided to the operation of anti-discrimination legislation, the terms are not used extensively in the chapter as they can suggest that the limitations are merely permissions to engage in discrimination that the government was forced to provide due to political pressure. The term 'protections' is preferred as it more accurately recognizes that the limitations to the operation of anti-discrimination legislation are typically aimed at ensuring that a variety of important rights are appropriately respected.

12 See Nicolae V. Dură, 'The Right to Religion: An Evaluation of the Texts of the Main Binding International and European Juridical Instruments', Chapter 2 of this volume.

importance of many other rights, significant features of these instruments indicate that the state should be particularly committed to ensuring that the right to religious liberty is appropriately protected.[13] The *Declaration on the Elimination of All Forms of Intolerance and of Discrimination Based on Religion or Belief* (1981 Declaration), for example, is dedicated to recognizing the importance of the right to religious liberty and ensuring that it is appropriately protected.[14] Further, some international human rights instruments place particular restrictions on states in relation to their ability to limit the protection provided to rights such as the right to religious liberty.

Under the *International Covenant on Civil and Political Rights* (ICCPR), for example, there are only seven rights, including the right to religious liberty, that are non-derogable even in times of public emergency.[15] The Human Rights Committee has emphasized that this restriction the Covenant places on states 'underlines the great importance of non-derogable rights'.[16] The importance the Covenant attributes to the right to religious freedom is further illustrated through the other six non-derogable rights, which include the right to life, the right not to be tortured, and the right not to be enslaved.[17] Further support for the importance of the non-derogable rights is provided by the *Siracusa Principles on the Limitation and Derogation of Provisions in the International Covenant on Civil and Political Rights*, a document produced by the United Nations Economic and Social Council which clearly states that these rights (including the right to religious liberty) are 'not derogable under any conditions even for the asserted purpose of preserving the life of the nation'.[18]

13 It is accepted that the claim that a state should be particularly focused on protecting some human rights is contestable considering that international human rights instruments declare the equal importance of all human rights. A relevant illustration is the *Vienna Declaration and Programme of Action*, A/CONF.157/23 (12 July 1993) which states: 'All human rights are universal, indivisible and interdependent and interrelated. The international community must treat human rights globally in a fair and equal manner, on the same footing, and with the same emphasis': Art 5. One approach to such a criticism could be to simply argue that this view is wrong. For example, the Human Rights Committee would be justly condemned if it held that states must aim at protecting all the rights contained in the *International Covenant on Civil and Political Rights* (ICCPR) in a 'fair and equal manner, on the same footing, and with the same emphasis' and that states cannot consider that there is a significant difference in importance between rights in the ICCPR (such as the right a person has to receive just compensation in the event of unlawful arrest under Article 9(5) compared to the prohibition on torture under Article 7). An alternative response to the criticism could be to accept that all human rights are of equal importance but that states can legitimately adopt a nuanced approach to promoting human rights that takes account of a range of relevant factors and that, under this approach, adopting a particular emphasis on promoting religious liberty, equality or some other right is acceptable and consistent with an understanding that all rights are of equal importance.

14 Although the United Nations General Assembly committed to producing a convention on religious freedom, this has not yet occurred. For an explanation regarding why a convention on religious liberty has not yet been established and an evaluation of the merits of producing such a convention, see Malcolm Evans, 'Advancing Freedom of Religion or Belief: Agendas for Change' (2012) 1 *Oxford Journal of Law and Religion* (1) 6–9.

15 *International Covenant on Civil and Political Rights* (ICCPR), opened for signature 16 December 1966, 999 UNTS 171 (entered into force 23 March 1976), Art. 4.

16 Human Rights Committee, *General Comment No. 24: Issues Relating to Reservations Made Upon Ratification or Accession to the Covenant or the Optional Protocols Thereto, or in Relation to Declarations under Article 41 of the Covenant*, 52nd sess, UN Doc. CCPR/C/21/Rev.1/Add.6 (4 November 1994), para. 10.

17 ICCPR, Art. 4.

18 United Nations Economic and Social Council, United Nations Sub-Commission on Prevention of Discrimination and Protection of Minorities, *Siracusa Principles on the Limitation and Derogation of Provisions in the International Covenant on Civil and Political Rights*, Annex, UN Doc. E/CN.4/1984/4 (1984) [58].

The fundamental importance of the right to religious liberty is also frequently affirmed by international and national courts. The European Court of Human Rights, for example, emphasized the importance of religious liberty in *Kokkinakis v. Greece*, upholding the applicant's claim that his religious liberty had been violated when he was prosecuted under laws prohibiting proselytism.[19] The Court held that

> . . . freedom of thought, conscience and religion is one of the foundations of a 'democratic society' . . . It is, in its religious dimension, one of the most vital elements that go to make up the identity of believers and of their conception of life, but it is also a precious asset for atheists, agnostics, sceptics and the unconcerned. The pluralism indissociable from a democratic society, which has been dearly won over the centuries, depends on it.[20]

In *Christian Education South Africa v. Minister of Education* the Constitutional Court of South Africa considered the constitutionality of corporal punishment of students in Christian schools administered with parental consent.[21] Although the Court ultimately rejected the attempt by the schools to rely on religious liberty to justify corporal punishment, Justice Albie Sachs strongly emphasised the importance that should be given to religious freedom:

> The right to believe or not to believe, and to act or not to act according to his or her beliefs or non-beliefs, is one of the key ingredients of any person's dignity. Yet freedom of religion goes beyond protecting the inviolability of the individual conscience. For many believers, their relationship with God or creation is central to all their activities. It concerns their capacity to relate in an intensely meaningful fashion to their sense of themselves, their community and their universe. For millions in all walks of life, religion provides support and nurture and a framework for individual and social stability and growth. Religious belief has the capacity to awake concepts of self-worth and human dignity which form the cornerstone of human rights. It affects the believer's view of society and founds the distinction between right and wrong. It expresses itself in the affirmation and continuity of powerful traditions that frequently have an ancient character transcending historical epochs and national boundaries.[22]

The right to religious liberty is not an absolute right that can never be limited by the state.[23] Rather, a determination of what justice requires in a particular situation may involve a consideration of different, sometimes conflicting, human rights and, in some situations, other rights should be given priority.

19 *Kokkinakis v. Greece*, App. No. 14307/88 (ECtHR, 25 May 1993).

20 *Kokkinakis* § 31.

21 *Christian Education South Africa v. Minister of Education* [2000] 4 SA 757 (Constitutional Court) [1]–[5].

22 *Christian Education South Africa* [36].

23 Although the claim that absolute human rights exist is contested, some rights that are commonly considered to be absolute include the right not to be tortured and the right an innocent person has not to be intentionally killed. For a useful discussion of the claim that some human rights should be considered to be absolute see John Finnis, *Natural Law and Natural Rights* (Oxford University Press, 2nd edn, 2011), 223–226.

The legitimacy of the state being able to limit religious liberty is supported by international human rights instruments including the ICCPR, which declares that '[f]reedom to manifest one's religion or beliefs may be subject only to such limitations as are prescribed by law and are necessary to protect public safety, order, health, or morals or the fundamental rights and freedoms of others.'[24] The possibility of limiting religious freedom in appropriate situations was affirmed by the High Court of Australia in *Church of the New Faith v. Commissioner of Pay-Roll Tax (Vict)* (1983) 154 CLR 120, which decided that the Church of the New Faith should be regarded as a religion for the purposes of taxation. Mason ACJ and Brennan J held that

> . . . the area of legal immunity marked out by the concept of religion cannot extend to all conduct in which a person may engage in giving effect to his faith in the supernatural. The freedom to act in accordance with one's religious beliefs is not as inviolate as the freedom to believe, for general laws to preserve and protect society are not defeated by a plea of religious obligation to breach them . . . Religious conviction is not a solvent of legal obligation.[25]

A similar point was made by Kirby J in *Ermogenous v. Greek Orthodox Community of SA Inc* (2002) 209 CLR 95: 'Courts will seek to avoid entanglements in what are substantially issues of religious doctrine where there is no applicable legal norm or specific judicial competence. But courts will reject the notion that religious organizations, as such, are somehow above secular law and exempt from its rules.'[26]

That a state's decision to limit religious liberty must be supported by a strong justification was supported by the Human Rights Committee in a General Comment issued on ICCPR Article 18, dealing specifically with the obligations imposed on states in relation to respecting freedom of religion:

> [Article 18 permits] restrictions on the freedom to manifest religion or belief only if limitations are prescribed by law and are necessary to protect public safety, order, health or morals, or the fundamental rights and freedoms of others . . . In interpreting the scope of permissible limitation clauses, States parties should proceed from the need to protect the rights guaranteed under the Covenant, including the right to equality and non-discrimination on all grounds specified in articles 2, 3 and 26. Limitations imposed must be established by law and *must not be applied in a manner that would vitiate the rights guaranteed in article 18*. The Committee observes that paragraph 3 of article 18 is to be strictly interpreted: restrictions are not allowed on grounds not specified there, even if they would be allowed as restrictions to other rights protected in the Covenant, such as national security.[27]

24 ICCPR, Art. 18(3).

25 *Church of the New Faith v. Commissioner of Pay-Roll Tax (Vic)* (1983) 154 CLR 120, 135–136. See Carolyn Evans, *Legal Protection of Religious Freedom in Australia* (The Federation Press, 2012), 79–80, where Evans is critical of the reliance placed on *Cantwell v. Connecticut* (1940) 310 U.S. 296 to support what Evans referred to as the 'rather wide proposition' that general laws 'are not defeated by a plea of religious obligation to breach them', considering that the authority of the case had been undermined by the subsequent decision of *Wisconsin v. Yoder* (1972) 406 U.S. 205.

26 *Ermogenous v. Greek Orthodox Community of SA Inc* (2002) 209 CLR 95, 121.

27 Human Rights Committee, *General Comment No. 22: The Right to Freedom of Thought, Conscience and Religion*, 48th sess, UN Doc. CCPR/C/21/Rev.1/Add.4 (30 July 1993), para. 8 (emphasis added).

The Importance of Religious Schools to Religious Communities

The determination of the nature and scope of a particular religious commitment is essentially a theological issue that the state should generally avoid addressing. However, this does not mean that the comparative importance of religious commitments is an issue that the state cannot attempt to address in deciding how it should act in areas involving religious liberty. Instead, an evaluation of the importance of a religious commitment is essential in determining whether it is appropriate for the government to regulate an area, and if so, the nature of any permissible regulation. If the religious commitment is of substantial importance to the religious individual and their community then the state should only implement a measure that has the effect of limiting or prohibiting the religious activity if it can be justified by the importance of the objectives being pursued by the state. As Evans and Gaze noted in the context of anti-discrimination laws:

> The centrality of a particular activity to a religion is a key factor that needs to be taken into account when assessing whether non-discrimination laws should apply to that activity. This is a fraught issue because it requires legislatures or courts to make an assessment of religious practices, but it is still of crucial importance if religious freedom is to be respected. The hiring of staff in religiously run hospitals, schools and other institutions may well be important to many religions, but it usually does not have the central place of activities such as the selection and training of clergy, the language and symbolism of ritual, and the determination of membership of the religious community. Such core religious activities have a greater claim for freedom from regulation (including from the imposition of non-discrimination laws) than activities that are more peripheral. The imposition of non-discrimination law in those core areas also has more serious implications for religious freedom than does regulation of service provision. While a religion may simply withdraw from providing schools or hospitals (a danger that the state needs to be aware of when deciding how much to regulate a particular organization), a religion cannot stop ordaining clergy or conducting worship if regulatory burdens on these activities become oppressive.[28]

The views of commentators such as Evans and Gaze that the establishment and management of religious schools is not of the same fundamental importance to religious communities as activities such as the selection of religious leaders and the conduct of religious ceremonies would likely be true for most religious communities. However, even if religious schools are not critical to the existence of religious communities, it does not mean either that the establishment and maintenance of religious schools are not important expressions of religious faith or that they do not play a central role in the life of the religious communities. Indeed there are good grounds for considering that religious schools play a fundamentally important role in the wellbeing of many religious communities through their contribution to religious education, supporting the general religious community, and allowing religious adherents to fulfill a spiritual obligation to engage in charitable works.

Many religious communities establish religious schools to fulfill what they consider to be a spiritual obligation to educate members of the religious community – in particular children

28 Carolyn Evans and Beth Gaze, 'Between Religious Freedom and Equality: Complexity and Context' (2008) 49 *Harvard International Law Journal* 40, 47 (citations omitted).

of religious adherents – so that they know and are committed to their religion. This is not to disregard the other essential roles that educational institutions have of developing the skills, knowledge, and character of their students and employees for their benefit and for those within and outside of the religious community. However, many religious individuals understand that their religion imposes on them – either by explicit statements in holy texts or by necessary implication from the tenets of the religion – a fundamental obligation to be involved in educating others about their religion on the basis that the religious knowledge is of primary importance for the welfare of individuals both in living a fulfilled life and in properly preparing them for divine judgement after death. As May notes, 'Each religious heritage is precious, and it is a primary task of every tradition to hand on an intact understanding of it to successive generations.'[29]

The central importance of religious education to religious adherents is clearly recognized in ICCPR Article 18, which declares that parents have the right 'to ensure the religious and moral education of their children in conformity with their own convictions'.[30] The Human Rights Committee, in General Comment 22, confirmed that the establishment of religious schools is integral to the functioning of religious groups and that Article 18 explicitly protects the right of religious groups to establish religious schools.

> The freedom to manifest religion or belief may be exercised 'either individually or in community with others and in public or private'. The freedom to manifest religion or belief in worship, observance, practice and teaching encompasses a broad range of acts . . . the practice and teaching of religion or belief includes acts integral to the conduct by religious groups of their basic affairs, such as the freedom to choose their religious leaders, priests and teachers, *the freedom to establish seminaries or religious schools* and the freedom to prepare and distribute religious texts or publications.[31]

The establishment and management of religious schools allow the religious community to effectively teach their religious beliefs to their children and others interested in the religion. Establishing religious schools allows the religious community to be confident that their religion will be appropriately explained and defended in a wide range of subjects in which religious issues might arise – a result that is very unlikely to occur in a government school where subjects will probably be taught by teachers with little, or no, knowledge about the beliefs of the religion. Further, control over the school environment allows the religious group to incorporate a wide range of religious and cultural practices and symbols into the daily operation of the school, increasing the opportunities available to students, staff members, and others involved with the school to learn about their religion and participate in religious ceremonies. Such a situation will normally be superior – from the perspective of the religious community – to an approach where students attend government schools and receive their religious education at an external location outside school hours.

Religious schools are particularly important to many religious communities, as in most countries in the world, there are a wide variety of religious and non-religious worldviews competing for adherents. The establishment of their own religious schools is an effective

29 John D'Arcy May, 'Can Tolerance Be Taught?: Steps Towards Inter-religious Education' (2006) 54 *Journal of Religious Education* (4) 13–14.

30 ICCPR, Art. 18(4).

31 *General Comment 22* [4] (emphasis added).

way for the religious community to educate its children and other members of the community on the merits of their religion compared to alternative worldviews. Furthermore, many religious adherents throughout the world suffer ridicule, distrust, and even violence due to their religious commitments, especially where the religious community is a minority group.[32] Religious schools will often be one of the few locations where the religious community will be able to positively present their religion in an environment supportive of their religion's theological and ethical teachings. This ability to create a positive environment in which the religion can be understood and assessed illustrates the central importance that religious schools will often have in supporting religious communities.

It is also important to recognize that religious schools are often not just places of education, but religious communities established to create a supportive environment for the religious adherents where the religion can be taught, religious obligations met, and the religious community supported. Places of worship are incorporated into many religious schools, allowing religious ceremonies to be performed for staff and students attending the religious school and also for members of the wider religious community not formally a part of the religious school. Religious schools also often function as meeting places for the religious community to learn more about their faith and cultural traditions, engage in charitable work, meet the various challenges that their religious community is faced with, socialize with other members of the community, and meet friends and potential spouses from within the religious community. A narrow focus solely on the role religious schools play in providing an education to students fails to appreciate that religious schools play a much broader role and that, while most members of religious communities would consider the teaching aspect of schools to be essential, many would also consider that the other aspects of the operation of religious schools are an important part of their operation.

Religious schools are also often established by religious groups as a way of fulfilling a spiritual obligation to engage in charitable works. Numerous statements within the holy texts of various religions impose clear obligations on religious adherents to be involved in charitable work.[33] In this regard, Garvey used the example of the charitable work undertaken by the Catholic Church:

> Religious organizations like schools, hospitals, and Catholic Charities ... do their work because of their religious beliefs. Catholic Charities does adoptions because the gospel tells us to care for the weak and vulnerable. Catholic universities exist because the gospel tells us to teach all nations. Migration and Refugee Services lives out the teachings of the Sermon on the Mount and Matthew 25. This is the heart of the Christian religion. Serving others – not just Catholics; *all* others – is not just a recommendation. It's a requirement.[34]

32 For a detailed analysis of the oppression suffered by religious adherents throughout the world see, for example, the annual reports of the United States Commission on International Religious Freedom, most recently 2014, http://www.uscirf.gov/reports-briefs/annual-report/2014-annual-report (accessed 16 October 2015).

33 For example, see the Bhagavad Gita 17: 20–22 for Hinduism, see Deuteronomy 15:7–11 for Judaism; see Matthew 25:31–40 for Christianity and see the Quran 2:177 for Islam.

34 John Garvey, 'Religious Freedom and the Love of God' (speech delivered at the General Assembly of the United States Conference of Catholic Bishops, Atlanta, 12 June 2012), http://publicaffairs.cua.edu/releases/2012/garvey-bishops-address.cfm (accessed 16 October 2015).

Considering these factors, in most situations religious schools will be of substantial, and in some situations of critical, importance to the religious community. Consistent with the human rights instruments and the views of the Human Rights Committee members discussed above, the importance of religious liberty in the context of religious schools should be understood as imposing a strong obligation on the state to protect the ability of religious groups to establish and maintain religious schools and avoid acting in a way that undermines the operation of religious schools.

The Importance of Employment Decisions to Religious Schools

A significant way in which the state can protect the effective operation of religious schools is to provide them with sufficient freedom so that they can select staff members on the basis of their compatibility with the school's religion (their 'mission fit'). The ability to employ individuals with good mission fit is central to the ability of religious schools to provide an effective religious education in the classroom environment as religious adherents will probably have a more detailed understanding of the religion and, even more importantly, their personal commitment to the faith will make them more effective in presenting the religion in a persuasive manner. The employment of religious adherents in a variety of positions within a religious school also provides important opportunities to students and others involved with the school to continue learning about the religion in informal social discussions, to be inspired by the example set by how a committed religious adherent lives their life in conformity with the religion, and to obtain personal assistance in living an ethical life as understood by the religion.

Furthermore, for those religions that teach that only certain persons can perform religious ceremonies and other religious activities, it is particularly important that religious schools are able to employ only those persons for roles within the school involving these functions. A failure to provide this protection would likely result in schools abolishing these employment positions in order to avoid violating their religious commitments. Such a result would significantly impair the school's ability to provide an authentic religious environment for students, staff, and others involved with the school.

Adequate protection for the employment decisions of religious schools is also necessary to ensure that there are a sufficient number of religious adherents within the school to allow the religious identity of the school to be established and maintained. As Mortensen notes, the 'right to discriminate on religious grounds is essential to the freedom as the group could not exist as a distinctive religious entity without it'.[35] Such an identity is essential in helping the religious school recruit suitable employees in the future, obtain external support, and act as a source of motivation for employees. Being clearly identified as an organization that adheres to a particular worldview can be critical for a religious school's continued existence as it might be the central reason why it receives donations and why individuals are willing to undertake paid and voluntary work for the school.

Considering these reasons, the ability of religious schools to select employees compatible with the school's religion should be understood as an important aspect of the right to religious

35 Reid Mortensen, 'A Reconstruction of Religious Freedom and Equality: Gay, Lesbian and De Facto Rights and the Religious School in Queensland' (2003) 3 *Queensland University of Technology Law and Justice Journal* (2) 323.

liberty in the context of religious schools. Consequently, the state should be understood to be under a strong obligation to protect this aspect of the right to religious freedom and avoid limiting the ability of religious schools to select employees for mission fit unless there are sufficiently strong grounds to justify any limitation.

The Right to Religious Liberty and the General Exception Approach

Considering that the general exception approach allows religious schools to make employment decisions on all grounds except race, age and a person's responsibilities as a carer it would appear that the provisions are substantially compatible with the right to religious liberty. However, on closer examination there are some important issues to consider in determining if the general exception approach is consistent with the right to religious liberty.

The Merits of Excluding Some Grounds from the General Exception Approach

The current approach may violate the religious liberty of particular religious groups that consider the excluded grounds of race, age, and a person's responsibilities as a carer to be significant in making employment decisions for their schools. Some groups, for example, may want to exclude persons with these characteristics from their schools as they consider that such persons are of inferior worth on the basis of the particular characteristic. Such a situation would arise with racial supremacist groups that situate their worldview within a particular religion and want to exclude persons of different races from their schools due to their perceived inferiority.

Although such groups could argue that the failure by the state to provide adequate protection for their employment decisions is a violation of their religious liberty, the state would be justified in refusing to enact measures to allow the groups to make decisions on these grounds. Importantly it may not even be appropriate to regard the denial of protection to these groups as a violation of their religious liberty if it appears that the groups are fraudulently claiming religious status. Even if some of these groups could legitimately claim to be religious, then the state could easily justify its actions due to the importance of promoting racial equality, which would clearly fall within the permissible limitations on the right to religious liberty as it would involve protecting 'public safety, order, health, or morals or the fundamental rights and freedoms of others.'[36]

However, other religious groups with a strong commitment to racial equality may want to be able to make decisions on the basis of race to allow them to develop an internal environment that is an authentic expression of the group's religious and cultural identity. A Jewish group managing a religious school, for example, could operate on the understanding that the definition of a Jew can have both a religious and racial component. Such a group may want to employ persons satisfying their definition of a Jew to assist the school in effectively promoting the religious beliefs and culture of the Jewish people. Under the general exception approach adopted in NSW a school that made employment decision on these grounds may violate the prohibition on racial discrimination contained in *ADA 1977*.

This issue was considered by the Supreme Court of the United Kingdom in *R (on the application of E) v. Governing Body of Jewish Free School* [2009] UKSC 15 (*JFS*), which

36 ICCPR, Art. 18(3).

concerned a refusal by an Orthodox Jewish school to enrol a student whose mother's conversion to Judaism was not recognized as valid according to the Orthodox Jewish faith as understood by the Office of the Chief Rabbi, but was recognized as valid by other branches of the Jewish faith.[37] The school's decision could not be unlawful on the basis that it involved religious discrimination as religious schools were permitted under the *Equality Act 2006* (UK) to make decisions regarding the admission of students on the grounds of religion.[38] However, a majority of the Supreme Court held that the school's decision to exclude the student was made on the grounds of 'ethnic origin' and that this violated the legal prohibition on discrimination on the grounds of race, which was defined in the *Racial Relations Act 1976* (UK) as including 'colour, race, nationality or ethnic or national origins'.[39]

The judgment was controversial with some of the judges in dissent concerned that it would undermine the ability of Jewish groups to maintain religious schools. Lord Rodger, for example, stated that the 'decision of the majority means that there can in future be no Jewish faith schools which give preference to children because they are Jewish according to Jewish religious law and belief'.[40] Considering that 'race' is defined in *ADA 1977* as including 'colour, nationality, descent and ethnic, ethno-religious or national origin' the case demonstrates that a similar decision could be made by a NSW court in relation to both students and employees.[41]

The potential for the current provisions to undermine the ability of Jewish and other groups to maintain the religious composition of their staff body should be regarded as a significant failure of the general exception approach to appropriately respect the right to religious liberty.

The Significance of Widespread Disagreement within Religious Groups

The general exception approach can also be criticized on the basis that many religious communities are engaged in intense debate on a variety of theological and ethical matters and the state should not be seen to be supporting one side by providing protection that others in the religious community consider to be unnecessary, if not inappropriate. In some religious communities many adherents disagree on an extensive range of issues ranging from the restriction of religious leadership roles to male adherents, sexual ethics, and whether the particular religion's claim to be the truth is valid or whether the correct position should be that the truth is found in variety of different religious and non-religious worldviews that are all equally valid. As Evans and Gaze note, '[t]here is no single "religious schools" response to anti-discrimination law; differences arise both between and within religious communities about whether religious schools should have exceptions and whether they should use the exceptions that they currently have.'[42] Mortensen expands on this point with the example of the diversity that exists within Christianity:

> A surprising number of Christians . . . presented theologically informed reasons for the application of sexuality and marital status discrimination laws to employment decisions

37 *R (on the application of E) v. Governing Body of JFS* [2009] UKSC 15 [5]–[7].

38 *Equality Act 2006* (UK) ss 59(1)–(2).

39 *Race Relations Act 1976* (UK) s 3(1).

40 *JFS* [225].

41 *ADA 1977* s 4 (definition of 'race').

42 Carolyn Evans and Beth Gaze, 'Discrimination by Religious Schools: Views from the Coal Face' (2010) 34 *Melbourne University Law Review* (2) 395.

> in religious schools. They appealed to the principles of tolerance taught by Christ, the place of free will in the biblical tradition, the moral insignificance of sexual conduct, the malleability of Christian morals, and the need for churches to modernise.[43]

The Anglican Church provides a contemporary example of a religious community where there is currently widespread disagreement about the religious significance of characteristics like gender and sexuality. Similarly in the Catholic Church there is a high level of dissent among adherents from official Catholic teaching especially in areas involving issues of sexuality, human life, and the validity of other religions. The Victorian Independent Education Union, for example, in a government inquiry into Victorian discrimination laws stated that they had 'observed on many occasions' school employers and priests declining to follow official Catholic teaching which they considered to be 'uncaring, harmful, intolerant and in conflict with the social justice teachings of the Catholic Church'.[44]

It is undoubtedly true that there are significant divisions in most, probably all, religious communities of any significant size. However, division within a religious community should not be understood as reducing any support that could be provided to the general exception approach on the grounds of religious liberty. The right to religious liberty would be a very weak right if state and non-state actors could reject the applicability of the right to religious liberty simply because there are other individuals who identify as belonging to the same religious group who do not share the same theological or ethical commitments. Mortensen appropriately makes the point, stating that

> . . . if parliamentarians want their churches, or church schools, to exemplify them then they should take efforts to do so through the appropriate Synod, congregational meeting or school council. It is not proper for Christian parliamentarians, inactive or uninfluential in their own churches' forums, to exploit the privileged position they have in Parliament, and try to realise their religious beliefs by use of the coercive powers of government. Legislators exercising a public trust are not free to rely on their own religious convictions when crafting legislation for the State as a whole, especially when those convictions do not represent a strong mandate of the people they represent.[45]

As Mortensen states the appropriate response for religious adherents who disagree with the teachings of their religion is to attempt to change the doctrines of the religion through methods available within the religious group. If they are unsuccessful in changing the religion then they have the freedom to leave the religious group and either join an alternative religious group that more closely aligns with their beliefs or establish a new religion that is completely compatible with their theological commitments. Disagreement with the current teachings of a religion by some religious adherents should not be understood as weakening the ability of the religious group to claim protection for their beliefs on the ground of religious liberty. For these reasons the view that the general exception approach is not consistent with the right

43 Mortensen, supra note 35 at 330–331 (citations omitted).

44 Victorian Independent Education Union, *Submission to the Department of Justice Review of the Exceptions and Exemptions in the Equal Opportunity Act 1995* (2008), http://www.ieuvictas.org.au/files/3613/3163/9447/vieu_submission_to_exceptions_review_2.pdf [5.1.3] (accessed 16 October 2015).

45 Mortensen, supra note 35 at 331.

to religious liberty due to the widespread disagreement that exists within many religious communities should be rejected.

The Broad Scope of the Protection Provided to Religious Schools

The general exception approach can also be criticized for providing protection to religious schools far in excess of the level of protection required by the right to religious liberty. Religious groups want sufficient protection under anti-discrimination legislation so that they are able to hire, manage, and dismiss school employees according to the employee's mission fit. This importance placed by religious groups on being able to regulate the membership of their organizations was appropriately expressed by Anglicare in its submission to the Commonwealth Inquiry into the Consolidation of Commonwealth Anti-Discrimination Laws. Anglicare argued that they

> . . . cannot employ, at any level, someone who is hostile to or unsupportive of our mission, vision or values. Provided this is done in good faith, religious organisations such as ANGLICARE Sydney maintain the right to decide whether some or all of the positions offered by it carry such a 'faith dimension'. To allow for limitation of this right would be to seriously diminish the specific right to religious freedom. Without this requirement, we cannot maintain our character as a Christian organisation, or carry out our mission. In this respect it is in the same position as any organisation – be it a company, political party or environmental advocacy group. It is a well-accepted principle that all organisations require their employees to be capable of working towards the mission of their employing organisation while respecting the organisation's values.[46]

The general exception approach, however, provides far greater protection than what is required by religious groups. *ADA 1977* provides protection to 'private educational authorities' rather than to specifically religious schools. Such broad protection may potentially be justifiable on other grounds (for example, the right to privacy or freedom of association), but the provision of protection to schools not based on a religious or non-religious worldview cannot be justified on the grounds of religious liberty.[47] Additionally, the protection is provided to all religious schools regardless of whether they actually want the protection. Such an all-inclusive approach results in many religious schools that do not want protection being covered by the provisions. Further, the protection provided to religious schools automatically includes all employment positions and all grounds except for race, age, and a person's responsibilities as a carer. However, many religious schools that want to receive protections for their employment decisions may only want protection for a few central employment positions and only on a few grounds rather than the near complete protection currently provided.

A religious group managing a particular school, for example, may consider that the school's religious character can be adequately safeguarded through limiting the protection to employment positions that they consider to be of central importance to the religious identity

46 Anglicare Sydney, Submission No. 153 to the Commonwealth Attorney-General's Department, *Inquiry into the Consolidation of Commonwealth Anti-Discrimination Laws*, 1 February 2012, 11.

47 A broad definition of the term 'religion' to include both religious and non-religious worldviews is supported by a number of international human rights bodies. See, for example, *General Comment 22*.

of their school such as the principal, religious education teachers, and religious ministers.[48] Further, they may only want to be able to make employment decisions on the basis of religion and marital status on the understanding that according to their religion there is no relevant significance in the differences that exist for characteristics such as gender, race, and sexuality. Under the current approach such a school would be provided with additional protection that is unwanted and, more importantly, unjustifiable according to the right to religious liberty considering the religious commitments of the school.

A further way in which the current approach provides excessive protection to religious schools is that employment decisions receive protection regardless of the actual reason for the decision. The irrelevancy of the reasons motivating employment decisions allows religious schools to make adverse employment decisions on the basis of non-religious and unjustifiable grounds. As a consequence, under the general exception approach it is possible for a religious school to refuse to employ a person on almost all grounds for any reason – even if denying a person employment for that reason would contradict the explicit teachings of the school's religion. Therefore a manager of a Christian school could openly refuse to hire a woman for an employment position involving religious leadership within the school despite the school being based on a Christian denomination that is committed to gender equality in religious leadership positions. Such a decision might result in action being taken against the manager by others in the school or within the religious community; however, the relevant point is that this decision would not constitute discrimination under the general exception approach even though it is entirely contrary to the religion on which the school is based.

Similarly, employment decisions by religious school authorities based on a prejudiced understanding of the likely conduct that particular individuals might engage in would also be legal under the current approach. The Gay and Lesbian Rights Lobby emphasized this undesirable aspect of the general exception approach in relation to the ground of sexuality arguing that

> . . . people frequently act, or claim to act, in the honest belief that their discrimination against gay men and lesbians is justified, even necessary or good. Discrimination is usually based on ignorance and/or prejudice and frequently manifests in stereotyping. Prejudices may be honestly held. . . . An obvious example of a stereotype that may result in discrimination is the genuinely held belief that gay men are all paedophiles. This myth persists in the face of all evidence that child sexual abuse is overwhelmingly perpetrated by heterosexual male family members. Yet if true it would make gay men (and lesbians when they are tarred with the same brush) unsuitable for a wide range of occupations. This would include not only those directly working with children but any occupation in which they were likely to come into contact with children.[49]

48 The term 'religious minister' is used in a broad sense to refer to any person within a religious community who plays a central role in providing religious education and performing religious ceremonies (priests, imams, rabbis, etc.). It is accepted that for some religious groups a broad range of religious adherents can legitimately be regarded as religious ministers, while for other non-hierarchical religions the concept of a religious minister may have little, if any, meaning. In many situations the definitional difficulties regarding who should be regarded as a religious minister for a particular religious community will not be significant; however, the determination of who can appropriately be considered to be a 'religious minister' can be of critical importance in some situations.

49 Gay and Lesbian Rights Lobby Inc., Submission to the Attorney General's Department, *Law Reform Commission Report 92 (1999) Review of the Anti-Discrimination Act 1977 (NSW)* (2000), 14.

The extensive overreach of the protections provided under the current approach is a major flaw of the general exceptions approach. There is a clear need for a different approach that adapts the protection provided for the employment decisions of religious schools to the particular needs of each religious group, and which provides for ongoing, effective government review of employment decisions to ensure that religious schools are not abusing the protections provided.

The Violation of the Religious Liberty Rights of Employees

A further criticism of the general exception approach is that it can result in the right to religious liberty of persons of different religions being infringed as it allows managers of religious schools to make adverse employment decisions against persons because of their religion. For example, if a Buddhist mathematics teacher applied for employment at a religious school and was rejected on the grounds that she was Buddhist, she would appear to have a valid argument that her right to religious liberty has been violated as she has suffered a detriment on the grounds of her religious beliefs. The Sikh Interfaith Council of Victoria emphasized the potential for the protections to violate the religious liberty of individuals arguing that exceptions to anti-discrimination legislation

> . . . should not extend to allowing or sanctioning discrimination on the basis of a person's religion or adherence to a religious observance. All schools, regardless of whether they are state schools or private schools, receive significant funding from public revenue. Public revenue is collected and spent without discrimination as to a person's religion . . .. No Sikh or person of any other faith should be placed in a circumstance where they have to choose between their religion and their employment or education.[50]

The appropriate outcome of a conflict between an individual employee's religious liberty and the religious liberty of a religious group has been considered extensively in a range of national and international cases. The European Commission of Human Rights, for example, considered the issue in *X v. Denmark*, which involved a clergyman in the State Church of Denmark who claimed that his right of religious liberty had been violated when he was requested by his religious superiors 'under threat of sanctions to abandon a certain practice of christening'.[51] As the clergyman was not required to remain within the religious group the Commission held that there had been no violation of the right to religious liberty considering that a

> . . . church is an organised religious community based on identical or at least substantially similar views. Through the rights granted to its members under [the right to religious

50 Evidence to Scrutiny of Acts and Regulations Committee, Parliament of Victoria, Melbourne, *Inquiry into the Exceptions and Exemptions in the Equal Opportunity Act – Public Hearing* http://www.parliament.vic.gov.au/images/stories/committees/sarc/EOV/transcripts/5_August_-_Sikh_Interfaith.pdf, 5 August 2009 (G.S. Gill and J.S. Shergill, Sikh Interfaith Council of Victoria): 2–3 (accessed 16 October 2015).

51 *X v. Denmark* (1976) 5 DR 157 §1 [App. No. 7374/76 (ECmHR, 8 March 1976)]. Although the case specifically dealt with religious liberty in relation to a state church, Evans argues that the 'reasoning of the Commission in making this decision is important . . . in regard to the religious freedom of members of a Church, whether the Church is established or not': Carolyn Evans, *Freedom of Religion under the European Convention on Human Rights* (Oxford University Press, 2001), 85. This view is echoed by Ahdar and Leigh: Rex Ahdar and Ian Leigh, *Religious Freedom in the Liberal State* (Oxford University Press, 2nd edn, 2013), 393.

liberty] the church itself is protected in its right to manifest its religion, to organise and carry out worship, teaching practice and observance, and it is free to act out and enforce uniformity in these matters. Further, in a State church system its servants are employed for the purpose of applying and teaching a specific religion. Their individual freedom of thought, conscience or religion is exercised at the moment they accept or refuse employment as clergymen, and their right to leave the church guarantees their freedom of religion in case they oppose its teachings. In other words, the church is not obliged to provide religious freedom to its servants and members, as is the State as such for everyone within its jurisdiction.[52]

The significance of a person's religious liberty when working for a religious organization was recently reconsidered by the European Court of Human Rights in *Siebenhaar v. Germany*.[53] The case involved a Protestant kindergarten dismissing an employee after she converted to the religion of a group called the 'Universal Church', which had a range of incompatible doctrines, including a belief in reincarnation.[54] Importantly, unlike in *X v. Denmark* the option that the applicant had of resigning was not considered to be fatal to the claim that her right to religious liberty had been violated. However, on the facts of the case the Court held that there was no violation of the right to religious liberty as the requirement in her employment contract that she not convert to an incompatible religion was reasonable considering it had the legitimate aim of ensuring that the kindergarten was genuinely Protestant for the benefit of the parents, the children, and members of the public.[55]

The issue was also considered by the US Supreme Court in *Corporation of the Presiding Bishop of The Church of Jesus Christ of Latter-day Saints v. Amos*, which concerned the operation of a public gymnasium owned and operated by adherents of the Mormon faith who had established it in the hope that 'all who assemble here, and who come for the benefit of their health, and for physical blessings, [may] feel that they are in a house dedicated to the Lord.'[56] The managers of the gymnasium employed a building engineer who was subsequently dismissed on the basis that he did not conform to the requirements of the Mormon religion.[57] The employee's claim was dismissed as the Court was concerned that intervening in such cases might result in an excessive entanglement of the government in religious matters and that court intervention might impair the freedom of religious groups to make employment decisions they consider appropriate.[58] However, Justices Brennan

52 *X v. Denmark* §1.

53 *Siebenhaar v. Germany*, App. No 18136/02 (ECtHR, 3 February 2011).

54 *Siebenhaar* §§8–12; 15.

55 *Siebenhaar* §§24; 46–47. For a general discussion of the view that recent decisions of the European Court of Human Rights indicate that the Court is moving from a position where the right to leave a religious group prevents a member of the group claiming protection under the right to religious liberty to a position where a court will balance the applicant's right to religious liberty against other relevant considerations, including the rights of the religious organization, see Nicholas Bratza, 'The 'Precious Asset': Freedom of Religion Under the European Convention on Human Rights' (2012) 14 *Ecclesiastical Law Journal* (2) 261; Ian Leigh, 'Balancing Religious Autonomy and Other Human Rights under the European Convention' (2012) 1 *Oxford Journal of Law and Religion* (1), 109.

56 *Corporation of the Presiding Bishop of The Church of Jesus Christ of Latter-day Saints v. Amos* (1987) 483 U.S. 327, 330; 337.

57 *Amos* at 330.

58 *Amos* at 336, 343–345.

and Marshall did consider that the exception granted to the gymnasium from the operation of anti-discrimination legislation had the effect of undermining the religious liberty of individual employees and was an important consideration in determining how the case should be resolved. They held that the legal provision

> ... necessarily has the effect of burdening the religious liberty of prospective and current employees. An exemption says that a person may be put to the choice of either conforming to certain religious tenets or losing a job opportunity, a promotion, or, as in these cases, employment itself. The potential for coercion created by such a provision is in serious tension with our commitment to individual freedom of conscience in matters of religious belief.[59]

These cases support the view that denying a person employment within a religious organization because of the person's religion can be considered to be a significant violation of their right to religious liberty. In these circumstances both the religious school and the individual can legitimately rely on the right to religious liberty to claim that they should receive the support of the law. In many situations the law may be justified in adopting an approach that prioritizes the interests of the religious school over the religious individual, especially where the employment of individuals of different religions will undermine the religious identity and operation of the school. However, the excessively broad scope of the general exception approach allows religious schools to deny a person employment on the basis of their religion in situations that cannot be justified. Under the current provisions it is possible for religious schools to deny a person employment on the grounds of their religion for all employment positions within the school regardless of the actual teachings of the school's religion or the significance of the employment position within that school. This potential of the general exception approach to unjustifiably violate the religious liberty of individuals is a further significant criticism of the current approach.

The Relevance of Government Funding of Religious Schools

Religious schools in Australia receive substantial financial assistance from the Commonwealth and State governments. In the 2010–11 financial period non-government schools in NSW were provided with $2.2 billion in funding from the Commonwealth government and $853 million in funding from the NSW government for the recurring expenses of non-government schools.[60] A substantial amount of additional government funding is also available to non-government schools for other purposes, including improving school infrastructure through the capital grants program. The Commonwealth government in 2009, for example, allocated $1.35 billion for improving the infrastructure of non-government schools throughout Australia.[61]

59 *Amos* at 340–341 (citations omitted).

60 Productivity Commission Steering Committee for the Review of Government Service Provision, 'Report on Government Services 2013' (2013) http://www.pc.gov.au/__data/assets/pdf_file/0005/121784/government-services-2013-volume1.pdf 4.5 (accessed 16 October 2015).

61 Marilyn Harrington, 'Australian Government Funding for Schools Explained' (Background Note, Parliamentary Library, Parliament of Australia), http://www.pc.gov.au/research/ongoing/report-on-government-services/2013/2013 (accessed 1 November 2015).

The provision of such substantial government funding to religious schools is often used as a justification for limiting or removing any protection the state provides to the employment decisions of religious schools. The Victorian Scrutiny of Acts and Regulation Committee, in its review of the exceptions contained in the *Equal Opportunity Act 1995* (Vic), considered that

> . . . where public money is spent on activities that are argued to be excepted from equality rights, there is a responsibility to consider the people whose rights are limited to provide freedom of religion. While some minor limitations may be acceptable, it may be difficult to justify the religious exceptions at their current levels in a large number of publicly funded institutions such as non-government schools, because of the systemic impact on the employment and equality rights of women and gay teachers.[62]

Along similar lines Thornton argues: 'But why should private schools that are the recipients of considerable public funds be entitled to ignore the general law? If religious bodies claim that their freedom of religion justifies them discriminating against citizens by virtue of sex, sexuality or marital status, they should be precluded from receiving substantial moneys from the state. After all, it has been contributed by those selfsame citizens.'[63] A more detailed explanation of the merits of the criticism is provided by Mortensen:

> Once account is taken of the fact that most religious schools in Australia are major recipients of government funding, the issue can be seen to involve questions of distributive justice. And, continuing a typical liberal analysis of the collision of rights, the redistribution of wealth by government through taxation and education funding is often regarded as being legitimately subject to conditions of fair equality of opportunity. In these circumstances . . . [it is fair to demand] equal opportunity in employment for gays, lesbians and people in de facto relationships in all schools – State and non-State – which receive government funding . . . Furthermore, where equal opportunity is attached to the voluntary receipt of government funding no question of religious freedom arises. The school that wished to retain the freedom to discriminate on the ground of sexuality or marital status could do so by refusing funding, and the school that accepted funding would, in a legal sense, freely choose to do so on conditions of equal opportunity.[64]

Although it has widespread support the claim that the provision of government funding to religious schools justifies the limitation or removal of legal protection for the employment decisions of religious schools should be rejected. A major justification for not supporting

62 Scrutiny of Acts and Regulations Committee, Parliament of Victoria, *Exceptions and Exemptions to the Equal Opportunity Act 1995 – Options Paper* (2009), 128.

63 Margaret Thornton, 'Balancing religion and rights: the case against discrimination', *The Sydney Morning Herald*, 4 October 2009, http://www.smh.com.au/opinion/society-and-culture/balancing-religion-and-rights-the-case-against-discrimination-20091003-gh9y.html (accessed 16 October 2015).

64 Mortensen, supra note 35 at 331 (citations omitted). For a general discussion of the significance of government financial support in determining how anti-discrimination legislation should regulate religious organizations, see Jeff Spinner-Halev, 'Discrimination within Religious Schools' (2012) 1 *Journal of Law, Religion & State* (1) 45.

a criticism based on government funding is that it is inconsistent with how states interact with other individuals and groups within the community. Thornton argues that government funds should not usually be used to support groups that exclude community members, while Mortensen argues government funding should be subject to requirements regarding equality of opportunity; however, these arguments can apply as easily to the funding and protection provided to non-religious groups as they can to religious groups. States regularly provide financial support to different groups based on particular characteristics – such as race, gender and sexuality – without there being any understanding that the provision of state support undermines the group's ability to claim protection from the state in other areas, such as through being provided with the ability to preferentially employ persons who are compatible with the group's identity. If the state allowed an indigenous group to make employment decisions on the grounds of race to allow it to build an indigenous culture within the group, it is highly unlikely that government funding of the indigenous group would be considered by many to be a factor in favour of limiting or removing the indigenous group's freedom in employment decisions.

The view that the provision of government support to religious groups makes it more appropriate to subject such groups to government regulation involves a devaluing of the right to religious liberty compared to other human rights in a way that cannot be justified. Furthermore, considering that a majority of Australians identify as religious and make a substantial contribution to the funds available to the government through taxation, it is reasonable for them to expect that some government funding will be directed in a manner that they consider appropriate, including funding schools they establish and manage. On the need for the state to act impartially in providing government funds to community groups, the Anglican Diocese of Sydney, in its submission to the Commonwealth Inquiry into the Consolidation of Commonwealth Anti-Discrimination Laws, observed that

> . . . the Australian government funds organisations and activities on a regular basis that are directed to particular segments of the community or which are undertaken on the basis of particular social or cultural norms. There is no apparent reason for singling out religiously based organisations as somehow needing to become monochrome in their recruitment and service delivery.[65]

Critics of religious schools may claim that there is a significant difference between government support for religious groups and for other groups constituted on non-religious grounds that justifies governments in removing, limiting, or refusing to provide additional state protection for religious groups. However, those making such a claim should explicitly state the reasons for such a distinction. Critics often simply state that protection for the employment decisions of religious schools should be removed or limited if the schools are receiving government funding without justifying their position. Various explanations could be provided by such critics – for example, religions are irrational, they promote inappropriate ethical standards, they are inherently divisive, or that religious groups have not been disadvantaged to the same extent as other protected groups.

65 Anglican Diocese of Sydney, Submission No 178 to the Commonwealth Attorney-General's Department, *Inquiry into the Consolidation of Commonwealth Anti-Discrimination Laws* (2 February 2012), 15.

These criticisms may be true for some or all religious groups; however, the critical point is that these arguments can be legitimate grounds for denying these religious groups protection under anti-discrimination legislation *and* for denying them government funding. The mere provision of public funds should not be a factor in determining whether the state should provide a particular type of support to a group; rather it should be one of the possible results that may occur if the resolution of the issue is in favour of the state supporting the group. The central issue should be what involvement, if any, the state should have in supporting or limiting the operation of a group. If the state does consider it appropriate to support a group then a particular type of support – such as financial assistance – should not in itself be understood as an argument against additional state support – such as the provision of protection through anti-discrimination legislation for employment decisions to allow the group to protect its identity.

Conclusion

Due to the broad nature of the general exception approach it would satisfy the religious liberty claims of many religious groups that their religious schools need to be able to employ individuals according to their mission fit. There are, however, some significant problems with the general exception approach in consideration of religious liberty.

The current approach denies religious schools protection on the grounds of race, age, and a person's responsibilities as a carer. As illustrated in the *JFS* case these grounds can be important for some religious schools, and the failure to extend the protection to cover them can appropriately be regarded as a violation of religious freedom.

The provision of protection to religious schools that greatly exceeds what can be appropriately justified on the basis of religious liberty is the most significant criticism of the general exception approach. Providing protection to all 'private educational authorities' cannot be justified on the grounds of religious freedom. Similarly, automatically providing protection for the employment decisions of all religious schools for all employment positions on almost all grounds regardless of the reasons for the employment decision cannot be justified by the right to religious liberty, especially considering that such extensive protection will often not even be wanted by many religious schools.

A further problem with the general exception approach is that the protection it provides to religious schools will often result in an adverse employment decision being made against a person on the grounds of their religion. It is important to respect the religious liberty claims of the individuals who are adversely affected and recognize that the current approach has the potential to violate their religious liberty in situations where the school's religious commitments do not require the adverse employment decision to be made.

The right to religious liberty is of central importance in supporting the claim that the state should provide religious schools with the freedom to make employment decisions based on an individual's compatibility with the school's religion. Considering that the general exception approach cannot legitimately be considered to be consistent with the right to religious liberty, the merits of this approach are substantially undermined. Although a consideration of a range of other criteria is needed before a satisfactory conclusion on the merits of the current approach can be reached, the inconsistency of the general exception approach with the right to religious liberty pro

Religion and Same-Sex Marriage

7 Same-Sex Marriage

Exemptions for Celebrants and Religious Freedom

*Rex Ahdar**

Conscientious Objection to Same-Sex Marriage: Carving Exemptions

Same-sex marriage (SSM) has recently been legalized in several Western nations and is likely to become legal in others.[1] Where it has become legal, a recurrent issue has been the rights of those who usually conduct marriages to refuse to do so in the case of same-sex couples. Some religious ministers, clergy, marriage celebrants, commissioners, and registrars (hereafter collectively referred to as 'celebrants') may have a conscientious objection to conducting marriage ceremonies for people of the same sex. Their objection is usually grounded in sincere religious beliefs about the propriety of homosexual relationships.

This chapter considers the attempts to craft an exemption for such marriage celebrants based on solicitude for their religious convictions. My starting point is that no one ought to be forced to marry a couple against that person's religious beliefs or conscience. Where the celebrant refuses for this reason to perform a marriage, he or she should be permitted by the state to refuse. Ideally, the law ought to make it clear that there is no legal obligation on celebrants in such circumstances to conduct SSMs. Likewise, the relevant antidiscrimination laws that prohibit discrimination on the grounds of sexual orientation ought to explicitly exempt from performing SSMs those celebrants who wish to be exempted, who should be immune from civil suit.

Yet carving out a suitable exemption has proved rather harder to achieve than one might expect. This, at least, has been the experience in nations such as New Zealand, Canada, and England and Wales. Other nations have also experienced teething troubles. In Denmark and Norway the state churches negotiated a path to allow objecting clergy to refuse to conduct SSM. But it is these three English-speaking countries that form the focus of this chapter.[2]

One of the key dividing lines in the case for exemptions is between religious marriage celebrants – that is the ministers, priests, pastors, rabbis, imams, and other religious leaders appointed by their church, synagogue, temple (or other religious body) – and state-employed

* An abbreviated form of this chapter appeared as 'Solemnisation of Same-sex Marriage and Religious Freedom' in (2014) 16 *Ecclesiastical Law Journal* (3) 283–305. The sections of this chapter that were so published are included here with the knowledge and permission of the ELJ Editor.

1 Same-sex marriage is legal in Argentina, Belgium, Brazil, Canada, Denmark, England/Wales, Finland, France, Greenland, Iceland, Ireland, Luxembourg, Mexico (some jurisdictions), The Netherlands, New Zealand, Norway, Portugal, Scotland, South Africa, Spain, Sweden, the United States, and Uruguay. 'Gay Marriage around the World', *Pew Research Center Religion & Public Life*, 26 June 2015, http://www.pewforum.org/2015/06/26/gay-marriage-around-the-world-2013/.

2 For an illuminating exploration of the treatment of the issue in four countries – Canada, Scotland, the Netherlands, and South Africa – see Bruce MacDougall, Elsje Bonthuys, Kenneth Norrie and Marjohn van den Brink,

marriage officials. The former receive much greater protection than the latter; indeed, religiously devout state or civil marriage celebrants are likely to receive no exemption at all.

This chapter does not consider the case for exemption for those who have a conscientious objection to participating in or being involved in the SSM event outside of the actual solemnization itself. Thus, caterers, photographers, musicians, florists, chauffeurs, those who hire out reception halls or rent bridal and honeymoon suites, and so on, remain a topic for further investigation.[3]

New Zealand

New Zealand became the thirteenth nation to legalize SSM when it passed the Marriage (Definition of Marriage) Act 2013 on 19 April 2013.[4] The question of religious freedom for those church ministers and other marriage celebrants who did not wish to conduct SSMs featured prominently in the public debate.[5] Critics of the Bill, such as the conservative lobby organization, Family First,[6] the newly-formed Conservative Party[7] and many Church leaders,[8] as well as the New Zealand Law Society,[9] voiced doubts about the adequacy of legal protection for celebrants with conscientious objections to conducting SSMs. The promoter of the Bill,[10] Labour MP Louisa Wall, gave repeated assurances that the religious freedom of conscientious objectors would be respected. 'Section 29 of the Marriage Act [1955] remains in place and makes it clear that once a marriage licence is obtained by a couple it does not oblige a minister or celebrant to marry that couple . . . Because we have freedom of religion

---

'Conscientious Objection to Creating Same-Sex Unions: An International Analysis', (2012) 1 *Canadian Journal of Human Rights* (1) 127–164. For South Africa, see also Pieter Coertzen, 'Marriages, Civil Unions, Partnerships, and Religion in South Africa after 1996', Chapter 8 of this volume.

3 For discussion of the position of participants other than celebrants in a same-sex marriage, see for example Ira Lupu and Robert Tuttle, 'Same-Sex Family Equality and Religious Freedom', (2010) 5 *Northwestern Journal of Law & Social Policy* (2) 274–306.

4 Public Act 2013, No 20. The Act came into force on 19 August 2013: s 2. The Bill was passed by 77 votes to 44 by way of a free (conscience) vote.

5 See Matthew Backhouse, 'Wall: Gay Marriage Bill Will Allow Choice', *New Zealand Herald*, 10 March 2013. Louisa Wall MP commented: 'The select committee was very clear, and I agree, that no celebrant ever should be forced. Why would you want a celebrant at a beautiful celebration actually not wanting to be there? It doesn't make any sense.'

6 Backhouse, 'Wall: Gay Marriage Bill . . .', supra note 5.

7 See Colin Craig, the Conservative Party leader, quoted in Backhouse, 'Wall: Gay Marriage Bill . . .', supra note 5.

8 Bronwyn Torrie, 'Bishops Damn Gay Marriage in Letter', *Dominion Post*, 21 August 2012, http://www.stuff.co.nz/dominion-post/news/7513602/Bishops-damn-gay-marriage-in-letter (accessed 1 January 2016) (NZ Catholic bishops oppose SSM); Simon Collins, 'Gay Weddings Ban: Churches Say No', *NZ Herald*, 23 April 2013; Media Release from 70 Church Leaders Regarding the Marriage Amendment Bill, 3 October 2012 (joint statement by 70 church leaders including Catholic bishops and heads of the Baptist, Open Brethren, Seventh-day Adventist, Wesleyan Methodist, Assemblies of God, Elim, and New Life Churches), http://www.scoop.co.nz/stories/PO1208/S00472/church-leaders-unite-to-speak-up-on-marriage-amendment-bill.htm (accessed 1 November 2015).

9 'Complex technical issues in drafting of same-sex Marriage Bill', NZ Law Society, http://www.familylaw.org.nz/public/media-releases/2012/complex-technical-issues-in-drafting-of-same-sex-marriage-bill (accessed 1 November 2015).

10 This was a Private Member's Bill not a Government Bill.

in New Zealand, no religious body is bound to marry a couple if that marriage is at odds with its religious belief.'[11] The Select Committee that considered the Bill was well aware of the concern:

> A large number of people and organizations have expressed their concern that, were this bill to pass, celebrants could not lawfully refuse to solemnise a marriage that would conflict with their religious beliefs . . . We accept the right of people to hold religious and cultural beliefs, and we make no attempt to dissuade people from holding them. It is our intention that the passage of this bill *should not impact negatively upon people's religious freedoms*. The Marriage Act enables people to become legally married; it does not ascribe moral or religious values to marriage. The bill seeks to extend the legal right to marry to same-sex couples; *it does not seek to interfere with people's religious freedoms*.[12]

Accordingly, the Committee wished 'to clarify beyond doubt'[13] that no marriage celebrant who was a minister of religion was obliged to solemnize a marriage if that would contravene the religious beliefs of the religious body to which he or she belonged. The exemption in its final form reads:

> **29. Licence authorizes but not obliges marriage celebrant to solemnise marriage**
>
> (1) A marriage licence shall authorise but not oblige any marriage celebrant to solemnise the marriage to which it relates.
>
> (2) Without limiting the generality of subsection (1), no celebrant who is a minister of religion recognised by a religious body enumerated in Schedule 1, and no celebrant who is a person nominated to solemnise marriages by an approved organisation, is obliged to solemnise a marriage if solemnising that marriage would contravene the religious beliefs of the religious body or the religious beliefs or philosophical or humanitarian convictions of the approved organisation.

Despite the Committee's hope that this version would provide the necessary clarity that the Ministry of Justice and Crown Law advisers sought, a flaw still remained. The problem, as I saw it,[14] was that the exemption was not worded widely enough.

11 First Reading, 683 *New Zealand Parliamentary Debates* (*NZPD*) 4914, 29 August 2012. MP Wall continued: 'For Churches and religious institutions, such discrimination would be justified under section 5 of the New Zealand Bill of Rights Act 1990, based on the right to freedom of religion – specifically, the manifestation of religion and belief – under section 15 of that Act.' At the Second Reading, 688 *NZPD* 8524, 13 March 2013, Wall reiterated: 'Freedom of religion is an individual right and I support the Government Administration Committee's recommendation to strengthen section 29 of the Marriage Act to make it clear that there is no compulsion for a minister to perform a marriage that he or she does not feel comfortable about.' The same assurance was pronounced by her at the Third Reading: 689 *NZPD* 8483, 17 April 2013.

12 Government Administration Committee Report, 27 February 2013, at 3 (emphasis added).

13 Government Administration Committee Report at 3.

14 See Rex Ahdar, 'Gay Marriage and Preserving Religious Freedom for Celebrants', *Pundit*, 14 March 2013, http://www.pundit.co.nz/content/gay-marriage-and-preserving-religious-freedom-for-celebrants (accessed 1 November 2015).

First, marriage celebrants who are independent, that is, not members of any of the listed religious bodies,[15] or any approved organization,[16] are not protected. Yet some 45 percent of marriages are conducted by these independent marriage celebrants (with 23 percent by registrars at a state registry office and 32 percent conducted by a church or approved organization marriage celebrant).[17] Independent marriage celebrants are persons that the Registrar-General is satisfied 'will conscientiously perform the duties of a marriage celebrant' and 'it is in the interests of the public generally, or of a particular community (whether defined by geography, interest, belief, or some other factor)' that they be so appointed.[18] Such persons may well have defined beliefs that generate a conscientious objection to SSM. For them, it is conceivable that they may find it difficult or impossible to 'conscientiously perform' a SSM. It was erroneous then, as Ian Bassett pointed out,[19] for the Ministry of Justice to recommend that independent celebrants be excluded from the benefit of the conscientious objection exemption in s 29(2).[20] The Ministry's response was that, in contrast to ministers of religion, independent celebrants (and registrars) are appointed by the government 'to perform a public function, not to promote their own religious or personal beliefs'.[21] (I shall respond to this reasoning in the section on Canada, below.)

Second, and perhaps even more importantly, ministers of religion of designated religious bodies may not be protected either. Religious ministers within tightly knit homogeneous denominations such as the Open Brethren, Seventh-day Adventists, or Elim (Pentecostal) Churches are not vulnerable. Rather, it is a religious minister whose more-heterogeneous denomination is divided on the issue of gay marriage that may not be able to point to any authoritative ruling, precept, custom, or teaching of his or her denomination that clearly states that only heterosexual marriage is right and acceptable. The mainstream Protestant denominations – Presbyterian, Methodist, and Anglican – have struggled to formulate a clear policy on this matter.[22]

15 The designated religious bodies in Schedule 1 of the Marriage Act 1955 are Baptists, the Church of England, Congregational Independents, the Greek Orthodox Church, all Hebrew Congregations, the Lutheran Churches, the Methodist Church, the Presbyterian Church, the Roman Catholic Church, the Salvation Army.

16 Marriage Act 1955, s 10(4).

17 Government Administration Committee Report, at 4; Chris Auchinvole (National), Second Reading debate, 688 *NZPD* 8533, 13 March 2013.

18 Marriage Act 1955, s 11(3)(a)(b).

19 Legal Opinion by New Zealand barrister, Ian Bassett, for *Family First NZ*, 6 March 2013, at 7–14, http://bob-mccoskrie.com/wp-content/uploads/2013/03/Legal-Opinion-6-March-Marriage-Act-Amendment-Bill.pdf (accessed 1 November 2015).

20 Ministry of Justice, *Departmental Report for the Government Administration Committee*, 13 February 2013, at 49: 'We recommend that the exemption extend to religious bodies and approved organisations but not to independent marriage celebrants or registrars. A key purpose of religious bodies and most approved organisations is to promote religious beliefs. Section 5 of the NZBORA [NZ Bill of Rights Act 1990] allows rights affirmed under the NZBORA to be justifiably limited. Accordingly, an exemption could be justified where it would be contrary to the recognised purpose of religious bodies and approved organisations to require their celebrants to solemnise certain marriages.', http://www.parliament.nz/resource/en-nz/50SCGA_ADV_00DBHOH_BILL11528_1_A318744/1f0e3c63c8f26cab9c115a4dfe68f18e45949633 (accessed 1 November 2015).

21 *Departmental Report* . . ., supra note 20 at 50: 'In contrast, independent marriage celebrants and registrars are appointed by the Registrar-General to perform a public function, not to promote their own religious or personal beliefs. It appears unlikely that they could lawfully refuse to solemnise a marriage on religious grounds under s 5 of the NZBORA.'

22 Isaac Davison 'Church Groups at Odds over their Definitions of Marriage', *NZ Herald*, 15 November 2012, http://www.nzherald.co.nz/nz/news/article.cfm?c_id=1&objectid=10847505 (accessed 1 January 2016).

In the Presbyterian Church of Aotearoa New Zealand (PCANZ), the long-running battle over the ordination of gay clergy is a poignant reminder of how contentious matters of sexual practice and sexual orientation are.[23] The Presbyterians debated the issue of SSM at their 2012 General Assembly. There were 'strong feelings'[24] on each side of the issue. Nonetheless, and over the dissent registered by some, the Assembly passed a resolution affirming that the Church 'upheld the historic Christian understanding of marriage as the loving, faithful union of a man and a woman'.[25] The Assembly narrowly declined, however, to adopt a proposal that would have prohibited ministers from administering marriage ceremonies between same-sex couples. The motion to pass this no-SSM resolution failed by just one vote to achieve the necessary 60 percent threshold.

Louisa Wall, in her second reading speech on the SSM bill, noted this failure by the General Assembly and praised it as 'a positive step' that would allow a Presbyterian minister (such as the outspoken lesbian minister, the Reverend Margaret Mayman, at a central Wellington Presbyterian church) to marry a same-sex couple.[26] The Moderator of the PCANZ had, indeed, observed that if SSM was to be legalized, 'ministers will have the flexibility to marry same-sex couples.'[27] The Moderator asked, two days before the right to conduct SSM came into force, for a temporary ban to preserve the Church's 'peace and unity'.[28]

Other denominations have yet to grasp the nettle. The Anglican Church announced that its ministers could not conduct same-sex weddings pending a report from a commission chaired by the former Governor-General, Sir Anand Satyanand, at its General Synod in Paihia in May 2014.[29] The Synod passed a resolution that would 'create a pathway towards the blessing of same-gender relationships, while upholding the traditional doctrine of marriages'.[30]

Meanwhile, a conservative Anglican minister who declined to marry a gay couple could not point to any ruling of the regional or national diocese that clearly states that marriage is only for opposite-sex couples or that SSM contravenes the religious beliefs or tenets of that religious body. The blessing of the same-sex nuptials might contravene the religious beliefs of his own congregation, a sizeable conservative sector of New Zealand Anglicanism, and of numerous Anglicans across the country – but that is not the same thing. One MP commented that she would personally appear as a witness in support of any minister embroiled in litigation to state that that minister 'had the right to deny a same-sex couple solemnisation of

23 See for example Rex Ahdar, *Worlds Colliding: Conservative Christians and the Law* (Ashgate 2001), Chapter 9. On the same dispute in the Anglican Church of New Zealand, see Ian Wishart, 'Church vs State: Gay Ordination Dispute Heads to Court', *Investigate*, February/March 2012,13–18.

24 'Church Supports Marriage between Man and Woman', *PCANZ Media Release*, 11 October 2012, http://www.presbyterian.org.nz/speaking-out/what-we039ve-said/media-releases/church-supports-marriage-between-man-and-woman (accessed 21 October 2015).

25 General Assembly News, 6 October 2102: 'Church Says No to Same-Sex Marriage': http://presbyterian.org.nz/sites/default/files/ga12/saturday/Church_says_no_to_same_sex_marriage.pdf (accessed 21 October 2015).

26 Second Reading 688 *NZPD* 8524, 13 March 2013.

27 'Church supports marriage between man and woman.'

28 Simon Collins, 'Presbyterian Head Seeks Gay-Wedding Ban for Unity's Sake', *NZ Herald*, 17 August 2013, http://www.nzherald.co.nz/nz/news/article.cfm?c_id=1&objectid=10913508 (accessed 1 January 2016).

29 Collins, supra note 28.

30 'Pathway to same-gender blessings', *AnglicanTaonga*, 14 May 2014, http://anglicantaonga.org.nz/News/General-Synod/forward. Full Text: 'A Way Forward – The Full Synod Text, http://www.anglicantaonga.org.nz/Features/Extra/Anga (both accessed 21 October 2015).

their wedding.'[31] But such a well-intentioned gesture would be largely ineffectual and little solace for any minister of religion who had to defend his or her position.

Even if the New Zealand Anglican Church should eventually decide that solemnization of SSM is allowed, particular Anglican clergy who dissent from that official line ought to still be protected. The right of religious freedom protects the religious liberty of all who practice religion, not just those whose beliefs accord with the official teaching of that denomination or group.[32] Those holding eccentric, idiosyncratic, or even heretical religious beliefs – beliefs which are at odds with the majority of those of that faith, that are inconsistent with received church doctrine or contrary to the views of the church hierarchy (if any such hierarchy exists) – ought to be protected too. Religious freedom is not just for the 'orthodox' or those who happen to abide by the views of the majority of co-religionists or the pronouncements of the ecclesiastical or ruling elite. Appellate courts have acknowledged this. The Supreme Court of Canada stated that: 'An "expert" or an authority on religious law is not a surrogate for an individual's affirmation of what his or her religious beliefs are.'[33] Lord Nicholls in the House of Lords observed:

> The court is concerned to ensure an assertion of religious belief is made in good faith: 'neither fictitious, nor capricious, and that it is not an artifice', to adopt the felicitous phrase of Iacobucci J in the decision of the Supreme Court of Canada in *Syndicat Northcrest v Amselem* . . . But, emphatically, it is not for the court to embark on an inquiry into the asserted belief and judge its 'validity' by some objective standard such as the source material upon which the claimant founds his belief or the orthodox teaching of the religion in question or the extent to which the claimant's belief conforms to or differs from the views of others professing the same religion. Freedom of religion protects the subjective belief of an individual . . . religious belief is intensely personal and can easily vary from one individual to another. Each individual is at liberty to hold his own religious beliefs, however irrational or inconsistent they may seem to some, however surprising.[34]

In a case in which a Jehovah's Witness's pacifist beliefs were challenged because other members of his faith felt able to work in an armaments factory, whereas he did not, the U.S. Supreme Court stated:

> The guarantee of free exercise of religion is not limited to beliefs which are shared by all the members of a religious sect. Particularly in this sensitive area, it is not within the judicial function and judicial competence to inquire whether the petitioner or his fellow worker more correctly perceived the commands of their common faith.[35]

31 Ruth Dyson (Labour), Second Reading, 688 *NZPD* 8528, 13 March 2013.

32 See, for example, *Thomas v. Review Board*, 450 U.S. 707, 715–716 (1981); *R (on the application of Williamson) v. Secretary of State for Education and Employment* [2002] EWCA Civ 1820 at 233. See further Rex Ahdar and Ian Leigh, *Religious Freedom in the Liberal State* (Oxford University Press, 2nd edn, 2013), 175, 195.

33 *Syndicat Northcrest v. Amselem*, 2004 SCC 47 at 54 per Iaccobucci J (for the majority).

34 *R (on the application of Williamson) v. Secretary of State for Education and Employment* [2005] UKHL 15 at 22.

35 *Thomas*, 450 U.S. at 715–716, per Burger CJ.

In light of this I proposed an amendment to s 29(2):[36]

> Without limiting the generality of subsection (1), no celebrant who is a minister of religion recognised by a religious body enumerated in Schedule 1, and no celebrant who is a person nominated to solemnize marriages by an approved organisation, is obliged to solemnize a marriage if solemnizing that marriage would contravene the religious beliefs **of that celebrant**.

This change was not adopted, however. So, for now, the position of conservative church ministers within the mainstream Protestant denominations in New Zealand remains precarious.

Canada

In 2004 the Supreme Court of Canada was asked to hear a reference on the Federal Government's proposed legislation to extend marriage to same-sex couples. One of the four questions in *Reference Re Same-Sex Marriage* was 'if the Proposed Act were adopted, religious officials could be required to perform same-sex marriages contrary to their religious beliefs.'[37] The Court was in no doubt:

> If a promulgated statute were to enact compulsion, we conclude that such compulsion would almost certainly run afoul of the *Charter* guarantee of freedom of religion, given the expansive protection afforded to religion by s. 2(*a*) of the *Charter* . . . The performance of religious rites is a fundamental aspect of religious practice. It therefore seems clear that state compulsion on religious officials to perform same-sex marriages contrary to their religious beliefs would violate the guarantee of freedom of religion under s. 2(*a*) of the *Charter*. It also seems apparent that, absent exceptional circumstances which we cannot at present foresee, such a violation could not be justified under s. 1 of the *Charter*.[38]

The Court also determined that the legalization of SSM was consistent with the Canadian *Charter of Rights and Freedoms* 1982.[39]

The bill to legalize SSM, Bill C-38, was introduced to the House of Commons on 1 February 2005 and was passed by that House on 28 June 2005, 158 to 133 votes, with 32 MPs abstaining.[40] The Senate passed the Bill by 47–21 votes on 19 July 2005, and it received the Royal Assent on 20 July 2005. The Civil Marriage Act 2005[41] defines civil marriage as 'the lawful union of two persons to the exclusion of all others'.[42] An attempt by the incoming Conservative Government to restore the traditional opposite-sex definition of marriage in December 2006 was defeated in the House of Commons.[43]

36 *Departmental Report* . . . , supra note 20.
37 *Reference re Same-Sex Marriage* 2004 SCC 79.
38 *Reference re Same-Sex Marriage* at 56–58.
39 *Reference re Same-Sex Marriage* at 5, 43.
40 For the history of the legislation, see the Parliament of Canada website, Commentary by Mary C Hurley, 'Bill C-38. 'The Civil Marriage Act': http://www.parl.gc.ca/About/Parliament/LegislativeSummaries/bills_ls.asp?ls=c38&Parl=38&Ses=1#creligiousmarriagetxt. (accessed 21 October 2015).
41 Civil Marriage Act, SC 2005, c. 33.
42 Civil Marriage Act 2005, s. 2.
43 By 175 to 123 votes, 7 December 2006. The vote was a free vote.

Religious freedom for clergy and other religious ministers featured prominently in the parliamentary debates on Bill C-38. The Prime Minister and Liberal Party leader, Paul Martin, addressed this concern in his second reading speech:

> First, some have claimed that, once this bill becomes law, religious freedoms will be less than fully protected. This is demonstrably untrue. As it pertains to marriage, the government's legislation affirms the charter guarantee: that religious officials are free to perform such ceremonies in accordance with the beliefs of their faith.
>
> In this, we are guided by the ruling of the Supreme Court of Canada, which makes clear that in no church, no synagogue, no mosque, no temple – in no religious house will those who disagree with same sex unions be compelled to perform them. Period. That is why this legislation is about civil marriage, not religious marriage.
>
> Moreover, and this is crucially important, the Supreme Court has declared unanimously: 'the guarantee of religious freedom in section 2(a) of the *Charter* is broad enough to protect religious officials from being compelled by the state to perform civil or religious same-sex marriages that are contrary to their religious beliefs.'
>
> The facts are plain. Religious leaders who preside over marriage ceremonies must and will be guided by what they believe. If they do not wish to celebrate marriages for same sex couples, that is their right. The Supreme Court says so and the charter says so.[44]

The Leader of the Opposition and Conservative party leader, Stephen Harper, was not convinced: 'The so-called protection that the government has offered for even basic religious freedom is, frankly, laughably inadequate.' The Bill provided 'one meagre clause to protect religious freedom, a clause which states that religious officials will not be forced to solemnize marriages.'[45] Yet, he continued, 'the Supreme Court of Canada has already ruled that this clause is *ultra vires*. It falls within the provincial responsibility for the solemnization of marriage.'[46] The Government's proposal, in his view, fell well short of comprehensive protection:

> The government's constitutionally useless clause purports to protect churches and religious officials from being forced to solemnize same sex marriages against their beliefs, but this threat has always been only one of many possibilities. We note the Prime Minister did not choose to address a single other possibility. What churches, temples, synagogues and mosques fear today is not immediately the future threat of forced solemnization, but dozens of other threats to religious freedom, some of which have already begun to arrive and some of which will arrive more quickly in the wake of this bill.[47]

44 38th Parliament, 1st Session, House of Commons Debates, 1525, 16 February 2005. The quoted passage is from *Reference re Same-Sex Marriage* [2004] 3 SCR 698, 2004 SCC 79 at 60.

45 38th Parliament, 1st Session, House of Commons Debates, 1605, 16 February 2005. The Supreme Court in *Reference re Same-Sex Marriage* 2004 SCC 79 at 39 held that, pursuant to s. 92(12) of the Constitution Act 1867, only the Provincial legislatures, not the Federal Parliament, may legislate exemptions to solemnisation of marriage requirements.

46 House of Commons Debates, 1605, supra note 45.

47 House of Commons Debates, 1605, supra note 45.

The Opposition Leader proffered the following further protections to anticipate future challenges:

> There are things, of course, that are within the federal sphere that can protect religious freedom. Parliament can ensure that no religious body will have its charitable status challenged because of its beliefs or practices regarding them. Parliament could ensure that beliefs and practices regarding marriage will not affect the eligibility of a church, synagogue, temple or religious organization to receive federal funds, for example, federal funds for seniors' housing or for immigration projects run by a church. Parliament could ensure that the Canadian Human Rights Act or the Broadcasting Act are not interpreted in a way that would prevent the expression of religious beliefs regarding marriage. Should the bill survive second reading, we will propose amendments in areas like these to ensure that in all areas subject to federal jurisdiction nobody will be discriminated against on the basis of their religious beliefs or practices regarding marriage.[48]

In the end, none of these additional protections floated by the Opposition – bar one – were taken up. The one concession was a new clause in the Preamble (when the Bill returned from the Legislative Committee) to assuage concerns about freedom of expression: 'Whereas it is not against the public interest to hold and publicly express diverse views on marriage.' Even here, the wording is somewhat hesitant and coy, preferring the term 'diverse' to 'traditional', 'conservative' or some other epithet indicating positive endorsement of heterosexual-only marriage.

The Civil Marriage Act, in its final form, states:

> **Preamble**
>
> WHEREAS nothing in this Act affects the guarantee of freedom of conscience and religion and, in particular, the freedom of members of religious groups to hold and declare their religious beliefs and the freedom of officials of religious groups to refuse to perform marriages that are not in accordance with their religious beliefs . . .
>
> **3.** It is recognized that officials of religious groups are free to refuse to perform marriages that are not in accordance with their religious beliefs.
>
> **3.1** For greater certainty, no person or organization shall be deprived of any benefit, or be subject to any obligation or sanction, under any law of the Parliament of Canada solely by reason of their exercise, in respect of marriage between persons of the same sex, of the freedom of conscience and religion guaranteed under the Canadian Charter of Rights and Freedoms in respect of marriage as the union of a man and woman to the exclusion of all others based on that guaranteed freedom.

Originally, the Bill just contained section 3, the 'one meagre clause' that Stephen Harper alluded to above.[49] Section 3.1 was added after the Bill came back from the Legislative Committee.[50]

48 House of Commons Debates, 1605, supra note 45.

49 See quotation accompanying footnote 45.

50 As reported to the House of Commons on 16 June 2005.

Clearly, officials of religious bodies are protected. Are registrars or, as they are called in Canada, marriage commissioners, also protected? Can they legitimately decline on grounds of conscience or religion from officiating at SSMs?

The question was explored by the Saskatchewan Court of Appeal in *Re Marriage Commissioners appointed under the Marriage Act 1955*.[51] The Saskatchewan Marriage Act provides that various listed religious clergy and officials may solemnize marriages, as well as marriage commissioners appointed by the minister. Following the legalization of SSM, some marriage commissioners in Saskatchewan refused to solemnize SSM on the basis that they could not do so without violating their religious beliefs.[52] Mr. Orville Nichols was one.[53] He lodged a human rights complaint against the Saskatchewan Government alleging religious discrimination under the province's human rights law. In turn, a human rights complaint was filed against him, alleging that he had acted in a discriminatory manner by refusing to perform a SSM ceremony. The Human Rights Tribunal upheld the latter complaint, and Nichols lost his appeal in the Court of Queen's Bench.[54]

In light of all this, the Province submitted two questions to the Court of Appeal. The first concerned an exemption for those commissioners appointed *before* the change in the law occurred, the so-called 'Grandfathering Option'. The second question concerned an exemption for all commissioners regardless of when they were appointed, the 'Comprehensive Option'.[55] The Grandfathering Option is below, whilst the Comprehensive Option is the provision below minus the words in bold:

> **28.1 (1)** Notwithstanding *The Saskatchewan Human Rights Code*, a marriage commissioner **who was appointed on or before November 5, 2004** is not required to solemnize a marriage if to do so would be contrary to the marriage commissioner's religious beliefs.[56]

The significance of 'November 5, 2004' is that this was the date on which the Saskatchewan Queen's Bench struck down the ban upon SSM in Saskatchewan.[57] That court held that a denial of a marriage license to a same-sex couple would violate their equality rights provided in section 15(1) of the *Charter*. Accordingly, marriage commissioners thereafter were told by the Director of the Marriage Unit that they must perform SSM ceremonies. The Grandfathering Option is clearly a more narrowly-tailored exemption designed to exempt those commissioners appointed *before* the date of the legalization of SSM. But, Nichols's hopes were to be dashed when the court observed

> Although the *Grandfathering Option* has a more narrow reach than the *Comprehensive Option*, this difference is not of enough significance to place it on different constitutional

51 *Re Marriage Commissioners appointed under the Marriage Act 1955* 2011 SKCA 3; (2011) 327 DLR (4th) 669.

52 Following the legalisation of SSM, eight commissioners had resigned and three lodged human rights complaints against the Saskatchewan Government: *Marriage Commissioners* at 11, 13.

53 *Marriage Commissioners* at 13.

54 *Nichols v. Saskatchewan* (Human Rights Commission) 2009 SKQB 299.

55 *Marriage Commissioners* at 18. The options are in the form of proposed amendments to the Marriage Act 1995, ss 199 c. M-4.1.

56 The Grandfathering Option also requires that Commissioners who seek the benefit of the exemption file a written notice with the Director of the Marriage Unit in the Ministry of Justice and Attorney General within three months of the section coming into force: s. 28.1(2)(3).

57 *NW v. Canada* (Attorney General) 2004 SKQB 434.

> ground. The root obligation of a marriage commissioner is to solemnize marriages in keeping with how the concept of marriage is legally defined from time to time. Commissioners who were appointed before the Queen's Bench decision recognizing the legality of same-sex marriage in this jurisdiction are in no meaningfully different position than those appointed after the decision was rendered.[58]

The court first had to decide whether the exemptions (as formulated in the proposed section 28) infringed the *Charter* guarantee of equality:

> **15.(1)** Every individual is equal before and under the law and has the right to the equal protection and equal benefit of the law without discrimination and, in particular, without discrimination based on race, national or ethnic origin, colour, religion, sex, age or mental or physical disability.

It was clear that the purpose of the two options was to accommodate the religious beliefs of certain marriage commissioners.[59] The court rejected the submission that their purpose was to deny same-sex couples the right to marry. Next, although facially neutral, did the options have the *effect* of denying same-sex couples equal protection or benefit of the new law? They did. First, gay and lesbian individuals would be treated differently to other people and this negative differential treatment was due to their sexual orientation.[60] Sexual orientation is not a ground mentioned in section 15 but has been recognized as a protected ground analogous to those enumerated in the section.[61] It was argued that the infringement would be minimal as a same-sex couple turned away by a commissioner could easily find another one prepared to officiate.[62] The court was not persuaded. First, and 'most importantly,'[63] this argument downplayed the serious offence that such a refusal might have upon a gay or lesbian person seeking to be wed. These effects could 'be expected to be very significant and genuinely offensive',[64] even 'devastating'.[65] Further, it was possible that the pool of non-objecting commissioners might not be large enough to ensure same-sex couples' demand could be met, and this potential dearth of eligible commissioners would be exacerbated in remote rural areas.[66]

The different treatment would, secondly, also create a disadvantage by perpetuating prejudice or stereotyping about the worthiness of same-sex unions and this 'would clearly be a retrograde step'.[67]

Rather optimistically it was contended that the Supreme Court in *Reference Re Same-Sex Marriage* had *already* determined that legislative initiatives of the sort at issue

58 *Marriage Commissioners* at 23.
59 *Marriage Commissioners* at 36.
60 *Marriage Commissioners* at 39, 44.
61 *Marriage Commissioners* at 39. The Supreme Court recognized sexual orientation as a qualifying analogous ground under s. 15 in *Egan v. Canada* [1885] 2 SCR 513 at 528; *Vriend v. Alberta* [1998] 1 SCR 493 at 13.
62 *Marriage Commissioners* at 40.
63 *Marriage Commissioners* at 41.
64 *Marriage Commissioners* at 41.
65 *Marriage Commissioners* at 105 per Smith and Vancise JJA (concurring).
66 *Marriage Commissioners* at 42–43.
67 *Marriage Commissioners* at 45.

here passed constitutional muster. Did not the Court say that the state could not oblige officials *of any sort* to solemnize same-sex marriages contrary to their personal religious beliefs?[68] This was, replied the Saskatchewan Court of Appeal, a misreading of the decision, for it was abundantly clear that the Supreme Court's approval of exemptions for 'religious officials' was referring only to ministers of religion holding formal positions in religious communities, and not marriage commissioners.[69]

Turning to the second stage of the *Charter* analysis: was the curtailment of the equality rights of same sex couples justifiable in terms of section 1 of the *Charter*? Applying the usual framework, the first requirement is that the objective of the impugned law must be of sufficient importance to warrant limiting a *Charter* right or freedom. The broad goal of both options was the accommodation of the religious beliefs of the marriage commissioners. One could characterize the goal of the options as the denial of the rights of same-sex couples but that way of stating the objective was unhelpful. So, correctly stated, was the objective of sufficient importance? It 'seem[ed] clear enough'[70] that it was.

The second requirement is the proportionality analysis. This in turn subdivides into three matters. First, was there a rational connection between the impugned law and its objective? Exempting commissioners was clearly rationally connected to the goal of accommodating such commissioners' religious beliefs.[71] Second, did the law impair rights and freedoms as little as possible in order to meet its goal? Here the exemptions foundered. The court raised the possibility of a 'single entry point' system.[72] This corrals would-be married couples towards a bureaucratic official or some central office, rather than permitting them to directly contact a marriage commissioner.

> What if the request for the services of a marriage commissioner involved completion of a form indicating, not just the time and place of the proposed ceremony, but also the genders of the two people planning to marry? (This information is presumably already available in the system in that, in order to obtain a marriage licence, people planning to marry must present identification documents which would typically, or perhaps always, reveal their genders.) Assume too that the Director operated *a simple internal system* whereby a commissioner who did not want to perform same-sex marriage ceremonies because of his or her religious beliefs could make that fact known to the Director. In this sort of arrangement, the Director's office could reply to a request for marriage services by privately taking into account the religious beliefs of commissioners and then providing, to the couple planning to marry, a list of commissioners in the relevant geographical area who would be available on the planned date of the wedding and who would be prepared to officiate. The accommodation of commissioners who did not want to be involved in a same-sex ceremony would not be apparent to the couple proposing to wed and there would be no risk of the couple approaching a commissioner and being refused services because of their sexual orientation.[73]

68 *Marriage Commissioners* at 48.
69 *Marriage Commissioners* at 49.
70 *Marriage Commissioners* at 77.
71 *Marriage Commissioners* at 82.
72 *Marriage Commissioners* at 85.
73 *Marriage Commissioners* at 86 (emphasis added).

Counsel for the marriage commissioners conceded that this kind of procedure *did* represent a less restrictive means of attaining the objectives the commissioners sought. This system fell 'within the range of reasonable alternatives'[74] and, in the court's view, did not appear to be 'impractical, overly costly or administratively unworkable.'[75] The court cautioned that its positive endorsement of a single entry point system was 'not necessarily a determination that *any* such system would ultimately pass full constitutional muster.'[76] Rather, the concrete features of any *particular* system would still need to be evaluated to see if it met the *Charter* standard.

The third inquiry seeks to determine whether the benefits of the impugned law are proportionate to the negative effects of it upon citizens' guaranteed rights or freedoms. The salutary effect of the exemptions is that they permit marriage commissioners to avoid a violation of their consciences or religious convictions. But this was given modest weight, for reasons I will return to shortly. The deleterious effects upon same-sex couples, by contrast, loomed much larger. There was, again, the 'perpetuat[ion of] a brand of discrimination which our national community has only recently begun to successfully overcome.'[77] Second, the denial of marriage by certain commissioners was 'devastating' to the individuals concerned and had a more generalized 'ripple' effect upon the gay community as a whole.[78] Third, the exemptions would 'undercut the basic principle that governmental services must be provided on an impartial and non-discriminatory basis.'[79] The 'proud tradition'[80] of impartial civil servants was undermined. Persons who 'voluntarily chose to assume' a public office, becoming part of 'the apparatus of the state',[81] could not expect to shape that office to conform to their personal scruples. It was the other way around:

> Marriage commissioners do not act as private citizens when they discharge their official duties. Rather, they serve as agents of the Province and act on its behalf and its behalf only. Accordingly, a system that would make marriage services available according to the personal religious beliefs of commissioners is highly problematic. It would undercut the basic principle that governmental services must be provided on an impartial and non-discriminatory basis.[82]

It was then 'readily apparent'[83] that the positive effects of the exemptions did not outweigh their negative effects and thus the third aspect (like the second) of the proportionality analysis had not been satisfied.

In the balancing of negative and positive effects the court gave rather short shrift to the benefits of respecting the commissioners' religious liberty. The following paragraph is telling:

> [I]n considering the benefits of the *Options*, it is also important to note that the freedom of religion interests they accommodate *do not lie at the heart* of s. 2(a) of the *Charter*. In

74 *Marriage Commissioners* at 84.
75 *Marriage Commissioners* at 87.
76 *Marriage Commissioners* at 89 (emphasis added).
77 *Marriage Commissioners* at 94.
78 *Marriage Commissioners* at 95–6.
79 *Marriage Commissioners* at 98.
80 *Marriage Commissioners* at 97.
81 *Marriage Commissioners* at 97.
82 *Marriage Commissioners* at 98.
83 *Marriage Commissioners* at 99.

> other words, the *Options* are concerned only with the ability of marriage commissioners to *act* on their beliefs in the world at large. They do not in any way concern the freedom of commissioners to *hold* the religious beliefs they choose or to worship as they wish. This reality means the benefits flowing from the *Options* are less significant than they might appear on the surface.[84]

For the court, the religious freedom interests of the commissioners 'do not lie at the heart' of this right. They are, after all, still entirely 'free to worship as they wish'. This stance resonates with the tenuous 'core' versus 'peripheral' religious beliefs and practices distinction.[85] According to this view, declining to do one's everyday job because it offends one's religious scruples is regrettable but fairly 'small beer' for the commissioners can still attend their church, pray, read their Bible and go about their usual avowedly religious rituals. Restricting an aspect of one's secular labor is, when said and done, comparatively insignificant compared with the circumscribing of the fundamental and patently 'religious' duties of one's faith. According to this blinkered conception of religious free exercise, the former is a mere indirect curtailment of a secondary or peripheral religious matter whereas the latter represents a direct incursion upon a primary or central religious activity.

Furthermore, in the court's understanding, the right to *hold* religious beliefs is acknowledged and, indeed, inviolable, but *acting* upon them is another matter. Here the perennial 'belief/action' distinction rears its unsightly head once more.[86] Acting upon one's beliefs must be circumscribed in the interests of society and to protect the rights of others. But do not be alarmed, for one still can hold to that belief. This mindset, with its attenuated conception of religious exercise (protecting core but not peripheral religious matters, beliefs but not necessarily actions that manifest such beliefs), is made explicit in the concurring opinion of Smith JA:

> [W]hile the right to hold certain religious beliefs, and to engage in particular rites and practices, lie at the core of the right to religious freedom protected by s. 2(a) of the *Charter*, Canadian constitutional jurisprudence has consistently distinguished between the right to *hold* certain beliefs and the right to *act* on those beliefs, particularly as one moves out of the *fundamental area* of religious rites and practices and when acting on a religious belief harms or infringes the rights of others. See, for example, the analysis in *Trinity Western University v. British Columbia College of Teachers* . . . where the [Supreme] Court was at great pains to distinguish between the right of education students to hold negative and stereotypical *beliefs* about gays and lesbians, held to be protected by s. 2(a), from the right to discriminate against others, based on those beliefs, by implication, not protected. At the very least, the protection of s. 2(a) of the *Charter*, like s. 2(b) encompasses a range of activities that diminish, as they recede from a *fundamental core*, in constitutional value[87]
>
> (emphasis added).

84 *Marriage Commissioners* at 93.

85 See Ahdar and Leigh, *Religious Freedom*, supra note 32 at 173–175 for criticism of this dichotomy.

86 See Ahdar and Leigh, *Religious Freedom*, supra note 32 at 163–165.

87 *Marriage Commissioners* at 146 (Vancise JA concurring) (italics added).

From this narrow perspective, secular labor by a state-employed official is very far removed from rituals or liturgical conduct undertaken by a religious official. Earlier in his opinion, Smith JA had emphasized that marriage commissioners were carefully devised by the legislature to be 'non-religious, civil, as opposed to religious'[88] celebrants. The legislation amply provided for a long list of religious celebrants whereas marriage commissioners conducting a civil, non-religious ceremony were there as a distinctly *secular* alternative to cater for those who did not wish to have their marriage conducted in a religious setting or with any religious connotations.[89]

The assertion that marriage commissioners are state employees and therefore must conform to the state's juridical norms does not take the argument very far. For another norm, alongside state impartiality in the provision of public services, is government accommodation of its civil servants' consciences. As Geoffrey Trotter puts it: 'Rights-bearing citizens do not lose their human rights when they enter public employment.'[90] To focus exclusively on the state's obligation to same-sex couples is to neglect the position of the flesh-and-blood providers of the marriage services. Officiating is not (yet) done by 'robots and computers', and as long as the state acts through its citizens their rights must also be taken into consideration.[91] As an employer, the state must attempt to reasonably accommodate the sincere religious convictions of its employees. To ignore the duty of reasonable accommodation is to adopt a stark, take-it-or-leave-it stance: religious commissioners must reform their beliefs to agree with the state, or take their beliefs with them and leave government employment.[92] Rigid denial of an exemption for devout marriage commissioners would simply lead to the exclusion of many religious persons from this branch of the public service, an outcome that seems at odds with the usual espoused political aim of tolerance and inclusion of *all* citizens.[93]

The Saskatchewan court believed that exemptions for marriage commissioners (permitting them to decline to conduct SSMs) would 'clearly be a retrograde step – a step that would perpetuate disadvantage and involve stereotypes about the worthiness of same-sex unions.'[94] Bruce MacDougall charged that to allow refusals only in relation to the conduct of SSM (and not refusals to marry, say, opposite-race or divorced couples) would demonstrate that the state was not trying to accommodate religious consciences in general but rather was 'simply supportive of religious hostility to homosexuals, ie, homophobia'.[95] But these criticisms are misplaced, for they conflate the state with its myriad employees.[96] The granting of an exemption for devout commissioners does not demonstrate that the state necessarily accepts the views of those commissioners. When the state allows doctors and nurses the right of conscientious objection from participation

88 *Marriage Commissioners* at 123.

89 *Marriage Commissioners* at 123–124.

90 Geoffrey Trotter, 'The Right to Decline Performance of Same-Sex Civil Marriages: The Duty to Accommodate Public Servants – A Response to Professor Bruce MacDougall', (2007) 70 Saskatchewan Law Review (2) 385.

91 Trotter, 'The Right to Decline . . .', supra note 90 at 385.

92 Trotter, 'The Right to Decline . . .', supra note 90 at 366–367, 392.

93 Trotter, 'The Right to Decline . . .', supra note 90 at 366–367, 392.

94 Marriage Commissioners at 45, also 142, per Smith JA.

95 Bruce MacDougall, 'Refusing to Officiate at Same-Sex Civil Marriages' (2006) 69 Saskatchewan Law Review (2) 358.

96 Trotter, 'The Right to Decline . . .', supra note 90 at 374.

in abortion procedures, the state is not accepting or endorsing the stance of those objectors on the merits of abortion.[97] By permitting religious civil servants to opt out of conducting SSMs, the legislature or court does not, as MacDougall argued, in effect, accept the religious 'version' of the issue.[98] Rather, an accommodation sends out the message that the state has solicitude for the consciences of its employees. If anything, the legislature has already decisively rejected the religious stance on the issue by legalizing SSM. An exemption is a departure from the official 'version' that SSM is now accepted and meets the societal threshold meriting full legal recognition. As for the accusation of homophobia, a physician who withdraws from abortion is not (one would hope) motivated by *animus* against the woman seeking the procedure, but is simply unable in good conscience to provide the service herself or himself.[99]

Smith JA was puzzled and wondered how conducting a marriage for a same-sex couple infringed a devout marriage commissioner's religious freedom at all. From the testimony of the objecting commissioners and religious experts it appeared that officiating at a SSM would offend the religious beliefs of devout commissioners because to so perform the ceremony 'would constitute condonation or approval of same-sex relationships', something they found contrary to their (unchallenged) sincere beliefs.[100] Smith JA was unable to see how officiating at a civil ceremony carried any implication or connotation that the marriage commissioner who officiates necessarily approved of these types of union.[101] By stark contrast, refusing to perform a SSM 'without doubt expresses *condemnation* of same sex unions and practices as socially harmful and perverse'.[102] Performing the ceremony when asked 'might well be neutral [whereas] refusing to do so is an overtly discriminatory act' that engenders psychological anguish and reinforces age-old prejudice.[103]

As a matter of logic it is difficult to see how performing *x* is neutral while refusing to perform *x* is discriminatory and expresses condemnation of those seeking *x*. Furthermore, this approach over-emphasizes the external appearance of conduct at the expense of the internal attitude of the moral agent towards the conduct. For example, eating pork may well be a neutral act for most citizens but for certain people it violates deeply held religious beliefs. A central thrust of freedom of religion and conscience is protection of the individual's conscience, or the safeguarding the person's subjective religious sensibilities. It may be hard to comprehend how undertaking a secular task can be freighted with religious meaning, but much mundane activity is religiously significant for many religionists.[104] So, to say that '[t]he performance of a civil marriage by a marriage commissioner . . . is not a religious rite or practice' and that '[n]or does the requirement to do so limit or restrict religious belief'[105] is to miss the point.

Even if, continued Smith JA, the performance of SSMs by devout marriage commissioners did restrict their religious freedom, it would do so 'only in a secondary way' and the curtailment would arguably be 'trivial or insubstantial, in that it is interference that does not

97 Trotter, 'The Right to Decline . . .', supra note 90.
98 MacDougall, 'Refusing to Officiate . . .', supra note 95 at 365.
99 Trotter, 'Right to Decline . . .', supra note 90 at 371.
100 *Marriage Commissioners* at 132.
101 *Marriage Commissioners* at 142.
102 *Marriage Commissioners* at 142 (italics in original).
103 *Marriage Commissioners* at 142.
104 See Ahdar and Leigh, *Religious Freedom*, supra note 32, Chapter 10.
105 *Marriage Commissioners* at 147.

threaten actual religious beliefs or conduct.'[106] And thus 'to the extent that this is so, it does not even fall within the protection of s. 2(a) of the *Charter*.'[107] This simply demonstrates that the judge has an attenuated understanding of just what constitutes the manifestation of one's religion.

Although Saskatchewan rejected a statutory exemption for marriage commissioners, Prince Edward Island passed an exemption in 2005 permitting commissioners to refuse to solemnize SSMs.[108]

United Kingdom

Following a public consultation on SSM which began in March 2012 – that elicited 228,000 responses and 19 petitions, the largest response ever received to a Government consultation[109] – the Minister for Women and Equalities, Maria Miller, introduced the Bill to legalize SSM in England and Wales on 24 January 2013. The Bill was given the Royal Assent on 17 July 2013. The Marriage (Same Sex Couples) Act 2013 states with stark simplicity 'marriage of same sex couples is lawful.'[110]

Simplicity, however, is not a feature of the statutory provisions for clergy and other marriage celebrants who seek an exemption from conducting SSM on grounds of conscience. Churches expressed serious concerns about their right to refuse to marry same-sex couples. The Government's response was the so-called 'quadruple lock', a fourfold bundle of provisions designed to make it clear that clergy and other religious officials would not be compelled to conduct SSMs.[111] Part of the complexity is due to the special position of the Church of England as the established church.[112] This status means its Canons (church law) form part of the law of the land. The Church can amend or repeal primary legislation through a Measure passed by its Synod, provided the Measure is later approved by parliament and receives the Royal Assent. Most pertinently, its clergy are under a common law duty to marry a parishioner in his or her parish church. The Church in Wales is still under a similar duty by virtue of its previously being established (it having been disestablished in 1920).

The Government's report on the public consultation, 'Equal Marriage', made it clear that no religious organization or its ministers would be forced to conduct marriage ceremonies for same-sex couples.[113] This assurance was consistently reiterated throughout the entire parliamentary passage of the Bill. In the House of Commons second reading, the sponsoring Minister stated

> I have been true to my word and ensured that there is clear protection for all religious organisations and ministers who are opposed to this measure. All religious

106 *Marriage Commissioners* at 148.

107 *Marriage Commissioners* at 148.

108 Marriage Act (Prince Edward Island), RSPEI 1988, c. M-3, s. 11.1 (added by An Act to Amend the Marriage Act, SPEI 2005, c. 12, s 7. The section reads: '**11.1** For greater certainty, a person who is authorized to solemnize marriage under this Act may refuse to solemnize a marriage that is not in accordance with that person's religious beliefs.'

109 *Equal Marriage: The Government's Response* (London, December 2012) at para. 1.1.

110 The Marriage (Same Sex Couples) Act 2013, Section 1.

111 *Equal Marriage*, supra note 109 at paras 4.19–4.20.

112 See *Equal Marriage* at paras 1.4 and 4.21–4.23.

113 *Equal Marriage* at paras 1.3 and 4.18–4.27.

> organisations – whether they be Jewish, Muslim, Christian or any other – will be able to decide for themselves if they want to conduct same-sex marriages. The Bill provides for and promotes religious freedom through the Government's quadruple lock. These protections are absolutely carved on the face of the Bill and are the foundation on which the legislation is built.[114]

The Quadruple Lock

The first of the four provisions to protect the religious freedom of marriage celebrants is an express non-compulsion provision. Part 2 of the Act, headed 'Religious protection', opens with section 2:

> **2. Marriage according to religious rites: no compulsion to solemnize etc**
>
> (1) A person may not be compelled by any means (including by the enforcement of a contract or a statutory or other legal requirement) to –
>
> (a) undertake an opt-in activity, or
> (b) refrain from undertaking an opt-out activity.
>
> (2) A person may not be compelled by any means (including by the enforcement of a contract or a statutory or other legal requirement) –
>
> (a) to conduct a relevant marriage,
> (b) to be present at, carry out, or otherwise participate in, a relevant marriage, or
> (c) to consent to a relevant marriage being conducted,
>
> where the reason for the person not doing that thing is that the relevant marriage concerns a same sex couple.

The right to not be forced to conduct a 'relevant marriage' in section 2(2) refers to 'a marriage between same-sex couples.'[115]

Second, the statute sets out an opt-in system so that religious organizations or individual ministers who wish to conduct marriages for same-sex couples will need to take positive steps before they can do so. It will be unlawful for religious bodies or their ministers to marry same-sex couples unless the requisite opt-in requirements have been complied with. An 'opt in' activity is further defined in a detailed table in section 2(3). If a religious organization has decided not to opt-in, then none of its ministers will be able to conduct a SSM.[116] If such an organization has chosen to conduct SSM, its individual ministers are still under no compulsion to conduct one unless they decide to do so.[117]

Third, there are two special provisions to safeguard the position of the established church. First the Church of England's current stance on SSM (opposing it) might fall foul

114 Maria Miller, House of Commons Debates (HC Deb), Second Reading, 5 February 2013, vol. 558, col. 129.
115 Marriage (Same Sex Couples) Act 2013, s 2(4).
116 Maria Miller, HC Deb, 11 December 2012, vol. 555, col. 156.
117 Miller, HC Deb, 11 December 2012, vol. 555, col. 156.

of centuries-old legislation, the Clergy Act 1533, that requires that church law be consistent with the law of the land. So when SSM was legalized the Church's position might violate ordinary secular law and be subject to nullification on that basis. A special provision would, however, avert this clash and allow the inconsistency between the Church's no-SSM-stance and the law's affirmative policy in favour of SSM to continue. Thus, we have section 1(3):

> **1(3)** No Canon of the Church of England is contrary to section 3 of the Submission of the Clergy Act 1533 (which provides that no Canons shall be contrary to the Royal Prerogative or the customs, laws or statutes of this realm) by virtue of its making provision about marriage being the union of one man with one woman.

Then, there is explicit recognition that it is illegal for the established church to marry same-sex couples:

> **1(4)** Any duty of a member of the clergy to solemnize marriages (and any corresponding right of persons to have their marriages solemnized by members of the clergy) is not extended by this Act to marriages of same sex couples.

The term 'a member of the clergy' is a clerk in Holy Orders of the Church of England or the Church in Wales.[118]

Fourth, the Equality Act 2010 was amended to explicitly state that it is not unlawful discrimination for a person to refuse to conduct a SSM.[119]

The Unpicking of the Locks?

There were many members who foresaw the real potential for a disappointed same sex-couple to take a successful claim to the European Court of Human Rights.[120] For instance, Sir Tony Baldry, the Second Church Estate Commissioner for the Church of England cautioned:

> Before I leave the question of the locks, let me be clear that we think that the Government have done their best in these, given their intention to introduce same-sex marriage. But . . . there is *an inevitable degree of risk in all this*, given that it would ultimately be for the courts, and in particular the Strasbourg court, to decide whether provisions in the legislation are compatible with the European convention on human rights. There is absolutely no doubt that once marriage is redefined in this very fundamental way, a number of new legal questions will arise and *no one can be sure what the eventual outcome will be.* The Government believe that this is a risk worth taking. The Church of England does not.

118 Marriage (Same Sex Couples) Act 2013, s 1(5).

119 Marriage (Same Sex Couples) Act 2013, s 2(5)(6). Section 110 provides that A does not contravene section 110 if A does not conduct a SSM. Schedule 3 to the Equality Act (services and public functions) now has a new Part 6A that contains the exemption for SSM, namely: '25A(1). A person does not contravene section 29 only because the person – (a) does not conduct a relevant marriage. . .'

120 See for example Robert Flello (Labour), HC Deb, 5 February 2013, vol. 558, col. 146; Jim Shannon (Democratic Unionist), HC Deb, 5 February 2013, vol. 558, col. 165; Graham Brady (Conservative), HC Deb, 5 February 2013, vol. 558, col. 172; Fiona Bruce (Con), HC Deb, 5 February 2013, vol. 558, col. 194.

> As I understand it, the Roman Catholic Church does not, and nor do a number of other faith groups, including the Muslim faith . . . I simply reiterate that there is no way in which any of us can know just how robust these protections will be until they are tested in the courts.[121]

'It is abundantly plain to most Conservative Members,' charged Sir Roger Gale in blunter fashion, 'that the product of the Bill will end up before the European Court of Human Rights and that people of faith will find that faith trampled upon.'[122] The Bill was a veritable 'Pandora's box of endless litigation', warned another.[123] Labour MP Michael McCann, blasted:

> I am damn sure – as sure as the sun rises in the morning – that a same-sex couple will go to a church or synagogue and demand to be married, their demand will be refused and they will go to court; and we in turn will have to wait to see what new case law is created. By that time, it is possible that none of us will be serving in the House – we may have left politics altogether or indeed left this mortal coil – but in that set of circumstances people will look back and ask, 'How did we get into this mess?' They will look back in *Hansard* and say, 'It's because we made a bad law in 2013, and some politician said at the time that there was a quadruple lock, underpinned by case law.'[124]

In response, proponents of the Bill conceded that no one could totally rule out future litigation, for no law could prevent an individual filing an application with a court.[125] Those who sought 'a cast iron guarantee'[126] were seeking the impossible.[127] Yet, it was the Minister herself who had fuelled such an expectation when she confidently assured the House that 'the system of locks will iron-clad the protection'[128] religious bodies sought against being forced to conduct SSM. Others were only a little less categorical and relied upon the advice of the Attorney-General to the effect that 'case law in the European Court of Human Rights makes it infinitesimally unlikely that any such challenge would succeed.'[129] Lord Pannick had assured the Public Bill Committee by written memorandum that: 'For the European Court of Human Rights to compel a religious body or its adherents to conduct a religious marriage of a same sex couple would require a legal miracle much greater than the parting of the Red Sea.'[130] As the Minister explained, 'The Government's legal position has confirmed that, with appropriate legislative drafting, the chance of a successful legal challenge through domestic or European courts is negligible.'[131] And again, 'It is simply

121 HC Deb, 5 February 2013, vol. 558, cols. 144–5 (emphasis added).
122 HC Deb, 5 February 2013, vol. 558, col. 152.
123 Stewart Jackson (Con), HC Deb, 5 February 2013, vol. 558, col. 201.
124 HC Deb, 5 February 2013, vol. 558, col. 180.
125 Hugh Robertson, HC Deb, 28 February 2013, vol. 558, col. 280.
126 Such as Sir Gerald Kaufman (Lab), HC Deb, 5 February 2013, vol. 558, col. 125.
127 As noted, for example, by Lord Alli, House of Lords debates (HL Deb), 19 June 2013, col. 274.
128 Maria Miller, HC Deb, 11 December 2012, vol. 555, col. 156.
129 Margot James (Lab), HC Deb, 5 February 2013, vol. 558 col. 163.
130 Quoted in the speech by Hugh Robertson, HC Deb, 28 February 2013, vol. 558, col. 280.
131 Maria Miller, HC Deb, 11 December 2012, vol. 555, col. 156.

inconceivable that the Court would require a faith group to conduct same-sex marriages in breach of its own doctrines.'[132] Lord Faulks did 'not share the enthusiasm of some noble Lords for the Strasbourg jurisprudence' and whilst some of his colleagues predicted that it was 'inconceivable' that there would be a challenge, he was 'not as confident as they are – few lawyers are'.[133] Lord Brennan agreed with that sentiment adding 'it would be naïve to assume that the problems that have been raised by other barristers will not encounter serious disputation in our courts and in Strasbourg.'[134]

Lords Faulks and Brennan were to be vindicated with alacrity. Within just one month of the Act's passing, the homosexual couple chosen by the Government to promote the SSM legislation announced they were taking a case to Strasbourg to force the Church of England (to which they belonged) to marry them in their local parish of Danbury, Essex.[135] It is difficult to forecast how the European Court of Human Rights would rule to such UK applicants. Some members were never persuaded that the quadruple locks ('Fort Knox locks' as one member mocked)[136] would not be 'picked' by the Strasbourg court.[137]

In *Schalk and Kopf v. Austria,* the European Court of Human Rights held that the introduction of legislation permitting SSM was a matter for each state.[138] It also noted the incontestable sociological fact that 'a rapid evolution of social attitudes towards same sex couples had taken place in many member states' over the last decade.[139] This might suggest a readiness to recognize a right for same-sex couples to be married by religious as well as civil bodies. But the right of religious group autonomy under Article 9 has also been consistently and forcefully affirmed.[140] In the recent *Good Shepherd* case, the Grand Chamber reaffirmed the right of a religious community to determine matters of internal governance,[141] including the duties of members of its clergy.[142]

For now at least, the locks do appear to be reasonably secure from Strasbourg attack. Unpicking from future UK Parliaments is a different matter. As Lord Naseby reminded: 'Safeguards are not met by quadruple locks. Locks can be undone by any fiendishly good legislator anywhere in the world'.[143] Including, one might gratuitously add, those that inhabit Westminster.

132 Maria Miller, HC Deb, 5 February 2013, vol. 558, col. 131 (quoting 'the eminent QCs Lord Pannick, Baroness Kennedy and Lord Lester').

133 HL Deb, 4 June 2013, col. 1067.

134 HL Deb, 4 June 2013, col. 1070.

135 John Bingham, 'First Couple Consider Legal Challenge to Church's Gay Marriage Opt-Out', *Daily Telegraph*, 2 August 2013, http://www.telegraph.co.uk/news/religion/10219802/First-couple-consider-legal-challenge-to-Churchs-gay-marriage-opt-out.html (accessed 1 January 2016).

136 Jim Shannon HC Deb, 28 February 2013, col. 292.

137 For example Jim Shannon HC Deb, 5 February 2013, col. 165; Graham Brady (Con), HC Deb, 5 February 2013, col 172.

138 *Schalk and Kopf v. Austria*, App. No. 30141/04 (ECtHR, 24 June 2010), §§ 101–110.

139 *Schalk and Kopf* at § 93.

140 Ahdar and Leigh, *Religious Freedom*, supra note 32, Chapter 11, especially at 377–378 and 396–399.

141 *Sindicatul 'Pastorul Cel Bun' v. Romania*, App. No. 2330/09 (ECtHR Grand Chamber, 9 July 2013), §§ 162–168.

142 *Sindicatul* § 4 per Wojtyczek J (concurring).

143 HL Deb, 3 June 2013, col. 997.

Exemptions for Registrars?

Regarding marriage registrars, Conservative MP David Burrowes moved an amendment to protect them during the second reading in the House of Commons.[144] The Bill (clause 2 (4) (b)) expressly stated that those entitled to immunity from conducting SSMs '[did] not include a registrar'. Some MPs considered this was a serious flaw. The amendment, if adopted, 'would ensure that the legislation matches the Government's aspiration to provide freedom of conscience and would enable us to have a liberal, tolerant society that respects different views, including those of registrars. They would also protect existing registrars from being faced with a choice between a violation of conscience and losing their livelihood.'[145]

The well-known case of the Islington Borough Council Registrar, Lillian Ladele, whose claim went all the way to the European Court of Human Rights,[146] was the prime example mentioned in the House. It will be recalled that Mrs Ladele, a Christian, had intimated that, due to her sincere religious convictions, she did not feel able to conduct a civil partnership ceremony for any same-sex couple seeking one. She had become a Registrar of Births, Deaths and Marriages in 2002, and two years later the UK Parliament passed the Civil Partnership Act 2004, which came into effect in December 2005. Islington Borough Council could have accommodated her conscientious position without interruption of service and without any offense to those seeking civil partnerships. There were more than sufficient registrars who did not share her views to cover these duties. Other UK councils had organized their roster of registrars to ensure that no objecting registrars would be forced to comply and that no client would face any embarrassing refusal. However, Islington Council's decision not to do so was found by both the Employment Appeal Tribunal and the Court of Appeal to be lawful since it was acting in pursuit of a self-made equality policy entitled (with no apparently intended irony) 'Dignity for All'.[147] The disciplinary proceedings instituted by the Council against Ladele for gross misconduct were upheld and her claim of religious discrimination was dismissed.[148] The European Court of Human Rights upheld the Court of Appeal decision in January 2013 and so the Strasbourg judgment was fresh in the parliamentarians' minds during the SSM debate.

To return to the Burrowes amendment, it read:

> New clause 2 – Conscientious objection –
>
> (1) Subject to subsections (2) and (3) of this section, no registrar shall be under any duty, whether by contract or by any statutory or other legal requirement, to conduct, be present at, carry out, participate in, or consent to the taking place of, a relevant marriage ceremony to which he has a conscientious objection.

144 The first version (Amendment 11) was moved and debated at length at the Public Bill Committee stage on 26 February 2013, col. 220. The revised version was debated on 20 May 2013, col. 926 et seq. There is a useful summary in the House of Lords Library Notes, Marriage (Same Sex Couples) Bill (HL Bill 29 of 2013–14), 30 May 2013, LLN 2013/011.

145 David Burrowes, HC Deb, 26 February 2013, col. 224.

146 *Eweida v. United Kingdom*, App. Nos. 48420/10, 59842/10, 51671/10, 36516/10 (ECtHR, 15 January 2013).

147 *London Borough of Islington v. Ladele* [2008] EAT Case No. UKEAT/0453/08/RN (10 December 2008); *Ladele v London Borough of Islington* [2009] EWCA 1357; [2010] 1 WLR 955 (CA).

148 Ladele's religious discrimination claim had been upheld at first instance by the Employment Tribunal: *Ladele v. London Borough of Islington* [2008] ET, Case No. 2203694/2007 (20 May 2008). For further analysis see Ahdar and Leigh, *Religious Freedom*, supra note 32 at 356–357.

(2) Nothing in subsection (1) shall affect the duty of each registration authority to ensure that there is a sufficient number of relevant marriage registrars for its area to carry out in that area the functions of relevant marriage registrars.
(3) The conscientious objection must be based on a sincerely-held religious or other belief.
(4) In any legal proceedings the burden of proof of conscientious objection shall rest on the person claiming to rely on it.[149]

There was also a similar amendment (new clause 3) to implement *transitional* protection to preserve the right of conscientious objection for registrars *already* employed.[150] The Netherlands, noted several MPs, had such a transitional exemption provision.[151]

The conscientious objection provision makes it clear that no client would be denied a civil marriage ceremony due to a want of suitable registrars, and so a registrar would be unable to claim protection if no one could cover for him or her in that particular locality. Objecting registrars would also have the onus of proving their refusal was grounded in sincere religious or other beliefs. Some members drew the analogy with surgeons who were allowed, under the conscientious objection provision in the abortion legislation, to abstain from participation in abortions.[152]

Opponents of the new conscientious objection clause echoed the arguments from the Saskatchewan case, *Marriage Commissioners*, discussed earlier. Labour MP Kate Green, for instance, contended: 'We are talking about someone who is performing a state function. They cannot pick and choose when acting as an agent of the state to what extent they are prepared to fulfil the function that they are required to perform.'[153] As for the prospect that some registrars might be forced to choose between their beliefs and their livelihood, this was 'regrettable', but 'one of the things that [went] with being a public servant is that one has to fulfil the requirements of the law of the land as it stands at the time.'[154] The analogy between objecting registrars and surgeons refusing to do abortions was misplaced, countered one MP. The registrar's sole duty was to conduct marriage whereas a surgeon had many duties, among which abortion was a 'tiny part' of what they might be called to undertake.[155]

David Burrowes did not press the permanent exemption (new clause 2) to a vote but did put up the transitional exemption provision (new clause 3). The amendment was lost by 340 to 150 votes.[156]

149 HC Deb, 20 May 2013, vol. 563, col. 926.

150 HC Deb, 20 May 2013, vol. 536, col. 926: 'New clause 3 – Conscientious objection: transitional arrangements – (1) No person shall be under any duty, whether by contract or by statutory or other legal requirement, to conduct a marriage to which he has a conscientious objection if he is employed as a registrar of marriages on the date this Act comes in force.'

151 David Burrowes, HC Deb, 20 May 2013, vol. 536, col. 929 and 20 May 2013, vol. 536, col. 929; Jim Shannon (Democratic Unionist), HC Deb, 20 May 2013, vol. 536, col. 954.

152 Jim Shannon, HC Deb, 26 February 2013, vol. 536, col. 232 and David Burrowes, HC Deb, 20 May 2013, vol. 536, col. 929. The conscientious objection exemption for medical practitioners is in section 4 of the Abortion Act 1967.

153 HC Deb, 26 February 2013, vol. 536, col 225. See also the Minister for Sport and Tourism, Hugh Robertson (Con), HC Deb, 26 February 2013, vol. 536, col. 234.

154 Kate Green, HC Deb, 26 February 2013, vol. 536, col. 226,

155 Stephen Williams (Liberal Democrat), HC Deb, 20 May 2013, vol. 563, col. 934. This overlooks the fact that registrars also attend to the registration of births and deaths, hence their full title.

156 HC Deb, 20 May 2013, vol. 563, col. 966.

Conclusion

It is fitting that clergy and other religious ministers have been granted exemptions to permit them to refuse to solemnize SSMs in those countries that have legalized marriages by same-sex couples. This core facet of religious group autonomy has been guaranteed in the wake of considerable pressure from churches (and other religious communities) to have the right to solemnize marriages in accordance with the religious community's beliefs and customs preserved. Whether future parliaments or courts will overturn this exemption is difficult to assess. Three, and even two, decades ago one would have been hard pressed to find many who would have confidently predicted that SSM itself would be legalized.

In New Zealand, the protection for religious ministers is weakened by the requirement that the religious body to which the minister belongs must have an express and clear rule on the matter. This is a problem for conservative pastors and priests in those denominations that are still vigorously debating the issue and struggling to come to a clear resolution either in favor of or against the solemnization of SSM.

The attempt to extend protection to civil marriage celebrants has been rejected in each country that has sought to do so. It was expressly considered and rejected in the Westminster parliament. Indeed, the attempt by Saskatchewan to introduce an exemption for civil celebrants was ruled to be unconstitutional by that province's Court of Appeal. The case for protection for those who were *already* celebrants when SSM was legalized would seem to be stronger than those appointed *after* the law came in. But even in that situation, an exemption has been rejected. The operative reasoning has been that those who work for the state must abide by official public norms. There is no room for devout public servants to pick and choose which citizens it will serve when it comes to solemnizing marriage (or civil unions for that matter). There is a strange amnesia at work here insofar as the obligation of the state to accommodate the religious conscience of its servants is forgotten. It is a safe prediction that devout religious persons (who hold to 'traditional' sexual ethics) will withdraw from this area of the civil service.

But it might not come to this. The Saskatchewan Court of Appeal approved in principle a 'single entry point' system. Here, by way of a quick and simple bureaucratic process, a sensible reconciliation of the competing rights can be attained: same-sex couples may obtain a state-sanctioned ceremony without enduring rejection or embarrassment, and devout marriage commissioners can retain their jobs and avert a violation of their conscience. If the hard-won right of religious liberty is to be preserved in increasingly secular Western societies, creative solutions such as these will need to be found.

8 Marriages, Civil Unions, Partnerships, and Religion in South Africa after 1996

Pieter Coertzen

Antecedents of South African Marriage Law

Roman and Germanic law played an important role in the legal foundations of marriage in the Western world. In the years 1100–1580 the Roman Catholic Church established its jurisdiction over the institution of marriage by declaring marriage to be a sacrament and by establishing various theocratic requirements for marriage.[1] By 1580, in the time of Roman Dutch Family Law, the Protestant Reformation played an important role with regard to the view of marriage. This has been characterized by some as an increasing secularization[2] of marriage. In fact, however, though marriage was no longer seen as a sacrament, it was still seen as a divine institution. At the same time the roles of the state and legal institutions were also acknowledged. The Political Ordinance of the States of Holland, issued 1 April 1580, mandated that either a minister of the church or an official of the state had to conduct a marriage. The church and the state each had a role to play.

All of this was part of the 'Christian' family law inheritance of South Africa, 'Christian' because of the Reformation view of the relationship between church and state in which the state was seen as both the protector of and ruler over the church by way of legislation and policy. The legislation of the state was seen to portray 'Christian values'. This is most probably the reason why legal writings on family law in South Africa, while recognizing civil marriages, civil unions, and customary marriages and also discussing Jewish, Muslim, and Hindu marriages as systems of religious marriages, say nothing about Christian marriages. Apparently it is taken for granted that the historical Marriage Act (and the legal position in terms of the 1996 South African Constitution) portrays Christian values. This, however, must be questioned.

Before 1994 South African family law acknowledged only monogamous civil marriages of heterosexual persons, conducted and registered in accordance with the marriage law. The Bill of Rights in the 1996 Constitution – stating the right to equality, human dignity, and freedom of conscience, religion, thought, belief and opinion – brought about many changes with regard to marriage in South Africa. It brought forward calls that polygyny be recognized, that due to the high divorce rate the definition of marriage as a life-long union be revised, and that the definition of marriage as restricted to between a man and a woman be amended.[3] For

1 Ann Skelton, Marita Carnelley, Sonia Human, Jacobus Abraham Robinson and Bradley S. Smith, eds, *Familiereg in Suid-Afrika* (Oxford University Press Southern Africa 2011), 12–15. English version, *Family Law in South Africa* (Oxford University Press Southern Africa 2010).

2 Skelton et al., *Familiereg in Suid-Afrika* at 13.

3 D.S.P. Cronjé and Jacqueline Heaton, *South African Family Law* (LexisNexis Butterworths, 2nd edn, 2004), 17.

Christians, this presented a significant challenge, to seriously rethink and clearly formulate the Christian position on marriage and how it fits into the legal world of South Africa.

Marriage Law in South Africa

The 1996 Constitution

The current Constitution of the Republic of South Africa, which has been referred to as the 'birth certificate' of a new South Africa,[4] was promulgated by Nelson Mandela on 10 December 1996. The country's fifth constitution, it 'was the result of a long and inclusive negotiation process'[5] following the country's first non-racial elections. This document determines in Article 15(1) that 'everyone has the right to freedom of conscience, religion, thought, belief and opinion.'[6] By the provisions of Article 15(3)(a), 'This section does not prevent legislation recognising (i) marriages concluded under any tradition, or a system of religious, personal or family law; or (ii) systems of personal and family law under any tradition, or adhered to by persons professing a particular religion.'[7] Marriage is also mentioned in Article 9:

> (1) Everyone is equal before the law and has the right to equal protection and benefit of the law. (2) Equality includes the full and equal enjoyment of all rights and freedoms. To promote the achievement of equality, legislative and other measures designed to protect or advance persons, or categories of persons, disadvantaged by unfair discrimination may be taken. (3) The State may not unfairly discriminate directly or indirectly against anyone on one or more grounds, including race, gender, sex, pregnancy, marital status, ethnic or social origin, colour, sexual orientation, age disability, religion, conscience, belief, culture, language and birth. (4) No person may unfairly discriminate directly or indirectly against anyone on one or more grounds in terms of subsection (3). National legislation must be enacted to prevent or prohibit unfair discrimination. (5) Discrimination on one or more of the grounds listed in subsection (3) is unfair unless it is established that the discrimination is fair.[8]

Laws Regarding Cohabitation

South African law recognizes three forms of cohabiting relationships. Another such relationship, the domestic or life partnership, is not regulated by law.

1. Civil Marriage

In South Africa civil marriages are traditionally defined as the legally recognized union between one man and one woman to the exclusion of all other persons.[9]

4 Constitutional Court of South Africa, *The Constitution: The History of the Constitution,* http://www.constitutionalcourt.org.za/site/theconstitution/history.htm#apartheid (accessed 21 October 2015).

5 Constitutional Court of South Africa, *The Constitution: The Ccertification Process,* http://www.constitutionalcourt.org.za/site/theconstitution/thecertificationprocess.htm (accessed 21 October 2015).

6 The Constitution of the Republic of South Africa [hereinafter SA Const.], 1996, Act 108 of 1996, Art 15(1).

7 SA Const., Art 15(3)(i) and (ii).

8 SA Const., Art 9(1–5).

9 *Seedat's Executors v. Master (Natal)* 1917 AD 302 op 309; Marriage Act 25 of 1961.

2. African Customary Marriage

Before the coming into operation of the law on the Recognition of Customary Marriages, Act 120 of 1998 on 15 November 2000[10] (some legal scholars give the date as 15 November 1998),[11] South African law did not see customary marriages as legally valid. Two reasons were given for this view, namely that customary marriages were seen as polygyny, and they were not solemnized according to the Marriage Act. Customary marriages are between indigenous persons of South Africa and are entered into in accordance with the culture and customs of those persons.[12] For certain purposes, such as the registration of births and deaths and for the definition of a marriage for the sake of childcare, lawmakers before 1998 gave limited recognition to customary marriages. The Customary Marriages Act gives full legal recognition to customary marriages regardless of when they were concluded and regardless of how many customary wives a husband has. In general, the Act preserves the old customary law requirements and consequences for customary marriages concluded prior to the commencement of the Act, while it creates different requirements and consequences (which are in many respects similar to those applying to civil marriages) for customary marriages entered into after its coming into operation.[13]

Questions are asked about the constitutionality of the Recognition of Customary Marriages Act 120 of 1998. The Constitution in Article 9(3) and (4) enshrines the right not to be unfairly discriminated against on grounds of culture. Article 30 affords everyone the right to participate in the cultural life of their choice, while Article 31(1)(a) provides that persons belonging to a cultural community may not be denied the right to enjoy their culture. These rights, however, may not be exercised in a way which is inconsistent with provisions of the Bill of Rights. Customary law is part of culture, and the recognition of customary marriages invokes the right to culture and the right not to be unfairly discriminated against on grounds of culture. The problem then arises that some of the elements of culture are seen to be unfair discrimination against women on grounds of sex and gender, infringing on their right to dignity.

Article 15(3)(b) of the Constitution also comes into play, when it allows for marriages under any tradition, or system of personal and family law under any tradition. The Recognition of Customary Marriages Act falls squarely under Article 15(3), which provides that legislation recognizing the particular marriages or systems of law must be consistent with the rights contained in Article 15 and other provisions of the Constitution. Once again, it is claimed that the practices regarding customary marriages, such as the rules on the acquisition and administration of house and family property, the practice of *lobola* ('bride price'), and the practice of polygyny, may infringe on sex and gender equality and violate the right to dignity unjustifiably.[14]

10 Cronjé and Heaton, supra note 3 at 191.

11 Skelton et al., *Familiereg in Suid-Afrika*, supra note 1 at 200.

12 Recognition of Customary Marriages, Act 120 of 1998. For a discussion and references on whether customary marriage applies only to black people in South Africa or whether it also applies to other indigenous peoples, such as Namas, Bushmen, and Griquas, see Cronjé and Heaton, supra note 3 at 191 n.3.

13 Cronjé and Heaton, supra note 3 at 191.

14 Cronjé and Heaton, supra note 3 at 208–211.

3. Civil Union

The Civil Union Act 17 of 2006 provides a framework for people of the same gender to formalize and legalize their relationship through a civil union.[15] Some argue that this Act regulates only the monogamous union of two persons of the same gender.[16] It is not always clear from the Act itself that it provides for heterosexual unions as well.[17] The law describes a civil union as 'the voluntary union of two persons who are both 18 years of age or older, which is solemnised and registered by way of either a marriage or a civil partnership, in accordance with the procedures prescribed [in the Civil Union Act], to the exclusion while it lasts, of all others'.[18] A marriage or a partnership in accordance with the Civil Union Act has the same consequences as a marriage according to the Marriage Act. Any reference to the term 'marriage', 'man', 'wife', 'spouse' in any other law, including common law, includes a civil union or a party to a civil union. Furthermore there are unique prescriptions with regard to the formal and material legal requirements for civil unions, such as that an *ex officio* marriage officer or a religious marriage officer can conduct a civil union. The same requirements regarding blood and family relations apply to both marriages and civil unions. The Civil Union Act also allows for *ex officio* marriage officers to refuse to conduct civil unions on grounds of conscience, religion, and faith.[19]

The fact that the mentioned marriages and unions are regulated by law means that the persons in the relationship enjoy certain rights and duties with regard to matters such as privacy, dwelling(s) and property(s), pension funds, medical aid schemes, insurance, and the right to support. They also have rights and duties with regard to children, immigration, inheritance, subsistence, compensation in case of injuries at work or of illness, and protection against violence.[20]

Before 27 April 1994, the law paid very little attention to alternative family structures because civil marriage was the only state-recognized option available. The concept of civil marriage had two key elements: (1) A marriage was a monogamous relationship between heterosexual persons. (2) A marriage was civil in the sense that this type of marriage was sanctioned by the state in that it was conducted according to the Marriage Act.

In 1983, in *Ismael v. Ismael*, the Appeal Court declared a marriage to be 'the legally recognized voluntary union for life of one man and one woman to the exclusion of all others while it lasts'.[21]

The new Constitution of 1996 with the Bill of Rights had an immediate and drastic influence on the marriage situation in South Africa. This was effected especially through the equality clauses and the Equality Act. For the first time in South Africa every person could claim equality before the law and equal protection by the law. Apart from equality, the Bill of Rights also prohibited unfair discrimination, *inter alia*, on grounds of race, religion, and sexual orientation. The implication of this was that in due course the judicial recognition of marriage as an exclusive heterosexual institution came under attack. A string of court cases followed in which the rights of spouses were gradually extended to partners of the same sex.

15 Skelton et al., *Familiereg in Suid-Afrika* supra note 1 at 196–197.

16 Civil Union Act 17 of 2006.

17 Skelton et al., *Familiereg in Suid-Afrika* supra note 1 at 189.

18 Skelton et al., *Familiereg in Suid-Afrika* supra note 1 at 189.

19 Skelton et al., *Familiereg in Suid-Afrika* supra note 1 at 197.

20 Women's Legal Centre, *Ken U Regte 'n Maklike Gids tot Huwelike en verhoudings* [*Know Your Rights: A Quick Guide to Marriage and Relationships*] (2007), 1–25.

21 *Ismael v. Ismael* 1983 (1) SA 1006 (A).

Judicially, recognition of same-sex marriage began in 2002 when a lesbian couple, Marié Adriaana Fourie and Cecelia Johanna Bonthuys, asked the High Court of the Transvaal in Pretoria, currently the Northern Gauteng High Court, for an order to force the Minister of the Interior to register their marriage in terms of the Marriage Act. When the High Court rejected the request the couple sought other routes to have their marriage legally recognised. Finally on 1 December 2005 the highest court in South Africa, the Constitutional Court, made a decision that paved the way for marriages between same-sex couples to be legally registered. The Court ruled that the common law description of a marriage as a monogamous relationship between heterosexual persons was inconsistent with the Constitution and was invalid to the extent that it did not allow for same sex couples to enjoy the same status, advantages and responsibilities awarded through marriage to heterosexual couples.[22] The Court also ruled that Article 31(1) of the Marriage Act, which contains the marriage formula, is equally unconstitutional because it contained words like 'husband' and 'wife' instead of a gender neutral term like 'spouse'.[23] The court suspended its ruling for twelve months to give the legislature time to prepare the necessary legislation for same sex-couples to get married.[24] Should that not happen within a year's time, the Court ruled that Article 30(1) of the marriage law must be read as if it provided for spouses to get married.[25]

On 30 November of 2006 the Civil Union Act of 2006 took effect. The aim of the act was to regulate the solemnization and registration of civil unions and to provide for the results of such unions. In the Act a civil union is described as 'the voluntary union of two persons who are both 18 years of age or older, which is solemnised and registered by way of either a marriage or a civil partnership, in accordance with the procedures prescribed [in the Civil Union Act], to the exclusion while it lasts, of all other'.[26]

The Constitutional Court also ruled that religious institutions would remain undisturbed in their ability to perform marriage ceremonies according to their own tenets, celebrating, if they desired, heterosexual marriages only. 'The principle of reasonable accommodation could be applied by the state to ensure that civil marriage officers who had sincere religious objections to officiating at same sex marriages would not themselves be obliged to do so if this resulted in a violation of their conscience.'[27]

With reference to its holding in *Christian Education v. Minister of Education,* the Court observed the following:

> The underlying problem in any open and democratic society based on human dignity, equality and freedom in which conscientious and religious freedom has to be regarded with appropriate seriousness, is how far such democracy can and must go in allowing members of religious communities to define for themselves which laws they will obey and which not. Such society can cohere only if all its participants accept that certain basic norms and standards are binding. Accordingly, believers cannot claim an

22 *Minister of Home Affairs and Another v. Fourie and Another* [*Fourie*] (CCT 60/04) [2005] ZACC 19; 2006 (3) BCLR 355 (CC); 2006 (1) SA 524 (CC) (1 December 2005) at para. 162 (2.b).

23 *Fourie* at para. 162 (2.c).

24 *Fourie* at para. 162 (2.d).

25 *Fourie* at para. 162 (2.e).

26 Civil Union Act, Art 1.

27 Justice Sachs, *Minister of Home Affairs v. Fourie* at para 159.

> automatic right to be exempted by their beliefs from the laws of the land. At the same time, *the State should, wherever reasonably possible, seek to avoid putting believers to extremely painful and intensely burdensome choices of either being true to their faith or else respectful of the law.*[28]
>
> (Emphasis in original.)

4. Domestic Partnership

As in many other countries of the world, domestic partnerships, also called 'life partnerships',[29] have become increasingly common in South Africa. Legal thinking about these kinds of relationships developed after 1994, when people began to see marriage as only one of several forms for a union between people.[30] Couples who prefer not to marry or who cannot marry but desire a permanent stable monogamous relationship with the same responsibilities and duties as married couples may choose to consider themselves to be in such a partnership.[31] Economic reasons, the need for procreation, or an aversion to the legal restrictions or the religious requirements of a marriage may motivate a preference for just living together in a domestic partnership rather than entering into a formal marriage.

In South Africa there is currently no law regulating domestic partnerships, which implies that such partnerships are not recognized or protected by law. The result is that the consequences which usually flow from a civil or customary marriage are not applicable to domestic partnerships. There is also no or very little legal protection for such partnerships in terms of the common law.[32] The partners must make a contract with one another, which is then known as a co-habitation contract, or they must make use of other legal aids, which are usually insufficient, in order to apply some of the consequences of a civil marriage or a civil partnership to a domestic partnership. If a couple makes use of a contract, their rights and duties will be dependent on the express stipulations of the contract. In January 2008 a draft Domestic-Partnership Bill was published. When this bill is promulgated, it will regulate the legal position of domestic partnerships.

In spite of the absence of a law with regard to domestic partnerships, the courts of the land, especially after 1994 and the Bill of Rights in the Constitution, have begun to give greater recognition to domestic partnerships. Nevertheless, the fact remains that, as of late 2014, the legal position with regard to domestic partnerships remained inconsistent and fragmented, and same-sex couples and heterosexual couples in domestic partnerships were treated differently.[33]

As no other forms of marriage or union are valid under South African law, couples who want to live in a legally recognized relationship are limited to one of the above mentioned forms of marriage or union.

28 *Fourie* at para. 159, fn 160, citing *Christian Education South Africa v. Minister of Education* 2000 (4) SA 757 (CC); 2000 (10) 1051 (CC) at para. 76.

29 Cronjé and Heaton, supra note 3 at 234.

30 Skelton et al., *Familiereg in Suid-Afrika*, supra note 1 at 229.

31 Women's Legal Centre, supra note 20 at 22.

32 *Volks NO v. Robinson* 55; SARHK2006:110, 111, in Skelton et al., *Familiereg in Suid-Afrika*, supra note 1 at 22.

33 Skelton et al., *Familiereg in Suid-Afrika*, supra note 1 at 229.

Marriage and Religion in Modern South Africa

Marriage and the Church

General Synod 2004 of the Dutch Reformed Church in South Africa was presented with a report concerning homosexuality expressing the view that the Bible is not a historical or scientific handbook that gave us 'full knowledge' of every aspect of reality. It was therefore, said the report, the task of the Church, while remaining loyal to the confession that the Bible is the Word of God, to consider how Scripture must be interpreted in a specific time. This resulted in a new report about homosexuality, brought before the Synod, containing the views of experts and members with a homosexual orientation as well as the opinions of members who had been freed from homosexualism. The Synod was asked to take note of the fact that there is not unanimity in the Church about homosexuality. The Synod was also asked to consider whether the negative views about homosexuality in Scripture can be applied to homosexuality in general and specifically to homosexuals in permanent relationships of love and trust. It was stated before the Synod that all persons, apart from their sexual orientation, were objects of God's love, and they should be accepted as full members of the Church solely on ground of their faith. All homosexual as well as heterosexual promiscuity was condemned, and an unequivocal apology was made to all homosexuals and their families where the love of God was not made visible in the Church's treatment of them in the past.[34]

In the years after 2004 the Dutch Reformed Church and other churches in South Africa have often been taken to task because of their views on homosexuality and same-sex marriages. In some cases it was homosexual persons who threatened to take the churches to court for discrimination against them in not allowing them into the preaching office in the church or for not recognizing their same-sex marriages, or for dismissing a homosexual employee of the church. They claim that the attitude of churches and religions towards homosexual persons and against Civil Unions, and the exclusion of these persons and unions, violate their human rights. According to arguments such as those made by homosexual TV producer and former pastor Pieter Cilliers, author of an autobiography[35] praised for its role in pioneering discussion of homosexuality and the church, it is a matter of a battle between human rights and equality on the one hand and religious rights on the other hand, and the fact that religions claim that it is their right to discriminate against homosexual persons.[36] The rights of religious believers to regulate their affairs according to deeply held beliefs do not have weight in such discussions.

Marriage and Voluntary Associations

As this discussion was going on in churches in South Africa and in the same year (2005) that the *Fourie* case was heard, the South African Human Rights Commission (SAHRC) conducted a public enquiry after it received complaints alleging violations of the rights to equality and dignity from persons excluded from joining voluntary associations (VAs). The

34 See Piet Strauss, *Kerkwees in die Branding. Die Nederduitse Gereformeerde Kerk in algemene sinodale verband 1994–2011* (2013), manuscript at http://www.ajol.info/index.php/actat/article/view/102539 (accessed 21 October 2015).

35 Pieter Cilliers, *'n Kas is vir Klere* (Human & Rousseau 2007), translated into English as *Pilgrim* (Protea Boekhuis 2013).

36 *Die Burger*, BY, Saturday 8 June 2013, 3.

purpose of the enquiry was to enable the SAHRC to hear representations of all interested parties and to reflect on the relevant constitutional and statutory provisions in order to suggest a set of principles that would achieve an appropriate balance between associational rights and the rights of equality and dignity. The context of the enquiry required the balancing of two distinct sets of rights. On the one hand there are the fundamental rights to be treated equally, not to be unfairly discriminated against and the rights to dignity. On the other hand are the cluster of rights, sometimes collectively called associational rights, which include freedom of association, freedom of religion, freedom to practice and use one's language, religion, and culture, and the right to associate in cultural, religious and linguistic communities.

In the end the SAHRC recommended that VAs that wanted to implement exclusionary policies had to take certain guidelines or legal principles into account. A church or a religion that sets up rules of not allowing practicing homosexuals into the preaching office or not employing them, or that refuses to acknowledge civil unions would be good examples of such VAs. The guidelines they recommended are that the VA:

(i) Identify the right or interest that it seeks to protect, such as the faith identity or the spirituality of the church.
(ii) Identify the rights that may be infringed or limited by the adoption of a certain policy, such as the constitutional rights of practicing homosexuals in terms of Article 9(3) of the Constitution.
(iii) Determine alternative ways of achieving its objectives.
(iv) Adopt the alternative that achieves its objectives without unreasonably and unfairly limiting or restricting rights.
(v) Maintain reasons as to why a particular method or means was adopted and other alternatives discarded or disregarded.[37]

This would mean that proper decisions would be made at the outset and would reflect the necessary deliberation and balancing that needs to be done in order to arrive at a constitutionally permissible conclusion.

One of the oral presentations made during this process was that of S.C. Woolman, Professor of Law at the University of Pretoria, who made his presentation in his personal capacity and on behalf of the South African Board of Jewish Education, SABJE. Much of what he said can also be applicable for churches and religions in South Africa in their relationship to Civil Unions and Lifelong partnerships. As Professor Woolman explained,

> All the schools controlled by the SABJE are, in terms of the South African Schools Act, designated as independent schools. The SABJE has a history of allowing non-Jewish children to attend their schools and employing non-Jewish educators. Their schools however insist that all students admitted to the schools must adhere to and abide by the requirements of a Jewish education, undertake Hebrew language instructions, observe Jewish religious instructions and participate in all school sponsored religious events. The application forms make it clear that the goals of the schools are to inculcate respect for the Jewish religion, its traditions, customs and institutions and to further the Zionist aims of the Jewish people. Parents and pupils admitted to the schools are required to

37 South African Human Rights Commission, *The Exclusionary Policies of Voluntary Associations: Constitutional Considerations* (2006), 31, http://www.gov.za/sites/www.gov.za/files/exclusionary%20polices%20of%20voluntary%20associations.pdf (accessed 21 October 2015).

> abide by the policies and participate in all activities of the school. Thus, while the SABJE schools do not exclude non-Jewish children and non-Jewish educators, their admission is controlled in order to maintain the Jewish identity of the school.[38]

In Professor Woolman's view, the school's admission policies do not amount to unfair discrimination, and if there is differentiation on a specified ground, 'the admission policy constitutes fair discrimination as it is grounded in the legitimate objectives of the SABJE and its schools.'[39]

> [Woolman] conceded that the admission policy, which provides that an applicant who refuses to take Hebrew classes or Jewish religious instructions should be refused admission, could be interpreted as either imposing indirect burdens or withholding benefits from a student on grounds of religion. If this is the case, then the differentiation is deemed to be discrimination, and according to section 9 of the Constitution and the Equality Act, the onus of proving fairness rests on the school. According to Prof. Woolman the discriminatory admissions policy is necessary to achieve the object of SABJE of offering a Jewish education, including Hebrew language classes and Jewish religious instructions. He also pointed out that in the urban centre of Johannesburg, a child in a position to afford private school fees has a great array of options opened to him or her. There is no compulsion either directly or indirectly for non-Jewish children to seek admission to SABJE controlled schools.
>
> Based on the decision of *Van Dijkhorst J in Wittman v Deutscher Schulverein*, he concludes that the constitutional right to set up and run an independent school grounded in culture, language or religion inevitably includes the right to exclude students who do not wish to adhere to school requirements that are grounded in language, culture or religion. Given the clear choice enjoyed by non-Jewish children to attend other private schools, the restrictive admission policies impact marginally on their dignity. The restrictive admission policies are however necessary in order to preserve the cultural, and religious character of the schools. Professor Woolman also referred to whether SABJE could limit entrance of non-Jewish students in order to preserve its objectives. The question is hypothetical in respect of the operations of the SABJE schools but very pertinent for the purposes of the SAHRC report. Prof. Woolman concluded that the only proper basis for a completely exclusionary practice would be to prevent 'capture'. He defined capture as the legitimate fear that the new members of the community could, after having obtained sufficient numbers, move to fundamentally alter the character of the school.
>
> [Notes omitted.][40]

Religious Marriage

Many religious people in South Africa, from Jewish, Muslim, and Hindu traditions, live according to their religious family law. This should have been the case with Christianity as well, but Christianity is not treated as a separate religious legal system with its own identity in the courts or in the legal handbooks in South Africa. It is simply accepted that the Marriage Act portrays Christian values.

38 *Exclusionary Policies* . . . supra note 37 at 7.

39 *Exclusionary Policies* . . . supra note 37 at 7.

40 *Exclusionary Policies* . . . supra note 37 at 7–8.

The Supreme Court of Appeal in the 1983 case *Ismael v. Ismael* held that the marriage law in South Africa was rooted in Christianity, and that any marriage which did not comply with such values was invalid.[41] This view is not correct and must be questioned. The reason for the view probably lies in history, in the so called Constantinian relationship between church and state. This view entails that from the time of Constantine the state protected the Christian religion but at the same time also ruled over the religion. Christian religion was used to legitimize the laws and the policies of the state. It was accepted that the marriage law of the state portrayed the Christian view of marriage. Since this was often favorable for Christianity, the Church accepted this view and never really asked the question whether a law of the state could be dangerous for the faith identity of the Church.

Exactly this danger is addressed in the *Barmen Declaration* of 1934 when the Church in Germany had to make a stand against the policies of National Socialism. This resulted in the wording of Articles 17 and 18 of the Declaration:

> (17) The Christian Church is the congregation of brethren in which Jesus Christ acts presently as the Lord in Word and sacrament through the Holy Spirit. As the Church of pardoned sinners, it has to testify in the midst of a sinful world, with its faith as with its obedience, with its message as with its order, that it is solely his property, and that it lives and wants to live solely from his comfort and from his direction in the expectation of his appearance.
>
> (18) We reject the false doctrine, as though the Church were permitted to abandon the form of its message and order to its own pleasure or to changes in prevailing ideological and political convictions.'[42]

The Civil Marriage Act in South Africa portrays the civil values of society which can be questioned in many ways and can certainly not be said truly to portray Christian convictions and values. Christians in South Africa therefore would profit from taking up the opportunity which the new Constitution[43] of the country offers to develop Christian legal rules for Christian religious marriages in South Africa.

The other religions mentioned above have legal rules and institutions for the marriage of their followers, even though their religious marriages are not recognized by law in South Africa.[44] The religious rules for the various marriages are applied by unofficial religious institutions. It is the task of the Beth Din for the Jews and the Ulama for the Muslims to apply the religious rules. For the South African Hindus the Maha Sabha is the largest overarching body to which Hindu organizations in South Africa belong.[45] It has happened that South African courts have recognized the consequences of these invalid religious marriages in accordance with the rules of the religion concerned. Lesala Mofokeng writes in this regard, 'It must be borne in mind that the courts have recognised certain aspects of the consequences of religious marriages other than Christian marriages, albeit that they are invalid.'[46]

41 *Ismael v. Ismael* 1983 (1) SA 1006 (A).

42 *Theological Declaration of Barmen*, http://www.sacred-texts.com/chr/barmenhtm (accessed 4 November 2013).

43 SA Const., Art. 31.

44 Lesala L. Mofokeng, *Legal Pluralism in South Africa: Aspects of African Customary, Muslim and Hindu Family Law* (Van Schaik Publishers 2009), 25.

45 Skelton et al., *Familiereg in Suid-Afrika*, supra note 1 at 213.

46 Mofokeng, supra note 44 at 25.

Legal scholars argue that the new constitutional dispensation in South Africa, with the values of human dignity, equality, and freedom as the cornerstones of democracy, requires that the religious rules according to which people live and how these rules are adhered to in the religious bodies be looked at anew in the light of the Constitution. Article 15 of the Constitution, read together with Articles 30, 31, 181(1)(c), and 185, recognizes and protects the cultural and religious diversity of South African society. Many of the arguments in favour of customary marriages and the law on the Recognition of Customary Marriages[47] can also be used to argue for the right of religious marriages to be legally recognized. The way in which a distinction is made between customary marriages and religious marriages is in contradiction to the constitutional right of equality before the law as well as to the right to equal protection and benefit by the law.[48]

In the same way as has been provided for customary marriages, provision should be made for the legal recognition of a plurality of religious marriages in the South African legal system. One of the arguments for the recognition of a plurality of religious marriages is that the claim to legal pluralism according to sections/Articles 15, 30, 31, and 39(1) of the Constitution is of little value unless it is substantiated by real legal pluralism. An important part of religious freedom is that people who claim that right must also have the right and the opportunity to exercise that right according to their convictions and in doing this no particular legal system should be given preferential treatment over any other. 'The freedom of religion clause should be interpreted in a manner that would guarantee linguistic and religious communities the right to have their private law matters regulated in accordance with the personal laws of their choice, provided they do not conflict with the spirit and values of the Constitution.'[49] It is important that the religions themselves take up this challenge and start the process for the legal recognition of religious marriages. If they do not, they will have to be satisfied with the way they are treated by the laws of the land and the fact that they are judged by the courts of the land in terms of the existing laws of the state.

For the Christian religion there is ample space and much necessity to write Christian principles and values into a Christian religious legal framework for marriages. One of the challenges for Christians will be to develop a view of marriage that is in accordance with what the Bible teaches. In Christianity, as in many other religions and societies, marriage is often seen as a patriarchal institution in which the man is the head of the home and also of the wife and she is completely subjected to the husband. The question is whether the relationship between men and women, and especially between a Christian husband and his Christian wife, must always be seen in such a way or does Scripture show another way for people who are in Christ?

It is the view of this author that an appropriate text for answering this question is found in the writings of the Apostle Paul to the Ephesians. In Ephesians 5 and 6 we can find the so-called 'house rules' of a Christian style of life – relations between husbands and wives (5:22–30), parents and children (6:1–4), owners and slaves (6:5–9) – all of which must be seen against the call in Ephesians 5:18 that Christians must be filled with the Holy Spirit.[50] This in turn must again be seen against the background of verses such as Ephesians 1:23:

47 Act 120 of 1998.

48 Skelton et al., *Familiereg in Suid-Afrika*, supra note 1 at 213–215; Cronjé and Heaton, supra note 3 at 223.

49 Mofokeng, supra note 44 at 163.

50 Heinrich Schlier, *Der Brief an der Epheser. Ein Kommentar* (Patmos Verlag 1957), 250 ff.

'The Church is Christ's body, the completion of him who himself completes all things everywhere.'[51] And Ephesians 4:15–16:

> By speaking the truth in a spirit of love, we must grow up in every way to Christ, who is the head. Under his control all different parts of the body fit together, and the whole body is held together by every joint with which it is provided. So when each separate part works as it should the whole body grows and builds itself up through love.

This brings us to Ephesians 5:21, where Paul writes, 'Submit yourselves to one another, because of your reverence for Christ.' For Christian husbands and wives the new life in Christ does not mean a total submission of only the wife to the husband but a submission of both the husband to the wife and of the wife to the husband because they revere Christ. What this reciprocal submission means for each is spelt out in the following verses of Ephesians 5, ending with verse 33: '[E]very husband must love his wife as himself, and every wife must respect her husband.'

The words of Ephesians 5:21 are words that must be taken very seriously if Christians want to rethink the foundations and principles of a Christian marriage in our times. A Christian marriage must be built on a fundamental reciprocal relationship of submission and service between both husband and wife to each other out of reverence for Christ.

The Way Forward

In July 2014, the United Nations launched the *Free and Equal* campaign for global public education, to raise awareness of homophobic violence and discrimination, and to promote greater respect for the rights of lesbian, gay, bisexual, transgender, and intersex (LGBTI) people everywhere. In speaking in favor of the campaign, Archbishop Desmond Tutu remarked that not necessarily everything that is written in the Bible is true, that he cannot worship a homophobic God, and that he refuses to go to a homophobic heaven and would rather go to the other place.[52] Such words, especially coming from someone with the stature of Archbishop Tutu, seem less than helpful in finding a legal and civil balance between the religious rights of voluntary associations and the rights of LGBTI people.

Certainly, from their side, churches and religions should not just issue a blank rejection of all LGBTI members of their organizations. All human beings have a right to be members of a church or a religion and to enjoy the full membership rights, to be regarded in their dignity as persons, to be taken seriously and treated with respect. And Christians are under obligation to show love and compassion for all.

At the same time, the constitutional right to freedom of religion and freedom of association allows churches and religions to set up and run their organizations according to their deepest religious convictions. This inevitably implies the right to exclude persons who do not desire to adhere to the religious requirements for membership that are grounded in the organization's faith convictions.

Churches do have the religious freedom and right to confess and exercise their belief in Scripture and its authority. They also have the right to decide on their confessions of faith and which religious order they want to have in the church or religion and how the

51 *Good News for Modern Man: The New Testament in Today's English Version* (American Bible Society, 2nd edn, 1966).

52 *Die Burger*, Saturday 27 July 2013, 1.

decisions to exercise these rights must be taken in order to be valid in the church and not in contravention of the Constitution. Churches and religions also have the right to define their requirements for membership and to expect that any member or prospective member must comply with the requirements to become a member or to stay a member of the church. On the grounds of their faith identity, churches also have the right to terminate the membership of existing members who act in contravention of the membership requirements on matters, for instance, such as immorality, greediness, adultery, the worshipping of idols, robbery, slander, drunkenness, deceitfulness, and the practice of homosexuality. Churches are often reluctant to act against members who contravene such membership requirements, and this opens them to the justifiable criticism that they do not live up to their faith convictions.

Churches and religions also have the right to determine the requirements for office bearers and other persons in their service in accordance with their faith identity. Many religious organizations, for instance, have strict rules of not allowing women as office bearers. It is their right to take and keep this position. They must however be able to show why their view is an integral part of their faith identity. If a religious organization does not avail itself of and explicitly express its faith identity, and it is brought before a court, the court has no choice but to apply the laws of the land as they are. At the same time, a religious organization has the right to protect its religion and religious convictions and values. One could say it has the right to protect its faith identity against capturing, which means that the church or religion can take preventive measures to protect its faith identity against those who want to change that identity for their own benefit.

It is very important that churches and religions clearly identify and state their faith identity on, for instance, requirements for membership as well as their requirements for employees in accordance with their faith identity. They must do this when they allow new members and when they set up contracts of employment. If they do not do this they will be judged in a court of law according to the existing laws of the land.

Religious organizations cannot deny membership to believing persons of homosexual orientation, nor can they not allow such persons to be eligible for offices in accordance with the organization's expressed rules. Churches or religions can, however, expect homosexual members to comply with the requirements for membership and eligibility for an office in order to protect the organization's faith identity. Such a policy will not amount to unfair discrimination; to the contrary it will constitute fair discrimination as it is grounded in the legitimate and expressed faith identity of the church or religion. Expecting homosexual members to remain celibate can be seen as imposing indirect burdens or withholding benefits of a church or religion. If this is the case the differentiation is deemed to be discrimination according to section 9 of the Constitution and the Equality Act. This places the onus of proving fairness on the religious organization, which will have to show that the discrimination is necessary in order to protect and promote its expressed faith identity. There are churches that provide membership for practicing homosexuals and homosexual partners, so that it can be said that there is no compulsion for practicing homosexuals to seek membership of a church for whom the practicing of homosexualism is against its faith identity.

These are rights that churches and religions have, and they may profess and exercise these rights in terms of Article 15 of the Constitution. While religious organizations must respect the fact that there are people who fundamentally disagree with them on many issues, they can also rightfully expect that their right to freedom of religion will be respected by those who fundamentally differ from them, especially if these people insist that their own rights must be accepted by churches. It is a matter of finding the balance between the individual rights of equity and dignity and the associational right to freedom of religion.

9 A Fissure within the Human Rights System?

Same-Sex Marriage Claims and Religious Freedom of Speech

Ursula C. Basset

The Transformative Power of Same-Sex Marriage

Whoever thought that same-sex marriage was exclusively an issue concerning the right to marry of individuals with a determinate sexual orientation evidently underestimated the impact of redefining marriage.

First, marriage has always been a cornerstone of family law.[1] The shift in the meaning of marriage unavoidably implies a modification of the rights, duties, and juristic affiliations traditionally attached to marriage: legal filiation, kinship, legal obligations stemming from family relations, succession laws, social benefits, and many others. So, at the outset, to redefine marriage implies a deep reform of almost every legal institution bound with marriage, as comparative studies from Spain,[2] France[3] and Argentina[4] show, and as is indicated by the observations of Lord Dear during the debate in the United Kingdom's House of Lords[5] and the opinion of the United States Supreme Court in *Windsor.*[6]

However, the expansive power of the redefinition of marriage does not stop at the gate of the human rights system. The latter was built on the premises of a heterosexual definition of marriage.[7] Any intent to read a right to same-sex marriage into the human

1 Lynn Wardle, 'The Morality of Marriage and the Transformative Power of Inclusion', in Lynn Wardle, ed., *What's the Harm?* (University Press of America 2009), 207–238.

2 D. José Luis Bazán, *Informe sobre el impacto de la ley española del matrimonio entre personas del mismo sexo en el derecho interno* (Profesionales por la Ética – Servicio Jurídico 2009), http://www.profesionalesetica.org/wp-content/uploads/2010/01/Informe-sobre-el-impacto-de-la-ley-del-matrimonio-entre-personas-del-mismo-sexo-VF2.pdf (accessed 23 October 2015).

3 Hugues Fulchiron, 'La reconnaissance de la famille homosexuelle: étude d'impact', *Recueil Dalloz*, 18 January 2013.

4 Ursula C. Basset, 'How the Battle to Redefine Marriage Affected Family Law in Argentina', (2013) 27 *Brigham Young University Journal of Public Law* (2), 529–540.

5 Parliamentary Business, Publications & Records, House of Lords, Monday, 3 June 2013, Marriage (Same Sex Couples Bill), Second Reading: col. 942, 3.25 pm, Lord Dear: 'This House is asked to debate and examine a Bill that has not yet come anywhere near identifying all the consequences of change. The official government estimate of the numbers of amendments to existing legislation that would follow should the Bill become law is, in their words, at least 8,000 and they are still counting' http://www.publications.parliament.uk/pa/ld201314/ldhansrd/text/130603-0001.htm#13060312000364 (accessed 22 October 2015).

6 *United States v. Windsor*, 133 S.Ct. 2675, 2683 (2013): 'The enactment's comprehensive definition of marriage for purposes of all federal statutes and other regulations or directives covered by its terms . . . does control over 1,000 federal laws in which marital or spousal status is addressed as a matter of federal law.'

7 This was the interpretation of the European Court of Human Rights in the ruling *Schalk and Kopf v. Austria*, App. no. 30141/04 (ECtHR, 24 June 2010), §§ 54–55:

rights treaties[8] relies invariably upon either avoiding language which expressly refers to opposite-sex couples or calling for a progressive interpretation of the original wording.[9] Each alternative causes a structural imbalance in the previously harmonious human rights system.

For one thing, the clash between religious liberty in the public sphere and the same-sex marriage paradigm is a notorious outcome of the debate.[10] The long list of publications cited throughout this chapter is vivid proof of concern as to how to address these new tensions between the redefinition of marriage on the one hand and religious liberty and freedom of speech on the other.

> The Court notes that Article 12 grants the right to marry to 'men and women'. The French version provides 'l'homme et la femme ont le droit de se marier'. Furthermore, Article 12 grants the right to found a family . . . The Court observes that, looked at in isolation, the wording of Article 12 might be interpreted so as not to exclude the marriage between two men or two women. However, in contrast, all other substantive Articles of the Convention grant rights and freedoms to 'everyone' or state that 'no one' is to be subjected to certain types of prohibited treatment. The choice of wording in Article 12 must thus be regarded as deliberate. Moreover, regard must be had to the historical context in which the Convention was adopted. In the 1950s marriage was clearly understood in the traditional sense of being a union between partners of different sex.

Nevertheless, in paragraphs 61–4 the majority vote of the Court opened the door to a progressive interpretation: 'the Court would no longer consider [that] the right to marry enshrined in Article 12 must in all circumstances be limited to marriage between two persons of the opposite sex.' However, the Court did not impose 'an obligation on the respondent Government to grant a same-sex couple like the applicants access to marriage'. Judge Malinverni, joined by Judge Kovler, issued a concurring opinion in which, relying on the Vienna Convention on the Law of Treaties, he concluded that it could not be inferred that Article 12, read jointly with Article 9 of the Charter, applied to same-sex couples. See also Robert John Araujo, S.J., 'Marriage, Relationship, and International Law: The Incoherence of the Argument for Same-Sex Marriage', in Lynn D. Wardle, Mark Strasser, William C. Duncan and David Orgon Coolidge, eds, *Marriage and Same-Sex Unions. A Debate* (Praeger 2003), 367–379.

8 While other rights are recognized as extending to 'every human being', each time the right to marry is mentioned in international treaties, it is ascribed to men and women. The sexual differentiation appears to be significant only in the case of the right to marry. See for instance Article16.1, UDHR; Article 10, ICESCR; Article 23.2 ICCPR; Articles 9 and 16, CEDAW; Article 17.2, ACHR; Article 12, ECHR. (The CFR, however, uses gender-neutral wording in its Article 9).

9 This was invariably the case in Argentina's challenges to Article 172, which established that marriage could be contracted between a man and a woman. A synthesis of those challenges can be consulted in Ursula Basset, 'Ley 26.618 de matrimonio "gender neutral" ', *Doctrina Judicial*, La Ley, 2010/36 (2482–2491).

10 To quote only a few instances of concern: Douglas Laycock, Anthony R. Picarello, Jr., and Robin Fretwell Wilson, eds, *Same-Sex Marriage and Religious Liberty: Emerging Conflicts* (Rowman & Littlefield 2008); Gordon A. Babst, Emily R. Gill and Jason Pierceson, *Moral Argument, Religion, and Same-Sex Marriage: Advancing the Public Good* (Lexington Books 2009); Roger Severino, 'Or for Poorer? How Same-Sex Marriage Threatens Religious Liberty', (2007) 30 *Harvard Journal of Law and Public Policy* (3), 939–982; Thomas C. Berg, 'What Same-Sex Marriage and Religious-Liberty Claims Have in Common', (2010) 5 *Northwestern Journal of Law & Social Policy* (2), 205–235; Andrew Koppelman, 'You Can't Hurry Love: Why Antidiscrimination Protections for Gay People Should Have Religious Exemptions', (2006) 72 *Brooklyn Law Review* (1), 125–146; George W. Dent, Jr., 'Civil Rights for Whom?: Gay Rights versus Religious Freedom', (2006) 95 *Kentucky Law Journal* 553; Michael J. Perry, 'Christians, the Bible, and Same-Sex Unions: An Argument for Political Self-Restraint', (2001) 36 *Wake Forest Law Review* 449–485; Colleen Theresa Rutledge, 'Caught in the Crossfire: How Catholic Charities of Boston Was Victim to the Clash between Gay Rights and Religious Freedom', (2008) 15 *Duke Journal of Gender Law & Policy* (1/2) 297–314; Ira C. Lupu and Robert W. Tuttle, 'Same-Sex Family Equality and Religious Freedom', (2010) 5 *Northwestern Journal of Law & Social Policy* (2) 273–306.

Third, there is a cultural shift to which many authors have pointed. Some speak of 'culture wars'.[11] Others see a deep chasm running through our societies.[12] Still, the most significant effect of the redefinition of marriage is one we should reflect upon thoroughly, for its yet uncertain implications. Two great contemporary minds signaled the anthropologic impact of gender neutrality. The French anthropologist Françoise Héritier put it this way:

> La différence des sexes – à la fois anatomique, physiologique et fonctionnelle – est à la base de la création de l'opposition fondamentale qui permet de penser. Car penser c'est d'abord classer, et classer c'est d'abord discriminer. Ceci est un *fait* irréductible: de même que l'on ne peut nier l'opposition du jour et de la nuit, on ne peut pas davantage décréter que la différence des sexes n'existe pas.[13]

More recently, Julia Kristeva, a Bulgarian-French psychoanalyst, debating on the impact of same-sex marriage in that field, said: 'C'est la parentalité, avec hétérosexualité en nous, qui est 'la part problématique': l'hétérosexualité est le problème des problèmes, le fondement de la tiercéité, et en ce sens le problème personnel et universel par excellence.'[14]

If these thinkers were right, our discussions about religious freedom and marriage would become a pale epiphenomenon compared with the depth of the challenges we will be facing.

These introductory considerations are offered with the sole purpose of showing the framework of the concrete issues we are dealing with. If the social norm of sexual diversity (heteronormativity) is supplanted by one of gender neutrality, we will probably have to adapt our *Weltanschauungs*. This new principle (gender neutrality) will be the cornerstone to which we will have to adapt – the note by which we will be required to tune – not only in private law, but also in the human rights system, and probably, as Mme Héritier implied, in the very foundations of how we conceive reality.

As a matter of fact, this has been the path Argentina has been traveling. Every single law touching upon any issue related with family, identity, procreation, or similar subjects has contained a provision expressly enshrining the general principle that the law should be interpreted consistently with gender equality.[15] This clause acts as a paramount principle,[16] ensuring that the text can never

11 Charles P. Kindregan, Jr., 'Same-Sex Marriage: The Cultural Wars and Lessons of Legal History', (2004) 38 *Family Law Quarterly* (2) 427–447; Richard F. Duncan, 'Wigstock and the Kulturkampf: Supreme Court Storytelling, the Culture War, and *Romer v. Evans*', (1996) 72 *Notre Dame Law Review* (2) 345–372.

12 William Duncan analyzes the effect of the same-sex marriage debate on the American governmental system in 'Redefinition of Marriage and the Rule of Law', in Lynn Wardle, ed., *What's the Harm?* (University Press of America 2009), 375–387. As the editor (Lynn Wardle) put it: 'It is hard to overstate the potential impact of legalization of same-sex marriage . . .', 208.

13 Interview published in the French Catholic newspaper *La Croix*, 9 November 1998. Roughly translated: 'The difference between sexes is anatomical, psychological and functional. It poses the basis of the opposition that makes it possible to think. To think is to classify, and to classify means to discriminate. This remains an indisputable fact: as one cannot deny the difference between day and night, one cannot decide that the difference of sexes does not exist.' See http://www.la-croix.com/Archives/1998–11–09/Pacte-civil-de-solidarite-_NP_-1998–11–09–462502 (accessed 23 October 2015).

14 Julia Kristeva, 'Métamorphoses de la parentalité', 73ème Congrès des Psychanalystes de Langue Française, *Le Paternel* 9, 12 May 2013, http://www.kristeva.fr/metamorphoses.html (accessed 23 October 2015). In English: 'The problematic part is parenthood with heterosexuality. Heterosexuality is the problem of problems, the foundation of otherness, the personal and universal problem par excellence.'

15 See Basset, 'How the Battle to Redefine Marriage . . .' supra note 4.

16 For instance, Law 26.618, which introduces same-sex marriages, states in its Article 2: 'Ninguna norma del ordenamiento jurídico argentino podrá ser interpretada ni aplicada en el sentido de limitar, restringir, excluir o

be read as contradictory to gender neutrality claims. One comes to fear that even the paramount interest of the child might be eclipsed when opposed to equality claims (in some cases in fact, it already has been, and not only at a national level, but in the Inter-American human rights system).[17]

After same sex marriage was introduced, several inconsistencies concerning family law were signalled by many jurists. By 2011 a group of scholars had been commissioned to draft a new Civil and Commercial Code.[18] The title regulating family relations tried to adjust every norm to the gender neutral paradigm, stating gender neutrality as the main principle that presides over family relations.[19] That title begins with two principles: liberty and equality. These two titles are meant to be the key to family law. And they are phrased as a prohibition to interpret any norm in such a way that it could restrict equality in couples of the same or different sex.[20] Paternity presumptions, artificial reproductive techniques, adoption and parental responsibility were adapted so as to admit homoparentality and eventually, multiparental relationships.[21] Furthermore, in a recent case, a woman in a lesbian couple was fertilized with the sperm of a man, a friend of the couple, who wanted to become a father to the child. The registry office issued a birth certificate in which all three of them were given the status of legal parents.[22] The choices of the parents set the scenario for the child's life, yet those

---

suprimir el ejercicio o goce de los mismos derechos y obligaciones, tanto al matrimonio constituido por personas del mismo sexo como al formado por DOS (2) personas de distinto sexo.' (No norm of the Argentine juridical system can be interpreted nor applied in the sense of limiting, restricting, excluding or suppressing the exercise and enjoyment of the same rights and obligations, whether the marriage is entered by persons of the same or diverse sex.) See also, Ley 26.743 on gender identity: 'Articulo 13–Aplicación. Toda norma, reglamentación o procedimiento deberá respetar el derecho humano a la identidad de género de las personas. Ninguna norma, reglamentación o procedimiento podrá limitar, restringir, excluir o suprimir el ejercicio del derecho a la identidad de género de las personas, debiendo interpretarse y aplicarse las normas siempre a favor del acceso al mismo.' (Article 13–Application. Every norm, regulation or proceeding shall respect the Human Right to gender identity. No norm shall limit, restrict, exclude or suppress the exercise and enjoyment of gender identity right. This right shall be interpreted favoring the access to the fulfillment of that right.'

And furthermore, the Ley 26.862, on Reproductive Techniques, enshrines gender equality in its Article 6, a): 'Articulo 6–Funciones. El Ministerio de Salud de la Nación, sin perjuicio de sus funciones como autoridad de aplicación y para llevar a cabo el objeto de la presente, deberá: a) Arbitrar las medidas necesarias para asegurar el derecho al acceso igualitario de todos los beneficiarios a las prácticas normadas por la presente. . .' (The National Ministry of Health Issues . . . shall ensure the right to equal access to all beneficiaries. . .).

17 See Inter-American Court of Human Rights case *Atala Riffo v. Chile*, 24 February 2012, paras 132–40. See also Ursula C. Basset, 'The Changing Standard of the "Best Interests of the Child" and its Impact on the Exercise of Parenting and on Children', (2012) 2 *International Journal of the Jurisprudence of the Family* 407–436: 425–426.

18 Decree 191/2011.

19 Ricardo L. Lorenzetti, Elena Highton and Aida R. Kemelmajer, *Fundamentos del Anteproyecto de Código Civil y Comercial de la Nación*' (Rubinzal Culzoni 2012), 555.

20 Art. 402, Código Civil y Comercial de la Nación Argentina: 'Interpretación y aplicación de las normas. Ninguna norma puede ser interpretada ni aplicada en el sentido de limitar restringir, excluir o suprimir la igualdad de derechos y obligaciones de los integrantes el matrimonio y los efectos que este produce, sea constituido por dos personas de distinto o igual sexo.' ('Interpretation and application of norms. No norm can be interpreted or applied in such a sense that it limits, restricts, excludes, or suppresses equality of rights and obligations of the spouses and the effects marriage produces, be it between persons of the same sex or different sexes'.)

21 The Civil and Commercial Code recognizes no more than two 'natural parents' (Art. 558, 'La filiación puede tener lugar por naturaleza . . . Ninguna persona puede tener más de dos vínculos filiales' (No person may have more than two parents; however multiparentality is possible through adoption) (Art. 621, 624, 628, for instance) or new institutions regulating parental responsibility.

22 See Jessica Weiss, 'Argentina Schools the U.S. on Gay Rights, Allows Child To Legally Have Three Parents', *MiamiNewTimes*,30April2014,http://www.miaminewtimes.com/news/argentina-schools-the-us-on-gay-rights-allows-child-to-legally-have-three-parents-7583088, (accessed 5 August 2015). In Spanish: http://es.reuters.com/article/entertainmentNews/idESKBN0NF21G20150424.

choices might not be questioned because they stem out of a human right for individuals to decide without any admissible limitation how to configure their adult lives. The new Civil and Commercial Code entered in force on 1 August 2015.[23]

In the two former paragraphs we have seen how the key principle of gender equality re-configured family relations. How would such a principle work if opposed to religious freedom? In Argentina, we still do not have answers. While private law has undergone rapid changes, religious freedom has not yet emerged as a relevant subject. This asynchrony could be explained by certain political and social developments[24] that cannot be analyzed within the frame of this chapter. To profitably analyze this question, let us examine instead recent developments in the European community and in the Inter-American human rights system.

Developments in Europe[25]

The definition of what is contained in the European Convention on Human Rights[26] depends upon monitoring committees and the rulings of the European Court of Human Rights, as both have the power to reinterpret the Convention. There follow some examples concerning hate speech and sexual orientation.

In 2009, an independent NGO, the European Union Agency for Fundamental Rights (FRA), which is financed by the European Union as a special agency,[27] published a two-part report on *Homophobia and Discrimination on Grounds of Sexual Orientation.*[28] The Foreword to Part II ('The Social Situation') of the report notes developments in 2008, including a UN declaration calling for the global decriminalization of homosexuality and condemnation of human rights violations based on sexual orientation or gender identity, and a proposal by the European Commission for stronger EU wide protection against discrimination on all grounds. It then warns: 'The social situation . . . is worrying. In recent years a series of events in EU Member States, such as the banning of Pride marches, hate speech from politicians and intolerant statements by religious leaders, have sent alarming signals . . .'[29] Evaluating such

23 According to Ley 26.994, passed 1 October 2014.

24 On the one hand, the election of an Argentinian Pope has increased the popularity of the Catholic Church. On the other hand, there has been a political use of the fact: most politicians have made a stop in Rome in the last months. That is why, relating to this matter, Argentina is not the best example. However, during the same-sex marriage debate and afterwards, verbal attacks on the Catholic Church have been frequent. Since economy is a concerning issue and politics has taken the center of the scene, there is a very peculiar microclimate in which religion coexists with opposing legal choices: concessions are sometimes made by both sides.

25 See, additionally, Mark Hill QC, 'Freedom of Religion: Strasbourg and Luxembourg Compared', Chapter 3 of this volume.

26 Convention for the Protection of Human Rights and Fundamental Freedoms, *entered into force*, 21 September 1970, 213 U.N.T.S. 222, http://www.echr.coe.int/NR/rdonlyres/D5CC24A7-DC13–4318-B457–5C9014916D7A/0/Convention_ENG.pdf (accessed 2 November 2015).

27 See European Union Agency for Fundamental Rights (FRA), *Finance and Budget*, http://fra.europa.eu/en/about-fra/finance-and-budget (accessed 23 October 2015).

28 European Union Agency for Fundamental Rights (FRA), *Homophobia and Discrimination on Grounds of Sexual Orientation and Gender Identity in the EU Member States. Part I. Legal Analysis* (2009), http://fra.europa.eu/sites/default/files/fra_uploads/1127-FRA_hdgso_report_Part1_en.pdf (accessed 23 October 2015) and *Homophobia and Discrimination on Grounds of Sexual Orientation and Gender Identity in the EU Member States. Part II. The Social Situation* (2009), http://fra.europa.eu/sites/default/files/fra_uploads/397-FRA_hdgso_report _ part2_en.pdf (accessed 2 November 2015).

29 FRA Report *Part II. The Social Situation*, supra note 27 at 3.

speech includes consideration of 'articulation of patterns examining anti-LGTB statements and other homophobic expressions that may not, strictly speaking, all fall under a legal definition of hate speech'.[30] Remarks by which homosexuality is viewed as an immoral inclination and references to family values or certain moral values were included within these problematic 'articulation patterns'. For the authors of this report, such derogatory remarks need to be addressed in a proper legal framework. They suggest that statements of that sort are comparable to hate speech.

In July 2013 the European Court of Human Rights released a *Factsheet* entitled *Hate speech* [reissued, updated June 2015].[31] This document and the cases it describes reflect a continued tension between various fundamental freedoms and pressures to further affirmations of gender equality when contrasted with freedom of speech. The Factsheet explains that, when dealing with cases concerning incitement to hatred and freedom of expression, the Court 'uses two approaches which are provided for by the European Convention on Human Rights':

- the approach of exclusion from the protection of the Convention, provided for by Article 17 (prohibition of abuse of rights), where the comments in question amount to hate speech and negate the fundamental values of the Convention; and
- the approach of setting restrictions on protection, provided for by Article 10, paragraph 2, of the Convention (this approach is adopted where the speech in question, although it is hate speech, is not apt to destroy the fundamental values of the Convention). [Notes omitted.]

Hate speech is a complex issue and quite difficult to define. The 2009 FRA report mentioned above, offers this definition, as applied to discrimination on grounds of sexual orientation:

> The term 'hate speech', as used in this section, includes a broader spectrum of verbal acts drawing upon or expressing homophobia and/or transphobia in degrading or disrespectful public discourse . . . [I]t is possible to identify at least three types of hate speech as having particular importance in a homophobic context: hate speech by public figures, hate speech by public religious figures and hate speech published, often anonymously, on the Internet.[32]

The ECtHR in the 2006 case of *Erbakan v. Turkey*[33] characterized hate speech and appropriate societal reaction to it in this way, as expressly cited in the 2015 *Hate speech* factsheet:

> . . . [T]olerance and respect for the equal dignity of all human beings constitute the foundations of a democratic, pluralistic society. That being so, as a matter of principle it may be considered necessary in certain democratic societies to sanction or even prevent all forms of expression which spread, incite, promote or justify hatred based on

30 FRA Report *Part II. The Social Situation*, supra note 27 at 46.

31 European Court of Human Rights Press Unit, *Factsheet – Hate speech*, June 2015, http://www.echr.coe.int/Documents/FS_Hate_speech_ENG.pdf (accessed 23 October 2015).

32 FRA, Homophobia and Discrimination . . . Part II. The Social Situation, supra note 27 at 46.

33 Erbakan v. Turkey, App. no. 59405/00 (ECtHR, 6 July 2006). The case did not confront the gender equality quest or the protection of sexual minorities, but a division between 'believers and non-believers' (les 'croyants' et les 'non-croyants') in an aggressive discourse (§ 30). We include the citation because of the relevance assigned to it in the Hate Speech report.

intolerance . . . provided that any 'formalities', 'conditions', 'restrictions' or 'penalties' imposed are proportionate to the legitimate aim pursued.[34]

This is the approach the ECtHR followed in February 2012 when it, for the first time, issued a judgment concerning hate speech towards homosexual people in *Vejdeland and Others v. Sweden.*[35] In this case the Court concluded that discrimination based on sexual orientation was as serious as discrimination based on 'race, origin and colour' and that therefore a government might permissibly conclude that interference with freedom of expression in instances of negative speech about homosexuality might be necessary in a democratic society for the protection of the reputation and rights of others. The applicants had distributed leaflets in a secondary school which stated that homosexuality was a 'deviant sexual proclivity', and that it had a 'morally destructive effect on the substance of society'. They claimed that their purpose was to start a debate in which views other than those usually presented in schools were brought forward for consideration. This decision implies that a narrow interpretation of freedom of speech may be adopted in matters concerning same-sex marriage or homosexual orientation.

To this point we have reviewed European standards concerning so-called 'hate speech'. In the case of hate speech, freedom of religion is examined from the perspective of the rights and dignity of sexual minorities, that is, when the expression of religious belief is offensive to sexual minorities. In the next paragraphs, we will move on to examine the European standards on the protection of religious persons and groups when they are the target of a speech offensive to their beliefs.

In its Recommendation 1805 (2007), *Blasphemy, religious insults and hate speech against persons on ground of their religion,*[36] the Parliamentary Assembly of the Council of Europe (PACE) considered that blasphemy, as an insult to a religion, should not be deemed a criminal offense. 'Religious groups must tolerate, as must other groups, critical public statements and debate about their activities, teachings and beliefs . . . provided that such criticism does not amount to intentional and gratuitous insults or hate speech and does not constitute incitement to disturb the peace or to violence and discrimination against adherents of a particular religion' (§ 5). This Recommendation also called for a 'wide margin of appreciation' when regulating matters liable to offend intimate 'personal convictions within the sphere of morals or, especially, religion' (§ 8). PACE considered that national law should only penalize expressions about religious matters which 'intentionally and severely disturb public order and call for public violence' (§ 15).

If compared, the protection of sexual minorities when they are targeted by a harmful religious speech is remarkably stronger than the protection of religious persons and groups when they are targeted by any other group of society. While sexual minorities have a right to criminally pursue such offenses in many states,[37] religious persons and groups 'must tolerate'

34 Erbakan § 56. There is a large amount of scientific literature dealing with this matter. See, for example, Michael Herz and Peter Molnar, The Content and Context of Hate Speech: Rethinking Regulation and Responses (Cambridge University Press 2012); and Ann Weber, Manual on Hate Speech (Council of Europe 2009), 3.

35 Vejdeland and Others v. Sweden, App. no. 1813/07 (ECtHR, 9 February 2012).

36 Parliamentary Assembly of the Council of Europe [PACE], Recommendation 1805 (2007), *Blasphemy, religious insults and hate speech against persons on ground of their religion*, http://assembly.coe.int/nw/xml/XRef/Xref-XML2HTML-en.asp?fileid=17569&lang=en (accessed 23 October 2015).

37 Criminalization of hate speech is frequently bound with equality reforms concerning marriage. This was the case in Argentina. When sexual orientation is at issue, there is increasing demand for the criminalization of such offenses, in order to make enforcement more efficient, as in the case of the Bill C-250 in Canada, which expanded

offense.[38] Why are two human rights so deeply embedded in personal dignity, identity, and integrity dealt with in such different manners?

This double standard perhaps results from historical discrimination against gays and lesbians that has to be repaired. In order to grant a wider protection to people not yet identified in the relevant texts of treaties as a 'suspect class', it might seem necessary to articulate a distinct set of doctrines for them. The assertion of a right to freedom of religion or belief, on the other hand, is evidently misconstrued as an identity issue.[39] Human rights law should explore ways of convergence and dialogue, so that both rights (the right to express one's sexual orientation in the public sphere and the right to express one's own belief) find new, more equal balances.

Developments in the Americas

The human rights instrument of the Organization of American States (OAS)[40] is the American Convention on Human Rights (ACHR).[41] Unlike in Europe, where freedom of thought, conscience, and religion are treated in one article of the Convention (Art. 9, ECHR) and freedom of expression is treated in another (Art. 10, ECHR), the Inter-American system of human rights has a specific provision referring to freedom of conscience and religion (Art. 12, ACHR) and another one on freedom of thought and expression (Art. 13, ACHR).[42] The two different approaches to the issue are also manifest in the wording. The concern of the ACHR relating to all four freedoms (conscience, religion, thought, and expression) is expansive, with lengthy paragraphs outlining general rights, specific rights, and restrictions.

Specifically, Article 13, paragraph 5, reads as follows:

> *Any propaganda for war and any advocacy of national, racial, or religious hatred that constitute incitements to lawless violence or to any other similar action against any person or group of persons on any grounds including those of race, color, religion, language, or national origin shall be considered as offenses punishable by law.* [43]

On the one hand, there is an evident concern expressed by the very detailed wording of the two articles (ACHR 12, 13) granting those freedoms. On the other hand, the restriction

---

hate speech to cover sexual orientation shortly after same-sex marriage was legalized. This view is implicit in the FRA report, above.

38 See PACE Recommendation § 5.

39 See, for example, the International Convention on the Rights of the Child (CRC), which in Article 20(3) asserts that a child deprived of family environment should be assured alternative care, for which 'due regard shall be paid to the desirability of continuity in a child's upbringing and to the child's ethnic, religious, cultural and linguistic background' http://www.ohchr.org/en/professionalinterest/pages/crc.aspx. (accessed 23 October 2015).

40 The Organization of American States comprises all 35 independent states of the Americas. See http://www.oas.org/en/ (accessed 23 October 2015).

41 The American Convention on Human Rights (ACHR) was adopted at the Inter-American Specialized Conference on Human Rights in San José, Costa Rica, 22 November 1969, http://www.cidh.org/Basicos/English/Basic3.American%20Convention.htm (accessed 23 October 2015). Two OAS organs are responsible for overseeing ACHR, the Inter-American Commission on Human Rights (IACHR) http://www.oas.org/en/iachr/, and the Inter-American Court of Human Rights (Corte IDH or IACourtHR), http://www.corteidh.or.cr/ (both accessed 23 October 2015).

42 Héctor Gross Espiell, *La Convención Americana y la Convención Europea de Derechos. Análisis Comparativo* (Editorial Jurídica de Chile 1991), 100–102.

43 ACHR, supra note 39 at Art. 3 para. 5.

grounds for any propaganda or advocacy are detailed without any open clauses. Compared with Article 1 ACHR, which forbids all kinds of discrimination, and therefore adds at the end of its first paragraph an open clause ('or any other social condition'),[44] the enumeration of Article 13 is closed (race, color, religion, language or national offenses).[45]

The Inter-American Court (IACourtHR) considers itself, like the European Court of Human Rights, to be the living instrument to interpret the text of the ACHR, so these limited grounds could be expanded by the way of an evolutionary interpretation and the *pro homine* principle. By its judgments, the Court has determined freedom of conscience and religion to be the basis of a democratic society.[46] Any limitation of freedom of thought is restrictively interpreted.[47]

Relevant case law on freedom of religion is yet to come. The IACourtHR dealt with only one case, *Olmedo Bustos v. Chile*, and this case is not directly relevant to our purposes, since it dealt more with prior censorship than with the duty of the state to protect religious freedom. Chile had forbidden the exhibition of the film *The Last Temptation of Christ* because it offended the Catholic majority in the country. However, the petitioners alleged a breach of their religious freedom. They felt that prohibiting them from watching the film because of prior censorship limited their freedom of religion.[48] The Court, while disregarding any violation of the freedom of religion in the present case,[49] did undertake to define the extent and relevance of freedom of religion:

> According to Article 12 of the Convention, the right to freedom of conscience and religion allows everyone to maintain, change, profess and disseminate his religion or beliefs. This right is one of the foundations of democratic society. In its religious dimension, it constitutes a far-reaching element in the protection of the convictions of those who profess a religion and in their way of life.[50]

This is a strong wording on the meaning of freedom of conscience and religion: it is considered to be the basis of a democratic society (compare to the European approach in the *Erbakan*

44 'The States Parties to this Convention undertake to respect the rights and freedoms recognized herein and to ensure to all persons subject to their jurisdiction the free and full exercise of those rights and freedoms, without any discrimination for reasons of race, color, sex, language, religion, political or other opinion, national or social origin, economic status, birth, or any other social condition.' ACHR Art. 1 para. 1.

45 'Any . . . advocacy of national, racial, or religious hatred that constitute incitements to lawless violence or to any other similar action against any person or group of persons on any grounds including those of race, color, religion, language, or national origin shall be considered as offenses punishable by law,' ACHR Art. 13 para. 5.

46 See, for instance, *Masacres de Río Negro v. Guatemala*. Excepción Preliminar, Fondo, Reparaciones y Costas. Judgment of 4 September 2012, Series C No. 250 para. 154: 'Este derecho es uno de los cimientos de la sociedad democrática.' (This right constitutes the basis of a democratic society.)

47 See *'La Última Tentación de Cristo' (Olmedo Bustos y otros) v. Chile.Fondo*, Reparaciones y Costas. Judgment of 5 February 2001. Series C, No. 73.

48 '[A]s he is not a Catholic, he considers that his freedom of conscience was violated, because a group of people of a specific religion attempted to impose their own vision about what others may see.' IACourtHR, *Olmedo Bustos v. Chile*. Judgment of 5 February 2001, para. 45 b.

49 'In this case, however, there is no evidence to prove that any of the freedoms embodied in Article 12 of the Convention have been violated. Indeed, the Court understands that the prohibition of the exhibition of the film "The Last Temptation of Christ" did not impair or deprive anyone of their right to maintain, change, profess or disseminate their religion or beliefs with total freedom.' *Olmedo Bustos*, para. 79.

50 *Olmedo Bustos*, para. 79.

case,[51] in which tolerance was 'the foundation of a democratic society').[52] It encompasses the right to maintain, profess, and disseminate one's religious beliefs. Nevertheless, the *Olmedo-Bustos* case does not provide anything upon which to build a hypothesis concerning a conflict between equality claims and freedom of religion. For this, a leading case on sexual orientation must be examined.

The IACourtHR made the news worldwide in 2012 with the case *Atala Riffo v. Chile*,[53] the first case to treat sexual orientation as a suspect category of discrimination in the Inter-American system. This case is important as a model of interaction of the clash of rights between sexual orientation and a very sensitive right: in this case the best interests of the child. The Supreme Court of Chile had awarded custody of the three daughters of Chilean Judge Karen Atala Riffo to her ex-husband after her lesbian orientation was made public. Atala had made her sexual orientation public in many ways, and in a Catholic and traditional Chile of the 1990s, the girls had apparently experienced social rejection because of their mother's lifestyle choice. The Chilean court asserted that Atala's lesbian relationship put the development of her children at risk. According to the IACourtHR, however, sexual orientation includes not only the right of choosing one's own lifestyle[54] but also of expressing that choice in the public sphere,[55] and 'potential social stigma due to the mother or father's sexual orientation cannot be considered as a valid "harm" for the purposes of determining the child's best interests . . . Ms. Atala had no reason to suffer the consequences of the girls allegedly being discriminated against in their community due to her sexual orientation.'[56]

In the eyes of the Court, the harm to the child's best interests because of social rejection 'cannot be considered' valid. Moreover, Judge Atala, in her right to exert her sexual orientation publicly and privately, does not have 'to suffer the consequences' of any social harm her children might suffer. In the clash of rights between the best interests of children and the rights to exert sexual orientation, the second prevails upon the first. Even in case of harm to children, a parent should not suffer the consequences of being responsible for the harm, and the harm should not be considered as a limit or impediment to the rights of a parent to publicly express her sexual orientation. The Court also implies that to admit the best interests argument would imply a form of legitimation of the social discrimination.[57] In short,

> The child's best interest cannot be used to justify discrimination against the parents based on their sexual orientation. Therefore, the judge cannot take this social condition into consideration as an element in a custody ruling.[58]

The analysis of the interaction between the best interests of the child and the right to choose and live the adult's sexual orientation weaves in and out throughout the *Atala Riffo*

51 The cultural attitudes and problems in Europe, especially in Turkey, concerning religious freedom are quite different. Let us recall that the *Erbakan* case did not deal with an offensive discourse against sexual minorities, and yet it was cited in the Hate Speech factsheet of the ECtHR. See supra note 32.

52 See also, and more recently, IACourtHR, case *Masacres de Río Negro v. Guatemala*, supra note 46.

53 *Atala Riffo and daughters v. Chile*, IACourtHR, Judgment 24 February 2012.

54 *Atala Riffo*, para. 133.

55 *Atala Riffo*, para 139.

56 *Atala Riffo*, para. 121.

57 See, for instance, para. 139: 'Furthermore, if sexual orientation is an essential component of a person's identity, it was not reasonable to require Ms Atala to put her life and family project on hold.'

58 *Atala Riffo*, para. 110.

judgment: sometimes the Court says that it should be analyzed on a case-by-case basis and not '*in abstracto*'; sometimes the Court claims there is no proven harm; sometimes it says that the harm to the children cannot be imposed or argued as a way to restrict the rights of the mother to her sexual orientation. Whatever the analysis of the issue, the relevant matter is that when dealing with one of the most cherished rights of the human rights system, 'the best interests of the child', the IACourtHR in several instances considers that this right cannot be 'used' or even 'considered' when opposed to a sexual orientation claim.

At present there is no other case dealing with sexual orientation matters in the Court. An upcoming case deals more with social rights (pension of a homosexual partner)[59] and not with a clash of rights between sexual orientation and other human rights. However, *Atala Riffo* might well provide a sample of the IACourtHR line of reasoning in this matter.

It would seem that OAS organs have not shared the concerns of the ACHR drafting commission when it comes to religious freedom. Beyond the case law, the OAS General Assembly, while adopting no resolution to grant liberty of conscience, religion or thought, has taken great pains to protect sexual orientation.[60]

There is no monitoring of freedom of conscience or religion. Even though there is special rapporteurship on freedom of expression, it is not concerned with freedom of conscience or

59 *Angel Alberto Duque v. Colombia*, Case 12.841. See OAS Press Release, 'IACHR Takes Case involving Colombia to the Inter-American Court', 1 December 2014, http://www.oas.org/en/iachr/media_center/PReleases/2014/144.asp (accessed 23 October 2015).

60 Resolutions on sexual orientation and gender issues were adopted by the General Assembly of the OAS in 2008, 2009, 2010, 2011, 2012, and 2013. Most of these replicate the content and language of AG/RES. 2721 (XLII-O/12): 'Human Rights, Sexual Orientation, and Gender Identity'. In June 2013 the OAS adopted Resolution AG/RES 2807 (XLIII-O/13), *Human Rights, Sexual Orientation, and Gender Identity and Expression*, which contains the following resolutions:

1. To condemn all forms of discrimination against persons by reason of their sexual orientation and gender identity or expression, and [urges] the states within the parameters of the legal institutions of their domestic systems to eliminate, where they exist, barriers faced by lesbians, gays, and bisexual, transsexual, and intersex (LGBTI) persons in equal access to political participation and in other areas of public life, and to avoid interferences in their private life.'
2. To encourage member states to consider, within the parameters of the legal institutions of their domestic systems, adopting public policies against discrimination by reason of sexual orientation and gender identity or expression.
3. To condemn acts of violence and human rights violations committed against persons by reason of their sexual orientation and gender identity or expression; and to urge states to strengthen their national institutions with a view to preventing and investigating these acts and violations and ensuring due judicial protection for victims on an equal footing and that the perpetrators are brought to justice.
4. In addition, to encourage states, within their institutional capacities, to produce data on homophobic and transphobic violence, with a view to fostering public policies that protect the human rights of lesbians, gays, and bisexual, transsexual, and intersex people (LGBTI).
5. To urge member states to ensure adequate protection for human rights defenders who work on the issue of acts of violence, discrimination, and human rights violations committed against individuals on the basis of their sexual orientation and gender identity or expression.
6. To urge member states to afford appropriate protection to intersex people and to implement policies and procedures, as appropriate, to ensure medical practices that are consistent with applicable human rights standards.
7. To request the Inter-American Commission on Human Rights (IACHR) to pay particular attention to its work plan titled "Rights of LGBTI People" and, in keeping with its established practice, to continue with its work to prepare a hemispheric study on the subject; and to urge member states to support the efforts of the Commission in this area.

religion.[61] However, by 2011, a special rapporteurship on the rights of lesbian, gay, bisexual, trans, and intersex persons (LGTBI) was created.[62] In the image carousel heading this entity's website[63] one image is of a group of people with a banner that confronts religion as an obstacle to equality.[64]

It seems therefore reasonable to conclude that freedom of thought, conscience, and religion is an underdeveloped right in the Inter-American system, and that, despite its golden cradle (in the detailed wording of Articles 12 and 13), there has not been any evolution in securing this right that might eventually collide with other more specifically and extensively protected rights.

At the same time, the IACourtHR has developed a suspect class to protect rights of gender and sexual orientation, apparently against even such a sensitive interest as the best interests of the child, which should not be 'considered' or 'used' to the restrict the expression rights of parent who is a member of this class, even with a showing of harm to the child. The question is, then, in a clash of religious freedom rights against sexual orientation rights, such as the right to same-sex marriage, would the Court apply the *Atala Riffo* case line of reasoning? Or would the Court claim, as in *Olmedo Bustos* that the right of freedom of religion is 'a foundation of a democratic society'?

The Equality Claim and New Risks

We may summarize by observing that the equality claim seems slowly to be growing into a fundamental principle to which other principles should defer. The promotion of liberties pertinent to gender issues is becoming a quest for the redefinition of other liberties against which the equality claim appears to be conceived as the preeminent one. In other words, analysis of the latest developments concerning gender seems to indicate that the road is being paved for the introduction of new inequalities. Where it has been recognized, same-sex marriage, as connected to 'gender equality', has often been accorded a heightened status of protection comparable to that afforded to other suspect categories expressly protected by the human-rights treaties. This produces an imbalance in the human rights system as well as new vulnerabilities.

It seems imperative, then, to pay particular attention to potential conflicts between protection of religious freedom, conscience, and speech and protection of sexual orientation

---

8. To request the IACHR to continue preparing a study on legislation and provisions in force in the OAS member states restricting the human rights of individuals by reason of their sexual orientation or gender identity or expression and to prepare, based on that study, a guide aimed at promoting the decriminalization of homosexuality and practices related to gender identity or expression.
9. To urge the member states that have not yet done so to consider signing, ratifying, or acceding to, as the case may be, the inter-American human rights instruments.
10. To request the Permanent Council to report to the General Assembly on the implementation of this resolution. Execution of the activities envisaged in this resolution will be subject to the availability of financial resources in the program-budget of the Organization and other resources.

61 See Organization of American States, Office of the General Rapporteur for Freedom of Expression, http://www.oas.org/en/iachr/expression/index.asp (accessed 23 October 2015).

62 Created by AG/RES. 2721 (XLII-O/12), 'Human Rights, Sexual Orientation, and Gender Identity', adopted at the second plenary session, held on 4 June 2012). See Organization of American States, Rights of Lesbian, Gay, Bisexual, Trans and Intersex Persons, http://www.oas.org/en/iachr/lgtbi/ (accessed 23 October 2015).

63 See http://www.oas.org/en/iachr/lgtbi/.

64 The banner addresses the issue of legal recognition of LGTBI couples: 'Ni el Estado ni la Iglesia me dirán a quién y cómo amar.' (Neither the State nor the Church will tell me who to love or how to love.)

where gender neutrality, transsexualism, or same-sex marriage are introduced. The line of reasoning of preponderance of one category over the other, or the line that goes along the prevailing of one category to the point of suppressing the other might be understandable as a transition from non-recognition of gender identity issues to their articulation in terms of juridical protection in the human rights system. However, theories and interpretation should evolve to a range of equal recognition.

Both rights, religious freedom and gender equality, are a component of the right to identity, and therefore both are constitutive of the right to human integrity and dignity, and the right to life. Allowing one of those rights to eat into the other might implicate a legitimation of new ways of undermining human rights under the pretence of applying them. And, therefore, new forms of discrimination would rise: two categories of people would be treated differently according to the preferred component of identity chosen by the interpreter of the law or the lawmaker as prevailing.

As long as societies cannot learn to live in peace and respect with those who are different or think differently without trying to impose the rule of sameness, new forms of violence will inevitably gain ground. To suppress any difference by treaty, statute, or case law, to try to suffocate in any way freedom of speech, religion, and thought, as long as it does not constitute an express call for violence or disruption of public order, is to contribute to this process.

Theoretical studies on violence against women have emphasized that between a victim and a perpetrator there is frequently only a thin line. Once victims are put in power, they sometimes recreate scenarios of violence, only this time as perpetrators.[65] Violence engenders violence. The LGTBI community has suffered various forms of discrimination and social segregation for a very long time. Members of this community now have the power to change their status. Precisely now, they are walking along a most precarious line. From sad experience, they know where the path of oppression, discrimination, disregard, and suppression of choice leads. To live and respect one another's institutions, lives, views, and beliefs is a principle of safety which, if applied thoughtfully and consistently, should keep everybody on the right side.

65 Lloyd Ohlin and Michael Tonry, "Family Violence in Perspective", in *Crime and Justice, Family Violence* (The University of Chicago Press 1989), 1–18 ; Karolin Eva Kappler, *Living with Paradoxes: Victims of Sexual Violence and Their Conduct of Everyday Life* (Springer 2012), 78–79.

10 A 'Bare . . . Purpose to Harm'?

Marriage and Catholic Conscience

*Helen M. Alvaré**

Finding Animus in the Rejection of Same-Sex Marriage

The United States Supreme Court's 2013 opinion in *United States v. Windsor*[1] strongly suggested that any view of marriage that excludes the possibility of same-sex unions is irrational, even hateful. Justice Kennedy's opinion for a five-Justice majority in the 2015 *Obergefell v. Hodges*,[2] did likewise. Ultimately, *Windsor* turned on the majority's holding that section three of the Federal Defense of Marriage Act ('DOMA'),[3] passed in 1996 by large majorities in both houses of Congress and signed into law by President Bill Clinton, reflected a 'bare desire to harm' same-sex couples, a legislative purpose which, the Court said, could never form the basis of a valid law, given the Constitution's guarantee of equality.[4] *Obergefell* rested for the most part upon a new interpretation of the Fourteenth Amendment's Due Process Clause – now held to include rights discerned by the 'new insight' and 'reasoned judgment' of five Justices.[5] A substantial portion of the majority's 'insight' consisted in its conclusion that denying a right to same-sex marriage 'demean[ed]' gay and lesbian citizens, even while opponents of same-sex marriage insisted that same-sex marriage itself 'demean[ed]'[6] an institution that had always linked marriage recognition primarily with the interests of children.

* The author would like to thank the George Mason Law School's summer research grant program, Brian Miller for his able research assistance and the comments offered by members of the symposium Freedom of Religion and Non-Discrimination: The Collision of Identities, held at Central European University, Budapest, Hungary, 7–8 June 2013, co-sponsored by the Department of Legal Studies (CEU), the International Center for Law and Religion Studies (Brigham Young University).

1 *United States v. Windsor*, 133 S.Ct. 2675 (2013).

2 *Obergefell v. Hodges*, 135 S.Ct. 2584 (2015). *Obergefell*, in finding a federal constitutional right to same-sex marriage, effectively overruled *Windsor*. See, for example, Kyle Duncan, 'Symposium: Overruling Windsor', *SCOTUSblog*, 27 June 2015, 2.38 pm, at http://www.scotusblog.com/2015/06/symposium-overruling-windsor/ (accessed 24 October 2015). For the author's preliminary thoughts on this ruling, see Helen M. Alvaré, 'A decision that's unfair and disenfranchising', *Crux: Covering All Things Catholic*, 26 June 2015), at http://www.cruxnow.com/life/2015/06/25/supreme-court-gay-marriage-is-constitutional/ (accessed 24 October 2015).

3 1 U.S.C. §7 (1996).

4 See *Windsor* at 2693: 'The Constitution's guarantee of equality must at the very least mean that a bare congressional desire to harm a politically unpopular group cannot justify disparate treatment of that group,' citing *Department of Agriculture v. Moreno*, 413 U.S. 528, 534–535 (1973).

5 *Obergefell* at 2598.

6 *Obergefell* at 2602 and 2594 respectively.

For many who oppose same-sex unions not out of any animus, but on the basis of sincerely held rational and religious beliefs, these judicial opinions are troubling. *Obergefell* compounds this sensation by misstating the First Amendment's Free Exercise guarantee as protecting only rights to 'advocate' and 'teach' religious beliefs that marriage and children are intrinsically intertwined,[7] ignoring religious citizens' constitutional rights also to practice and to live in accordance with religious beliefs.[8]

To a great many religious institutions and individuals marriage between a man and a woman provides unique social goods. This notion has been widely accepted for millennia. It is evident in the ways in which Christian teachings on marriage have shaped Western marriage law, including in the United States.[9] For many religious believers, moreover, opposite-sex marriage forms a central and nonseverable element of an understanding of self, God, and the world. Refusing a religious exemption – refusing, that is, to allow religious believers to avoid cooperating with laws recognizing same-sex marriage – is tantamount to denying them the right to practice their faith, or even insisting that they practice a different faith. This situation is more dramatic than even many supporters of Free Exercise are aware.

Faced with the possibility of running afoul of state laws requiring recognition of same-sex marriage, the question of religious exemptions becomes urgent. While the *Windsor* opinion did not directly address this question, the *Obergefell* majority did, alongside its alarmingly truncated version of the First Amendment.[10]

Already, religious actors may be pressured to cooperate with same-sex partnerships via various states' laws treating public accommodations, licensing, housing, education, employment, government grants, and tax exemptions.[11] Should a state dismiss religious objections as animus, or simply conclude that same-sex marriage recognition is, in every case, more "compelling" a state interest than religious freedom, the legal obligations facing religious actors will be amplified.

Catholic Belief and the Common Good

A variety of religions and religious actors have sought to avoid cooperating with same-sex marriage, including members of the Orthodox, Catholic, Muslim, Jewish, and Protestant faiths.[12] The Catholic situation post-*Windsor* and post-*Obergefell* merits particular attention because Roman Catholic dioceses and other institutions have frequently sought exemptions from same-sex marriage laws, and the dampening or silencing of Catholic witness on marriage is a matter

7 *Obergefell* at 2607.

8 *Burwell v. Hobby Lobby Stores, Inc.*, 134 S.Ct. 2751, 2769–2770 (2014).

9 See John Witte Jr., *From Sacrament to Contract: Marriage, Religion and Law in the Western Tradition* (Westminster John Knox Press, 2nd edn, 2012).

10 See supra note 7.

11 See the summary of potentially affected areas in Professors Robin Fretwell Wilson, Carl H. Esbeck, Edward McGlynn Gaffney, Jr., Thomas C. Berg and Richard W. Garnett, *Letter to the Honorable Pat Quinn, Governor of Illinois*, 18 December 2012, at http://mirrorofjustice.blogs.com/files/ill-letter-12–2012.pdf (accessed 24 October 2015).

12 See, for example, the statement of Orthodox, Catholic and Protestant leaders regarding same-sex marriage and other challenges to religious liberty at http://manhattandeclaration.org/#0 (accessed 24 October 2015). See also, Joe Winkler, 'Responses to Same-sex Marriage Decisions', 26 June 2013, at http://www.jta.org/2013/06/26/news-opinion/the-telegraph/responses-to-same-sex-marriage-decisions (accessed 24 October 2015).

of more than parochial interest. The Catholic Church claims that its teachings about marriage are closely linked with the common good. Indeed, a growing chorus of sociological and other literature supports ideas and practices about marriage which overlap significantly and normatively with Catholic teachings and practices.[13]

Allowing Catholic witness also matters profoundly to Catholic believers, but not for the limited reasons most observers believe. Of course it matters for Catholics' ability to live out and effectively transmit the meaning of marriage to their children; but it also matters because marriage is an irreplaceable archetype within Christian cosmology, closely linked to the meaning of the universe and of human life in the world. This is not intuitive for non-believers, but it is also not inexplicable. For Catholics, understanding 'marriage' is essential for comprehending the identity of God; God's way of loving; norms for human interactions; the meaning of the embodied human person; and the meaning of life, as mutual service in love. The Catholic conception of marriage is thus at one and the same time directly at odds with the meaning of marriage articulated by *Windsor* – with its excising of procreation and its focus upon on adults' sexual and emotional desires – *and* indispensable to Catholics' ability to understand, to live, and to transmit, an authentically Catholic life.

Catholics, then, must strenuously seek a religious exemption from cooperation with same-sex marriage laws. Yet today, legislatures could easily be less inclined to allow such an exemption. It could hardly be otherwise if the *Windsor* and *Obergefell* opinions mean what they say: that an 'opposite-sex-only' marriage norm is both irrational and intentionally hateful, and 'demeans' gay and lesbian citizens. Further, the *Windsor* majority took specific offense at some DOMA supporters' references to moral and religious values, DOMA's use of the language of 'defense' in its title, and DOMA's practical operation:[14] that is, marriages solemnized by sovereign states would not be recognized in a separate (federal) domain. A religious exemption to a same-sex marriage law features each of these qualities.

Following *Employment Division v. Smith*,[15] religious actors seeking exemptions from state laws will usually have to win them in the legislature. Judges will allow 'neutral laws of general applicability'[16] to stand, even if they burden religion, so long as the state can show that the law is rationally related to a legitimate state interest – the simplest constitutional test. A law defining marriage for all citizens of a state, as well as laws affecting employment benefits or public accommodations, will ordinarily be formally drafted as a neutral law of general applicability. Yet the findings of *Windsor* and *Obergefell* that opposite-sex-only laws are driven by animus could well dispose legislators to refuse religious exemptions; lawmakers do not want to be perceived as willing to license some citizens to wound others.

Windsor and *Obergefell* exacerbate the pressure on religious freedom even in states possessing more free-exercise-protective laws, for example states possessing state-level Religious Freedom Restoration Acts,[17] or judicial decisions interpreting state constitutions to

13 See the section on 'Living Together?' below.

14 *Windsor* at 2693.

15 *Employment Division, Department of Human Resources of Oregon v. Smith*, 494 U.S. 872 (1990).

16 *Smith* at 878–880.

17 See 'State legislative responses to Obergefell v. Hodges', *Ballotpedia: The Encyclopedia of American Politics*, 6 July 2015, at http://ballotpedia.org/State_legislative_responses_to_Obergefell_v._Hodges (accessed 2 November 2015).

require burdens on religion to be justified by 'compelling state interests.' They do so by defining marriage in a way that makes excluding same-sex couples appear the equivalent of denying their personhood.

In response to the current environment, this chapter sets forth Roman Catholic teachings on marriage relevant to the existence and shape of a religious exemption from same-sex marriage recognition, showing how these teachings are at odds with both same-sex marriage cases' claims about the meaning of state marriage recognition and how they ground a 'cosmology' – an understanding of the 'order of the universe' – by which Catholics are required to live. This material illustrates the degree of importance Catholics attach to freedom from coercion to recognize, support, facilitate, or cooperate with an opposing view of marriage.

It should be noted here that there are several extant proposals to protect religious freedom in the context of legalized same-sex marriage.[18] While these proposals perform several important functions, they do not attend to the cosmological scope of Catholic teachings about marriage. Further, because some were written pre-*Windsor*, they could not take into account the Supreme Court's insistence upon the animus underlying disagreement with legal same-sex marriage. Nor did they have the benefit of the Supreme Court's assertions about the meaning of state marriage recognition. They proceeded, rather, from the true but limited perspective that a number of religious actors hold that marriage is an opposite-sex institution, and will require legislative protection to preserve their religious liberty if same-sex marriage laws are passed. These proposals have in general not considered the related matter of how religions' teachings about marriage might substantively contribute to the common good. Due to their limited theological contents, these proposals are less demanding on behalf of religious freedom – less demanding to protect believers from charges of hateful animus, and less bold to insist that even a pluralistic society might benefit from religious witness to the meaning of marriage.

Windsor and *Obergefell:* The Majority's Reasoning and the Future Context for Religious Exemptions

Two closely intertwined aspects of *Windsor and Obergefell* have implications for religious liberty: the Court's definition of the legal meaning of marriage; and the Court's conclusion that DOMA's section three was motivated by a 'bare desire to harm.'

Windsor appears to turn upon the majority's conclusion that DOMA's section three violated the Equal Protection and Due Process guarantees of the U.S. Constitution because the legislation was motivated solely by a desire to harm persons; as a matter of law, in other words, the statute has no rational basis.[19] The majority's finding about the meaning of state marriage recognition formed a crucial part of its constitutional analysis. The Court found that states recognize marriage in order to benefit two people with an emotionally and sexually intimate

18 See, for example, Thomas C. Berg and Douglas Laycock, 'Protecting Same-Sex Marriage *and* Religious Liberty', Chapter 11 of this volume. See also Wilson et al., supra note 5, and Douglas Laycock, Thomas C. Berg, Bruce S. Ledewitz, Christopher C. Lund and Michael Perry, *Letter to Rep. Tom Cross*, 12 March 2013, at http://mirrorofjustice.blogs.com/files/illinois-republicans-2013.pdf (accessed 24 October 2015). See also Robin Fretwell Wilson, 'Insubstantial Burdens: The Case for Government Employee Exemptions to Same-Sex Marriage Laws', (2010) 5 *Northwestern Journal of Law and Social Policy* (2) 318–368.

19 *Windsor* at 2693.

partnership who wish to make a public commitment to one another. Marriage, then, can be formed by two people of the same-sex or of opposite sexes. This is the foundation for *Windsor*'s finding about animus. In other words, once marriage means what *Windsor* says it means, it becomes *per se* irrational to refuse to recognize as 'marriage' a committed, emotionally and sexually intimate partnership of any two persons. Opposition to such recognition is easily interpreted as the product of irrational and harmful animus, based upon sexual orientation.

The Meaning of State Marriage Recognition

Plaintiff Edith Windsor married Thea Spyer in Canada; the pair then moved to New York, which recognized the marriage. When Spyer died, because DOMA prevented federal estate tax law from recognizing Windsor as Spyer's 'spouse" (and as such entitled to a spousal tax deduction), Windsor owed $365,000 in federal estate taxes. Ms. Windsor sued to recover these, asserting that section three of DOMA violated the Constitution, and that the federal government should comply with New York's definition of 'marriage' and 'spouses.'[20]

After writing at length about the federal government's pre-DOMA practice of recognizing states' authority to define marriage for purposes of interpreting and applying federal laws, the *Windsor* majority declared, unexpectedly, that it would *not* rest its holding on federalism grounds. Rather, it proposed that its discussion of state authority over marriage served the purpose of highlighting the unusual quality of DOMA's refusing to accept states' marriage determinations. DOMA's break from a pattern of federal reliance on state marriage law also contributed to the majority's suspicion that something else was afoot – perhaps animus against lesbian or gay individuals or couples.

Woven throughout the majority's discussion – both of states' traditional marriage-recognition function and of the alleged animus undergirding DOMA – were numerous statements about the meaning and purpose of state marriage recognition, respecting both couples in general and same-sex couples in particular.

Windsor's opening line about states' marriage laws and the situation of the plaintiffs suggests, first, that marriage is a 'right' the state confers. ('When at first Windsor and Spyer longed to marry, neither New York nor any other State granted them that right.')[21] There is also, and by distinction, a small suggestion that marriage is a pre-existing reality that the state simply acknowledges – when the majority calls New York's decision to recognize same-sex marriage 'a new insight'[22] – as if the state had a pre-existing notion of marriage in its head and then realized that same-sex pairs conformed to it.

The Court also called marriage a way of defining oneself individually and as a partnership: two people 'define themselves by their commitment to each other.'[23] It is also a public affirmation of commitment between two people: 'New York came to acknowledge the urgency of this issue for same-sex couples who wanted to affirm their commitment to one another before their children, their family, their friends, and their community.'[24]

The Court appears to conclude that over and above the meaning that state marriage recognition possesses generally, there are additional meanings applicable to same-sex couples;

20 *Windsor* at 2682.
21 *Windsor* at 2689.
22 *Windsor* at 2689.
23 *Windsor* at 2689.
24 *Windsor* at 2689.

here, the focus was upon equality with opposite-sex pairs. The Court writes, for example, that marriage is an elevated status and a marker of dignity: 'two persons of the same sex might aspire to occupy the same status and dignity as that of a man and woman in lawful marriage.'[25] 'It is a path to pride in oneself individually and to pride in one's partnership with one other person, and toward living in and being seen to live in a partnership equal to that between opposite-sex persons.'[26] 'New York . . . decided that same-sex couples should have the right to marry and so live with pride in themselves and their union and in a status of equality with all other married persons.'[27]

It appears that the majority was also addressing only same-sex marriages when it wrote that marriage is a right that offers 'protection'; the Court referred to a 'class of persons that the laws of New York, and of 11 other States, have sought to protect.'[28] Further addressing same-sex couples, it opined that marriage is a vehicle for conferring 'dignity' and a 'status of immense import.'[29] Moving to even more profound concepts, it said that recognizing marriage between same-sex partners protects 'personhood and dignity',[30] although the attributes of personhood were not specified. Finally, the Court called marriage a means for same-sex couples to 'enhance their own liberty.'[31] Again, the attributes of liberty were not specified, but this could refer again to same-sex couples having a right to a status formerly enjoyed only by opposite-sex couples.

While the majority weaves the above-described attributes of state marriage-recognition throughout its opinion, at one point it strings together several observations about the significance of marriage recognition in *every* state. This paragraph therefore may have special significance for the Court. It begins by observing: 'States' interest in defining and regulating the marital relation, subject to constitutional guarantees, stems from the understanding that marriage is more than a routine classification for purposes of certain statutory benefits.'[32] Immediately after this, the Court says the following:

> Private, consensual sexual intimacy between two adult persons of the same sex may not be punished by the State, and it can form 'but one element in a personal bond that is more enduring.'[33]

This is a citation to the (also Justice Kennedy-authored) opinion in *Lawrence v. Texas,*[34] the case striking down Texas' ban on homosexual sodomy. The Court's choice to highlight sexual intimacy and *Lawrence* here – coming right on the heels of its statement that there is 'more' to states' 'understanding [of] marriage,' than benefits availability – seems to indicate that private consensual sexual intimacy is, in the Court's mind, the *first* important aspect of a state's interest in defining and regulating marriage. It is also worthy of note that in a paragraph devoted to '*[s]tates*' interest in defining and regulating the marital relation,' the first

25 *Windsor* at 2689.
26 *Windsor* at 2689.
27 *Windsor* at 2689.
28 *Windsor* at 2690.
29 *Windsor* at 2691.
30 *Windsor* at 2696.
31 *Windsor* at 2695.
32 *Windsor* at 2692.
33 *Windsor* at 2692, citing *Lawrence v. Texas*, 539 U.S. at 567.
34 *Lawrence v. Texas*, 539 U.S. 558 (2003).

interest comes from a *federal* source. Furthermore it is a portion of a federal source expressing the personal surmise of five federal justices – the idea that sexual intimacy only takes place within enduring personal relationships – not a legal conclusion.

In the second sentence in this paragraph devoted to states' interests in marriage recognition, the Court moves away from a discussion of the meaning of state marriage recognition generally, to the meaning of same-sex marriage recognition specifically. Immediately following the *Lawrence* reference, the majority asserts that New York's same-sex marriage law was '[seeking] to give further protection and dignity to that bond.'[35] Its next sentence is susceptible to too many meanings to construe definitively: 'For same-sex couples who wished to be married, the State acted to give their lawful conduct a lawful status.'[36] By 'lawful conduct,' it is not clear whether the Court intended to refer to their sexual intimacy, thus continuing to spotlight the importance of sexual intercourse to marriage. The Court might also have been referring to their marriage ceremony or their living 'as if' married even before they were legally able to achieve a state-recognized marriage. Or perhaps the Court was simply reminding readers that same-sex couples' cohabiting, and their sexual intimacies, are legal everywhere, post-*Lawrence*.

Next in the Court's description of what state marriage recognition is (beyond a classification for purposes of distributing benefits) comes another reference to the same-sex couple's 'intimate' relationship and to its equality with marriages between opposite-sex couples. The Court wrote: '[t]his status is a far-reaching legal acknowledgment of the intimate relationship between two people, a relationship deemed by the State worthy of dignity in the community equal with all other marriages.'[37] Again, no state sources are cited.

Finally, the majority opined – and again without citing any supporting state sources – that New York decided to recognize same-sex marriages on the basis of reflections about 'both the community's considered perspective on the historical roots of the institution of marriage and its evolving understanding of the meaning of equality.'[38]

Speaking further about the meaning of state marriage recognition respecting same-sex couples, the *Windsor* majority claimed that states intend marriage recognition to affirm the 'integrity and closeness' of the household of children living with two adults of the same sex, as well as their 'concord with other families in their community' and 'concord with other families . . . in their daily lives.'[39] It is not perfectly clear from the context whether the Court is using 'concord' to indicate 'peace' or 'equality' or perhaps 'similarity' with other families in a community – presumably families headed by two adults of opposite sexes. Again, no supporting state sources, or sources of any kind, are cited here.

The material in the *Windsor* opinion concerning the meaning of marriage recognition at state law is both extensive and scattered. Yet a few of its notable characteristics can be summarized. First, it is an account which owes nothing to state law sources or even to the myriad prior Supreme Court decisions dependent upon the meaning of marriage in state law – all of which feature procreation as an automatic and important state interest.[40] This is obviously

35 *Windsor* at 2692.
36 *Windsor* at 2692.
37 *Windsor* at 2692.
38 *Windsor* at 2692–2693.
39 *Windsor* at 2694.
40 For a summary of the Court's extensive record of approving states' interests in the procreative aspects of opposite-sex marriage, see 'Brief of Amicus Curiae Helen M. Alvaré in Support of Hollingsworth and Bipartisan Legal Advisory Group Addressing the Merits and Supporting Reversal, In the Supreme Court of the United States, Nos. 12–144, 12–307, *Hollingsworth v. Perry*, and *United States v. Windsor*.'

curious considering the majority's lengthy treatment of the importance of states' sovereignty respecting marriage recognition.

Second, *Windsor* ignores completely the most hotly debated subject matter in the same-sex marriage controversy: the relationship between state marriage recognition and linking children with the parents who gave them life. Perhaps the Supreme Court ignored this material on the understanding that it was speaking strictly about the meaning of marriage in those states which had chosen to recognize same-sex marriages – in which case perhaps the Court could assume that the state claimed no interest in linking children with their biological parents. But the *Windsor* Court did not indicate that its consideration of the meaning of state marriage recognition was thus limited; rather, it spoke *generally* about 'The States' interest in defining and regulating the marital relation.'[41] If the latter is true, then it is stunning that the Court left out children's interests in being reared by their natural parents, not only because the subject figures so largely in the same-sex marriage debate, but also because the Court has repeatedly, robustly, and over the course of more than 120 years, highlighted and strongly affirmed states' interests in linking marriage with both procreation and childrearing.[42]

Windsor's treatment of state marriage recognition focuses instead upon a range of claimed adult interests in marriage: self-definition, specifically as a person committed in a special emotional and sexual way to one other person; affirmations of a sexual relationship; dignity and personhood; and affirmation of the equality of same-sex and opposite-sex pairs.[43] The merits of this recently emerging adult- and emotion-centric vision of marriage are hotly contested, particularly as it interrelates with marriage stability, the welfare of the less-privileged, and children's welfare.[44]

To the extent that the *Windsor* Court considered children at all, it was only in relation to the subset of those children living with two adults of the same sex, that is, those children presently living with two adults of the same sex *who are also their parents*. But the majority of children (about 86 percent) living with two adults of the same sex were conceived in a prior heterosexual encounter and have a legal mother who is female and a legal father who is male.[45] The Court opines, without citing any sources, that this subset of children will have difficulty gaining a sense of family unity and equality with other families who do not have same-sex parents, if state and federal law treat their parents' marriages differently.[46]

Obergefell's treatment of the 'meaning' of marriage – also penned by Justice Kennedy for a five-Justice majority – was quite similar. Marriage is a governmental entitlement of enormous psychic and material importance; an individual's dignity,[47] liberty,[48] social status,[49] and even personhood[50] are closely bound to the receipt of a state license recognizing an

41 *Windsor* at 2392.

42 See Alvaré Amicus, *Hollingsworth*, supra note 40 at 9–15.

43 *Windsor* 2694.

44 See 'Living Together? *Reasons to Continue*' below.

45 Mark Regnerus, 'How different are the adult children of parents who have same-sex relationships? Findings from the new family structures study', (2012) 41 *Social Science Research* 752; Garry J. Gates, 'Family Focus on . . . LGBT Families: Family formation and raising children among same-sex couples', (2011) *National Council on Family Relations Report*, Issue FF51.

46 *Windsor* at 2694.

47 *Windsor* at 2594.

48 *Windsor* at 2593.

49 *Windsor* at 2613.

50 *Windsor* at 2602.

emotional and sexual bond with another person as 'marriage'. To deny marriage is to condemn a person to emotional hell.[51] After Justice Kennedy called state-recognized marriage a 'transcendent' reality,[52] an answer to the 'universal fear that a lonely person might call out only to find no one there',[53] a 'profound' union embodying the 'highest ideals of love, fidelity, devotion, sacrifice and family',[54] he wrote that to be denied marriage is to be 'condemned to live in loneliness, excluded from one of civilization's oldest institutions'.[55]

'A Bare . . . Desire to Harm'

The *Windsor* Court offered several grounds for its conclusion that section three of DOMA reflected a 'bare . . . desire to harm'[56] same-sex couples.

First, DOMA's refusal to grant federal same-sex marriage recognition was an 'unusual deviation from the usual tradition of recognizing and accepting state definitions of marriage'.[57] It called this choice a '[d]iscrimination[] of an unusual character,' requiring 'careful consideration'.[58] Eventually the majority held that DOMA's 'unusual' character constituted 'strong evidence of a law having the purpose and effect of disapproval' of the class of same-sex couples married in the eyes of their state's law.[59] The Court further commented here that because marriage law is state law, federal lawmakers passing marriage-related laws are charged with knowing that they are affecting people's 'daily lives and customs'.[60]

The Court then took three paths from its observations about DOMA's novelty and personal impacts, to its conclusion that DOMA springs from a 'bare congressional desire to harm a politically unpopular group.'[61]

The first path is indicated by the Court's frequently intertwining, in this part of the opinion, material identifying the meaning of state marriage recognition with material about congressional purpose. Given what the Court proposes marriage recognition *to mean* (recognition of emotional and sexual commitment; identity enhancement; and a marker of 'dignity,' 'equality,' and 'personhood'), federal lawmakers' 'no' in response to a state's 'yes', is a no to the dignity, equality, and personhood of same-sex attracted persons and couples. If the Court is right about the meaning of marriage, then it is irrational to refuse 'marriage' to a type of couple (same-sex) whose behaviors, desires, and natures (dignified, persons, equal) fall within the meaning of state marriage recognition.

51 Michael Cobb, 'The Supreme Court's Lonely Hearts Club', *The New York Times*, 30 June 2015, http://www.nytimes.com/2015/06/30/opinion/the-supreme-courts-lonely-hearts-club.html (accessed 24 October 2015). See also Andrew Koppelman, 'The Supreme Court Made the Right Call on Marriage Equality – But They Did it the Wrong Way', *Salon*, 29 June 2015, http://www.salon.com/2015/06/29/the_supreme_court_made_the_right_call_on_marriage_equality_%E2%80%94_but_they_did_it_the_wrong_way/ (accessed 24 October 2015).

52 *Windsor* at 2590.

53 *Windsor* at 2600.

54 *Windsor* at 2608.

55 *Windsor* at 2608.

56 *Windsor* at 2693 (quoting *Department of Agriculture v. Moreno*, 413 U.S. 528, 534–53 (1973)).

57 *Windsor* at 2693.

58 *Windsor* at 2693.

59 *Windsor* at 2693.

60 *Windsor* at 2693.

61 *Windsor* at 2693.

The second path to the Court's conclusion that Congress enacted DOMA with a bare desire to harm involves the Court's interpretation of DOMA's legislative history. The Court's entire legislative history analysis is as follows:

> The history of DOMA's enactment and its own text demonstrate that interference with the equal dignity of same-sex marriages, a dignity conferred by the States in the exercise of their sovereign power, was more than an incidental effect of the federal statute. It was its essence. The House Report announced its conclusion that 'it is both appropriate and necessary for Congress to do what it can to defend the institution of traditional heterosexual marriage . . . H. R. 3396 is appropriately entitled the 'Defense of Marriage Act.' The effort to redefine 'marriage' to extend to homosexual couples is a truly radical proposal that would fundamentally alter the institution of marriage.' H. R. Rep. No. 104–664, pp. 12–13 (1996). The House concluded that DOMA expresses 'both moral disapproval of homosexuality, and a moral conviction that heterosexuality better comports with traditional (especially Judeo- Christian) morality.' *Id.*, at 16 (footnote deleted). The stated purpose of the law was to promote an 'interest in protecting the traditional moral teachings reflected in heterosexual-only marriage laws.' *Ibid.* Were there any doubt of this far-reaching purpose, the title of the Act confirms it: The Defense of Marriage.[62]

Following this paragraph, the Court writes that the 'arguments put forward by BLAG [the Bipartisan Legal Advisory Group, the congressional group intervening in the case following the Executive's refusal to defend DOMA]' are 'just as candid about the congressional purpose to influence or interfere with state sovereign choices about who may be married.'[63] Yet none of BLAG's arguments about congressional purpose are actually articulated here or elsewhere in *Windsor*. Rather, one sentence after referring to BLAG's arguments on congressional purpose, the Court wrote simply that 'The congressional goal was "to put a thumb on the scales and influence a state's decision as to how to shape its own marriage laws".'[64] But BLAG never said this. Rather, this is language from a First Circuit DOMA opinion.[65] Furthermore, a look at the only piece of legislative history actually cited by the *Windsor* majority – the House Judiciary Report – reveals numerous statements disclaiming such animus while highlighting children's interests, as will be considered below.

The *Windsor* Court further considered the significance of DOMA's defining marriage for *every* federal law referencing marriage or spouses, without 'identified connection to any particular area of federal law.'[66] It interpreted this choice as a further indication of Congress' purpose to make a 'subset of state-sanctioned marriages . . . unequal.'[67] In other words, the Court suggested that its animus analysis might have concluded differently had federal lawmakers considered the

62 *Windsor* at 2693.

63 *Windsor* at 2693.

64 *Windsor* at 2693 (citing *Massachusetts v. U.S. Department of Health and Human Services*, 682 F. 3d. 1, 12–13 (2012)).

65 *Massachusetts v. U.S. Dep't of Health & Human Servs.*, 682 F.3d 1, 12–13 (1st Cir. 2012) ('. . . Congress' effort to put a thumb on the scales and influence a state's decision as to how to shape its own marriage laws does bear on how the justifications are assessed.')

66 *Windsor* at 2694.

67 *Windsor* at 2694.

wisdom of retaining an opposite-sexed understanding of marriage, for *each* of the approximately 1,000 affected federal laws.

The third path to the majority's conclusion about DOMA's purpose was its description of the *personal* harms it claimed that DOMA visited on same-sex couples and children in their households. In this part of its opinion, the Court cited no sources save *Lawrence's* reference to same-sex couples' 'moral and sexual choices'.[68] It appears therefore that the majority conflated its intuitions about personal harms with a congressional purpose to harm. The language is highly emotional, and definitive. The Court claimed, for example, that DOMA communicates to same-sex couples that their otherwise valid marriages are 'second-tier' and 'unworthy'; it renders their situations 'unstable' and 'humiliates tens of thousands of children now being raised by same-sex couples'.[69]

More than a few aspects of *Windsor*'s animus analysis suggest that Court had paved the way for judges in the future to find a purpose to harm in the simple fact of disagreement with a state's legally recognizing same-sex marriage. This prediction was fulfilled in *Obergefell,* where the denial of same-sex marriage was simply constitutionally equated with demeaning gay and lesbian citizens.[70] As noted above, this dynamic threatens the potential success of religious freedom exemptions to same-sex marriage laws. The first aspect, as already noted above, is the Court's conclusion about the meaning of state marriage recognition. If the Court means what it says about the animus underlying 'same-sex marriage denying', then a refusal to recognize marriage between two emotionally-committed, sexually-intimate persons is irrational, and points toward discriminatory animus.

Second, the Court could easily have characterized DOMA's, or any state's opposite-sex-marriage only laws, as proportionate to the unprecedented nature of the precipitating events: for DOMA, the decision by one state (Hawaii) to redefine marriage so as to contradict the meaning nearly always and everywhere held, not only in the United States, but globally and historically;[71] for state laws, the movement to impose same-sex marriage upon unwilling citizens via judicial opinions and unpopular legislative action. Pre-*Obergefell*, without DOMA, mandatory federal recognition of same-sex marriage change would affect the meaning and application of more than 1,000 federal laws, every one of which was drafted on the assumption that marriage is an opposite-sexed institution. The Court could easily have reasoned otherwise about DOMA's broad effect, drawing for example the reasonable conclusion that Congress acted rationally to preserve the understanding upon which all federal laws were based, a move which did not foreclose later redefining marriage for purposes of *particular* federal laws, after congressional consideration of the impact of including same-sex couples within the ambit of that particular law. This process had begun to unfold pre-*Windsor* in the form of bills like S. 296 (to alter federal immigration laws to allow same-sex partners to immigrate on the same basis as opposite-sex spouses).[72]

68 *Windsor* at 2694.

69 *Windsor* at 2694.

70 See *Obergefell* at 2594, 2602.

71 *Baehr v. Miike*, 910 P.2d 1996, 80 Haw. 341 (1996).

72 See The Uniting American Families Act, S. 296 (113th Cong., 1st Sess.) (A Bill to 'amend the Immigration and Nationality Act to . . . permit[] permanent partners of United States citizens and lawful permanent residents to obtain lawful permanent resident status in the same manner as spouses of citizens and lawful permanent residents . . .').

Also concerning the matter of DOMA's allegedly 'unusual' nature, the majority overlooked entirely the federal government's earlier refusal to accept a state's redefining marriage in the only other historical case which could claim equal moment: polygamy. In 1894, the U.S. government refused to allow Utah to join the union until it had agreed never to permit polygamy in its laws.[73] Justice Scalia raised this point in his *Windsor* dissent.[74]

Third – regarding the use of legislative history – the majority consulted only a tiny fraction of the legislative material treating DOMA's 'purpose.' First, the majority suggested that a reference in the House Report to DOMA's 'moral' purpose indicated unacceptable animus. Yet Congress regularly invokes moral and even religious language to support legislation, without any suggestion of unacceptable animus. Former House Speaker Pelosi, for example has asserted that a saint recognized by the Catholic Church (St. Joseph) might intervene to assist the passage of Health Care Reform;[75] that the DREAM Act (concerning immigration) is 'the right thing to do – both economically for our country and morally;'[76] and that the Healthy, Hunger-Free Kids Act was 'the right moral thing for us to do'.[77] Even the opinion arguably most relevant to the majority's scrutiny of moral purpose, *Lawrence v. Texas*, stated only that moral purposes *alone* were insufficient to constitute a rational basis for a law criminalizing homosexual sodomy.[78] And even that conclusion is called into question by Justice Scalia's *Lawrence* dissent pointing out that more than a few still-extant state laws are grounded solely upon moral rationales.[79]

Furthermore, the legislative history of DOMA is replete with legislative purposes separate from morality. These included, for example: the uncertainties of interpreting and applying to same-sex marriages federal law intended to cover opposite-sex pairs; migrating couples' choice-of-law; and a desire to preserve nationally a vision of marriage intrinsically inclusive of children and their interest in linkage with their parents.[80]

On this last point, while the *Windsor* majority stated that the word 'defense' in DOMA's title indicated harmful animus, the section of the House Report from which the majority plucked its leading quotations on this point was largely devoted to describing the links between opposite-sex marriage and children's interests, particularly their interests in maintaining connections with their birth-parents. In fact, surrounding the majority opinion's selected quotations from pages 12, 13, and 16 of the House Report about 'defend[ing]'

73 See Act of July 16, 1894, ch. 138, § 3, 28 Stat. 108.

74 *Windsor* at 2705 (Scalia, J., dissenting).

75 Real Clear Politics Video, 'Pelosi Prays to St. Joseph to Pass Health Care', 19 March 2012, http://www.realclearpolitics.com/video/2010/03/19/pelosi_prays_to_st_joseph_to_pass_health_care.html (accessed 24 October 2015).

76 Nancy Pelosi, 'DREAM Act Passes 216–198', 8 December 2012, at http://www.democraticleader.gov/newsroom/dream-act-passes-216–198/ (accessed 2 November 2015).

77 Jeff Winkler, 'Democrats Urge Congress to Pass the Healthy, Hunger-Free Kids Act', *The Daily Caller*, 11 November 2010, http://dailycaller.com/2010/11/30/democrats-urge-congress-to-pass-healthy-hunger-free-kids-act/#ixzz2dW0BfkkP (accessed 24 October 2015).

78 *Lawrence v. Texas*, 539 U.S. 558, 571 (2003) ('The condemnation has been shaped by religious beliefs, conceptions of right and acceptable behavior, and respect for the traditional family . . . The issue is whether the majority may use the power of the State to enforce these views on the whole society through operation of the criminal law. 'Our obligation is to define the liberty of all, not to mandate our own moral code')

79 *Lawrence* at 589–592 (Scalia, J., dissenting).

80 House Report Rep. No. 104–664 (1996) at 12–18 [H.R.].

marriage and 'traditional . . . morality', were statements on pages 13 and 14 and 15, and 33 about children as the *primary* congressional motivation to 'defend' marriage. These congressional statements included:

- 'At bottom, civil society has an interest in maintaining and protecting the institution of heterosexual marriage because it has a deep and abiding interest in encouraging responsible procreation and child-rearing.'[81]
- 'Simply put, government has an interest in marriage because it has an interest in children.'[82]
- 'And from this nexus between marriage and children springs the true source of society's interest in safeguarding the institution of marriage . . .'[83]
- 'Were it not for the possibility of begetting children inherent in heterosexual unions, society would have no particular interest in encouraging citizens to come together in a committed relationship.'[84]
- '[B]ecause America, like nearly every known human society, is concerned about its children, our government has a special obligation to ensure that we preserve and protect the institution of marriage.'[85]
- 'There are, then, significant practical reasons why government affords preferential status to the institution of heterosexual marriage. These reasons – procreation and child-rearing – are in accord with nature and hence have a moral component.'[86]
- 'Rather, [traditional marriage laws] have been the unbroken rule and tradition in this and other countries primarily because they are conducive to the objectives of procreation and responsible childrearing.'[87]

The House Report even addressed the matter of animus directly:

> It would be incomprehensible for any court to conclude that traditional marriage laws are (as the Supreme Court concluded regarding Amendment 2 [in *Romer v. Evans*[88]]) motivated by animus toward homosexuals. Rather, they have been the unbroken rule and tradition in this (and other) countries primarily because they are conducive to the objectives of procreation and responsible child-rearing.[89]

Fourth, part of the majority's 'animus' analysis included blaming federal lawmakers for legislating about 'domestic relations' – because this area affects the 'daily lives and customs' of people.[90] This argument is clearly a make-weight. Federal laws play a crucial role in many domestic relations arenas, including importantly, child-support,[91] marriage and fatherhood

81 H.R., supra note 80 at 13.
82 H.R. at 14.
83 H.R. at 14.
84 H.R. at 14.
85 H.R. at 14.
86 H.R. at 15.
87 H.R. at 33.
88 *Romer v. Evans*, 517 U.S. 620 (1996) (striking Colorado law banning sexual orientation antidiscrimination standards).
89 H.R. at 33.
90 *Windsor* at 2693.
91 The Child Support Recovery Act 18 U.S.C. § 228; The Personal Responsibility and Work Opportunity Reconciliation Act, Pub. L. 104–193 (1996).

promotion,[92] and family and medical leave.[93] Further federal rules in these areas not only *influence* local domestic relations bureaucracies and employers, and parental and children's behavior – they are often *decisive*. Still, they have failed neither federalism nor other constitutional tests.

Windsor's conclusions about the meaning of state marriage recognition, and about the animus allegedly undergirding DOMA, set up a difficult environment for religions. Religious actors opposed to same-sex marriage would need protection analogous to what DOMA provided to the federal government: a right, in one's own domain to recognize marriage as opposite-sexed only.

While *Windsor's* majority promised that '[t]his opinion and its holding are confined' to 'those whom the State, by its marriage laws, sought to protect in personhood and dignity,' the tone and the substance of its opinion portend otherwise. *Windsor* provided a template for legislators and judges to create same-sex marriage recognition laws: claim deference to state authority regarding marriage while defining marriage strictly by their own personal lights; ignore prior judicial decisions approvingly linking marriage-recognition to children's interests; and employ deeply emotional and human rights language to characterize both the meaning of marriage and the results of denying marriage to same-sex pairs and the children in their households. Justice Kennedy's opinion in *Obergefell*, then, accepted Justice Kennedy's *Windsor* invitation.

Marriage in the Roman Catholic Tradition

It is common to hear that same-sex marriage will create a legal clash with Catholics' religious freedom, based upon summary references to the Catholic Church's scripturally based opposition to homosexual sexual practices.[94] Yet Catholic arguments against forced cooperation with same-sex marriage are focused upon the meaning of marriage, not upon the moral status of sexual practices. They engage the question of same-sex marriage only as a logical conclusion to their reasoning about what marriage is by nature, and in light of scripture and theological tradition.

The essence of the Catholic position is this: the Catechism of the Catholic Church ('the Catechism') – its 'statement of the Church's faith and of Catholic doctrine, attested to or illumined by Sacred Scripture, the Apostolic Tradition, and the church's Magisterium,' 'declare[d] . . . to be a sure norm for teaching the faith'[95] – devotes 66 (1601–1666) paragraphs to the meaning of marriage and only three (2357–2359) to the question of the morality of homosexual sexual intercourse. One of these three paragraphs on homosexual behavior primarily concerns the requirement to treat homosexual persons with 'respect, compassion and sensitivity,'[96] avoiding 'every sign of unjust discrimination.'[97] None of the paragraphs

92 The Claims Resolution Act of 2010 (Pub. L. 111–291) (2010)) provides funding of $150 million in each of five years for healthy marriage promotion and responsible fatherhood. Each year, $75 million may be used for activities promoting fatherhood, such as counseling, mentoring, marriage education, enhancing relationship skills, parenting, and activities to foster economic stability.

93 The Family and Medical Leave Act, 29 U.S.C., Chapter 28.

94 See Genesis 19:5–8; Leviticus 18:22–23; Leviticus 20:13; 1 Timothy 1:9–10; Romans 1:26–27.

95 Pope John Paul II, *Fidei Depositum* (Apostolic Constitution on the Publication of the Catechism of the Catholic Church), 11 Oct 1992, ¶ 3 ('The Doctrinal Value of the Text').

96 See Catechism of the Catholic Church ¶¶ 2357–59.

97 Catechism ¶ 2358.

on homosexuality appear under the banner of teachings about 'marriage.' The only practical point of overlap between the 'marriage' and the 'homosexuality' portions of the Catechism is the observation in paragraph 2357 that homosexual sex is intrinsically closed to life;[98] paragraphs 1652 and 1653 on marriage state that marriage must be open to life. The official statements on same-sex marriage by Catholic bishops' conferences, not only in the United States but also in Europe, reveal these twin characteristics: respect for homosexual persons, and lengthy attention to the full meaning of marriage.[99]

Marriage as a Glimpse of the Person of God

Catholics believe that marriage is intended to offer a glimpse of God's self as Trinity – Father, Son, and Holy Spirit – three persons united in a relationship of endless love. This relationship is reflected in the marital union of the man and the woman – body and soul – and the fact that this union is the unique place where the Creator located new human life. In the words of the highest doctrinal body of the universal Catholic Church, the Congregation for the Doctrine of the Faith (CDF), the 'complementarity of the sexes . . . reflects the inner unity of the Creator,'[100] and '"the image and likeness" of God constitutes the immutable *basis of all Christian anthropology.*'[101] By 'Christian anthropology' the Church means understanding facets of the human person in light of God: humans' origins, divine likeness, structure, purpose, destiny, and relations with God and other persons.

Catholics, then, are called to live in loving communion, like God; and marriage is the first and fundamental dimension of this call.[102] John Paul II's apostolic exhortation of the family explains this further: men's and women's complementarity 'on all levels,' 'body . . . character . . . heart, intelligence. . . will . . . soul', their 'communion rooted in natural bonds of flesh and blood . . .,' images the Trinitarian God, who is a "mystery of personal loving communion."[103]

God's creative power is also imaged in the man and the woman together. The Catechism states that: 'the union of male and female imitates God's fecundity.'[104] Children are the 'living testimony of the full, reciprocal self-giving of the spouses.'[105]

98 Catechism ¶ 2357.

99 See, for example, U.S. Conference of Catholic Bishops, *Love and Life in the Divine Plan* (2009), http://www.usccb.org/issues-and-action/marriage-and-family/marriage/love-and-life/upload/pastoral-letter-marriage-love-and-life-in-the-divine-plan.pdf (accessed 24 October 2015). Executive Committee of the Bishops' Conference of Spain, Nota sobre el matrimonio y el fallo del Tribunal Constitucional (8 November 2012), http://www.conferenciaepiscopal.es/index.php/documentos-ejecutivo/3275-nota-sobre-el-matrimonio-y-el-fallo-del-tribunal-constitucional.html (accessed 24 October 2015). The Bishops' Conference of France, 'Élargir le mariage aux personnes de même sexe? Ouvrons le débat!' (September 2012), http://bit.ly/1Q16eu5 (accessed 2 November 2015).

100 Congregation for the Doctrine of the Faith (CDF), *Letter to the Bishops of the Catholic Church on the Pastoral Care of Homosexual Persons* ¶ 6 (1986).

101 Love and Responsibility, *On the Collaboration of Men and Women, in the Church and in the World* (2004), 5 (citing John Paul II, *Apostolic Letter Mulieris Dignitatem* (On the Dignity of Women) (15 August 1988)), ¶ 6.

102 *Mulieris Dignitatem* ¶ 7 (1988).

103 *Familiaris Consortio* ¶¶ 11, 19, 21.

104 Catechism ¶ 2335.

105 *Familiaris Consortio* ¶ 28.

Marriage as Humanity's Glimpse of God's Relationship with Human Beings

Statements by Pope Francis, the Catechism, and John Paul II's *Familiaris Consortio*, hold marriage to be indispensable for understanding the way in which God loves his people. Pope Francis called marriage an 'icon of God's love,' stating that 'When a man and a woman celebrate the sacrament of marriage, God is reflected in them.' 'As "one flesh", they become living icons of God's love in our world, building up the Church in unity and fidelity,' he said. 'The image of God is the married couple – not just the man, not just the woman, but both.'[106] The Catechism states that opposite-sex marriage 'becomes an image of the absolute and unfailing love with which God loves man',[107] the 'image and sign of the covenant which unites God and His people.'[108] Both point to the marital analogies and language featuring prominently in both the Old Testament descriptions of the covenant between God and Israel and in New Testament passages about God and the Church. God's relationship with Israel is captured in the language of fidelity, adultery, love and betrayal.[109] In the New Testament, reflecting on the unity of man and woman at the moment of the world's creation, the Apostle Paul exclaims: 'this mystery is a profound one, and I am saying that it refers to Christ and the Church' (*Eph.* 5:32). The very last book of the New Testament, the Book of Revelation, refers often to the 'bride' of God, the 'new Jerusalem,' (3:12; 21:2, 9–10) and the 'marriage' of the Lamb (19:7), referring to the relationship between God and his people.

Marriage as Instructions for how to Love One Another

Catholics understand sexual difference, and sexual complementarity, as pointing toward the meaning and purpose of life itself. This meaning is to love one another. Writes the CDF: Men's and women's 'capacity to love' others is a 'reflection and image of God who is Love' and 'disclosed in the spousal character of the body, in which the masculinity or femininity of the person is expressed.'[110] 'The human dimension of sexuality is inseparable from the theological dimension.'[111] "'Sexually differentiated, complementary marriage is not only a sign of human persons' essentially relational nature but is the norm of all relationships, which is love. Marriage is simply the 'primordial' expression,[112] the symbolically and physically and temporally complete (*e.g.* 'one-flesh,' and 'until death do us part') expression, and the most evidently fruitful expression, of the norm of love. It embodies the 'ethos' which must characterize the life of Christians.'[113]

106 Josephine McKenna, 'Pope Francis calls traditional marriage an icon of God's love', *Religion News Service* (2 April 2014), http://www.religionnews.com/2014/04/02/pope-francis-calls-traditional-marriage-icon-gods-love/ (accessed 24 October 2015).

107 Catechism ¶ 1604.

108 *Familiaris Consortio* ¶ 12.

109 Catechism ¶¶ 1611–1612.

110 *On the Collaboration of Men and Women*, supra note 101, ¶ 8.

111 *On the Collaboration of Men and Women* ¶ 8.

112 John Paul II, General Audience of 20 October 1982, http://www.ewtn.com/library/ papaldoc/jp2tb98.htm ('Marriage was also a part of this integral heritage – as can be deduced from the Letter to the Ephesians 5:21–33 – marriage, that is, as a primordial sacrament instituted from the beginning and linked with the sacrament of creation in its globality. The sacramentality of marriage is not merely a *model and figure* of the sacrament of the Church (of Christ and of the Church). It also constitutes an *essential part* of the new heritage, that of the sacrament of redemption, with which the Church is endowed in Christ.')

113 John Paul II, General Audience of 20 October 1982, supra note 112.

Marriage is Ordained Both for the Good of Spouses and for Procreation

In Catholic teaching marriage is 'by nature ordained [both to] the good of spouses and the procreation and education of offspring.'[114] Catholic doctrinal sources often trace the procreative aspect of marriage back to the Genesis passage wherein God commands the couple to '[b]e fruitful and multiply' (Gen. 1:28). In the 'procreation and education of offspring [marriage] finds its crowning glory.'[115]

Spousal friendship and children are regularly articulated together in a Catholic theology of marriage: 'true married love . . . without diminishment of the other ends' of marriage, is 'directed to disposing the spouses to cooperate valiantly with the love of the Creator.'[116] In 'this sense, the fundamental task of marriage and family is to be at the service of human life.'[117] The two goods of marriage cannot be separated 'without altering the couple's spiritual life and compromising the goods of marriage and the future of the family.'[118]

It is important to maintain the procreative aspect of marriage in Catholic teaching, not simply because 'all human generations come from this union,'[119] but also because it can help human beings avoid 'using' one another sexually – even if they possess every intention of avoiding 'use' – due to the strength of the sexual urge. In order to live what John Paul II called the 'personalistic norm' of love[120] – 'to love one another as I have loved you' (John 13:34) – there can be no using one another as a means to an end, even of sexual pleasure. But because sex is the source of such intense pleasure it is too 'easy to go from the experience of pleasure, to the quest of pleasure for its own sake, to accepting it as the superlative value and proper basis for a norm of behavior.'[121] John Paul II reflects that it could even be 'unthinkable' to overcome the tendency to use another sexually, 'without a common good to which both are inclined . . . [a] good to which they are willing to subordinate themselves [], and one to the other, for its sake.'[122] This good is children.

Another aspect of the procreative nature of marriage concerns the rights of children. God's instituting of marriage ('This is why a man leaves his father and mother and clings to his wife, and the two of them become one body' (Gen. 2:24)) indicates that children have rights respecting their origins and their family life. They have the right to be created in an act worthy of a human person – an act of love – and to be reared by their mother and father in marriage.[123] Because God's 'image and likeness' come into being in the world, practically speaking, by means of procreation, and this is done by persons we call 'father' and 'mother' (as God is Father and Jesus had a mother and a heavenly father) it is possible to say that 'God himself is present in human fatherhood and motherhood.' Both He and they are the 'source of image and likeness' to God that humans bear. In the formulation of Pope John Paul II: 'the

114 Catechism ¶ 1601.

115 Catechism ¶ 1652.

116 Catechism ¶ 1652 (citing *Gaudium et Spes* (Constitution on the Church in the Modern World (1965)), 48, §§1 and 50.

117 Catechism ¶ 1653 (citing *Familiaris Consortio* ¶ 28).

118 Catechism ¶ 2363.

119 Catechism ¶ 2335.

120 John Paul II, *Love and Responsibility* (Ignatius Press 1993), 41.

121 *Love and Responsibility* at 43.

122 *Love and Responsibility* at 28.

123 Congregation for the Doctrine of the Faith, *Donum Vitae* ('Instruction on Respect for Human Life in its Origin and on the Dignity of Procreation: Replies to Certain Questions of the Day') Introduction, 5 (1987); see also Catechism ¶ 2376.

genealogy of the person [i.e. his or her actual relationship both to God, as image and likeness, and to the parents] is inscribed in the very biology of generation.'[124]

Consequently, no adult has a 'right' to a child. Every child is rather a gift.[125] Closely related, given the total union that marriage is and represents, spouses have a right to become a father and a mother 'only through each other.'[126]

Same-sex unions intrinsically exclude this procreative dimension. Also, they are increasingly associated with recourse to artificial reproductive technologies,[127] which will, in every case, partly or completely dissociate the child from his or her parents, and his or her origins in an act of love.

For Marriage, not Animus Against Persons

Two elements of Catholic teaching, while they do not directly concern the meaning of marriage, seem important to raise when considering religious freedom post-*Windsor*. The first concerns relationships *other* than same-sex marriage, which contradict Catholic teachings about marriage. The second concerns the volume of Catholic doctrine strenuously asserting the equal dignity of same-sex attracted persons.

First, more than a few types of intimate relationships contradict Catholic teachings about marriage and the family. Same-sex unions are not a discrete target. Indeed, 'offenses against the dignity of marriage' or 'attempted partnerships which deny the truth of marriage' are several, including sexual union before marriage, sex closed to procreation by artificial contraception, adultery, divorce, polygamy, remarriage, or what Church documents call 'free unions,' *i.e.* sexual liaisons without formal entry into marriage.[128] As the CDF's 'Letter to the Bishops of the Catholic Church on the Pastoral Care of Homosexual Persons' states: 'Christians who are homosexual are called, *as all of us are*, to a chaste life.'[129]

Second, in document after document, and decade after decade, authoritative Catholic sources repeat the imperative to respect homosexual persons and to condemn unjust discrimination. The Catechism's summary of Church teaching in this area states unequivocally that homosexual persons 'must be accepted with respect, compassion and sensitivity. Every sign of unjust discrimination in their regard should be avoided . . . These persons are called to fulfill God's will in their lives.'[130]

The broader framework for this statement was constructed in 1965 at Vatican II, in the important document, *Gaudium et Spes*, where the basis for the equality and dignity of all human persons was set forth: 'Since all men possess a rational soul and are created in God's likeness, since they have the same nature and origin, have been redeemed by Christ and enjoy the same divine calling and destiny, the basic equality of all must receive increasingly

124 John Paul II, *Gratissimam Sane*, Letter to Families (1994), at ¶ 9.

125 Catechism ¶ 2378.

126 Catechism ¶ 2376.

127 See, for example, Gay Parent: LGBT Magazine, *Assisted Reproduction Resources* (2013), http://www.gayparentmag.com/assisted-reproduction (accessed 2 November 2015).

128 Catechism ¶ 1653.

129 CDF, 'Letter to the Bishops of the Catholic Church on the Pastoral Care of Homosexual Persons' (1986), para. 12, http://www.vatican.va/roman_curia/congregations/cfaith/documents/rc_con_cfaith_doc_19861001_ homosexual- persons_en.html (accessed 2 November 2015).

130 Catechism ¶ 2358.

greater recognition . . . [E]very type of discrimination . . . is to be overcome and eradicated as contrary to God's intent.'[131]

Ten years later, speaking specifically about same-sex attracted persons, the CDF's *Persona Humana* (Declaration on Certain Questions Concerning Sexual Ethics) concluded: 'They must be accepted with respect, compassion and sensitivity. Every sign of unjust discrimination in their regard should be avoided.[132]

In 1986 the CDF, headed by then Cardinal Joseph Ratzinger, issued its *Letter to Bishops on the Pastoral Care of Homosexual Persons*, asserting: 'It is *deplorable* that homosexual persons have been and are the object of violent malice in speech or in action. Such treatment deserves condemnation . . . The intrinsic dignity of each person must always be respected in word, *in action and in law*.'[133]

Even in the doctrinal statements banning Christians from approving homosexual acts, there appear admonitions to affirm the dignity of homosexual persons. In 2003 the CDF stated: 'Moral conscience requires that, in every occasion, Christians give witness to the whole moral truth, which is contradicted both by approval of homosexual acts *and* by unjust discrimination against homosexual persons.'[134]

Living Together?

This section considers why citizens and legislatures might *wish* to allow exemptions for religious actors. I will address these possibilities from a Catholic perspective, acknowledge significant hurdles, and consider already existing conscience proposals.

Practical Obstacles

In an era of constitutionalized same-sex marriage, it doubtless will be very difficult for religious actors to gain exemptions. Scholars writing about same-sex marriage and religious liberty have frankly acknowledged as much. In the words of activist Chai Feldblum: 'The most pressing question for LGBT people probably is not 'How can we be sure that we are adequately considering and taking into account the beliefs of those who believe we are immoral and sinful?'[135] Even a more reflective observer, such as constitutional scholar Douglas Laycock, predicted: 'The most likely political outcome is that if the gay-rights movement becomes strong enough to enact general recognition of same-sex marriage, it will simply roll over its opponents on all these collateral questions.'[136] Rabbi Marc Stern agreed: 'The remaining question is whether champions of tolerance are prepared to tolerate proponents of a different ethical vision. I think the answer will be no.'[137] Thus far, Laycock and Stern have proved correct. State laws have provided little protection for religious conscience.[138]

131 *Gaudium et Spes*, supra note 116 at 29.

132 Sacred Congregation for the Doctrine of the Faith (Prefect, Angelo Cardinal Seper), *Persona Humana*, Declaration on Certain Questions Concerning Sexual Ethics VIII (1975) (emphasis added).

133 CDF, 'Letter to the Bishops', supra note 129 at para. 10 (emphasis added).

134 CDF, *Considerations Regarding Proposals to Give Legal Recognition to Unions Between Homosexual Persons* (2003), ¶ 5.

135 Chai Feldblum, 'Moral Conflict and Conflicting Liberties', in Douglas Laycock, Anthony R. Picarello, Jr., and Robin Fretwell Wilson, eds, *Same-sex Marriage and Religious Liberty: Emerging Conflicts* (Rowman & Littlefield 2008): 26.

136 Laycock, Picarello, and Wilson, *Same-sex Marriage and Religious Liberty* at 196.

137 Marc Stern, 'Same-Sex Marriage and the Churches', in Laycock, Picarello, and Wilson at 57.

138 See Appendix A, a summary of state exemptions, in Wilson et al., supra note 11.

Another obstacle to legal protections for religious freedom is the difficulty of articulating thick Catholic teachings in a way that conveys the weight of the burdens on Catholic life posed by forced cooperation with same-sex marriage. The underlying theology, while commonplace in Catholic educational and sacramental contexts, is not commonplace in the public square. This difficulty is compounded not only by widespread disagreement with Catholic marital and sexual norms, but also by the inconsistent witness of some Catholics themselves, whether in the areas of divorce, cohabitation, or same-sex marriage. In the current environment, Catholic teaching can seem impossibly idealistic: fewer Americans understand marriage as a child-focused institution, or view sex as marked by its link with new human life.

Reasons to Continue

At the same time that Americans are cynical about the marriage ideals espoused by Catholics (and others), they continue to support religion and religious freedom.[139] They are also increasingly aware of rising intolerance globally for religious freedom, according to some accounts, and are susceptible to an enhanced awareness of America's accomplishment on this matter.[140] United States citizens are not physically harmed for their free exercise of religion; still there are reasons to conclude that religious liberty is more threatened in the United States today than it was in the recent past[141] – the religious backlash against the federal government's mandate requiring religious actors to provide contraception and early abortifacient insurance;[142] the federal government's (unanimously rejected) claim in the *Hosanna Tabor Evangelical Lutheran Church and School v. Equal Employment Opportunity Commission* [143] litigation that the Constitution has no 'ministerial exemption' to federal employment laws; federal agencies' stripping high-performing religious charities of federal grants for anti-trafficking and health care services, following the creation of new administrative requirements to cooperate with abortion or contraception;[144] the closing or reorganization of religious social services in response to same-sex marriage

139 See Frank Newport, *God is Alive and Well: The Future of Religion in America* (Gallup Press, 2012), 10–11. (The author, Gallup polling's Editor in Chief, summarizes decades of polling about religion in the United States. He concludes that there is a very low percentage of Americans who claim there is no God (6–8 percent), about 40 percent who currently attend services approximately weekly, and about 60 percent who believe religion 'can answer life's problems.')

140 See United States Commission on International Religious Freedom, Annual Report, 2013, http://www.uscirf.gov/sites/default/files/resources/2013%20USCIRF%20Annual%20Report%20(2).pdf and 2014 (a 15-year retrospective) at http://www.uscirf.gov/sites/default/files/USCIRF%202014%20Annual%20Report%20PDF.pdf. (accessed 2 November 2015).

141 Barna Group, 'Americans Concerned about Religious Freedom', 18 January 2013, https://www.barna.org/barna-update/5-barna-update/601-most-americans-are-concerned-about-restrictions-in-religious-freedom#.VjRbvrerS9I (accessed 2 November 2015).

142 See, for example, Archbishop William E. Lori, Russell D. Moore, et al., *Standing Together for Religious Freedom,* an Open Letter to the Obama Administration and the U.S. Congress (2 July 2013) (more than 100 prominent national religious leaders and scholars), http://www.usccb.org/issues-and-action/religious-liberty/upload/standing-together-for-religious-freedom.pdf (accessed 24 October 2015).

143 *Hosanna Tabor v. EEOC*, 132 S.Ct. 694 (2012).

144 For a summary of some of these events in 2011–2012, see Helen Alvaré, 'No Compelling Interest, the 'Birth Control' Mandate and Religious Freedom', (2013) 58 *Villanova Law Review* (3) 388–390.

recognition laws[145] and government subpoenas demanding disclosure about ministers' sermons concerning human sexuality.[146]

Pro-Marriage, not Anti-Person

As we have seen, the basis of a Catholic request for an exemption from cooperating with same-sex marriage is an understanding of marriage, not any animus against persons. This posture is made visible and credible by the witness of Catholic practice, including the history and the size of Catholic outreach worldwide to homosexuals suffering from AIDS. In the U.S. Church established the National Catholic AIDS Network which, by 2008, had 1,600 agencies providing services to AIDS sufferers, including residential facilities and mental health services.[147] Worldwide, as of 2008, the Catholic Church remained the largest private provider of AIDS care, providing 'anti-retroviral treatment, home-care visits and counseling to one in four of the world's 33.3 million AIDS patients.'[148] This is too significant a commitment to dismiss with the bare assertion that Catholic opposition to state-recognized same-sex marriage is the only important marker of Catholic disposition toward homosexual persons.

A Voice for Preserving the Weight of Sex, due to its Relationship with Existence Itself

In the United States today, the 'price' of sex has declined, in large part because of the availability of drugs and devices to disconnect sex and pregnancy.[149] The consequences – more sex outside the context of relationships, more non-marital and unwanted pregnancies, non-marital births, and abortions, and fewer marriages – have been felt largely by the most vulnerable Americans, women, minorities, the poor and the children of the poor.[150] It seems reasonable to propose that even if some wish to elevate relationships which are intrinsically unrelated to procreation – as a remedy for past discrimination and a means of social affirmation – social space should be preserved for a voice which advocates preserving the links between sex and marriage and children. This is an essential aspect of the marriage message of religious actors. Many people, not just religious adherents, are benefitted when the links between sex and marriage and children are preserved; the least-advantaged could benefit most.

145 See U.S. Conference of Catholic Bishops, *USCCB Fact Sheet: Discrimination Against Catholic Adoption Services: Religious Liberty Under Attack* (2013), http://www.usccb.org/issues-and-action/religious-liberty/upload/Catholic-Adoption-Services-Fact-Sheet-Updated.pdf (accessed 2 November 2015).

146 Eugene Volokh, 'Is it Constitutional For a Court to Enforce a Subpoena of Ministers' Sermons?', *The Washington Post,* (15 October 2014), http://www.washingtonpost.com/news/volokh-conspiracy/wp/2014/10/15/is-it-constitutional-for-a-court-to-enforce-a-subpoena-of-ministers-sermons/ (accessed 24 October 2015).

147 Brittany Stahl, *AIDS and the Catholic Church* (Pavement Pieces 2008), http://journalism.nyu.edu/publishing/archives/pavement/city/aids-and-the-catholic-church/index.html (accessed 24 October 2015).

148 Michelle Faul, 'Catholic AIDS Workers, Pope Echoing us on Condoms', *USA Today* (1 December 2010), http://usatoday30.usatoday.com/news/religion/2010–12–01-Africacondoms01_ST_N.htm (accessed 24 October 2015).

149 See Roy F. Baumeister and Kathleen D. Vohs, 'Sexual Economics: Sex as Female Resource for Social Exchange in Heterosexual Interactions', (2004) 8 *Personality and Social Psychology Review* (4) 339–363.

150 George A. Akerlof, Janet L. Yellen and Michael L. Katz, 'An Analysis of Out-of-Wedlock Childbearing in the United States', (1996) 111 *The Quarterly Journal of Economics* (2) 277–317; W. Bradford Wilcox and Andrew J. Cherlin, 'The Marginalization of Marriage in Middle America', *Brookings*, 10 August 2011, http://www.brookings.edu/research/papers/2011/08/10-strengthen-marriage-wilcox-cherlin (accessed 24 October 2015).

A Witness to the Body/Soul Connection

Arguments for same-sex marriage assume that a lack of sexual complementarity between a couple, and the absence of procreative potential, are meaningless; only emotional intention counts. Americans generally are increasingly receptive to this message. But the facts on the ground tell a different story, of young women in particular who suffer depression due to experiencing sex outside the context of a relationship,[151] of psychological distress following women's encounters with pornography and rape – each of which is also destructive of women's emotional and spiritual equanimity.[152] In short, there is room in American law and culture for the proposal at the heart of Catholic teaching about sex and marriage: that how one attends to the human body affects the entire human person and the common good.

Marriage is about more than Emotion

Judge Richard Posner has opined that the growing acceptance of homosexual marriage seems 'a natural consequence of the sexual revolution that began in the 1960s.'[153] This 'revolution' was essentially constituted by the separation of what was previously bound together: love, sex, marriage, and children.[154] Not surprisingly, the meaning of marriage also shifted during this period, from an enterprise importantly bound up with children, to what leading American sociologists Andrew Cherlin and W. Bradford Wilcox often call a 'soulmate union,' a highly emotional enterprise. For participants, it also signals personal accomplishment (gaining enforceable trust and pleasant company from a soulmate) and social status.[155] Such a view of marriage, however, is linked with increasing rates of divorce, which, in addition to creating difficulties for children, appear to cause lingering harms for adults and for society in general as well.[156] Recent literature highlights the difficulties faced by ex-spouses, unmarried parents, or former in-laws, when they become sick or elderly without an intact family.[157]

151 Mark Regnerus and Jeremy Uecker, *Premarital Sex in America: How Young Americans Meet, Mate, and Think about Marrying* (Oxford University Press USA 2011), 137–48; Miriam Grossman, M.D., *Unprotected* (Penguin Group USA 2007).

152 Ann Wolbert Burgess, 'Rape Trauma Syndrome', (2006) 1 *Behavioral Sciences & the Law* (3) 97–113, ; Geoff Steurer, *The Effect of Pornography on the Spouse of an Addict*, http://salifeline.org/the-effect-of-pornography-on-the-spouse-of-an-addict/ (accessed 24 October 2015); Nicole P. Yuan, Mary P. Koss and Mirto Stone, 'The Psychological Consequences of Sexual Trauma', *National Online Resource on Violence Against Women* (2011), http://www.vawnet.org/applied-research-papers/print-document.php?doc_id=349 (accessed 24 October 2015).

153 Richard A. Posner, 'How Gay Marriage Became Legitimate: A Revisionist History of a Social Revolution', *The New Republic*, 24 July 2013, http://www.newrepublic.com/article/113816/how-gay-marriage-became-legitimate (accessed 24 October 2015).

154 Andrew J. Cherlin, *The Marriage Go-Round: The State of Marriage and the Family in America Today* (Vintage Books 2010), 185.

155 Andrew J. Cherlin, 'The Deinstitutionalization of American Marriage', (2004) 66 Journal of *Marriage & Fam*ily (4) 848–861; W. Bradford Wilcox, 'The Evolution of Divorce', *National Affairs* (Fall 2009), http://www.nationalaffairs.com/publications/detail/the-evolution-of-divorce (accessed 24 October 2015); Cherlin, *The Marriage Go-Round*, supra note 154.

156 See Andrew J. Cherlin and W. Bradford Wilcox, *The Marginalization of Marriage in Middle America* (2011), http://www.brookings.edu/research/papers/2011/08/10-strengthen-marriage-wilcox-cherlin (accessed 24 October 2015); Charles Murray, *Coming Apart: The State of White America, 1960–2010* (Crown Forum/Random House 2012), 149–167.

157 I-Fen Lin, and Susan L. Brown, 'Unmarried Boomers Confront Old Age: A National Portrait', (2012) 52 *The Gerontologist* (2) 153–165.

Same-sex marriage proponents strenuously encourage the notion that marriage is largely an emotional enterprise, a personal accomplishment, and a marker of status. Even a society eager to communicate non-discrimination to lesbian and gay individuals and couples, however, may wish to maintain the uniqueness and visibility of a view of marriage linking marriage intrinsically to the concrete well-being of others – to children, to aging adults, and to the community.

Current Proposals from Religious Freedom Actors Regarding Exemptions

The most well-developed proposals regarding religious exemptions to same-sex marriage laws have come from two groups of law professors, one led by Professor Robin Wilson (which remains officially neutral on legalizing same sex marriage), and one led by Professor Douglas Laycock, which supports same-sex marriage recognition.[158]

Both proposals expertly summarize the relevant laws which, when combined with same-sex marriage recognition, might burden religious actors. These include, for example laws treating public accommodations, tax exemptions, the receipt of public benefits, or non-discrimination generally. They also identify the kinds of jobs, positions and services more likely to be the sources of requests for exemptions, and offer proposed language addressing specific cases.

The solutions offered in these proposals for the coexistence of same-sex marriage and religious liberty involve, in the case of employees whose jobs are directed to granting licenses or performing marriages, an opt out, but only to the point where there is no 'inconvenience or delay,' and another official is promptly available.

With regard to others who might be implicated in cooperating or affirming same-sex marriages – e.g. counselors, employers offering benefits, businesses supplying things used in weddings, housing providers – these persons and groups too, could opt out so long as they did not create a substantial hardship for one of the parties to the same-sex marriage. Respecting businesses, only small businesses (five or fewer employees) would get significant conscience protection (so long as this did not create a substantial hardship) and even then only if the owner of the business primarily performed the task or service in question.

I commend the proposals' depiction of current and potential struggles between same-sex marriage and religious freedom, as well as their attention to the needs of all citizens to live with a sense of dignity and normalcy in their communities. However, I would add material conveying the full scope of the meaning of marriage in various religious traditions, which would better communicate that the request for exemption is not motivated by harmful animus, and at the same time would indicate the degree of importance religious actors attach to living in accordance with their teachings about marriage. Failure to include such material risks underestimating the weight of the burden on free exercise created by forced cooperation with same-sex marriage. This seems to influence the willingness, for example, to cut off conscience protection where larger businesses are involved. It also informs the suggested limitation on the right to conscientious objection – 'until' conscience causes significant hardship to the would-be customer. However, requiring the religious person's cooperation *precisely at that point* seems to render him or her the 'but for causation' of licensing the same-sex couple, or supplying their wedding celebration, and so on. In the Catholic view, this behavior would

158 Wilson et al., supra note 11; Laycock et al., *Letter to Rep. Tom Cross*, supra note 18. See also Berg and Laycock: Chapter 11 of this volume.

not only probably constitute 'material cooperation,'[159] but would also give scandal by helping to normalize an understanding of marriage at odds not only with Catholic teaching, but with the various social goods outlined above.

I would also more clearly highlight, in any proposal, the line between religious opposition to redefining marriage, and religion's insistence upon recognizing the dignity of homosexual persons. I would tie this specifically to the presence of a defined list – such as the lists already suggested in the Wilson and Laycock letters – of matters constituting 'cooperation' with same-sex marriage (housing, employment benefits, etc.), as distinguished from other transactions involving persons or couples with same-sex attraction. This is helpful for overcoming fears that religious exemptions would be exploited for the purpose of refusing, for example, to interact at all professionally or commercially with same-sex attracted persons or couples. Fears of this type of exploitation are expressed by same-sex marriage advocates in a bid to dampen enthusiasm for proposals to grant *any* religious exemptions to same-sex marriage laws.

Finally, from a Catholic perspective, an 'advance notice' requirement might be a superior model as compared with 'conscience protection until hardship'. Such a regime has several virtues. It prevents same-sex couples from personal encounters or confrontations with conscientious objectors. It respects the profound and 'cosmological' character of Catholic teaching about marriage by preventing cooperation in more situations, while simultaneously performing a more public witness to the goods of opposite-sex marriage and the rights of objectors to speak out. And it would likely ensure – because of its public visibility – that only those persons who are sincerely religiously burdened by cooperation with same-sex marriage, and sincerely committed to opposite-sex marriage as a matter of religious faith, would undertake to exercise their right of conscience so publicly. Its obvious downside is the way it marks out religious businesses for potential ridicule and even harm. Depending upon the social and legal environment, and the precise way advance notice was given, these risks could be too great.

159 Material cooperation is actual assistance with another's wrongdoing, without approving it. See CDF, *Considerations Regarding Proposals to Give Legal Recognition to Unions between Homosexual Persons*, supra note 134 at 5.

11 Protecting Same-Sex Marriage *and* Religious Liberty

*Thomas C. Berg and Douglas Laycock**

Introduction

A legal system that respects and protects the liberty of its citizens should protect the liberty of both sides in the dispute over same-sex marriage. That is, it should protect the right of same-sex couples to marry, and it should also protect the right of churches, synagogues, mosques, and other religious organizations not to recognize those marriages.

This chapter is written in terms of U.S. law, and we do not presume to tell other nations how to govern themselves. But we believe that the proposals in this chapter are the best interpretation of U.S. law, not merely because we can support them with U.S. legal arguments, but also because they are normatively attractive and fair to all citizens.

The Right to Marry

The U.S. Supreme Court was correct to uphold same-sex couples' right to civil marriage in *Obergefell v. Hodges*.[1] The choice of whom to marry is one of the most intimate and personal decisions that any human being can make. Government should not interfere with that choice without a very important reason. Nor should government leave a substantial class of people with no one, on any realistic view of the matter, that they can legally marry. A state's refusal to permit same-sex civil marriages, and state or federal refusal to recognize such marriages in states where they were already permitted, *prima facie* violates both the Due Process Clause and the Equal Protection Clause. At the very least, some form of heightened scrutiny is required.

The Court has long recognized 'the right to marry' as a right 'of fundamental importance'.[2] It is a 'fundamental freedom' and 'one of the 'basic civil rights of man'.[3] It is protected from

* This chapter is derived from amicus curiae briefs that we filed in *Obergefell v. Hodges*, 135 S. Ct. 2584 (2015), *United States v. Windsor*, 133 S. Ct. 2675 (2013), and *Hollingsworth v. Perry*, 133 S. Ct. 2652 (2013). Only the briefs speak for the organization and individuals who joined those briefs as amici. We take positions here that go beyond the positions adopted by some of those amici. This chapter also expands on arguments in Douglas Laycock and Thomas C. Berg, 'Protecting Same-Sex Marriage and Religious Liberty', (2013) 99 *Virginia Law Review Online* 1, http://www.virginialawreview.org/volumes/content/protecting-same-sex-marriage-and-religious-liberty (accessed 11 December 2015). This chapter was substantially completed before the Supreme Court's decision in *Obergefell*; it has been lightly updated after that decision.

1 *Obergefell v. Hodges*, 135 S. Ct. 2584 (2015).

2 *Zablocki v. Redhail*, 434 U.S. 374, 383 (1978).

3 *Loving v. Virginia*, 388 U.S. 1, 12 (1967) (quoting *Skinner v. Oklahoma*, 316 U.S. 535, 541 (1942)).

discrimination, as in *Loving v. Virginia*,[4] which struck down legal restrictions on interracial marriage, and it has long been understood to be part of the liberty protected by the Due Process Clause.[5] That is, the right to marry is both an equality right (no discrimination) and a liberty right (it cannot be prohibited even by non-discriminatory laws). The Court has said that marriage is a relationship that is 'intimate to the degree of being sacred'.[6]

The Court has unanimously protected the right to marry even for prisoners.[7] Laws prohibiting same-sex marriage deprived law-abiding gays and lesbians of a right so fundamental that it is protected even for incarcerated felons.

Denying Marriage Equality to Protect Children

The alleged government interests offered in defense of this deprivation did not fit the laws they were offered to justify. They did not come close. Just as marriage is about much more than sexual intercourse,[8] so it is about much more than procreation. Few if any married couples experience their marriage as exclusively, or even primarily, about procreation. Children are one important part of most marriages, and no part at all of many others. The government's interest in protecting children is undoubtedly important. But the claim that that interest was the reason for opposite-sex-only marriage did not fit the existing marriage laws, or the social understanding of marriage, or the lived experience of millions of married couples, all of which treat marriage as first and foremost a relationship between two adult spouses. The Supreme Court summarily rejected the states' argument that marriage is only about reproduction, calling that argument 'counterintuitive,' 'unrealistic,' 'wholly illogical,' and without 'a foundation'.[9]

The attempt to justify the prohibition on same-sex marriage as a means of protecting children also failed on its own terms. If the only or principal purpose of state recognition of marriage were to enable children to live with two biological parents, then that policy has manifestly failed, at least in the United States, where high divorce rates and high rates of children born to unwed mothers leave vast numbers of children growing up with one or both biological parents absent. A theoretical government interest, not remotely implemented in practice, could not be a basis for denying a group of people the fundamental right to marry.

Moreover, as the Supreme Court recognized in *Zablocki v. Redhail*, denying the right to marry does little or nothing to prevent procreation.[10] Same-sex couples raise children resulting from assisted reproduction and from failed attempts to go straight – attempts generally induced by societal pressure and discrimination. They raise children from adoption, and they raise children as foster parents. Denying these couples the stability, commitment, and financial benefits of legally recognized civil marriage does nothing to protect any of these children, and in various contexts it affirmatively harms them. In striking down the Defense of Marriage Act in *United States v. Windsor*, the Court emphasized that the federal

4 *Loving* at 1.
5 *Meyer v. Nebraska*, 262 U.S. 390, 399 (1923).
6 *Griswold v. Connecticut*, 381 U.S. 479, 486 (1965).
7 *Turner v. Safley*, 482 U.S. 78, 94–100 (1987).
8 *Lawrence v. Texas*, 539 U.S. 558, 567 (2003).
9 *Obergefell* at 2607.
10 *Zablocki* at 390.

government's refusal to recognize marriages that were valid under state law 'br[ought] financial harm to children of same-sex couples' in multiple ways and also made it 'more difficult for the children to understand the integrity and closeness of their own family and its concord with other families in their community and in their daily lives'.[11] State denials of marriage created similar harms, especially since, in the wake of *Windsor*, the many marriage benefits provided by federal law were triggered only when the relevant state recognized a couple as spouses rather than simply domestic partners.[12] Prohibiting same-sex marriage to protect children was counterproductive, and just as inconsistent with the lived experience of same-sex couples with children as with the experience of childless couples and opposite-sex couples.

Thus, the principal reasons offered to justify the bans on same-sex civil marriage were insufficient to justify such a profound intrusion into the fundamental right to marry.

Denying Marriage Equality to Protect Religious Liberty

Bans on same-sex marriage have also been defended on the ground that they protect the religious liberty of those with conscientious objections to same-sex marriage. We agree that significant religious liberty issues will follow in the wake of same-sex civil marriage. But it is not an appropriate response to prohibit same-sex civil marriage in order to avoid addressing issues of religious liberty. No one can have a right to deprive others of *their* important liberty as a prophylactic means of protecting his own important liberty. Just as one's right to extend an arm ends where another's nose begins, so each claim to liberty in our system must be defined in a way that is consistent with the equal and sometimes conflicting liberty of others. Religious liberty, properly interpreted and enforced, can protect the right of religious organizations and religious believers to live their own lives in accordance with their faith. But it cannot give them any right or power to deprive others of the corresponding right to live the most intimate portions of *their* lives according to *their* own deepest values.

The mere recognition of same-sex civil marriage *by the state* presents no issue of religious liberty. 'For the Free Exercise Clause is written in terms of what the government cannot do to the individual, not in terms of what the individual can exact from the government.'[13] A conscientious objector can raise a free exercise claim only when the government has restricted, discriminated against, or penalized the objector's own religiously motivated behavior.[14]

Religious liberty issues begin not when a same-sex couple marries, but when the state pressures religious organizations or believers to recognize or facilitate that marriage in ways that would require them to violate their religious commitments. In the U.S. Supreme Court's

11 *United States v. Windsor*, 133 S. Ct. 2675, 2695, 2694 (2013).

12 *Garden State Equality v. Dow*, 79 A.3d 1036, 1042 (N.J. 2013).

13 *Lyng v. Northwest Indian Cemetery Protective Association*, 485 U.S. 439, 451 (1988) (internal quotation omitted).

14 See *Lyng* at 450–452 (finding no burden on religious exercise from building of road on government land, even though resulting noise would interfere with longstanding religious use of the land); *Bowen v. Roy*, 476 U.S. 693, 699–701 (1986) (finding no burden on religious exercise from government's internal use of social security number to maintain records on plaintiffs' child, despite claims that spiritual harms to child would result).

recent cases on same-sex marriage, we urged the Court to acknowledge these issues and commit itself to addressing them.[15] But the existence of these issues could not justify denying millions of other Americans the fundamental right to marry.

We teach our children that the United States is committed to 'liberty and justice *for all*'.[16] We must protect religious liberty *and* the right to marry.

Parallel Claims to Protect Identity

Same-sex civil marriage is a great advance for human liberty. But failure to attend to the religious liberty implications can create a whole new set of problems for the liberties of those religious organizations and believers who cannot conscientiously recognize or facilitate such marriages. The gain for human liberty will be severely compromised if same-sex couples now force religious dissenters to violate their conscience in the same way that those dissenters, when they had the power to do so, used to force same-sex couples to hide in the closet. And that is what will happen, unless the courts protect religious liberty as well and as vigorously as they protect same-sex civil marriage.

There is a sad irony to the bitter conflict between the supporters of same-sex civil marriage and the religious organizations and believers committed to the view that marriage is for opposite-sex couples only. Sexual minorities and religious minorities make essentially parallel claims on the larger society, and the strongest features of the case for same-sex civil marriage make an equally strong case for protecting the religious liberty of dissenters. These parallels have been elaborated by scholars who work principally on religious liberty[17] and also by scholars who work principally on sexual orientation.[18]

First, both same-sex couples and committed religious believers argue that some aspects of human identity are so fundamental that they should be left to each individual, free of all nonessential regulation, even when manifested in conduct. For same-sex couples, the conduct at issue is to join personal commitment and sexual expression in a multi-faceted intimate relationship with the person they love. For religious believers, the conduct at issue is to live and act consistently with the demands made by the Being that they believe made us all and holds the whole world together.

No person who wants to enter a same-sex marriage can change his sexual orientation by any act of will, and no religious believer can change his understanding of divine command by any act of will. Religious beliefs can change over time; far less commonly, sexual orientation can change over time. But these things do not change because government says they must, or because the individual decides they should; for most people, one's sexual orientation and one's understanding of what God commands are experienced as involuntary, beyond

15 See Douglas Laycock and Thomas C. Berg, amicus brief filed on behalf of Douglas Laycock and others in support of the same-sex couples in *Obergefell*; Marc D. Stern, Thomas C. Berg, and Douglas Laycock, amicus brief filed on behalf of the American Jewish Committee in support of the same-sex couples in *Windsor* and *Hollingsworth v. Perry*, 133 S. Ct. 2652 (2013). These briefs are available at http://sblog.s3.amazonaws.com/wp-content/uploads/2015/03/14–556tsacLaycock.pdf and http://sblog.s3.amazonaws.com/wp-content/uploads/2013/03/Marriage-Cases-AJC-Brief-Final.pdf, respectively (both accessed 11 December 2015), and on Westlaw.

16 This phrase (with emphasis added) is from the Pledge of Allegiance, specified in 4 U.S.C. § 4 (2012), and recited each morning by most school children in the United States.

17 See Thomas C. Berg, 'What Same-Sex-Marriage and Religious-Liberty Claimants Have in Common', (2010) 5 *Northwestern Journal of Law and Social Policy* (2) 212–226.

18 See William N. Eskridge, Jr., 'A Jurisprudence of "Coming Out": Religion, Homosexuality, and Collisions of Liberty and Equality in America', (1997) 106 *Yale Law Journal* (8) 2416–2430.

individual control. The same-sex partners cannot change their sexual orientation, and the religious believer cannot change God's mind.

In finding rights to same-sex civil marriage, courts have rejected the argument that marriage is simply conduct, presumptively subject to state regulation. They have rejected a distinction between sexual orientation and sexual conduct because, they have correctly found, both the orientation and the conduct that follows from that orientation are central to a person's identity.[19]

Religious believers face similar attempts to distinguish their religious beliefs from the conduct based on those beliefs, and to treat their conduct as subject to any and all state regulation. This is the premise of the U.S. Supreme Court's decision refusing to protect religiously motivated conduct from burdens imposed by generally applicable laws.[20] But believers cannot fail to act on God's will, and it is no more reasonable for the state to demand that they do so than for the state to demand celibacy of all gays and lesbians. Both religious believers and same-sex couples feel compelled to act on those things constitutive of their identity, and they face parallel legal objections to their actions.

Both same-sex couples and religious dissenters also seek to live out their identities in ways that are public in the sense of being socially apparent and socially acknowledged. Same-sex couples claim a right beyond private behavior in the bedroom: they claim the right to participate in the social institution of civil marriage. Religious believers likewise claim a right to follow their faith not just in worship services, but in the charitable work of their religious organizations and in their daily lives.

Finally, both same-sex couples and religious dissenters face the problem that what they experience as among the highest virtues is condemned by others as a grave evil. Where same-sex couples see loving commitments of mutual care and support, many religious believers see disordered conduct that violates natural law and scriptural command. And where those religious believers see obedience to a loving God who undoubtedly knows best when he lays down rules for human conduct, many supporters of gay rights see intolerance, bigotry, and hate. Because gays and lesbians and religious conservatives are each viewed as evil by a substantial portion of the population, each is subject to substantial risks of intolerant and unjustifiably burdensome regulation.

The classically American solution to this problem is to protect the liberty of both sides. There is no reason to let either side oppress the other. Same-sex couples should not be denied the right to civil marriage. Now that that right is secured, same-sex couples should not be allowed to force dissenting religious organizations to recognize or facilitate their marriages.

The Right to Religious Liberty

Judicial Intervention and Judicial Responsibility

Twelve U.S. jurisdictions enacted same-sex civil marriage by popular decisions (legislation, initiative, or referendum); all 12 also enacted religious liberty protections for religious organizations that do not recognize same-sex marriages.[21]

19 See *In re Marriage Cases*, 183 P.3d 384, 442–443 (Cal. 2008); *Kerrigan v. Commissioner of Public Health*, 957 A.2d 407, 438 (Conn. 2008); *Varnum v. Brien*, 763 N.W.2d 862, 885, 893 (Iowa 2009).

20 *Employment Division, Department of Human Resources of Oregon v. Smith*, 494 U.S. 872 (1990). Even the *Smith* approach leaves room for protecting religiously motivated conduct from laws that are not neutral, or not generally applicable, as we discuss in 'Laws with Secular Exceptions', below.

21 The following are ordinary legislative enactments unless otherwise indicated. See 13 Del. Code § 106(e), 13 Del. Code § 1504 note (Michie Supp. 2014); D.C. Official Code § 46–406 (LexisNexis Supp. 2015); Hawaii

The situation is very different in the states where same-sex marriage was recognized judicially, by interpretation of the state or federal constitution. No legislation was ever enacted to protect religious liberty with respect to marriage in Iowa[22] or Massachusetts,[23] states whose courts ordered recognition of same-sex marriage well before the Supreme Court's *Windsor* decision struck down the federal Defense of Marriage Act in 2013. Nor is there religious liberty legislation in any of the 19 states where federal or state courts ordered recognition of same-sex marriage after *Windsor* and before *Obergefell*.[24] In California, where court-ordered marriage equality prevailed after a long battle, there is an extremely narrow statutory provision that protects only the right of clergy not to perform the wedding ceremony.[25] Only Maine has so far enacted such a narrow exemption through a political rather than judicial process, and that happened as part of an initiative and referendum, bypassing the legislature.

Rev. Stat. §§ 572–12.1, 572–12.2, 572B-4, 572B-9.5 (LexisNexis 2015); 750 Ill. Comp. Stat. §5/209 (a-5), (a-10) (Thomson Reuters 2014); Me. Rev. Stat. tit. 19-A § 655.3 (Thomson Reuters 2014) (ballot initiative); Md. Code Ann., Fam. Law § 2–201 note (LexisNexis Supp. 2015) (legislation challenged and approved by referendum); Minn. Stat. §§ 363A.26, 517.01, 517.03 (subd. 1), 517.08 (subd. 1a), 517.09, 518.07 (2014); N.H. Rev. Stat. Ann. § 457:37 (LexisNexis Supp. 2015); N.Y. Dom. Rel. Law §§ 10-b, 11 (LexisNexis Supp. 2015); R.I. Gen. L. § 15–3–6.1 (LexisNexis Supp. 2015); Vt. Stat. Ann. tit. 8, § 4501(b) (LexisNexis 2013), tit. 9, § 4502(*l*) (LexisNexis 2014), tit. 18, § 5144(b) (LexisNexis Supp. 2015); Wash. Rev. Code §§ 26.04.010, 26.04.900 (2014) (legislation challenged and approved by referendum). The Delaware and Maryland religious liberty provisions, codified as notes to code sections, appear in the printed statutes but do not readily appear on Westlaw. To find these provisions on Westlaw, retrieve the code section, click on the 'History' tab at the top of the screen, and then click on 'Editor's and Revisor's Notes'.

22 The judicial decision was *Varnum v. Brien*, 763 N.W.2d 862 (Iowa 2009).

23 The judicial decision was *Goodridge v. Department of Public Health*, 798 N.E.2d 941 (Mass. 2003).

24 See 'National Conference of State Legislatures, Same-Sex Marriage Laws' (26 June 2015), http://www.ncsl.org/research/human-services/same-sex-marriage-laws.aspx (accessed 11 December 2015) (identifying these states and reviewing the history of legislation and litigation). Legislation and judicial decisions are also collected in appendices to the Court's opinion in *Obergefell* at 2608–2610.

25 Cal. Fam. Code § 400(a) (Deering Supp. 2015). The first judicial decision, recognizing marriage equality, was *In re Marriage Cases*, 183 P.3d 384 (Cal. 2008). This decision was overturned by an amendment to the state constitution, passed by initiative and a vote of the people. Cal. Const., Art. I, § 7.5 (commonly referred to as Proposition 8, its label on the ballot). A federal district court held that this amendment to the *state* constitution violated the *federal* Constitution. *Perry v. Schwarzenegger*, 704 F. Supp. 2d 921 (N.D. Cal. 2010), aff'd sub nom. *Perry v. Brown*, 671 F.3d 1052 (9th Cir. 2012), vacated sub nom. *Hollingsworth v. Perry*, 133 S. Ct. 2652 (2013). The Supreme Court of the United States held that no federal court had jurisdiction to decide the merits of an appeal from this district-court judgment, because the defendant state officials had not appealed and the private citizens who had intervened to defend Proposition 8 lacked standing to do so, *Hollingsworth* at 2661–2668. The Supreme Court vacated the judgment of the court of appeals, id. at 2668, but it did not vacate the judgment of the district court, apparently because it believed that there had been a live controversy in that court. The plaintiffs had sought marriage licenses, which the defendant officials had refused to issue, even as they declined to defend the constitutionality of their refusal. See id. at 2660.

The district court had issued a state-wide injunction against enforcement of Proposition 8. 704 F. Supp. 2d at 1004. Under controlling Ninth Circuit authority, the district court had no authority to issue such a state-wide injunction, because the only plaintiffs were two same-sex couples who had not filed a class action. See *Los Angeles Haven Hospice, Inc. v. Sebelius*, 638 F.3d 644, 664–65 (9th Cir. 2011); *Meinhold v. U.S. Dept. of Defense*, 34 F.3d 1469, 1480 (9th Cir. 1994). For further exploration of this issue, see Douglas Laycock, *Modern American Remedies: Cases and Materials* 275–76 (4th edn, 2010). But no one had appealed that issue either – certainly no one with standing. And the defendant state officials were eager to comply. So the decision of a federal district court in an individual action effectively resolved the issue for the whole state. Had the litigation been in state court, the private citizens who had sponsored Proposition 8 would have had standing to defend it in court. *Perry v. Brown*, 265 P.3d 1002 (Cal. 2011). Any lingering sense that there had not been a full and fair opportunity to litigate is of course mooted by the completed litigation in *Obergefell*.

Among the judicial-recognition states, only Connecticut gives robust protection similar to that enacted in most of the legislative-recognition states.[26]

There will probably be religious liberty legislation in response to *Obergefell* in some deeply conservative ('red' or Republican) states. But the 12 jurisdictions that enacted marriage equality with religious liberty protections legislatively were all liberal ('blue' or mostly Democratic) states. Now that *Obergefell* has been decided, it is quite unlikely that any other liberal states will enact religious liberty legislation with respect to marriage.

The reason is clear. When a legislature considered same-sex civil marriage legislation, there were supporters and opponents and undecided legislators. Sometimes there were supporters who also cared about religious liberty. Often there were undecideds or even opponents who would become supporters if adequate provision were made for religious liberty. In the democratic bargaining that is part of a functioning legislative process, bills emerged that protected same-sex civil marriage *and* religious liberty.

The religious liberty provisions were sometimes inserted or redrafted at the last minute. They were sometimes poorly drafted, incomplete, and ambiguous. Most of them are far from ideal. But most of them at least attempt to provide meaningful protection for the liberty of religious organizations.

This bargaining process could break down when there was lopsided support for same-sex civil marriage. And it has entirely broken down now that same-sex civil marriage has become national law through a judicial decision on constitutional grounds. Those who would have added religious liberty protections to a civil marriage bill are deprived of a legislative vehicle and deprived of bargaining power. Once same-sex marriage arrives judicially, the legislatures usually do not attend to the specific issues of religious liberty raised by the court's decision.

This dynamic appeared dramatically in New Jersey. After a state court ordered recognition of same-sex marriage[27] and the state abandoned its appeal, some supporters introduced legislation to confirm the decision and make it more secure. But the legislation was pulled after 'many advocates [objected that it] would add religious restrictions [that is, exemptions] that are not addressed by the court decision, originally concessions made to win votes for an earlier version of the legislation'.[28] Having secured marriage rights judicially, advocates had no further need to grant concessions on religious liberty.

When there are no exemptions specifically addressed to the issues raised by same-sex marriage, those issues are left to litigation under the general religious liberty provisions of state and federal constitutions and state and federal Religious Freedom Restoration Acts (RFRAs).[29] Enforcing those provisions is the responsibility of courts.

The lesson is clear. Now that the U.S. Supreme Court has constitutionalized same-sex civil marriage for the country, courts must attend to the resulting issues of religious liberty. The Supreme Court's decision has made it far less likely that legislatures in liberal or moderate states will do so. Legislatures in conservative states may pass specific exemptions – but protection for religious liberty should not depend on whether the practice needing protection is popular in the particular state.

26 Conn. Gen. Stat. Ann. §§ 46b-22b, 46b-35a, 46b-35b (2015). The judicial decision was *Kerrigan v. Commissioner of Public Health*, 957 A.2d 407 (Conn. 2008).

27 *Garden State Equality v. Dow*, 82 A.3d 336 (N.J. Super. 2013).

28 Matt Friedman, 'N.J. Senate Pulls Gay-Marriage Bill', *NJ.com* (16 December 2013), http://www.nj.com/politics/index.ssf/2013/12/nj_senate_pulls_gay_marriage_bill.html (accessed 11 December 2015).

29 For a discussion of RFRA, see infra notes 70 and 71 and accompanying text.

The only parties before the Court in *Obergefell* were same-sex couples and state officials; no question of religious liberty was presented within the scope of that case. We filed a brief urging the Court to indicate clearly that it recognized the religious liberty issues that would arise in the wake of its decision, that the lower courts should address those issues, and that the Supreme Court would address those issues in due course.

What the Court actually said was more murky than clear. The Court recognized that opposition to same-sex marriage is often based on 'decent and honorable religious or philosophical premises,' that religious organizations and believers 'may continue to advocate' their position, and that the First Amendment would protect them as they 'seek to teach' their principles.[30] It rather conspicuously did not say that the law would protect them as they sought to *act* on their principles. But neither did it say that the law would not protect them. The Court concluded each of these passages by saying that 'the State' could not act on these religious principles to refuse marriage equality. The serious questions of religious liberty were left for another day, and appropriately so in a legal system based on the precedential effect of judicial decisions in concrete cases and controversies between parties actually before the court.

Civil Marriage and Religious Marriage

Judges focused on discriminatory definitions of civil marriage have often failed to appreciate the range of religious liberty issues raised by same-sex marriage. The question is not simply whether clergy must perform same-sex wedding ceremonies, although that is certainly important. And the issues posed are not simply the result of existing anti-discrimination laws. Same-sex marriage raises new problems.

The religious disagreement over marriage equality begins with a disagreement over the nature of marriage. Marriage is a deeply personal human relationship, a legal relationship, and a religious relationship. Advocates of marriage equality tend to see the personal and legal relationships as primary, but most religious organizations and many religious believers see the *religious* relationship as primary. Of course it is possible to distinguish the legal and religious relationships, and many nations do. But in U.S. law, and especially in U.S. culture, they are deeply intertwined. Now that the Supreme Court has invalidated discriminatory definitions of legal marriage – civil marriage in the more common usage – all courts must take greater pains not to interfere with the right of religious organizations to define religious marriage.

Civil marriage – the legal relationship – defines property rights, mutual duties of support, inheritance rights, pension rights, insurance coverage, social security benefits, tax liabilities, evidentiary privileges, rights to sue for personal injury or file for bankruptcy, and much more. As was recognized back in the first decision instituting marriage equality (that of Massachusetts), 'hundreds of statutes' create rules or authorize benefits on the basis of marriage.[31] Equality with respect to these important consequences of civil marriage – most of them financial consequences – is of course part of the reason that civil marriage equality is so important.

Marriage also has important symbolic value, both for the relationship between the two spouses and for the married couple's relationship to the larger society. Same-sex couples

30 *Obergefell* at 2602, 2607.
31 *Goodridge* at 941, 955.

want their relationships to be marriages and to be recognized as such. This symbolic value is important for couples married in church and for couples married by a judge. Couples who understand their marriage as a religious relationship may experience this symbolic value differently, but it is part of both religious and civil marriage.

The religious relationship thus overlaps with civil marriage, but it is very different. The focus is not on finances or legal obligations. Marriage is a sacrament in the Catholic faith and an important religious commitment in most other faiths. Marriage is ordained in both the Jewish and Christian scriptures, and it is described in terms of male and female.[32] Both scriptures repeatedly condemn adultery.[33]

Sex and sexual morality are central to religious marriage, but increasingly peripheral to legal provisions for civil marriage. Consensual sex has been deregulated, both in and out of marriage. Adultery and fornication are no longer crimes, and alienation of affections is no longer a tort.[34] It is possible, and of course extremely common in the United States, to have sex without marriage. And it is entirely possible, although presumably rare, to have a fully valid legal marriage without sex. Understandings about sex in a civil marriage are left to the married couple, and appropriately so. There is surprisingly little about sex among the hundreds of things defined by law as part of civil marriage.[35]

A state, or a court as a matter of constitutional interpretation, can change the legal definition of civil marriage. But neither a state nor a court can change the religious definition of religious marriage: that is up to the authorities in each religious tradition. Some synagogues, churches, mosques, and other religious organizations (such as religious social-service and educational institutions) will refuse to recognize same-sex marriages because, for them, marriage is a religious relationship at its foundation, and a same-sex marriage is religiously invalid or impossible.

It is this issue of religious recognition of same-sex civil marriages that generates novel issues of religious liberty. Conflicts have arisen, and will continue to arise, between religious teachings and laws prohibiting discrimination on the basis of sexual orientation, with or without same-sex marriage. But same-sex marriage will increase the frequency and religious

32 Genesis 2:24; Matthew 19:6.

33 See, for example, Exodus 20:14; Matthew 19:18.

34 Adultery is sexual intercourse between a married person and another who is not that person's spouse. Fornication is sexual intercourse between two unmarried persons. Both adultery and fornication were once crimes in most states. Those laws have now been widely repealed, and where such laws are still in effect, prosecutions are rare and the occasional exceptions arouse public criticism. Alienation of affections was the tort of inducing a married person to leave his or her spouse. It too has been abolished in most states, and in most of the remaining states, lawsuits are rare and the occasional judgments arouse public criticism. Most of the contemporary writing about the crimes and the tort is student work reacting to the very occasional cases. See, for example, Gabrielle Viator, Note, 'The Validity of Criminal Adultery Prohibitions after Lawrence v. Texas', (2006) 39 *Suffolk University Law Review* (3) 837 and n. 6 (collecting surviving adultery statutes from 23 states); id. at 842 and n. 40 (noting that already, by 1955, the American Law Institute said that adultery and fornication laws were 'dead-letter statutes,' by reason of general non-enforcement); Amanda Connor, Note, 'Is Your Bedroom a Private Place? Fornication and Fundamental Rights', (2009) 39 *New Mexico Law Review* (3) 522 (collecting surviving state fornication laws, and repeals and invalidations in other states); Jennifer E. McDougal, Comment, 'Legislating Morality: The Actions for Alienation of Affections and Criminal Conversation in North Carolina', (1998) 33 *Wake Forest Law Review* 163, 172–173 and nn. 77–80 (collecting repeals and judicial abolitions of the tort).

35 These distinctions between civil and religious marriage are further elaborated in Douglas Laycock, 'Afterword', in Douglas Laycock, Anthony R. Picarello, Jr., and Robin Fretwell Wilson, eds, *Same-Sex Marriage and Religious Liberty* (Rowman & Littlefield 2008), 202–203.

intensity of these conflicts. Once same-sex couples are civilly married, the existing discrimination laws suddenly apply to a relationship of profound religious significance, demanding that religious organizations and believers recognize a relationship that they believe to be both inherently religious and religiously invalid.

All of the state supreme courts and one of the federal appeals courts that rendered final judgments holding marriage discrimination unconstitutional carefully explained that they were changing only civil marriage and not religious marriage.[36] That explanation is important, but it has done little to assuage religious objections. In part this is because the culture often fails to make the distinction. And in part it is because those who oppose same-sex marriage on religious grounds understand civil marriage to rest on the foundation of religious marriage. For example, the conservative journal *First Things* recently complained that 'In the past, the state *recognized* marriage,' but that now, the state has '*redefined*' marriage, 'making it an institution entirely under the state's control'.[37] On this view, a civil marriage that departs too radically from the foundation of religious marriage is simply not a marriage. To treat it as though it were a marriage, for many religious organizations and believers, is to violate fundamental religious commitments. And when the inevitable lawsuits come, those charging churches and synagogues with discrimination will also be conflating civil marriage and religious marriage.

It is essential to distinguish the two relationships, and to commit to protecting the right to adhere to religious understandings of the religious relationship.

Specific Religious Conflicts

The only book devoted to the issue to date, *Same-Sex Marriage and Religious Liberty*,[38] collected contributions from seven scholars – four who supported same-sex marriage and three who did not. All seven agreed that legalizing same-sex civil marriage without providing robust religious exemptions would create widespread legal conflicts – conflicts that, as one contributor said, would work a 'sea change in American law' and 'reverberate across the legal and religious landscape'.[39]

Both as organizations and as individuals, those committed to traditional understandings of religious marriage sometimes refuse to recognize, assist, or facilitate same-sex marriages.

36 As to the state supreme courts, see *In re Marriage Cases*, 183 P.3d 384, 400, 407 n. 11, 434 (Cal. 2008); *Kerrigan v. Commissioner of Public Health*, 957 A.2d 407, 475 (Conn. 2008); *Varnum* at 905–906; *Goodridge* at 954, 965 n. 29; *Griego v. Oliver*, 316 P.3d 865, 871 (N.M. 2013). New Jersey's highest court did not explicitly make this distinction in its decision, which only denied a stay of the lower-court ruling against the state and thus was not a final judgment on the merits, *Garden State* (N.J. 2013), refusing to stay *Garden State* (N.J. Super. 2013).

The federal appeals court making the distinction was *Kitchen v. Herbert*, 755 F.3d 1193, 1227–1228 (10th Cir. 2014). But three other federal circuits did not mention the distinction, *Bostic v. Schaefer*, 760 F.3d 352 (4th Cir. 2014); *Baskin v. Bogan*, 766 F.3d 648 (7th Cir. 2014) (Posner, J.); and one of these suggested a negative disposition toward religious liberty claims. *Latta v. Otter*, 771 F.3d 456, 475 (9th Cir. 2014) (Reinhardt, J.) (stating that 'anti-discrimination laws . . . 'serv[e] compelling state interests of the highest order") (brackets in original; quotation omitted). The Supreme Court specified 'civil marriage' in one summary of its holding, *Obergefell* at 2605, but not in the other, id. at 2608, and it gave no attention to the distinction. We do not hazard a theory on why the federal courts have been so much less likely than state courts to make the civil-religious distinction explicit.

37 R.R. Reno, 'Government Marriage', *First Things* (December 2014), 3, 4 (emphases added).

38 Laycock, Picarello, and Wilson, supra note 35.

39 Marc D. Stern, 'Same-Sex Marriage and the Churches', in Laycock, Picarello, and Wilson, supra note 35 at 1.

Of course this means not performing the wedding ceremony or hosting the wedding reception. But it means much more than that.

Priests, pastors, rabbis, and imams may refuse to provide religious marriage counseling to same-sex couples. Religious colleges may refuse to provide married student housing to same-sex couples.[40] Churches and synagogues may refuse to employ persons married to same-sex spouses; such employees would be persistently and publicly flouting the religious teachings they would be hired to promote. Some religious organizations may hire such employees but refuse to provide spousal fringe benefits to the same-sex spouse.[41] Religious social service agencies may refuse to place children for adoption with same-sex couples. Already, Catholic Charities' branches in Illinois, Massachusetts, and the District of Columbia have closed their adoption units because of this issue.[42]

Religious colleges, summer camps, day care centers, retreat houses, counseling centers, meeting halls, and adoption agencies may be sued under public accommodations laws for refusing to offer their facilities or services to same-sex couples.[43] Or they may be penalized by loss of licensing,[44] accreditation,[45] government contracts,[46] access to public facilities,[47] or tax exemption.[48] Tax exemption is a particular concern because of the Supreme Court's decision in *Bob Jones University v. United States*,[49] rejecting a free exercise claim to tax exemption for a racially discriminatory religious college. The Court in *Bob Jones* was at pains to emphasize that it was considering only schools, not 'churches or other purely religious institutions,' and that it relied on the government's compelling interest 'in denying public support to racial discrimination in education'.[50] *Bob Jones* should not be extended to religious organizations that refuse to recognize same-sex civil marriages.

40 See *Levin v. Yeshiva University* 754 N.E.2d 1099 (N.Y. 2001) (holding that lesbian couple stated a legal claim challenging such a refusal).

41 See *Catholic Charities v. City of Portland*, 304 F.Supp.2d 77 (D. Me. 2004) (upholding ordinance forcing religious charity either to extend spousal benefits to registered same-sex couples or to lose access to all city housing and community development funds); Don Lattin, 'Charities Balk at Domestic Partner, Open Meeting Laws', *San Francisco Chronicle*, 10 July 1998, at A1 (describing how the Salvation Army lost $3.5 million in social service contracts with the City of San Francisco because it refused, on religious grounds, to provide benefits to the same-sex partners of its employees).

42 Laurie Goodstein, 'Illinois Bishops Drop Program over Bias Rule', *New York Times*, 19 December 2011, at A16.

43 See Stern, supra note 39 at 37–43 (assessing reach of public accommodation laws).

44 Stern at 19–22 (describing licensing issues in both commercial and not-for-profit sectors).

45 See Stern at 23–24 (describing accreditation disputes in various academic disciplines); D. Smith, 'Accreditation Committee Decides to Keep Religious Exemption', (2002) 33 *Monitor on Psychology* (1) 16 (describing a proposal of the American Psychology Association to revoke the accreditation of religious colleges and universities with statements of faith that preclude sex outside of marriage), http://www.apa.org/monitor/jan02/exemption.aspx (accessed 11 December 2015).

46 Lattin, supra note 41, at A1 (describing how the Salvation Army lost $3.5 million in social service contracts with the City of San Francisco).

47 See *Evans v. City of Berkeley*, 129 P.3d 394 (Cal. 2006) (upholding revocation of a boat berth at public marina due to Boy Scouts' refusal to pledge not to discriminate against gay members); *Boy Scouts of America v. Wyman*, 335 F.3d 80 (2d Cir. 2003) (holding that the Boy Scouts may be excluded from the state's combined charitable campaign for denying membership to openly gay individuals); Jonathan Turley, 'An Unholy Union: Same-Sex Marriage and the Use of Governmental Programs to Penalize Religious Groups with Unpopular Practices', in Laycock, Picarello, and Wilson, supra note 35, at 69–76 (assessing implications of these cases).

48 See Douglas W. Kmiec, 'Same-Sex Marriage and the Coming Antidiscrimination Campaigns Against Religion', in Laycock, Picarello, and Wilson, supra note 35, at 103 (describing the threat to tax exemption for religious organizations with objections to same-sex marriage); Turley, supra note 47, at 62–69 (same).

49 *Bob Jones University v. United States*, 461 U.S. 574, 602–604 (1983).

50 *Bob Jones* at 604 n. 29.

But other reasoning in *Bob Jones* shows why recognition of same-sex civil marriage without meaningful exemptions may affect religious liberty objections to gay-rights laws in both the marriage context and elsewhere. The Court held that prohibitions on racial discrimination in a 'myriad' of educational contexts showed a 'firm national policy' against such discrimination, one that could brook few or no exemptions in other contexts.[51] The same spillover effect may occur if marriage discrimination is equated in all respects with race discrimination and no meaningful exemptions are provided. The Solicitor General of the United States triggered alarms at the oral argument in *Obergefell* when, in response to a question, he said that tax exemption is 'certainly going to be an issue'.[52]

Disputes have also arisen, and will increase, concerning individuals who provide creative and personal services that directly assist or facilitate marriages. A wedding planner, or a wedding photographer, may refuse to plan or photograph a same-sex wedding, because she thinks she would be cooperating with evil in a ceremony that makes a mockery of the religious institution of marriage.[53] Counselors in private practice may refuse to counsel same-sex couples about their relationship difficulties, because they think the relationship is religiously prohibited or intrinsically disordered. Of course no same-sex couple would ever *want* to be counseled by such a counselor. But disputes have arisen in such cases, facilitated by professional societies and educational programs that treat commitment to the gay-rights view of these issues as a requirement of professional ethics.[54] Such efforts do not obtain counseling for same-sex couples, but they do threaten to drive from the helping professions all those who adhere to older religious understandings of marriage. This not only would violate the rights of religious persons seeking to be counselors; by shrinking the diversity of the counselor pool, it also threatens to deprive religious counselees of counselors whom they may find more sympathetic and who may more readily understand their situation and personal commitments.

These religious liberty disputes can arise across a wide range of factual circumstances. But they involve a discrete and bounded set of potential claimants: churches, synagogues, and other places of worship, not-for-profit organizations with strong religious commitments, and individuals in a few occupations offering personal services closely connected to marriage. What is newly at issue in the wake of same-sex marriage is the right to refuse religious recognition to civil marriages that are fundamentally inconsistent with religious definitions of marriage.

Doctrinal Tools to Protect Religious Liberty

In this section, we discuss the legal doctrines available in U.S. law for a court that wishes to protect religious liberty in a jurisdiction with same-sex marriage. The best solution is for states and the federal government to enact robust statutory religious liberty exemptions tailored to the

51 *Bob Jones* at 593.

52 Transcript of Oral Argument 38, in *Obergefell*.

53 *Elane Photography, LLC v. Willock*, 309 P.3d 53 (N.M. 2013) (upholding administrative determination that photographer had no right to refuse, on religious grounds, to photograph a same-sex commitment ceremony).

54 See *Ward v. Polite*, 667 F.3d 727 (6th Cir. 2012) (reversing summary judgment against counseling student expelled from graduate school for refusing to counsel with respect to problems in a same-sex relationship); Stern, supra note 39, at 22–23 (describing attempt by St. Cloud State University to require all social work students, as a condition of admission, to affirm the moral validity of same-sex relationships); 'Missouri State U. Settles Lawsuit Filed by Student', *St. Louis Post-Dispatch*, 9 November 2006, at D4 (describing settlement with social work student disciplined for refusing to write legislator in support of gay adoption).

context of marriage. But with or without that, more general guarantees of religious liberty can also be brought to bear.

Internal Decisions that Affect Faith and Mission

In *Hosanna-Tabor Evangelical Lutheran Church and School v. EEOC*,[55] the Supreme Court confirmed the longstanding rule that 'ministers' cannot sue their religious employers for employment discrimination. But *Hosanna-Tabor* does not merely recognize the ministerial exception to employment discrimination law, as important as that is. The decision rests on a broader principle: that government may not interfere 'with an internal church decision that affects the faith and mission of the church itself'.[56] This plainly covers the religious body's definition of marriage and its willingness or unwillingness to solemnize or celebrate a marriage, or to provide the space for doing so. But it also extends prima facie to the ongoing decision of whether to recognize, for purposes internal to the religious organization, a marriage solemnized elsewhere.

This right to define religious doctrine and apply that doctrine to internal decisions extends beyond places of worship. *Hosanna-Tabor* involved a religious school, and the lower courts have applied the doctrine to employees in positions of religious leadership in religious colleges,[57] nursing homes,[58] hospitals,[59] mission agencies,[60] and diocesan bureaucracies.[61]

The ministerial exception imposes an absolute bar to regulation within its scope. This may be an exception to the more common approach of strict scrutiny, or it may reflect a categorical judgment that the state never has a compelling interest in forcing an unwanted minister on an unwilling religious organization. There may be other internal decisions for which compelling interests are more readily conceivable or apparent – say, protecting children from physical or sexual abuse – and for which the appropriate standard of protection is strict scrutiny. But cases in which government will have a compelling interest in regulating religious decisions inside a religious organization must be quite rare. And religious recognition of religiously invalid marriages is not such a case.

Laws with Secular Exceptions

Some decisions are crucial to 'the faith and mission' of a religious organization or individual but cannot easily be characterized as 'internal'. This is often the case when religious organizations offer services to the general public, as when Catholic Charities places children for adoption, or a religious college admits students of many faiths and of none. Wherever the line is ultimately drawn between internal and external, decisions on the external side of the line are governed by the rule in *Employment Division v. Smith*.[62]

55 *Hosanna-Tabor v. Equal Employment Opportunity Commission*, 132 S. Ct. 694 (2012).

56 *Hosanna-Tabor* at 707. This broader principle is explored in Christopher C. Lund, 'Free Exercise Reconceived: The Logic and Limits of *Hosanna-Tabor*', (2014) 108 Northwestern University Law Review (4) 1183–1233.

57 *Petruska v. Gannon University*, 462 F.3d 294 (3d Cir. 2006); *EEOC v. Catholic University*, 83 F.3d 455 (D.C. Cir. 1996).

58 *Shaliehsabou v. Hebrew Home*, 363 F.3d 299 (4th Cir. 2004).

59 *Scharon v. St. Luke's Episcopal Presbyterian Hospitals*, 929 F.2d 360 (8th Cir. 1991).

60 *Natal v. Christian and Missionary Alliance*, 878 F.2d 1575 (1st Cir. 1989).

61 *Alicea-Hernandez v. Catholic Bishop*, 320 F.3d 698 (7th Cir. 2003).

62 *Smith*, supra note 20.

That rule is more protective than has sometimes been assumed. *Smith* held that the Free Exercise Clause creates no right to exemption from neutral and generally applicable laws, such as the 'across-the-board criminal prohibition' at issue in that case.[63] *Smith*'s understanding of 'generally applicable law' is indicated by its explanation of *Sherbert v. Verner*.[64] *Sherbert* held that a worker who lost her job for refusing to work on her Sabbath was constitutionally entitled to unemployment compensation. The state required her to be available for work or lose eligibility, but that rule contained 'at least some' secular exceptions.[65] And therefore, the Court said, the Constitution required a religious exception as well. Obviously there cannot be many acceptable reasons for refusing available work and claiming a government check instead, but there were 'at least some'. The implication is that even rather narrow secular exceptions make a law less than generally applicable.

The Court subsequently made clear that categorical exceptions are as relevant as individualized exceptions. In *Church of the Lukumi Babalu Aye, Inc. v. City of Hialeah*, it said that 'categories of selection are of paramount concern when a law has the incidental effect of burdening religious practice'.[66] The facts of *Lukumi* were extreme – the exceptions virtually swallowed the ostensible rule – but the Court was clear that its decision was not limited to such situations. The ordinances in *Lukumi* fell 'well below the minimum standard' of general applicability.[67]

Many laws of course contain exceptions or gaps in coverage. When a law exempts some category of secular conduct, but prohibits religious conduct that causes the same or similar alleged harms, the state 'devalues religious reasons for [the regulated conduct] by judging them to be of lesser import than nonreligious reasons'.[68] Sometimes explicitly, but always and inescapably implicitly, a secular exception without a religious exception indicates a 'value judgment' that secular motivations 'are important enough to overcome' the government's asserted interest, 'but that religious motivations are not'.[69] Those words were written by Samuel Alito, now a Justice of the Supreme Court, when he was a judge on a federal court of appeals. Not every federal judge has read *Smith* and *Lukumi* so carefully. But this reading from Justice Alito is the most faithful to the Supreme Court's opinions and to the underlying constitutional provision read in light of those opinions.

Some anti-discrimination laws are neutral and generally applicable under this standard, but others are not. If, for example, an anti-discrimination law exempts very small businesses, then the Constitution *prima facie* requires exemptions for religious conscience, subject to the compelling interest test. Religious liberty can be protected, in a wide range of cases, under the rule of *Employment Division v. Smith*.

State Constitutions and Federal and State Religious Liberty Statutes

With respect to federal law, the Religious Freedom Restoration Act (RFRA)[70] will protect against any substantial burdens imposed on religious liberty. RFRA was enacted to restore

63 *Smith* at 884.

64 *Sherbert v. Verner*, 374 U.S. 398 (1963).

65 *Smith* at 884.

66 *Church of the Lukumi Babalu Aye, Inc. v. City of Hialeah*, 508 U.S. 520, 542 (1993). See 508 U.S. at 543–544 (relying on categorical exclusions such as fishing, hunting, extermination, and euthanasia to show that ban on animal sacrifice was not generally applicable).

67 *Lukumi* at 543.

68 *Lukumi* at 537–538.

69 *Fraternal Order of Police v. City of Newark*, 170 F.3d 359, 366 (3d Cir. 1999) (Alito, J.).

70 42 U.S.C. §§ 2000bb to 2000bb-4 (2012).

religious freedom rights legislatively, against the risk that the constitutional rule of *Employment Division v. Smith* might be interpreted in the least protective manner.[71]

With respect to state law, additional protection for religious liberty is to be found in state constitutions and state Religious Freedom Restoration Acts (state RFRAs). Twenty-one states have by now (December 2015) enacted state RFRAs,[72] and in 11 additional states, courts have held that their state constitutions protect the exercise of religion from neutral and generally applicable laws.[73] That is, Congress and 32 states have rejected the unprotective half of the rule in *Employment Division v. Smith.*

These state-law protections for religious liberty are of course not the responsibility of the federal courts. New Mexico recently interpreted – almost certainly misinterpreted[74] – its state RFRA to provide no protection against discrimination suits by private litigants.[75] But the federal courts should at least not get in the way. When the Supreme Court invalidated state bans on same-sex civil marriage, it protected same-sex couples from discrimination by the state. It did not direct states to override the free exercise of religion by religious organizations or by individual believers. We wish the Court had indicated more explicitly that it did not mean to preclude state-law protections for religious liberty in this context, but we think it clear that the opinion has no such effect.

Federal Protection Against Neutral and Generally Applicable Laws

Some religious refusals to recognize same-sex marriages may be fundamental exercises of conscience, but may not be fairly viewed as 'internal decisions', and may be subject to a law with no exceptions – a law that is truly generally applicable. In such a case, the Supreme Court should be open to reconsidering the rule, announced in *Employment Division v. Smith,* that the Free Exercise Clause never requires religious exemptions from neutral and generally applicable laws.

As Justice Souter once explained, there are many reasons to reconsider this part of *Smith,* beginning with the fact that the rule was neither briefed nor argued.[76] Moreover, although 25 years have now elapsed, this part of *Smith* cannot be said to have become embedded in the law. *Smith*'s rule about generally applicable laws has been interpreted only in *Lukumi*, which would have come out the same way under any standard. *Smith* was merely a background assumption

71 On the background and interpretation of RFRA, see Douglas Laycock and Oliver S. Thomas, 'Interpreting the Religious Freedom Restoration Act', (1994) 73 *Texas Law Review* (2) 209–245; Thomas C. Berg, 'What Hath Congress Wrought? An Interpretive Guide to the Religious Freedom Restoration Act', (1994) 39 *Villanova Law Review* (1) 1–70.

72 Alabama, Arizona, Arkansas, Connecticut, Florida, Idaho, Illinois, Indiana, Kansas, Kentucky, Louisiana, Mississippi, Missouri, New Mexico, Oklahoma, Pennsylvania, Rhode Island, South Carolina, Tennessee, Texas, and Virginia. For citations, see Douglas Laycock, 'Religious Liberty and the Culture Wars,' 2014 *University of Illinois Law Review* (3) 845 n. 26; Ark. Code §§ 16-123-401 to 16-123-407 (Westlaw 2015); Ind. Code §§ 34-13-9-0.7 to 34-13-9-11 (Westlaw 2015). All of these are statutes, except for Alabama's, which is a constitutional amendment.

73 Alaska, Maine, Massachusetts, Michigan, Minnesota, Montana, New York, North Carolina, Ohio, Washington, and Wisconsin. For citations, see Laycock, supra note 72, at 844 n. 22. Kansas, Mississippi, and arguably Indiana and Tennessee have protective decisions under their state constitutions as well as a state RFRA. Id. at 844 nn. 22–23.

74 See Shruti Chaganti, Note, 'Why the Religious Freedom Restoration Act Provides a Defense in Suits by Private Plaintiffs', (2013) 99 *Virginia Law Review* (2) 343–374 (reviewing the drafting and legislative history of the federal statutory language that was copied into the New Mexico statute).

75 *Elane Photography,* supra note 53.

76 *Lukumi* at 571–577 (Souter, J., concurring in the judgment).

in *City of Boerne v. Flores*,[77] which interpreted a completely different clause of the Constitution. Individual Justices debated *Smith* in separate opinions, but *Smith* was not argued by the parties or interpreted by the Court.

Smith was not applied in *Locke v. Davey*.[78] The discriminatory ban on theology scholarships in that case was neither neutral nor generally applicable; it was upheld on the ground that the refusal to fund did not impose a cognizable burden on the exercise of religion.[79] *Smith* was not applied in *Gonzales v. O Centro Espirita Beneficente Uniao do Vegetal*,[80] *Burwell v. Hobby Lobby Stores, Inc.*,[81] or *Holt v. Hobbs*,[82] all of which were decided under federal religious liberty legislation, or in *Hosanna-Tabor*, which was decided under the separate doctrine about internal church decisions.

These are all the significant free exercise decisions since *Smith*. The Supreme Court's remaining citations to *Smith* are little more than passing references and occasional cursory resolutions of secondary issues that were left unexplored. It is not too late to have full briefing and argument on the rule announced in *Employment Division v. Smith*.

Heightened scrutiny of laws burdening the free exercise of religion would provide a means of protecting the essential interests of both same-sex couples and those with religious objections. In the example of adoption services, a court should consider whether comparable services are readily available from a secular adoption agency. If so, the court should conclude that there is no compelling interest in forcing religious adoption agencies to the hard choice of closing down or losing essential state funding, on the one hand, or repeatedly violating their religious teachings concerning the nature of marriage on the other. Similarly in the case of a wedding planner, there is no compelling interest in forcing her to close her business or violate her conscience if other wedding planners are reasonably available to the couple.

The *Smith* rule appears to mean that if a law is truly generally applicable, government can refuse religious exemptions whether or not it has a plausible reason, or any reason at all. By contrast, a rule like RFRA's, putting the government to proof of a strong interest, provides a means for taking account of the weight of the competing interests – in this case, religious liberty and the right of same-sex couples to marry. Such a rule would do justice more often than a rule of law that ignores that weighing.

Whether or not *Smith* is reconsidered, there are important tools available to protect religious liberty within *Smith* itself, in the doctrine of *Hosanna-Tabor*, in the federal RFRA, and in state law. The courts should use these tools to protect religious liberty with respect to marriage, and federal courts should make clear that state courts are free to use state law to the same end.

77 *City of Boerne v. Flores*, 521 U.S. 507 (1997) (holding the federal Religious Freedom Restoration Act invalid as applied to the states on the ground that it exceeded Congress's power to enforce the Fourteenth Amendment).

78 *Locke v. Davey*, 540 U.S. 712 (2004) (upholding a rule excluding theology majors from otherwise generally available scholarships).

79 *Locke* at 720–721.

80 *Gonzales v. O Centro Espirita Beneficente Uniao do Vegetal*, 546 U.S. 418 (2006) (protecting religious use of mildly hallucinogenic drug under Religious Freedom Restoration Act).

81 *Burwell v. Hobby Lobby Stores, Inc.*, 134 S. Ct. 2751 (2014) (protecting closely held businesses, under Religious Freedom Restoration Act, from having to provide employees with insurance coverage for contraceptives, including drugs and devices that the religious claimants believed to be abortifacients, when less restrictive means were available to serve government's interests).

82 *Holt v. Hobbs*, 135 S. Ct. 853 (2015) (protecting Muslim prisoner's right to grow a beard under the Religious Land Use and Institutionalized Persons Act).

Conclusion

12 Religion and Equality

Reconcilable Differences?

W. Cole Durham, Jr.

Old Tension, New Concern

The tension between liberty and equality is as old as liberal theory and no doubt much older. But it is resurfacing with particular salience in recent years as the battle front in contemporary culture wars has entered the domain of religion. The tension is more than just a zero-sum game pitting the scope of individual liberty against state regulations aimed at protecting and enforcing equality. It reflects more even than the general contraction of social space available for individual autonomy as a result of the expansion of the modern welfare state. Over the past half century, we have witnessed the rise of an egalitarian paradigm that shapes the mental landscape of thought about fundamental rights and has begun to eclipse an older liberty paradigm that underlies modern constitutionalism. Where Justice Holmes could quip that equal protection is the 'last resort of constitutional arguments',[1] a century later equality has become the cardinal constitutional value.[2] As a result, there is a deep concern that rights claims rooted in once axiomatic protections of religious liberty are being eroded and will lose their resonance and persuasive force, unless they can be recast in terms of equalitarian non-discrimination norms.

Nowhere is this more evident than in the domain of the current global debates about same-sex marriage and the 'sea-change' likely to ripple through countless other legal institutions and to 'reverberate across the legal and religious landscape'[3] as a result. Only a generation ago, the right to freedom of religion or belief seemed securely ensconced as a fundamental[4] and even a 'first'[5] freedom. It was understood to be paramount over majoritarian legislation

1 *Buck v. Bell,* 274 U.S. 200, 208 (1927) (Holmes J.). The relative disuse of equal protection arguments until the Warren Court era is well-documented. See Joseph Tussman and Jacobus tenBroek, 'The Equal Protection of the Laws', (1949) 37 *California Law Review* (3) 341–381; Erwin Chemerinsky, *Constitutional Law: Principles and Policies* (Aspen Publishers, 2nd edn, 2002), 642. But see Stephen A. Siegel, 'Justice Holmes, *Buck v. Bell,* and the History of Equal Protection,' (2005) 90 *Minnesota Law Review* (1) 106–243, arguing that equal protection played a more significant role in case law much earlier than Holmes's quip would suggest.

2 See, for example, Ronald Dworkin, *Taking Rights Seriously* (Harvard University Press 1977), 267 ('laws are needed to protect equality, and laws are inevitably compromises of liberty').

3 Marc D. Stern, 'Same-Sex Marriage and the Churches', in Douglas Laycock, Anthony R. Picarello, Jr., and Robin Fretwell Wilson, eds, *Same-Sex Marriage and Religious Liberty* (Rowman & Littlefield 2008), 1.

4 International Covenant on Civil and Political Rights (ICCPR), Art. 18; European Convention for the Protection of Human Rights and Fundamental Freedoms (ECHR), Art. 9.

5 Though early drafts of the United States' Bill of Rights placed the religion clause in a third amendment, the ultimate positioning of this right in the First Amendment by the time of its ratification is often viewed as confirmation that religious liberty is a 'first freedom'.

except in cases where that legislation reflected compelling state interests that could not be advanced in any less restrictive manner.[6] But this once preeminent liberty right is gradually being transformed into a non-discrimination norm, and one which many seem increasingly to give little or no weight in the balance when other non-discrimination interests are involved. To take a particularly prominent example, a major theme running through lower court cases striking down same-sex marriage bans in the United States has been the contention that such bans reflected mere animus not rising to the level of providing even a 'rational basis' for legislation.[7] Long-standing religious beliefs to the contrary count for little or nothing. This approach implicitly disparages religious concerns about same-sex marriage, and could significantly weaken the strength of freedom of religion claims likely to arise in the aftermath of determinations that same-sex marriage is legitimate and constitutionally protected. The United States Supreme Court's decision upholding same-sex marriage avoided such explicit disparagement, noting that opposition to same-sex marriage is often based on 'decent and honorable religious or philosophical premises,'[8] and leaving open the question of the extent to which believers will be protected in their right to engage in religion-based conduct which seeks to avoid involvement with or support for same-sex marriage. The Court affirmed the right of 'religious organizations and persons . . . [to continue support for] the family structure they have long revered,'[9] but left unanswered the question of what, beyond speech, people and institutions can *do* when they are conscientiously opposed to same-sex marriage.

This particular issue is representative of the larger set of questions running through this volume about how religious freedom and equality rights can be reconciled in the contemporary world. In the marriage area, the question going forward will be whether and the extent to which the religious liberty of those with religious objections to same-sex marriage can be reconciled with equality and non-discrimination on the basis of sexual orientation. But the more general theme pervades the volume. How is freedom of religion or belief to be reconciled with non-discrimination norms in international law?[10] How are religious freedom and anti-discrimination norms dealt with in the European Court of Human Rights and the European Court of Justice?[11] How can these norms be reconciled in the workplace?[12] These questions are linked in turn to much deeper questions at the level of theory about the limits of pluralism in contemporary societies. At the level of practice, the questions are even more direct: how is it possible to organize community life in a world characterized by such deep and intense difference of religious and secular world views? Can these differences be reconciled?

6 See, for example, *Sherbert v. Verner*, 374 U.S. 398 (1963) and *Wisconsin v. Yoder*, 406 U.S. 205 (1972) in the United States and comparable cases such as *Bayatyan v. Armenia*, App. No. 23459/03 (ECtHR Grand Chamber 7 July 2011) invoking European-style proportionality tests in other parts of the world.

7 See, for example *Baskin v. Bogan*, 766 F.3d 648, 666–667 (7th Cir. 2014); *Latta v. Otter*, 771 F.3d 456 (9th Cir. 2014).

8 *Obergefell v. Hodges*, 135 S.Ct. 2584, 2607 (2015). But see Helen Alvaré, Chapter 10 of this volume: 'The United States Supreme Court's 2013 opinion in *United States v. Windsor* strongly suggested that any view of marriage that excludes the possibility of same-sex unions is irrational, even hateful. Justice Kennedy's opinion for a five-Justice majority in the 2015 *Obergefell v. Hodges*, did likewise.' [Notes omitted.]

9 *Obergefell* at 2607.

10 See Nicolae Dură, 'The Right to Religion: An Evaluation of the Texts of the Main Binding International and European Juridical Instruments', Chapter 2 of this volume.

11 See Mark Hill QC, 'Freedom of Religion: Strasbourg and Luxembourg Compared', Chapter 3 of this volume.

12 See María J. Valero Estarellas, 'State Neutrality, Religion, and the Workplace in the Recent Case Law of the European Court of Human Rights', and Greg Walsh, 'Anti-Discrimination Legislation and Regulation of Employment Decisions of Religious Schools in Australia', Chapter 4 and Chapter 6 of this volume.

Ironically, the right to freedom of religion emerged historically at least in part as an answer to the question of how communities divided by deep differences in world views could nonetheless live together in peace. At the core of equalitarianism is a similar thrust to find peace amidst diversity by assuring equal respect for all. Can these deep strands of liberal theory be woven together in a way that will respect the dignity of both religious believers opposed to same-sex marriage and those committed to supporting it? Can religious liberty be reconciled with equality, or will secular equalitarianism unleash a new and paradoxical genre of discrimination: that is, discrimination against religious believers for non-conformity with equalitarian ideals? The essays in this volume have explored in a variety ways both differing possibilities for and complexities standing in the way of such reconciliation. This adds further reflections to these themes, addressing first obstacles that lie in the way of finding reconcilable differences, and then some of the practical types of reconciliations that have been found to be workable.

The Erosion of Liberty Rights

Liberty and equality have lived in productive tension for generations, and one can continue to hope that appropriate reconciliations can be found. But there are profound grounds for pessimism. The rise of the equality paradigm is linked to a sense that political freedom 'is undergoing a slow loss of relevance. It is fading away.'[13] The social processes underlying this paradigm shift seem deep and in many ways ineluctable, but if that decline continues, the lost commitment to liberty for all will ultimately undermine the possibility of viable pluralism.

Part of the problem, as noted by the famous German jurist and former Constitutional Court judge Ernst-Wolfgang Böckenförde is that 'A free, liberal, and democratic state can only be built and sustainable on a foundation that it itself is unable to create.'[14] Commenting on this quotation, Judge András Sajó of the European Court of Human Rights has stated, 'Without supportive and dedicated public conviction, or at least committed public institutions, freedom cannot survive.'[15] In his view, what he describes as 'the tragedy of liberty' lies in the fact that there is a recurring tendency for other passions and interests to overwhelm the desire for freedom.

> Freedom as non-intervention by the state, as independent personal enterprise, functions only if independence has already deeply rooted itself in people's consciousness and practice, so that they regard it as self-evident. This requires that there be something in the citizens' fundamental psychological constitution that resonates to the possibilities of freedom, something that requires the ability to resist, if necessary, the freedom-stifling efforts of other psychological needs and interests. . . . In a consumer society, the freedom to consume, or to satisfy one's narcissistic needs (the freedom of control over one's own body) differs from traditional psychological sources of individual political freedom. We face the possibility that freedom is far from a top priority on the modern socio-cultural

13 András Sajò, 'Liberty and its Competitors', in Renáta Uitz, ed., *Freedom and its Enemies: The Tragedy of Liberty* (Eleven International Publishing 2015), 1.

14 Ernst-Wolfgang ,Böckenförde, Die Entstehung des Staates als Vorgang der Säkularisation (1967), in Ernst-Wolfgang Böckenförde, *Recht, Staat, Freiheit: Studien zur Rechtsphilosophie, Staatstheorie und Verfassungsgeschichte* (Suhrkamp 1992), 112.

15 Sajò, supra note 13 at 8.

> agenda, particularly in the absence of psychological mechanisms that sustain efforts toward freedom.[16]

The story of Dostoevsky's Grand Inquisitor recurs all too often: the masses appear to prefer bread (understood to represent all material wants and needs) to freedom. The emotional burden of freedom can be too great. It is true that 'people still demand freedom for themselves fairly often, and sometimes at great cost.'[17] However, '[t]he freedom of others is not psychologically relevant, at least not beyond empathy (compassion) towards visible suffering caused by denial of freedom.'[18] The result is that '[f]reedom, particularly legal and political freedom, cannot be postulated as a powerful and lasting psychological need.'[19] The practical consequence has been that 'over the past twenty years it has been nearly impossible to win political battles with a freedom-oriented platform.'[20] And even where lip service is given to freedom, 'it can be stripped of all meaning with the help of selective redefinition, allowing freedom the appearance of being respected even while it is being ground away.'[21] Other constitutional values such as welfare, equality, and appeals to human dignity, tend to demote or erode the fading constitutional norm of liberty.[22]

This erosion can be particularly threatening to religious freedom, because religion can be perceived as one of the passions threatening freedom, and the other rival values to freedom may seem more alluring. Judge Sajó's summary of the plight of freedom reflects this ambivalence. 'It is conceivable,' he writes,

> that neither the nature of democracy, nor the culture of (post-)modernism, nor anti-liberal geopolitical threats (e.g., the rise of Asian economies or terrorism motivated by religious fundamentalism), nor the current narcissism of Western culture, is favorable to the priority of liberty. The emotional attractiveness of freedom is weak; the emotional temptations that turn people against it are more powerful. Freedom as a moral demand or virtue has not established itself as a firm guiding principle in the consciousness and lives of modern citizens.[23]

Because of the 'ambivalence of the sacred',[24] it is all too easy to see religion as a source of passion antithetical to liberty. But in the last analysis, it is only freely chosen religion, or freely chosen world views analogous to religion, both of which are protected by freedom of religion or belief, that can ultimately reinforce the commitment to freedom sufficiently to override the power of liberty's rivals. As Locke recognized long ago, it is not the homogeneity of beliefs that creates social stability, but gratitude for the assurance that one will be protected in his or her own beliefs, whatever they are. The erosion of liberty, and with it, religious liberty, threatens to undercut this crucial bond that ultimately secures pluralism.

16 Sajò at 8.
17 Sajò at 13.
18 Sajò at 14.
19 Sajò at 14.
20 Sajò at 15.
21 Sajò at 18.
22 Sajò at 18–19.
23 Sajò at 37.
24 R. Scott Appleby, *The Ambivalence of the Sacred: Religion, Violence, and Reconciliation* (Carnegie Commission on Preventing Deadly Conflict) (Rowman & Littlefield 1999).

The fundamental threat to religious freedom is not that it will be disavowed, though even that is beginning to happen with surprising frequency,[25] but that it will be eroded by exceptions made in the name of other state interests that are pursued with greater passion. Without vigorous religious freedom and its protection of deeply opposed world views, however, we could be left with a new and coercive equalitarianism, overly willing to sacrifice religious freedom to equalitarian demands, potentially increasing social polarization, and threatening to repeat the centuries-old pattern that seems to transform every belief system or ideology into an engine of intolerance as soon as it acquires power.

Equal protection is, of course, a fundamental value. The point is not to understate or downplay its importance, but to insist that freedom of religion or belief not be inappropriately downplayed at a time when the rise of the equality paradigm increases that risk. As Justice McLachlin of the Canadian Supreme Court has stated:

> The modern religious citizen is caught between two all-encompassing sets of commitments. The law faces the seemingly paradoxical task of asserting its own ultimate authority while carving out a space within itself in which individuals and communities can manifest alternate, and often competing, sets of ultimate commitments.[26]

As important as equality is, there are times when integrating the values of religious freedom and equality requires that differences be protected. Particularly when there are ways that both values can be promoted, or an alternative can be found that minimizes the collision between the two rights, appropriate accommodations should be found. As Dean Martha Minow has written,

> The struggles over exemptions from civil rights laws for religious groups reflect historic political battles, inspired but not dictated by ideals and hammered out through shifts in power from popular mobilization and changes of heart . . . Direct confrontation and conflicts will play a role in resolutions, but so should efforts at accommodation. Accommodation and negotiation can identify practical solutions where abstract principles sometimes cannot – and in the meantime, build mutual trust.[27]

Indeed, it is often precisely in the process of seeking to identify accommodations that new and better options can be found[28] and better possibilities for living with irreconcilable differences can be identified.

The Legitimacy of Exemptions

One of the major barriers to finding ways to reconcile deep differences is skepticism about the legitimacy of exemptions that are carved out to respect conscience-based concerns. This is not the place to revisit the extensive literature that has focused on this issue over the past

25 See, for example, Winnifred Fallers Sullivan, *The Impossibility of Religious Freedom* (Princeton University Press 2007); Elizabeth Shakman Hurd, *Beyond Religious Freedom: The New Global Politics of Religion* (Princeton University Press 2015).

26 Beverley McLachlin, 'Freedom of Religion and the Rule of Law: A Canadian Perspective, in Douglas Farrow, ed., *Recognizing Religion in a Secular Society: Essays in Pluralism, Religion and Public Policy* (McGill-Queen's University Press 2004), 12, 16.

27 Martha Minow, 'Should Religious Groups Be Exempt from Civil Rights Laws?', (2007) 48 *Boston College Law Review* (4) 847–848.

28 Minow at 844–845.

quarter century. But it is worth noting that the very idea of conceptualizing such carve-outs as 'exceptions' is problematic. There is, of course, a legalist or positivist view according to which law is understood fundamentally as legislation. Granting exceptions under this view appears to undermine the authority of law. When claims of conscience are the basis for such exceptions, the contention is that recognizing the exceptions makes the conscientious claimants a law unto themselves, thereby threatening anarchy.[29]

But conceptualizing religion-based accommodations as exceptions in this manner is problematic in several respects. In the first place, doing so exaggerates the extent to which the accommodation is seen as differential treatment that constitutes an equality violation. It assumes that the baseline against which differential treatment is assessed is the statute. If one takes a more wholistic or integralist view of the legal system as a whole, however, it is clear that the adjustment is necessary to construe the statute in a way that avoids a constitutional violation. The carve-out made by the accommodation is not a distinction made for an arbitrary reason that creates an anomalous legal exception,[30] but one driven by the need to take a fundamental constitutional norm – freedom of conscience – into account. Thus, the accommodation is not a case of treating like cases differently, but of treating different cases in a way that takes substantively relevant differences into account. It thereby effectuates an appropriate interpretation of the relevant legislative rule, taking into account its place (and its need to conform to) the overall constitutional system.[31] The baseline is not the statute considered in isolation, but the legal order taken as a whole, including the law, the requirement that the law conform to the constitution, and interpretation that assures that freedom and equality are balanced and reconciled in a way that gives optimal protection to both. Law 'curved' to accommodate exceptions does not subvert the rule of law, but confirms it. The integralist view has affinities to natural law, or at least neo-natural law,[32] in that it takes into account not only the law as 'posited' by the lawmaker, but also higher constitutional principles, and possibly a recognition that such principles may reflect constitutional axiology that goes beyond the 'positive' norms of constitutions and international human rights instruments alone. But one could be committed to an integralist view of law without necessarily being committed to the existence of transpositive (in the sense of trans-constitutional) norms.

The legalist view's rejection of exemptions is analogous to a physicist complaining that Einsteinian physics leads to inappropriate exceptions to the rules of Newtonian physics. In fact, space is curved in precisely the ways that Einsteinian physics predicts. Similarly, subconstitutional rules sometimes need to be 'curved' to take into account constitutional and possibly even more fundamental norms. It is true that some disruptive effect may be felt in certain areas of the legal system when the gravitational pull of more fundamental norms causes adaptations within certain bodies of law. But this does not show that there is something illegitimate about the reach

29 See, for example, *Employment Division, Department of Human Resources of Oregon v. Smith*, 494 U.S. 872 (1990).

30 *Smith* at 886. For the contrary view, see Frederick Mark Gedicks, 'The Normalized Free Exercise Clause: Three Abnormalities,' (2000) 75 *Indiana Law Journal* (1) 75, 77, 78.

31 On the contrast between legalist and integralist views of conscientious objection, see Javier Martínez-Torrón, 'Conscientious Objections: Protecting Freedom of Conscience Beyond Prejudice', in Silvio Ferrari, ed., *Routledge Handbook of Law and Religion* (Routledge 2015), 192–194.

32 The integralist approach also has resonances with Ronald Dworkin's theory of legal interpretation, which criticizes positivist legal theory by emphasizing a thicker 'law as integrity' conception of law that includes both posited legal norms and deeper principles. See Ronald Dworkin, *Law's Empire* (Belknap Press of Harvard University Press 1986). Of course, Dworkin's view itself would place more weight on equalitarian than libertarian principles. But an integralist conception could accommodate both.

of fundamental law. Rather, it confirms that new legislation is not totally free to transform the legal landscape in ways that fail to take more fundamental norms into account.[33]

From this perspective, it is not at all surprising to find exceptions built into the structure of legal norms. Indeed, it is difficult to know how a society can go about finding ways to respect deep differences in religion or world view without finding ways to make exceptions from majoritarian rules in order to accommodate such differences. In the United States, such exceptions have been built into the structure of law at three levels. First, in some cases, even after *Smith*, which held (subject itself to exceptions) that neutral and general laws override religious freedom claims, there are contexts in which courts retain authority on the basis of religious freedom concerns to strike down legislation or other state action.[34] Second, the legislative branch itself can adopt broad general norms such as the Religious Freedom Restoration Act (RFRA),[35] the Religious Land Use and Institutionalized Person Act (RLUIPA),[36] and state-level RFRAs.[37] Such legislation necessarily creates broad standards, because it is impossible to predict in advance all the ways that legislation and other state action can encroach on religious freedom rights. Third, the legislative branch may craft specific exemptions in particular contexts. Specific exemptions crafted for the labor area are familiar in both Europe[38] and the United States.[39] Note that both the second and third categories do not just create exceptions from legislation; they *are* legislation.

33 See Nicolae Dură, Chapter 2 of this volume, who characterizes religious freedom as 'a fundamental human right, foreseen at the same time by *jus divinum* (divine law), by *jus naturale* (natural law), and by *jus scriptum* (written law) . . . hence, its characteristic of *jus cogens* (peremptory norm, fundamental principle of international law).'

34 See, for example, *Hosanna Tabor Evangelical Lutheran Church and School v. Equal Employment Opportunity Commission*, 132 S.Ct. 694 (2012) and *Church of the Lukumi Babalu Aye, Inc. v. City of Hialeah*, 508 U.S. 520 (1993). More generally, under *Smith* general and neutral laws do not trump religious freedom claims (1) where belief alone (internal forum) as opposed to conduct is involved; (2) where ostensibly neutral laws target specific legal practices; (3) in 'hybrid right' situations, where religious liberty concerns combine with other rights, such as freedom of expression, to provide protection; (4) where the autonomy of religious communities is at stake (*Hosanna Tabor*); (5) in unemployment compensation cases not involving criminal violations (i.e., the *Smith* court did not overrule *Sherbert v. Verner*, 374 U.S. 398 (1963); and (6) where the law in question has categorical or individualized exceptions that undercut the generality and/or neutrality of the law (*Church of the Lukumi Babalu Aye*).

35 42 U.S.C.A. §§ 2000bb et seq.

36 42 U.S.C.A. § 2000cc.

37 See William W. Bassett, W. Cole Durham, Jr., and Robert T. Smith, *Religious Organizations and the Law* (4 vols) (West 2013 and 2016 forthcoming), §§ 2.63–2.64 (analyzing state RFRAs). See also Baptist Joint Committee for Religious Liberty, 'State RFRA Bill Tracker', http://bjconline.org/staterfratracker/ (updated 21 January 2016, accessed 26 January 2016), also 'Protect thy Neighbor: Legislation Tracker', *A Project of Americans United for Separation of Church and State*, http://www.protectthyneighbor.org/legislation, accessed 5 March 2016.

38 See the 'Employment Directive': 'Equal Treatment in Employment and Occupation', Council Directive 2000/78/EC of 27 November 2000, http://eur-lex.europa.eu/legal-content/EN/TXT/?uri=uriserv:c10823 (accessed 26 October 2015).

This General Framework Directive, which 'aims to ensure that persons of a particular religion or belief, disability, age or sexual orientation do not suffer from discrimination and instead enjoy equal treatment in the workplace', is a major part of EU labor law. It accompanies the Racial Equality Directive and the Equal Treatment Directive on gender. It is implemented in the United Kingdom with the Equality Act 2010, http://www.legislation.gov.uk/ukpga/2010/15/contents (accessed 26 October 2015). In Chapter 3 of this volume, Mark Hill QC provides excellent treatment of relevant cases decided by the European Court of Human Rights and the European Court of Justice.

39 Title VII's duty to reasonably accommodate religious practices in the workplace and its protection of the right of religious organization's to engage in preferential hiring practices. See, for example, Carl H. Esbeck, 'Federal Contractors, Title VII, and LGBT Employment Discrimination: Can Religious Organizations Continue to Staff on a Religious Basis?' (2015) 4 *Oxford Journal of Law and Religion* (3) 368–397.

As Robin Fretwell Wilson has noted, the generalized legislative exemptions play an important role in protecting minority faiths 'too unpopular to garner the political support necessary to secure a specific exemption in the political process'.[40] Specific exemptions often operate quite differently, and serve a variety of different purposes.[41] Significantly, where generalized exceptions leave assessment of specific cases to judicial institutions, specific exemptions make a legislative determination about how different interests should be balanced in the specific types of cases involved. Moreover, specific exemptions may play an important role in striking legislative compromises that allow reforms to move forward.[42] In this regard, it is significant that there were no states in the United States that adopted same-sex marriage legislation without simultaneously adopting religion-related exemptions.[43] In short, both at the level of theory, and in constitutional and legislative practice, exemptions play an important and legitimate role in finding ways for people coming from different orientations to find effective ways to live together.

Reconciling Differences in Same-Sex Marriage Legislation

Legislative compromises that have been struck in the field of same-sex marriage exemplify both the complexity and the potential for finding livable solutions. In Chapter 11 in this volume Professors Thomas Berg and Douglas Laycock present a particularly cogent case for reconciling liberty and equality concerns in the same-sex marriage context. Drawing on their experience working with a number of legislatures that have adopted same-sex marriage legislation and in writing major amicus briefs in the major U.S. same-sex marriage cases, their analysis emphasizes the importance of providing appropriate exemptions for religious believers when same-sex marriage is legalized. Before the decision in *Obergefell*,[44] this was a council of prudence. It was extremely difficult to attract the votes necessary to approve same-sex marriage if religious groups could not be assured that many of their key issues were not met. The political leverage in the United States will obviously shift, now that same-sex marriage has been mandated by the U.S. Supreme Court. But the practical issues remain, and if they are not effectively addressed, deep tensions will continue.

In their amicus briefs, Laycock and Berg have urged the Court both to approve same-sex marriage and to provide protections for religious believers who will suffer religious freedom infringements as a result. The difficulty, of course, is that since the claims of religious believers who were worried about future implications of same-sex marriage were not before the Court, such concerns could at best be addressed in non-binding dicta.

In fact, the Court has not handed down even dicta, other than to say that religious believers remain free to advocate their now-rejected views.[45] The inability to work out more refined compromises in the judicial setting is a serious limitation on the possibilities of

40 Robin Fretwell Wilson, 'When Governments Insulate Dissenters from Social Change: What *Hobby Lobby* and Abortion Conscience Clauses Teach about Specific Exemptions', (2014) 48 *UC Davis Law Review* (2) 719, citing Douglas Laycock, 'The Religious Exemption Debate', (2009) 11 *Rutgers Journal of Law and Religion* (Part 1) 162–163.

41 For thorough analysis of legislation creating specific exemptions, see Robin Fretwell Wilson, supra note 40.

42 See Wilson, supra note 40 at 720.

43 See Wilson, supra note 40 at 720.

44 *Obergefell v. Hodges*, supra note 8.

45 *Obergefell* at 2607.

finding 'reconcilable differences' in the same-sex marriage area by judicial decision alone.[46] Regardless of whether the same-sex marriage issue is addressed judicially or in the political sector, the fundamental tensions remain. Even where the issues have been dealt with legislatively, there are significant complexities. For example, in Chapter 7 of this volume Rex Ahdar addresses legislation providing statutory exemptions that protect the rights of clergy who conscientiously object to performing same-sex marriages. Based on review of legislation in New Zealand, Canada, and the United Kingdom, Ahdar shows that even this least controversial of all the accommodations recognized to date turns out to be very difficult to deal with legislatively, even though there is substantial consensus that this exemption is appropriate.[47] As Professor Pieter Coertzen explains in Chapter 8, this problem has been successfully addressed in South Africa.[48] However, many parliamentary bodies that have sought to provide religious freedom protections in this limited area have encountered difficulties. It is not altogether clear, for example, who should count as a member of the clergy authorized to perform marriages in the major denominations, and it is also not clear what the implications should be for others not from mainline denominations. This just touches the tip of the iceberg of the technical difficulties that appear in this limited area.

But, of course, there are many other difficulties that lie ahead as legal systems balance the religious freedom and non-discrimination claims in the same-sex marriage area. Professor Robin Fretwell Wilson has analyzed these issues at great length.[49] One way to examine the range of issues as they have been arising in the United States is to consider the recent

46 That is one of the important reasons why only two countries to date (the United States and Brazil) have approved same-sex marriage nation-wide by the judiciary alone. See Resolution 175 of Brazil's National Judicial Council of 14 May 2013, implementing decisions of the Supreme Federal Court (ADI 4277/DF and ADPF 132/RJ, 4 May 2011) and the Supreme Tribunal of Justice of 25 Oct. 2011 (R.E. 1.183.378-RS (2010/0036663–8) and discussion in Chapter 5 of this volume, 'Religious Freedom, Anti-Discrimination, and Minority Rights in Brazil', by Rodrigo Vitorino Souza Alves. South Africa's Constitutional Court is the only other nationally binding court to hold marriage laws banning same-sex marriage to be discriminatory. *Minister of Home Affairs v. Fourie*, 2006 (3) BCLR 355 (CC) (South Africa) [see discussion in Chapter 8 of this volume]. In doing so, however, the Constitutional Court left the legislature a number of options, including distinguishing same-sex unions from traditional marriage. *Fourie* at ¶ 147. All other jurisdictions approving same-sex marriage have done so through political processes, either legislatively or by referendum.

47 Rex Ahdar, 'Same-Sex Marriage: Exemptions for Celebrants and Religious Freedom,' Chapter 7 in this volume.

48 South Africa was the first country in the world to constitutionally proscribe discrimination on the basis of sex, gender, or sexual orientation. It was the fifth country in the world, the second country outside Europe and the first, and as of early 2016 the only, country in Africa to legalize same-sex marriage. As Professor Coertzen explains, same-sex marriage, by way of the *Fourie* case in the Constitutional Court, the Civil Union Act, and subsequent legislation, has been legal since 2006, and the principle of 'reasonable accommodation' protects both religious institutions and civil marriage officers 'in their ability to perform marriage ceremonies according to their own tenets, celebrating, if they desire, heterosexual marriages only'. Some constitutional scholars, however, have argued that this constitutes state-sanctioned discrimination in violation of the right to equality and is therefore unconstitutional. See, for example, Elsje Bonthuy, 'Irrational Accommodation: Conscience, Religion and Same-Sex Marriages in South Africa,' (2008) 123 *South African Law Journal* (3) 473–482.

49 See, for example, the citations (through February 2015) in Robin Fretwell Wilson, 'Bargaining for Civil Rights: Lessons from Mrs. Murphy for Same-Sex Marriage and LGBT Rights', (2015) 95 *Boston University Law Review* (3) 951–993. Also Robin Fretwell Wilson and Anthony Michael Kreis, 'Embracing Compromise: Marriage Equality and Religious Liberty in the Political Process', (2014) 15 *Georgetown Journal of Gender and the Law* (2) 485–541) and Robin Fretwell Wilson, 'The Calculus of Accommodation: Contraception, Abortion, Same-Sex Marriage, and Other Clashes Between Religion and the State' (Washington & Lee Legal Studies Paper No. 2012–31), (2012) 53 *Boston College Law Review* (4) 1417–1513.

'Utah compromise',[50] legislation for which Professor Wilson served as an advisor. It will be difficult to replicate the unique political situation that made this compromise possible, but it is worth taking a look at one of the most comprehensive treatments of the relevant issues to date.[51]

On the one hand, this compromise provided as much protection for LGBT groups as had been provided in most of the more liberal states that had previously approved same-sex marriage. The Utah legislation protects LGBT individuals from employment and housing discrimination, and provides reasonable workplace accommodations, including for transgender individuals, who have often been left unprotected elsewhere. Moreover, it provides a system that allows government officials who object to same-sex marriage to keep their jobs, while assuring that marriage will be available to all, even in rural areas, and will be provided in ways that do not single out LGBT individuals in ways that might be demeaning. At the same time, the Utah legislation provides more extensive protections for religious groups, assuring that the religious communities can remain true to their beliefs, and that the religious character of religiously affiliated institutions and religious buildings owned by denominations will be respected. The exemptions are crafted with sufficient breadth to cover religiously affiliated institutions, such as religiously affiliated schools and other similar bodies. It adds affiliates, religious associations, societies (including a special mention of the Boy Scouts) to existing carve-outs for small employers, religious corporations, and their direct subsidiaries.

The Utah compromise also included exemptions that had been adopted in all or virtually all other states that had approved same-sex legislation. Thus, it exempts clergy from officiating at same-sex marriage ceremonies if this is contrary to their religious beliefs, and it similarly exempts religious organizations from providing such services. It protects those who object to same-sex marriages from private law suits and public penalties. Somewhat less typical is an explicit provision exempting religious marriage counseling courses or retreats from the obligation to serve same-sex couples. It allows adoption agencies to maintain their existing placement policies, even if that means they do not provide adoption services for LGBT couples. In order to assure that marriage services would be available, while at the same time allowing government officials to opt out of participating in such ceremonies, the Utah law has a distinctive provision requiring political subdivisions of the state to designate willing clerks and also provides that no one's professional or business license would be revoked because of religious expressions made in non-professional settings.[52] Significantly,

50 Utah State Legislature, 'S.B. 296 Antidiscrimination and Religious Freedom Amendments' and 'S.B. 297 Protections for Religious Expression and Beliefs about Marriage, Family, or Sexuality'.

51 The range of issues that have been addressed in various states is neatly captured in a chart summarizing the issues, 'The Utah Compromise', prepared by Robin Fretwell Wilson. See also Robin Fretwell Wilson, 'Marriage of Necessity: Same-Sex Marriage and Religious Liberty Protections', (2014) 64 *Case Western Reserve Law Review* (3) 1161, and Summary of the Utah Compromise (24 March 2015), http://ssrn.com/abstract=2584543 (accessed 26 October 2015).

52 This was designed to take into account the fact that ecclesiastical leaders representing the Mormon Church, which does not have a professional clergy, might well make statements consistent with religious teachings while leading or addressing church services, and it was important to prevent their voluntary ecclesiastical service from being used as a basis for imposing sanctions in work settings. NB: The headquarters of The Church of Jesus Christ of Latter-day Saints (Mormon) is in Utah's capital, Salt Lake City, and according to a 2013 Gallup Survey, approximately 60 percent of the state population identified as Mormon. See 'Mormons and Jews', in Frank Newport, 'Mississippi and Alabama Most Protestant States in U.S., *Gallup*, 5 February 2015, http://www.gallup.com/poll/167120/mississippi-alabama-protestant-states.aspx (accessed 26 October 2015).

the protection for religious and political expression outside the workplace protected both religious and LGBT employees.

One can disagree with various provisions of the Utah compromise in detail, but it certainly helps to suggest the range of issues that authorizing same-sex marriage entails. A further set of complexities, not yet addressed specifically by Utah legislation, has to do with non-discrimination in public accommodations. This notion has uncertain boundaries, clearly including non-discrimination in facilities such as hotels and restaurants, but potentially extending to a host of other settings in which goods and services are provided.[53] A number of highly publicized and controversial cases fall in this area. Consider situations involving devoutly religious business owners who have a conscientious objection to providing services for same-sex marriage celebrations or apparent endorsement of homosexual unions. Of course, if the objection is not based in sincere religious beliefs, or if religion is really being used as a cloak for non-religious bigotry or animus, the wrongfulness of the discrimination seems clear. But where such invidious animus is absent, as where the business has a proven track record of serving LGBT clients when same-sex marriage is not involved, or on the other hand, where alternative service providers willing to serve same-sex marriage events are readily available, denying religious freedom claims seems much less justifiable. Yet courts and administrative tribunals have sustained discrimination claims against a photographer who refused on conscientious grounds to provide photography services at a same-sex commitment ceremony,[54] and bakers who refused to provide wedding cakes in connection with same-sex marriages.[55]

Same-Sex Marriage, Anti-Discrimination, and the Accreditation of Professionals

Another area in which significant tensions between religious beliefs about same-sex marriage and anti-discrimination norms can arise is in the area of accreditation of professionals. This can take the form of loss (or inability to obtain) licensing or direct denial of accreditation to religiously affiliated associations.[56] This type of issue has recently surfaced in Canada in connection with the proposed creation of a law school at a private religiously affiliated institution in British Columbia – Trinity Western University (TWU). The Federation of Canadian

53 See Marc Stern, 'Same-Sex Marriage and the Churches,' in Douglas Laycock, Anthony R. Picarello, Jr., and Robin Fretwell Wilson, eds, *Same-Sex Marriage and Religious Liberty* (Rowman & Littlefield 2008), Chapter 1, at 37–43 (analyzing the reach of public accommodation laws).

54 *Elane Photography v. Willock,* 309 P.3d 53 (2013), cert. denied, 134 S.Ct. 1787 (2014).

55 *Craig v. Masterpiece Cakeshop, Inc.,* Colorado Civil Rights Commission (2013) (Colorado Christian baker can be fined for refusing to design a cake for a same-sex wedding) and Colo. Ct. App. No. 14CA1351, 13 August 2015 (2015 WL 4760543) (affirming CRC order and rejecting coerced speech and free exercise claims); *In re Melissa Klein, Oregon BOLI (2015)* (Oregon bakery owners ordered to pay $135,000 in damages for emotional suffering resulting from discrimination on the basis of sexual orientation when they refused on conscientious grounds to provide a wedding cake); *Lee v. Ashers Baking Co Ltd & Anor* [2015] NICty 2 (Northern Ireland Equality Act violated when a baker cancelled an order for a cake that included a slogan saying 'support gay marriage' along with a picture of Bert and Ernie from Sesame Street and the logo of the Queerspace organization). See Frank Cranmer, 'Lee v Ashers Baking Co Ltd & Ors – an analysis', *Law & Religion UK*, 20 May 2015, http://www.lawandreligionuk.com/2015/05/20/lee-v-ashers-baking-co-ltd-ors-an-analysis/ (accessed 26 October 2015).

56 See Stern, supra note 53 at 19–22 (describing licensing issues) and 23–24 (describing accreditation disputes). D. Smith, 'Accreditation Committee Decides to Keep Religious Exemption', (2002) 33 *Monitor on Psychology* (1) 16 (describing a proposal of the American Psychology Association to revoke the accreditation of religious colleges and universities whose religious beliefs oppose sex outside of marriage), http://www.apa.org/monitor/jan02/exemption.aspx (accessed 26 October 2015).

Law Societies gave approval for creation of the law school in December 2013, but controversy has erupted because of this private university's requirement that its students sign a 'Community Covenant' that obligates community members to abstain from 'sexual intimacy that violates the sacredness of marriage between a man and a woman.'

Canadian law societies, which control whether individuals can practice law, are organized at the provincial level. The decisions of law societies in three Canadian provinces – Upper Canada (Ontario), British Columbia, and Nova Scotia – to refuse to accept the TWU law degree as a basis for entering the legal profession were challenged in court. In results that might be seen as paired opposites, a Nova Scotia court of first instance overturned the refusal of the Nova Scotia Barristers' Society's (NSBS) to accept the TWU law degree,[57] whereas an Ontario court sustained the decision of the Law Society of Upper Canada (LSUC) to deny accreditation to the law school.[58] Where the Nova Scotia court held that NSBS lacked jurisdiction to compel a private university to restructure the requirements of its program, the Ontario court reasoned that the LSUC's long-standing commitment to remove obstacles to entry into the bar sufficed to confer jurisdiction. The Nova Scotia court could see no reason to distinguish a prior Canadian Supreme Court decision[59] that had overturned a similar rejection of accreditation of TWU's program for training teachers. The Ontario court found that a law society was sufficiently different from an entity accrediting training for teachers that the case could be distinguished. Both courts agreed that the refusal to accept the TWU degree infringed the religious freedom. But where the Ontario court concluded that it was reasonable to take the discriminatory impact of TWU's Community Covenant into account in reaching its decision, the Nova Scotia court held that as a private institution, TWU was not guilty of unlawful discrimination under the Canadian Charter.[60]

Most fundamentally, however, while acknowledging that 'dealing with discrimination' and 'dealing effectively with diversity in the legal profession is a pressing and substantial purpose',[61] the Nova Scotia court found that the action by NSBS in refusing to accredit TWU 'does not rationally relate to the important objective of dealing with discrimination.'[62] By opening a law school, TWU would add approximately 60 law graduates per year into Canadian society, some small percentage of whom might end up in Nova Scotia. Any impact on under-representation of the LGBT community in the Nova Scotia bar was a 'stretch', and even if there was some salutary effect, 'placing a barrier before Evangelical Christians or those willing to associate with them, so that the proportion of LGBT lawyers is increased would be inappropriate and wrongheaded'.[63] Summarizing its position, the court concluded that '[t]here is an important difference between the failure to regulate against discrimination in the profession and the failure to sanction someone else, somewhere else, for legally exercising a religious freedom.'[64] The Ontario court, in contrast, concluded that there was discrimination, and that that LSUC had reasonably balanced the interests of those who would be excluded or deterred by the Community Covenant from TWU's student body against the sincerely-held religious beliefs of TWU and its prospective students.

57 *Trinity Western University v. Nova Scotia Barristers' Society*, 2015 NSSC 25 (CanLII) (28 January 2015).
58 *Trinity Western University v. The Law Society of Upper Canada*, 2015 ONSC 4250 (CanLII) (2 July 2, 2015).
59 *Trinity Western University v. British Columbia College of Teachers* [2001] 1 SCR 772, 2001 SCC 31.
60 *TWU v. Nova Scotia Barristers* at 124, ¶ 245.
61 *TWU v. Nova Scotia Barristers* at 123, ¶¶ 241–2.
62 *TWU v. Nova Scotia Barristers* at 124, ¶ 244.
63 *TWU v. Nova Scotia Barristers* at 125, ¶ 247.
64 *TWU v. Nova Scotia Barristers* at 128, ¶ 254.

In December 2015 the Supreme Court of British Columbia shifted the balance of the decisions in favor of TWU when it found that the Law Society of British Colombia (LSBC) had breached its duty of procedural fairness and had neglected to fully consider the school's rights under the Canadian Charter when it allowed a non-binding vote of society members to override an earlier vote by the society's Benchers (board of directors) approving accreditation of the TWU Law School. The court therefore quashed the LSBC decision and ordered the earlier vote of approval to be reinstated.[65]

This issue, and others like it, will continue to play out in Canadian courts and around the world. If the rise of the equalitarian paradigm means that equality automatically trumps other rights claims, the likely result is that the possibility of creating legal training institutions with distinctive religious voices will be forbidden, or at least severely impaired. This seems inconsistent with the creation of a pluralistic democracy in which the state has an obligation to remain neutral and to avoid creating 'a preferential public space that favours certain religious groups and is hostile to others.'[66] If the rise of the equality paradigm carries with it this type of ideological hardening of positions, the hope of finding possibilities for reconciling differences will obviously decline.

In the end, part of the problem is that the same-sex marriage issues remain highly polarized, and there are fears on all sides. LGBT groups fear that if religious exemptions are allowed, the 'cloak of religion' will be invoked to paper over ongoing bigotry and discrimination. Religious groups, on the other hand, fear that approval of same-sex marriage is just a temporary battle-front, and that religious institutions will continue to be attacked by LGBT forces so long as they retain any beliefs that question LGBT lifestyles. So long as everyone feels threatened, tensions will remain high. Finding a range of issues on which it is possible to 'live and let live' is vital for tension levels to decrease, and so that longer term patterns for common life in a shared community can be established.

Religious Autonomy and Labor Law

Moving beyond the sphere of same-sex marriage, it is important to reflect on broader social contexts in which accommodation of religion is likely to be significant. There is a tendency to think of individual conscience as the core of the right to freedom of religion or belief, and there is of course much to be said for that view. As a practical matter, however, for most human beings, religion is a collective activity, and if the religious autonomy of the community is undermined, this will have a direct impact on individual belief, both because the belief itself will be compromised, and because the religious institutions that protect distinctive beliefs *vis-à-vis* state power will be weakened.

For this reason, it is not surprising that the autonomy rights of religious communities – the freedom of the church – is one of the oldest and most fundamental aspects of religious freedom.[67] Rooted in the ontological divide separating temporal and spiritual issues, recognition of religious autonomy has taken on jurisdictional significance and has become one of the hallmarks of Western civilization. The protection of religious freedom through setting

65 *Trinity Western University v. Law Society of British Columbia*, 2015 BCSC 2326 (CanLII) (10 December 2015).

66 *Mouvement laïque québécois and Alain Simoneau v. City of Saguenay and Jean Tremblay*, 2015 SCC 16, para. 75.

67 Richard W. Garnett, 'The Freedom of the Church,' Notre Dame Law School Legal Studies Research Paper no. 06–12, http://papers.ssrn.com/sol3/papers.cfm?abstract_id=916336 (accessed 2 November 2015). Paul Horwitz, *First Amendment Institutions* (Harvard University Press 2013).

jurisdictional limits on the competence of the state is one of the profound consequences of the recognition of temporal/spiritual divide. But in a world in which modern welfare-states have grown omnicompetent, it is easy to forget the fundamental jurisdictional lines.

In the United States, this line is protected by the non-establishment clause of the First Amendment to the federal constitution, which prohibits excessive entanglement of law and religion. But it is also protected by a religious autonomy doctrine,[68] which protects the rights of religious communities to define their own doctrines. And because doctrines define ecclesiastical structure, religious autonomy also guarantees the right to organize religious affairs in accordance with beliefs. This includes the right to determine religious personnel. While American-style separation is less common in Europe, the fundamental right to autonomy of a religious community is well respected.[69]

The right to religious autonomy has been implicated in a spate of decisions on both sides of the Atlantic. In the 2012 case *Hosanna Tabor Evangelical Lutheran Church and School v. EEOC*,[70] the United States Supreme Court unanimously held that a religious community has a right to choose its own ecclesiastical personnel even when the individual in question has extensive secular responsibilities, and when anti-discrimination laws might protect the worker in non-religious contexts. At about the same time, similar cases were decided in the European Court of Human Rights.[71] These cases all make it clear that in the core domain of religious autonomy, where personnel of a religious community are charged with proclaiming or representing the faith, religious autonomy rights prevail over other labor law concerns.

However, it is unclear how far such autonomy protections extend in a horizontal direction from core religious institutions such as churches or synagogues or mosques to religiously affiliated bodies. Religious schools seem to be covered, but what of religious hospitals, religious media enterprises, or religiously owned businesses of other types? Similarly, it is unclear how far such autonomy protections extend in a vertical direction. They cover priests and pastors, teachers whose duties include religious instruction, and probably teachers more generally, but what of secretarial personnel, or individuals who perform largely secular tasks, such as gardeners or custodians? There is a tendency to think religious communities do not need any special protection when it comes to these 'lower level' personnel. The difficulty is that religious leaders recognize that workers at all levels in their organization may have spiritual impact. One of the leading Supreme Court cases in the United States affirmed the right of a religious community to terminate a custodian

68 For historical background on religious autonomy doctrines in the United States and Europe see Brett G. Scharffs, 'The Autonomy of Church and State', (2004) 2004 *Brigham Young University Law Review* (4) 1217–1348, and Carl Esbeck, 'Dissent and Disestablishment: The Church-State Settlement in the Early American Republic', (2004) 2004 *Brigham Young University Law Review* (4) 1385–1592. For further discussion of the link between non-establishment and church autonomy see Carl Esbeck, 'Establishment Clause Limits on Governmental Interference with Religious Organizations' (1984) 41 *Washington & Lee Law Review* (2) 347–420 and 'The Establishment Clause as a Structural Restraint on Governmental Power', (1998) 84 *Iowa Law Review* 1–113.

69 See generally Gerhard Robbers, ed., *Church Autonomy: A Comparative Survey* (Peter Lang 2002).

70 *Hosanna Tabor Evangelical Lutheran Church and School v. Equal Employment Opportunity Commission*, 132 S.Ct. 694 (2012)

71 See, for example, *Obst v. Germany*, App. No. 425/03 (ECtHR, 23 September 20100; *Schüth v. Germany*, App. No. 1620/03 (ECtHR, 23 September 2010); *Siebenhaar v. Germany*, App. No. 18136/02 (ECtHR, 3 February 2011); *Sindicatul 'Păstorul cel Bun' v. Romania*, App. No. 2330/09 (ECtHR Grand Chamber, 9 July 2013). These cases are discussed in this volume extensively by María J. Valero Estarellas (Chapter 4), and also by Ursula C. Basset (Chapter 9) and Helen Alvaré (Chapter 10).

who failed to live up to religious worthiness standards.[72] Religious communities and their leaders recognize that the example and influence of individuals in an organization may have spiritual significance that transcends their positions in an organizational flowchart. Secular courts should be wary about assuming that they should have a free hand in directing employment policies of what may appear to them as the 'merely secular' employees of religious communities.

One of the most significant issues in the domain of religious autonomy involves determining the extent to which secular courts retain jurisdiction to monitor abuses of religious autonomy. In the *Hosanna Tabor* decision, Justice Alito's concurrence emphasized that 'In order to probe the *real reason* for [an employee's] firing, a civil court – and perhaps a jury – would be required to make a judgment about church doctrine.'[73] This, the Court recognized, would be impermissible.

In the European cases, there has been a more pronounced tendency for secular courts to retain jurisdiction to control for abuses of religious autonomy. Thus, in *Siebenhaar*[74] and *Obst*,[75] the European Court of Human Rights affirmed protection of religious autonomy in the termination of a teacher in a Protestant school and a public affairs director for The Church of Jesus Christ of Latter-day Saints. But in *Schüth*,[76] religious autonomy protections were not sufficient to withstand an Article 8 privacy claim brought by the organist and choirmaster of his Catholic parish. Although it was clear that Schüth had engaged in extra-marital sexual conduct that violated Catholic Church moral standards, the European Court held that German courts had not sufficiently considered all the factors weighing for and against termination. In fact, the holding in *Schüth* is somewhat problematic, in that it is not clear what would happen in a similar case if German courts weighed all the considerations more completely and nonetheless concluded that church autonomy considerations should prevail. But it is clear that this approach authorizes fairly intrusive analysis of the significance of religious beliefs and religious worthiness for church employment.

The most recent case in this line is the European Court of Human Right's decision in *Fernandez Martínez v. Spain.*[77] In this case, the Catholic Church had allowed a priest who had married and begun raising a family to continue teaching for several years, but when this status was made public as a result of the priest's participation in a demonstration opposing the Church's celibacy rules, the priest's position was not renewed. The Grand Chamber concluded that Spanish courts had taken into account all the relevant factors and decided in favor of protecting the Church's autonomy in this matter, but by a surprisingly narrow 9–8 decision. The core of the dissenting positions was that the state had impermissibly delegated too much of the hiring and firing decision of Catholic religious instruction teachers to the discretion of the Catholic Church, and that the state was required to maintain stricter oversight when Article 8 rights were at stake. The dissenters noted that it was only when the priest's married status became public knowledge that his teaching position was not renewed, and while this was an understandable problem for the Church, it should not be a ground for

72 *Corporation of Presiding Bishop of The Church of Jesus Christ of Latter-day Saints v. Amos*, 483 U.S. 327 (1987).

73 *Hosanna Tabor* at 715 (Alito, J., concurring).

74 *Siebenhaar*, supra note 71.

75 *Obst*, supra note 71.

76 *Schüth*, supra note 71.

77 *Fernandez Martínez v. Spain*, App. No. 56030/07 (ECtHR Grand Chamber, 12 June 2014). See discussion by María J. Valero Estarellas in Chapter 4 of this volume.

termination by the state (despite an agreement with the Holy See to this effect). They claimed that there was no evidence that the priest taught religion in a manner that contradicted the doctrine of the Church (ignoring the fact that the priest's married status was religiously problematic). And finally, the dissenters thought that non-reappointment of the priest was drastic action, leaving him unemployed. According to the dissenters,

> Domestic courts in particular, when they are reviewing the compatibility of administrative acts with human rights standards, must conduct an in-depth examination of the circumstances of the case and a thorough balancing exercise to weigh up the competing interests, in accordance with the principle of proportionality.[78]

The challenge is that this approach would mean that secular courts have broad roving authority to second guess religious judgments that go to the core of structuring religious education systems. The problem is of course complicated in Spain, where religious teaching is being performed in public institutions. But the dissenters' approach would substantially disrupt a long-established system of cooperation between state and church institutions in Spain, designed to respect religious autonomy in the course of managing state cooperation with the church in providing religious instruction.

The problem of the 'competence of competences' – of which jurisdiction (church or state) has ultimate authority to define the limits of the other – is one with an ancient history. In the end, it is clear that the state is destined to have the last word. But in a constitutional world committed to states with limited powers, states should be as deferential as possible to religious autonomy concerns. In many cases, this is more than an issue of balancing. There are some issues, such as which doctrines a religious community should believe, and how the community should be structured, that lie beyond the province of the state. Balancing state concerns in domains that are beyond the proper purview of the state constitutes improper balancing. If every personnel choice made by a religious organization is subject to judicial oversight, the religious judgments of religious organizations will be chilled and deterred. Refined respect for autonomy entails recognizing that some decisions should be protected from judicial oversight.

The Importance of Reasonable Accommodation

The notion of providing reasonable accommodations of religious differences, notably in the workplace, but also in education, health care, and a variety of other contexts, is a widely recognized solution to otherwise intractable sources of religious friction.[79] In the United States, the obligation to provide 'reasonable accommodations' in the workplace was guaranteed by Title VII of our major Civil Rights Act. However, this important protection was subsequently weakened by case law that held that reasonable accommodations in the workplace need not be provided if they would entail more than a '*de minimis* burden' on employers.[80]

78 *Fernandez Martínez*, Joint dissenting opinion of Judges Spielmann, Sajò, Karakaş, Lemmens, Jäderblom, Vehabović, Dedov, and Saiz-Arnaiz § 18.

79 See the extensive discussion of 'State Neutrality, Religion, and the Workplace in the Recent Case Law of the European Court of Human Rights' by María J. Valero Estarellas, Chapter 4 of this volume. See also Greg Walsh's call for reform to the 'general exception approach' to protecting employment decisions of religious schools, in Chapter 6, 'Anti-Discrimination Legislation and Regulation of Employment Decisions of Religious Schools in Australia.'

80 *Trans World Airlines, Inc. v. Hardison*, 432 U.S. 64 (1977).

In his 2014 Interim Report to the General Assembly, the U.N. Special Rapporteur on Freedom of Religion or Belief, Heiner Bielefeldt, focused specifically on the challenge of protecting freedom of religion or belief in the workplace. In his words:

> The management of religious or belief diversity in the workplace constitutes a major challenge for today's employment policy. An increasingly diverse and mobile global workforce, expanded manufacturing demands and new production schedules can lead to conflicts between professional and religious identities and duties.[81]

The problems involve both direct and indirect discrimination (i.e., conduct that does not intentionally discriminate, but has discriminatory effects). The Special Rapporteur emphasized that this area is under-studied and 'merits further systematic exploration.'[82] Noting that the idea of 'reasonable accommodation' has now found international legal acceptance in the Convention on the Rights of Persons with Disabilities,[83] he suggests that the time has come to import this notion in a revitalized form back into the domain of dealing with religious tensions in the workplace. In his view, 'public and private employers, as well as other stakeholders, should be encouraged to further explore and expand the scope of reasonable accommodation beyond what is currently enforceable.'[84] This could help solve a variety of problems involving disputes about wearing religious clothing or jewelry, or performing tasks that violate religious beliefs.

Several of the chapters in this volume examine the issue of accommodation of religion in the workplace that the Special Rapporteur has raised. In Chapter 3, Mark Hill undertakes a careful analysis of differences in the ways that the European Court of Human Rights and the European Court of Justice address this important practical sphere. Differences in procedure can affect everything from the speed with which cases are heard to the extent to which the European courts defer to national jurisdictions, but it seems clear that both courts recognize the importance of finding reasonable accommodations. María Valero Estarellas in Chapter 4 also focuses on the European cases addressing religion in the workplace, but worries that the 'new elucidation of general principles may not result in a significant future strengthening of the amount of actual protection given to religious interests at work, unless the Court refines its balancing criteria'.[85] What seems clear is that case law in this area is only likely to proliferate, and the challenge will be to see whether it is possible to raise standards that will enhance protections in increasingly pluralistic workplace settings.

In many ways, the notion of reasonable accommodation raised by the Special Rapporteur and running through so much of this volume needs to be more fully elaborated at the level of both constitutional and subconstitutional law. In presenting his annual report to the United Nations, Special Rapporteur Bielefeldt emphasized that workplace issues present not only practical questions. They pose existential choices, both about everyday life but also about the

81 Heiner Bielefeldt, Interim report of the Special Rapporteur on freedom of religion or belief (Focus: Tackling religious intolerance and discrimination in the workplace), United Nations General Assembly, U.N. Doc. A/69/261, para. 23, 5 August 2014, http://www.ohchr.org/Documents/Issues/Religion/A.69.261.pdf (accessed 26 October 2015).

82 Bielefeldt report, para. 28.

83 Bielefeldt report, para. 62.

84 Bielefeldt report, para. 63.

85 See Valero Estarellas, Chapter 4, page 54, of this volume.

larger issues of reconciling religious liberty and equality values in our time. Professor Bielefeldt's report is significant both in its legal sophistication, and in its practical significance in suggesting workable public policy. But the practical power of the report, like his earlier reports, is grounded in its philosophical depth.

Historical turning points are shaped by existential choices. We resonate with the choices made at important historical moments. One thinks, for example, of the image of people walking through the Brandenburg Gate following the collapse of the Berlin Wall in 1989, or the Orange Revolution in Ukraine, or the crowds listening to Martin Luther King's 'I Have a Dream' speech. But, for most people, the moments of existential choice come in small-scale contexts. Most people find confirmation of their dignity at work. The dramatic historical moments in the history of protecting human rights will be emptied of meaning if these ideals cannot be translated into living reality in concrete settings.

The difficulty is that there is always a temptation to want to reconstruct our social worlds in terms that resonate with our own existential choices. Religious believers would love to see the world restructured in the image of their beliefs. Secular believers have the same preference. Moreover, everyone – whether majority or minority – feels that their existential choices and their preferred image of the world may be threatened. Globally, we are all minorities, but even in national settings that give us the illusion of being prevailing majorities, we can feel threatened. There is always the worry that the strength of our current positions, whatever it may be, may be eroded as times change. And for those experiencing what it is like to be a minority suffering discrimination, the situation is even worse.

What Professor Bielefeldt's report helps to remind us is that we live in a world with deep differences, in which peace can only be grounded on an obligation to respect everyone else's existential choices, within the limits of optimal equal liberty for all. This is true at the macro-level, but it is equally true at the micro-level of the workplace. It requires complex notions of both freedom and equality, which can only be accomplished with reasonable accommodation. It requires us to understand, as Professor Bielefeldt's report recognizes, that religious employers may have special needs that reflect autonomy in the structuring of their affairs. It also requires secular employers, both public and private, to understand that reasonable accommodations are in the ultimate interests of all. Reasonable accommodation is not a one-size fits all philosophy. It makes room for the real lives of real people, and real organizations.

It is vital to give substance to reasonable accommodation, because that reminds us of the obligation to protect freedom. Protecting existential choice requires complex yet substantive notions of both equality and freedom. In the end, equality rights will be jeopardized if freedom of religion norms is not respected. Such norms hold an important key to finding the compromises and the forms of mutual respect that make a common life possible in an increasingly pluralistic world.

Index

For Product Safety Concerns and Information please contact our EU representative GPSR@taylorandfrancis.com Taylor & Francis Verlag GmbH, Kaufingerstraße 24, 80331 München, Germany